The Bitcoin Dilemma

Colin L. Read

The Bitcoin Dilemma

Weighing the Economic and Environmental Costs and Benefits

Colin L. Read
Economics and Finance
SUNY Plattsburgh
Plattsburgh, NY, USA

ISBN 978-3-031-09140-7   ISBN 978-3-031-09138-4 (eBook)
https://doi.org/10.1007/978-3-031-09138-4

© The Editor(s) (if applicable) and The Author(s), under exclusive license to Springer Nature Switzerland AG 2022
This work is subject to copyright. All rights are solely and exclusively licensed by the Publisher, whether the whole or part of the material is concerned, specifically the rights of translation, reprinting, reuse of illustrations, recitation, broadcasting, reproduction on microfilms or in any other physical way, and transmission or information storage and retrieval, electronic adaptation, computer software, or by similar or dissimilar methodology now known or hereafter developed.
The use of general descriptive names, registered names, trademarks, service marks, etc. in this publication does not imply, even in the absence of a specific statement, that such names are exempt from the relevant protective laws and regulations and therefore free for general use.
The publisher, the authors, and the editors are safe to assume that the advice and information in this book are believed to be true and accurate at the date of publication. Neither the publisher nor the authors or the editors give a warranty, expressed or implied, with respect to the material contained herein or for any errors or omissions that may have been made. The publisher remains neutral with regard to jurisdictional claims in published maps and institutional affiliations.

Cover illustration: Eoneren

This Palgrave Macmillan imprint is published by the registered company Springer Nature Switzerland AG
The registered company address is: Gewerbestrasse 11, 6330 Cham, Switzerland

Preface

January 1, 2017, heralded in the modern era of bitcoin. Barely seven years after Satoshi Nakamoto mined the first bitcoin and then disappeared without ever tapping upwards of $50 billion of unspent bitcoin wealth, the digital currency transformed a hobby currency for self-professed nerds into a powerhouse banking alternative valued upwards of a trillion dollars. In the early nascent period, someone in Florida purchased two pizzas with enough bitcoin that would have made him a millionaire sixty-eight times over by 2021. By 2017, bitcoin had caught the fancy of many, and spawned new financial institutions that generated huge wealth for some, but left others, especially electricity ratepayers, poorer for it.

The story of bitcoin is one of trust, or more precisely, concerns about whether existing financial institutions could be trusted to provide banking and transaction services for the greater good. The world was introduced to bitcoin's creator Satoshi through a cryptic message on a bulletin board used by cypherpunks in the latter half of the first decade of a new millennium. The post on February 11, 2009, read "The root problem with conventional currency is all the trust that's required to make it work. The central bank must be trusted not to debase the currency, but the history of fiat currencies is full of breaches of that trust."[1]

Satoshi was soliciting help to prove the utility of a new digital coin. In the early days, millions of bitcoin were minted with special software on personal

---

[1] http://p2pfoundation.ning.com/forum/topics/bitcoin-open-source, accessed April 26, 2022.

computers and laptops, fifty coin at a time, six times an hour, 24/7/365. But, by 2016, bitcoin had gone corporate. A visionary Chinese company called Bitmain had designed and popularized a special-built machine, the Antminer S9, to much more efficiently mine this fast-emerging medium of exchange. Almost overnight, the digital currency world was transformed from the utopian conception of its creator and the domain of cypherpunks and hobby miners to one that bred greed and environmental disregard in a miner arms race as more and more mining machines compete for upwards of $1 billion of mining rewards every month.

These new machines used specially designed integrated circuit chips called Application Specific Integrated Circuits (ASIC) that were assembled 189 at a time in S9 miners, then in turn linked upwards of tens of thousands at a time in mining farms. They have revolutionized the blockchain, bitcoin, cryptocurrency, and financial markets to this day. These miners and farms beckoned in a new corporate era for the mining of bitcoin that changed the landscape almost overnight and caused the coin to diverge dramatically from the ideals espoused in *The Cypherpunk Manifesto* that inspired the creator of bitcoin. The visionary creator developed the essential ingredient for a new level of profit-seeking for multi-billion-dollar institutions that Satoshi would have abhorred.

In 2016, a small city in the most northern corner of upstate New York, a quicker drive to Montreal, Canada than any other American city, became ground-zero for bitcoin mining in the Americas. Power was so inexpensive in the city that quite literally every home was warmed with resistance heaters, mostly baseboards lining each room.

A Puerto-Rico registered bitcoin mining company named CoinMint came to town before Plattsburgh knew what was coming. As is typical in this industry, bitcoin entrepreneurs do not readily announce their business plan, but, even if they did, few would have understood it back then. CoinMint arranged for the municipally owned electric company to sell them 10 megawatts of electricity on an ongoing basis, enough electricity to power a typical town of 10,000, and far more than that consumed by any local manufacturer, a regional hospital, or the State University of New York campus in Plattsburgh. They set up shop in a converted dollar store at a semi-vacant strip mall and tried their best to remain below the radar screen.

In the year CoinMint came to town, a university professor of finance and economics was running for mayor. To teach both disciplines at the college level is unusual enough. But to teach Money and Banking on one hand, and energy economics and sustainability on the other was fortuitous. This professor-candidate had a degree in physics in hand before he went on to study economics at the London School of Economics, and earn a Ph.D. in economics at Queen's University in Kingston, Ontario. For good measure, he studied graduate level electrical engineering in cryptography and completed a law degree at the University of Connecticut, an MBA at the University of Alaska, and a Master of Accountancy at the University of Tulsa.

His eclectic background is unusual for a politician, but it was perfectly suited to understand this novel cryptocurrency bitcoin. When he ran for the mayor's office, he had no more awareness about what bitcoin was doing to his city than anybody else in Plattsburgh. Even his position as a Clinton County legislator did not expose him to what was happening under everybody's nose.

All that changed when he was elected mayor of the City of Plattsburgh and began serving a four-year term on January 1, 2017. From that point on was an odyssey of attempts to understand and regulate an industry as wild as Gold Fever a century and a half earlier. As he studied the industry and learned bitcoin installations were soon dotting his state, he discovered something that few realized. The design of bitcoin will continue to devour increasing amounts of electricity globally almost without limit, and bounded only by the popularity and price of bitcoin itself. It turns out that the incredible wealth bitcoin has created for some is paid for in higher electricity for us all and diluted bitcoin value for cryptocurrency owners.

In fact, as you will see, even innovations in better mining machines that are increasingly powerful and more energy efficient will only lead to greater amounts of power consumption, which already exceeds the consumption of any but the world's top two dozen electricity consuming countries. Just half a decade later, we know much more about bitcoin, but this story will reveal to you so much we don't yet know, including results few have acknowledged.

This is my story, the entire story of bitcoin and of cryptocurrencies in general, the good, the bad, and the ugly, and the story of our future. Few could have imagined this story to now, but we all have a chance to determine how the story ends.

Plattsburgh, USA
2022

Colin L. Read

About This Book

There are few innovations that have the potential to revolutionize commerce that which have evolved as quickly as bitcoin. This digital coin sparked a movement that may well redefine banking, transacting, and public recording of important transactions. But bitcoin can create problems if not handled with appropriate care and is downright dangerous if pitfalls are not noted and avoided. I take the reader through the various dimensions of bitcoin, beginning with its Cypherpunk roots that inspired Satoshi Nakamoto, a mysterious but brilliant coder who has since disappeared from the crypto world. Satoshi's libertarian vision was to allow people to transact with each other just as they once exchanged music and movies on peer-to-peer networks. Satoshi's creation is a robust and decentralized network that has grown in value to almost a trillion dollars and has spawned new institutions larger than many Satoshi hoped to replace. I describe Satoshi's creation and derive *The Bitcoin Dilemma* that, for the first time, shows why bitcoin's almost insatiable energy demand will likely induce another forty-three million tonnes of carbon dioxide emissions annually by 2030, and will rival the electricity demand of some of the world's most populous nations.

The reader will discover that the very nature of bitcoin rewards to its miners creates an untenable but unavoidable race-to-the-bottom in which mining farms demand more energy and faster machines. Meanwhile, energy efficiency improvements simply result in more miners rather than smarter mining or lower energy consumption. This disturbing result has, to now, been missed by the extensive literature on bitcoin and has profound ramifications as the world struggles to combat global warming. This inevitability is intrinsic in the Bitcoin Proof of Work design that cannot be easily treated without global regulatory coordination. I also chronicle the experiences of local communities when bitcoin mining comes to town, and the effects of mining on higher electricity costs for residential and commercial ratepayers, and show that we all pay many times over for profits generated by bitcoin miners.

The incredible opportunities of this industry will only be realized if our regulators, legislators, entrepreneurs, and general public garner a more complete and objective understanding of this and other Proof of Work mining techniques. I provide this broader perspective of the effects of bitcoin on commerce and the economy, electricity markets and the environment, and the challenges to regulators as they try to ameliorate *The Bitcoin Dilemma*. My analysis is based on my research as an economist, my position as a director of a large regional bank, my understanding as a technologist and as an environmental and sustainability researcher, and my experience as a mayor who had to develop public policy to address nuisances bitcoin creates.

Introduction

This is a story of a Cypherpunk ideology, so pure and well-intentioned that, when combined with the genius of bitcoin's creator, almost resulted in the dream of democratization of banking, transacting, and personal finance. Instead, these ideals were eventually coopted and corrupted to create unbridled profit and the concentration of power within a new set of institutions that rival the size of the financial monoliths cypherpunks and bitcoin's creator and messiah hoped to replace.

Bitcoin is the product of a genius, but one who, not unlike many innovative computer scientists in their own time, was suspicious of powerful economic institutions. Satoshi Nakamoto hoped to help create a utopian digital society in which we all share banking concepts, contracts, and currency in a way that could not be coopted by the large institutions that many of Satoshi's ilk believed had done so much damage to the economy in the first decade of a new millennium. This genius came out to the world for just a few short years, and has disappeared ever since. We cannot ask Satoshi whether bitcoin has become what was anticipated then, but we can imagine from Satoshi's own words.

Indeed, Satoshi's first words to the Cypherpunk public were a terse statement inviting interest in a new digital coin. It read "I've been working on a new electronic cash system that's fully peer-to-peer, with no trusted third party."[1] The Cypherpunk world knew little of the person behind this statement, but would soon realize the beauty of what Satoshi had designed. Few could have imagined the forces Satoshi's creation would unleash.

---

[1] https://www.metzdowd.com/pipermail/cryptography/2008-October/014810.html, accessed April 26, 2022.

Satoshi's visionary crypto processing protocol has spawned a dichotomy of opposing forces. The computer science and economics of cryptocurrency are complicated. Most commentators and advocates are specialists, and each argues fervently from their various perspectives. There is little middle ground established for generalists to comprehend and explain this fascinating innovation to the rest of us. This book strives to bridge the chasm between cypherpunks and environmentalists, libertarians and public policy wonks, politicians, and profiteers.

I treat half a dozen aspects of bitcoin, from the nature and utility of cryptocurrencies in general but bitcoin in particular. I look at the contradictions in bitcoin as perpetuated by the economics of its protocol, the tensions and competitions between cryptocurrencies, the question of who is served by the industry's finances, the clashes in defense of our environment, and reasonable paths on how to proceed. I begin each of these parts with a review of the literature that highlights clashing commentaries by experts in their fields and then proceed with what I hope is considered a thoughtful and objective analysis. In doing so, it is important to offer an important acknowledgment.

There are few innovations that have the potential to redefine commerce and have evolved so quickly than has bitcoin. Cryptocurrency's potential for banking, transacting, and public recording of important records is profound, but can create problems if not managed with appropriate care, and is downright dangerous if pitfalls are not noted and avoided. I take the reader through the various dimensions of bitcoin, beginning with its computer science roots that inspired Satoshi Nakamoto, a mysterious but brilliant coder who has since disappeared from the crypto world. Satoshi's libertarian ideal was to allow people to transact with each other just as they once exchanged music and movies on peer-to-peer networks over the Internet. Satoshi's creation is a robust and decentralized network that has grown in value from pennies to approaching a trillion dollars and has spawned institutions larger than most Satoshi hoped to replace. I also derive *The Bitcoin Dilemma* that, for the first time, shows why bitcoin's almost insatiable energy demand will likely produce millions of tonnes of carbon dioxide emissions annually by 2030 that will rival greenhouse gas emissions from some of the world's most populous nations.

The reader will discover that the nature of bitcoin rewards to its miners that authenticate bitcoin transactions and constitute the network creates an untenable but unavoidable race-to-the-bottom in which mining farms demand more energy and faster machines. Yet, energy efficiency improvements simply spawn even more mining rather than lower energy consumption in a mining arms race, with electricity the ammunition. This disturbing result has received scant treatment in the extensive literature on bitcoin. Yet, *The Bitcoin Dilemma* has profound ramifications on our collective carbon footprint as the world increasingly struggles to combat global warming.

For instance, *The Bitcoin Dilemma* is expected to increase annual greenhouse gas emissions by upwards of forty-three million metric tonnes by the end of the decade, while ratepayers pay billions more for their electricity. This energy consumption spiral is intrinsic in the bitcoin Proof of Work design that cannot be easily fixed without global regulatory coordination. I also chronicle problems at the local level by describing the experiences of communities when bitcoin mining comes to town, and the effects of mining on higher electricity costs for residential and commercial ratepayers.

The incredible opportunities of this industry will only be realized if our regulators, legislators, entrepreneurs, and general public garner a more complete and objective understanding of the Proof of Work mining techniques bitcoin employs. I provide this broader perspective of the effects of bitcoin on commerce and the economy, electricity markets and the environment, and the challenges of regulators to keep the best and ameliorate the rest of the bitcoin experience. My analysis is based on my research as an economist, my insights as a director of a large regional bank, my understanding as a technologist and as an environmental and sustainability researcher, and my public policy experience as a mayor who had to develop public policy to address nuisances bitcoin creates.

Often, institutions perpetuate and protect their power by fostering an impression that they are uniquely positioned to provide to us something of great value. Institutions are loath to reveal the secrets to their success, at least until they are so large and powerful that nothing can affect their trajectory. Bitcoin is at a point now when we must carefully consider its future. Now that bitcoin is dominated by large institutions that could not have been imagined when Satoshi created the coin, we must salvage the ideology and mystique of bitcoin and the beauty of computer science techniques that gave rise to it.

Some would have us marvel in the ability of a new generation of institutions to mine and speculate on bitcoin and make billions in the process. Our collective lack of understanding of both the benefits and the dramatic hidden costs of bitcoin mining requires us, ironically enough, to trust these new institutions that are now replacing financial institutions too-big-to-fail. Yet, the genius of Satoshi was based on the premise that trust in large financial institutions be replaced with democratic participation. Bitcoin is now at a crossroads as its aura becomes tarnished and our regulators become increasingly concerned. In this book, the reader shall see that the concepts that underpin bitcoin are not so deep as to defy understanding. Nor are the consequences of mining so benign that we can ignore them any longer.

In the first part, I begin with a description of the brilliance of Satoshi. The mystery and genius of bitcoin's creator is treated in some detail so you can see for yourself the insights Satoshi had. The bitcoin messiah is portrayed as a utopian creator of a digital movement that now goes well beyond bitcoin itself.

I document how bitcoin was inspired by discussions in computer science circles in the 1990s and 2000s, especially around privacy and encryption, and from some early attempts to develop a blockchain system that was difficult to corrupt and co-opt. They called themselves Cypherpunks, and their ideology was recorded in *The Cypherpunk Manifesto*. From these inspirations, Satoshi assembled strands of computer science innovations, from cryptography and blockchain, and interjected a personal philosophy regarding a digital currency that could replace institutions overseeing our transactions with a peer-to-peer network which rewards clients that oversee a new type of Internet-based transactions to ensure they are not corrupted.

I trace the early innovators that inspired Satoshi to create the first bitcoin protocol. We shall see that, at first, Satoshi worked with a handful of collaborators, and released a bitcoin client in 2009. This new digital currency software was initially run by only a small number of committed hobbyists. Satoshi believed that bitcoin would either fail or succeed spectacularly. Over the period that Satoshi was involved, until 2011, it was difficult to imagine which outcome would prevail. Bitcoin's design has protected it from vulnerabilities that have destroyed lesser coins but has also perpetuated problems that present bitcoin's greatest challenge.

What really accelerated bitcoin mining was not only the hype and increased acceptance the digital coin started to enjoy by 2013, but also innovations in mining that brought to processing significantly more powerful and specialized equipment, much to Satoshi's chagrin. Bitcoin soon went from a nascent hobbyist stage into a corporate phase, beginning in late 2016 with the invention of highly specialized processors that were priced out of reach of hobbyists, but not of corporations with access to venture capital funds.

At that point, the economics of the industry pivoted. In Part II, I show that the economics is mostly driven by an escalating bitcoin price, as is the market equilibrium amount of processing power and electricity consumed. We shall see that the economic model predicts very well the vast increase in electricity consumption once Satoshi's beloved decentralized network became institutionalized. Indeed, I show that electricity consumption can even rise faster than the rate of increase of bitcoin prices. Rather than enhancing the efficiency of the bitcoin network, the model shows that Moore's Law actually worsens bitcoin energy consumption. This law, named after Intel chief Gordon Moore's 1966 postulate that processor power doubles every eighteen months, merely accelerates the miner arms race, and worsens electricity consumption. This Bitcoin Dilemma presents an important public policy problem now that the electricity consumption from mining bitcoin has grown to rival the consumption of some major countries.

Unintended societal and industry vulnerabilities of bitcoin mining soon caused its industry footprint to extend well beyond what Satoshi could have prophesized, and now affects almost everybody. Economists lump such consequences suffered by unrelated parties as externalities, which refers to effects on others that are not resolved through the price mechanism. In such cases, one can internalize the externality by requiring its producer to pay the cost of their actions as they would any other factor of production. Alternately, when that is not possible, regulation can be imposed on an industry to ensure that it acts in a way that promotes the common good. In Part III, I analyze the effects of mining on local, state, and national governments. I also explore how bitcoin mining has affected other sectors in computing and other cryptocurrencies. Finally, I describe recent innovations in bitcoin and other cryptocurrencies that may ameliorate some of these industry concerns, if not perhaps local, state, and national nuisances.

Bitcoin mining has proven to be very lucrative to the precious few able to secure financing and especially the access to inexpensive electricity that is the ammunition in the bitcoin arms race. In doing so, they are able to generate for themselves almost unimaginable profits. In Part IV, I describe how the ideal of a digital currency to serve the greater good has instead bred a cult-like following of those seeking their share of annual revenues tallied in the tens of billions of dollars per year.

These *Crypto Bros* who have emerged to praise the wonders of profits generated from bitcoin would have surprised and dismayed Satoshi. Satoshi's dream was to bypass large and deep pocketed institutions, not create rampant speculation and monolithic financial powerhouses of a different sort. Satoshi was a true believer in an ideal that was designed to benefit everybody and toiled selflessly to bring the bitcoin concept to fruition. Indeed, the wealth created by Satoshi's own mining remains untapped today. Equally unspent is the human capital Satoshi created through bitcoin and its successors. Others, especially today, would have ridden that bandwagon of fame or wealth for as long as possible, but Satoshi walked away from the movement early on, and certainly before people would ponder how an innovation for the common good could be transposed into a profit-hungry movement.

Someday the world may have abundant renewable power. The hope is that day will arrive in time to avoid the cataclysmic problems associated with global warming arising from the burning of fossil fuels. Any unnecessary increase in electricity consumption merely amplifies this dismal prophecy. In Part V, I explore the link between bitcoin mining electricity consumption and greenhouse gas emissions. The chapters conclude that the additional burden on energy consumption is already making precarious the promises made by nations to curb greenhouse gas emissions.

However, we shall see that not only does bitcoin significantly worsen our climate change picture, and is doing so at an accelerating rate, even though crypto advocates often argue the opposite and claim that miners' consumption of electricity actually aids in electric grid efficiency. Their strategy to give the perception of environmental responsibility while simultaneously contributing heavily to environmental degradation is called *Greenwashing* and is described in Part V.

In Part VI, I conclude that the benefits of cryptocurrency usage are substantial, if not perhaps as revolutionary as Satoshi had hoped. It is important that the industry develops in a way that allows it to realize Satoshi's vision, but not in a way that damages others and its own aspirations in the process. Problems arise because of the externalities inherent in the design of bitcoin. It is too late to isolate bitcoin. Rather, we must anticipate the regulatory needs of an entire industry that did not exist a dozen years ago and began to burgeon just in the last few years.

This would be challenging enough for regulators in the best of times. But, regulation is far more challenging in an industry that practices a shock and awe style of intense marketing to ensure that their party and profits do not end. The last part of this book looks at ways to navigate the regulatory abyss.

Throughout the book, I contrast two competing and conflicting philosophies. One is the idealism of the group of self-described *cypherpunks* who were concerned about ever-encroaching government and large financially powerful institutions. They were skeptical of the corruption of profit and were concerned about an increasingly dystopian state. The polar opposite of the cypherpunks are the *Crypto Bros* who believe everybody could become cryptomillionaires if only they too accepted and subscribed to the unbridled markets of cryptocurrency with the faith and zeal any Ponzi scheme requires.

With a subject matter as complex as bitcoin, our best chance to place it into the proper context is through education and understanding. I hope that by the end of this book, you will understand much better the great innovation of bitcoin, but also the weaknesses of an idea that can both improve our commerce and harm our environment. That is our choice.

Contents

Part I   The Cypherpunk Bible

1	In the Beginning	5
2	The Creator	13
3	The Disciples	19
4	The Genesis Block	29

Part II   Cryptocurrency Corporatization

5	A New Testament	43
6	Public Ledgers, Private Wallets, and Crypto Vulnerabilities	55
7	Bitcoin Goes Corporate	69
8	The Fundamental Flaw of Bitcoin	77
9	The Bitcoin Dilemma	95

Part III   Cryptocurrency Consequences

10	Towns and Cities Against Noise and Power Hogs	107
11	No More Duffel Bags Full of Cash	113

12	States and Bitcoin	121
13	National Policy and Bitcoin	129
14	The Rise of Ethereum and Hobby Mining	137

Part IV Born-Again *Crypto Bros* and the Gospel of Profits

15	A Hard Fork in the Bitcoin Philosophy	155
16	The First Crypto Bros Millionaires	163
17	The Coin du Jour: The Rise of Initial Coin Offerings	175
18	Decentralized Finance	187
19	The Market Prognosis for Bitcoin	199

Part V Cryptocurrency and the Environment

20	Carbon Footprints	213
21	Greenwashing in the Bitcoin Industry	219
22	Infighting in the Crypto Bros Family	231

Part VI The Rewriting of the Cryptocurrency Bible

23	Central Banks Get into the Act	249
24	The Disruption of the Fractional Banking System	257
25	Shock and Awe and a Call for Regulatory Action	267
26	Bitcoin's Global Reach	273
27	Conclusion	281

Epilogue	287
Appendix	291
Glossary	297
References	311
Index	323

About the Author

Colin L. Read has been teaching economics and finance for forty years, most recently as a Professor of Economics and Finance at the State University of New York College at Plattsburgh. He obtained a B.Sc. in Physics from Simon Fraser University, pursued graduate studies in Economics at the London School of Economics and in the electrical engineering of cryptography, and completed a Ph.D. in urban economics and finance at Queen's University in Kingston, Ontario. He also completed an M.B.A. at the University of Alaska, a J.D. in law at the University of Connecticut, and a Master of Accountancy in Taxation at the University of Tulsa. He is a prolific author, with a dozen books in finance and economics, two dozen journal articles, and about 500 newspaper and magazine columns and blogs. His teaching is primarily in money and banking, environmental and resource economics, and sustainability. He is the principal of ESG Analytics Group that offers services to corporations and institutions concerned about their environmental footprint. He resides in Plattsburgh, NY with his wife, Natalie, a new dog, Isaac, and three cats, Ruth, Amelia, and Eleanor. He enjoys flying, electronics, and skiing as hobbies.

List of Figures

Fig. 5.1	The first bitcoin transaction gifted 10 bitcoin to Hal Finney	44
Fig. 5.2	The Evolution of the bitcoin Hash Rate with Improved Technologies	51
Fig. 8.1	The payback period for a typical miner	81
Fig. 8.2	Relationship between bitcoin hourly block reward and annual energy consumption	90
Fig. 8.3	Relationship between level of bitcoin rewards and energy consumption	91
Fig. 8.4	Regression Analysis Between the Logs of Bitcoin Block Reward and Energy Consumption	92
Fig. 10.1	Antminer S9 profits per month in Plattsburgh, New York	108
Fig. 19.1	Bitcoin mining block reward trend	203
Fig. 20.1	Projections of bitcoin energy consumption	218
Fig. 21.1	Energy costs for various power sources in New York state, ranked by cost	225
Fig. 23.1	Annual bitcoin transactions	253
Fig. 24.1	The Bank's T-Account	259
Fig. 27.1	Annual bitcoin transaction activity	284

Part I

The Cypherpunk Bible

Our understanding of bitcoin may be based on what we read, our fascination with innovative digital technologies, or perhaps our interest in computer science, digital wallets, monetary systems, economics, or finance. We likely view conventional cash from such a practical and utilitarian perspective. Yet, government issued money itself has a fascinating history for some and is considered the root of all evil by others.

The evolution of the U.S. dollar spans an arc that has decided presidential elections and caused riots in the streets. This evolution has resulted in great wealth for those who betted right and losses for those who did not. It created an epic schism in a fledgling United States, with Treasury Secretary Alexander Hamilton staking his political future on advocating for a national bank and currency, while the nation's founders Jefferson and Madison argued instead for State rather than Federal solutions to banking and commerce. Hamilton never saw his ideal of a people's currency come to fruition in his lifetime, and neither did Satoshi, for reasons I describe in these pages.

The Ideological Roots of Bitcoin

It should not be surprising that something as quintessential as money fuels passions and ideologies even today. The rise and evolution of bitcoin is no different, except its development and the various forks in the road it followed are all over a remarkably short period of time. Within half a dozen years since its release, bitcoin has been developed and proven, and has diverged significantly from its ideological root. Few purists were confident that bitcoin would catch on. Even Satoshi's comment on Valentine's Day of 2010 expressed some doubt: "I'm sure that in 20 years there will either be very large transaction volume or no volume."[1]

A dozen years since its creation, bitcoin exceeded even Satoshi's more optimistic prophecy of very large transaction volume, but perhaps for reasons and in ways that Satoshi could not have imagined nor approved. Like Hamilton, there may be a play someday about Satoshi the idealist. And, like Hamilton's story, it may not end well.

Such ideological roots of the first popular digital currency may be irrelevant to those who find bitcoin useful for speculation or transactions. But, unlike other digital currencies that compete successfully with bitcoin, the original ideologies that predated and influenced bitcoin and its creator resulted in features baked into the coin that represent both its inherent strength and its fundamental flaw. While other digital currencies have learned from its experiences, bitcoin is unique among them in that it follows a blueprint, perhaps even a bible or constitution, that is incredibly difficult to modify.

To its purists, bitcoin ought not stray too far from its ideal, even the coin has been coopted to enrich but a few, despite its democratic and proletariat goals. A protocol chiseled in stone from on high means that some unintended consequences bitcoin creates will likely never be repaired. Instead, regulation must protect us all from problematic aspects I identify in this book. We shall see the irony in this necessary conclusion, given Satoshi's clearly stated goal to create a medium of exchange beyond the control of government or the cooption of high finance.

So we may understand the implications of such an inalterable constitution on the utility of bitcoin, it is helpful to present the coin not only from sterile perspectives of computer science and engineering, but also through an economic analysis of inherent details embedded in the bitcoin protocol, and their social, political, and regulatory consequences. This gamut of forces that define our perceptions of the coin will also determine its future.

I begin with a description of a small and loosely defined but tightly knit social movement that strongly influenced Satoshi Nakamoto, bitcoin's designer. I then use some of Satoshi's own words and actions that help us better understand what bitcoin's creator subsequently embodied in the digital currency, both in spirit and computer code. Finally, I describe Satoshi as both human and myth, and discuss the brilliance of this genius, the democratization of transactions and banking, the mystery that surrounds Satoshi,

---

[1] https://bitcointalk.org/index.php?topic=48.msg329#msg329, accessed April 26, 2022.

and the ways the messiah's vision was subsequently warped into a method to concentrate incredible new wealth among a few.

I draw on statement from Satoshi and others of the potential for this new protocol. In this first section, the mystery and genius of Satoshi is described in some detail so you can see for yourself the insights bitcoin's originator had. Satoshi is portrayed as a creator of a utopian virtual marketplace that is now much bigger than bitcoin itself.

Genius is rarely produced in a vacuum. While there are concepts that predated bitcoin, only Satoshi brought these disparate computer science concepts together in a way that promised to revolutionize how we transact. In subsequent sections, I will demonstrate that Satoshi the creator could not have imagined just how bitcoin would capture our imagination, nor how the original bitcoin concept would be corrupted through the formation of huge institutions and the creation of almost unimaginable wealth in precisely the ways that caused Satoshi to mistrust existing economic institutions. Nor would Satoshi have fathomed the consequences of *The Bitcoin Dilemma* on global energy consumption and climate change. For now, let's begin with the Cypherpunks.

1

In the Beginning

You may recall the motto from the 1960s: "Don't trust anyone over thirty." The slogan was coined by Jack Weinberg, a University of California at Berkeley student, who responded when people inquired whether the Free Speech Movement he represented was controlled by sinister individuals behind the scenes.[1] Weinberg represented a movement that was brewing especially among young people in California in the 1960s. He answered that his movement does not trust anybody over thirty. The slogan persists because the forces that caused young Californians to distrust authority then is a timeless sociological phenomenon. It also profoundly influenced those who would lay the groundwork for bitcoin a generation later.

A movement fueled by mistrust of big institutions thrived, typically virtually, among a group of young Californian coders in the 1990s who labeled themselves *cypherpunks*. This term was not at all derogatory, but instead embodied principles to which tech-savvy twenty something (mostly) male children of those raised in the 1960s often subscribed.

Fans of the movie *Blade Runner* are familiar with the dystopian genre. Cypherpunks harbor a mistrust for large corporations, government, and *Big Brother*. They are technologically savvy, and the movement's proponents typically interact virtually. The gritty science fiction genre it celebrates has the protagonist constantly doing battle with those who would deprive us all of freedom of expression and thought. While its initial carnations may include

---

[1] https://en.wikipedia.org/wiki/Jack_Weinberg, retrieved March 7, 2022.

Isaac Asimov's *Robot* series, it could also date back to Star Trek and forward to *Blade* Runner and The *Matrix*.

Within this genre, heroes typically use technology to undermine the forces believed to have commandeered our freedom with oppressive technology. Our protagonist cypherpunks communicate through private channels, and their superior command of alternative technologies immunizes them from those who would undermine their freedom. Anonymity, interaction through encrypted virtual channels, and the ability to speak in a cypherhip lingo and code are their hallmarks, as are anime, Goth, urban decay, and creative coding. They are less tied to hardware, which often requires institutional substantial resources, and are instead drawn to software that can command these machines.

Cypherpunks interacted through computer games and late night correspondences on alternative social media sites such as Reddit, with little activity from early to late morning. They were hackers by avocation and have side hustles such as coding or web design as their vocation. They were anything but corporate, although now monolithic organizations such as Google employ them for their willingness to work long hours with passion, especially if they are afforded 20% of their time to work on the personal projects of their choice.

The Cypherpunk generation was proud and intelligent. Like many smart and well-educated young males, they were sympathetic to the writings of Ayn Rand and her sense of resourcefulness and self-sufficiency in spite of government and institutions determined to discourage independence and creativity. Indeed, they had faith in the marketplace for ideas and for democracy itself, albeit in a different and decentralized form than we see in a republic.

California, and especially those who grew up in and around Silicon Valley, was chock-full of such urban cypherhipsters. They were afforded a good education, with unsurpassed technological integrations. They belonged to computer clubs in high school and quickly absorbed leading-edge programming languages such as C++. They were also experts at hypertext coding and with cross-platform applications.

These cypherpunks were highly idealistic. Their libertarian predilection is to free markets, free speech, democracy, and libertarianism. They strove for a world of meritocracy in which people should be judged primarily by the product of their intelligence, not the breadth of their networks, family connections, or length of their resumes.

Early Ataris and Commodore 64s, gaming consoles, and then Apple IIs and PCs were the technologies they mastered. Perhaps with access to the ARPANet through their technologist parents, they learned early on how to share interests and ideas over the precursor of the Internet. Cypherpunks were early adopters of technology and hence often had a disproportionate influence in technological development. They were motivated by a personal sense of accomplishment and acceptance by other cypherpunks, and less motivated by money and the corrupting forces of major corporations and institutions. For cypherpunks, the opportunity to exchange with each other, through electronic bulletin boards, email, posts, and blogs, or, perhaps someday, through a cyber-based market allowed them to interact and exchange without the need to rely on existing institutions or corporations.

> ### The Cypherpunk Manifesto
>
> Cypherpunks shared a credo penned by a Berkeley mathematician in 1993 named Eric Hughes. His Cypherpunk Manifesto was headed with a statement "Privacy is necessary for an open society in the electronic age." Hughes went on:
>
>> "Therefore, privacy in an open society requires anonymous transaction systems. Until now, cash has been the primary such system. An anonymous transaction system is not a secret transaction system. An anonymous system empowers individuals to reveal their identity when desired and only when desired; this is the essence of privacy... Privacy in an open society also requires cryptography. If I say something, I want it heard only by those for whom I intend it. If the content of my speech is available to the world, I have no privacy. To encrypt is to indicate the desire for privacy, and to encrypt with weak cryptography is to indicate not too much desire for privacy. Furthermore, to reveal one's identity with assurance when the default is anonymity requires the cryptographic signature...We cannot expect governments, corporations, or other large, faceless organizations to grant us privacy out of their beneficence. It is to their advantage to speak of us, and we should expect that they will speak. To try to prevent their speech is to fight against the realities of information. Information does not just want to be free, it longs to be free. Information expands to fill the available storage space. Information is Rumor's younger, stronger cousin; Information is fleeter of foot, has more eyes, knows more, and understands less than Rumor. We must defend our own privacy if we expect to have any. We must come together and create systems which allow anonymous transactions to take place. People have been defending their own privacy for centuries with whispers, darkness, envelopes, closed doors, secret handshakes, and couriers. The technologies of the past did not allow for strong privacy, but electronic technologies do."
>
>> "We the Cypherpunks are dedicated to building anonymous systems. We are defending our privacy with cryptography, with anonymous mail forwarding systems, with digital signatures, and with electronic money."[2]

---

[2] https://nakamotoinstitute.org/cypherpunk-manifesto/, retrieved March 2, 2022.

One can easily imagine the motivation of the manifesto for cypherpunks to develop a way to communicate and exchange privately. In the 1990s, cypherpunks used their spare time to develop techniques that would afford them the privacy to interact without fear of *Big Brother* intercepting their communications. It was not so much that they had something to hide, but more a matter of principle and an ideology.

None can question the passion these Cypherpunks brought to their avocations in developing methods to communicate and exchange privately and digitally beyond the oversight of institutions. They were also incredibly adept at absorbing leading-edge theories of computer scientists and National Security Agency employees alike. This generation was remarkable in their facilities to combine disparate state-of-the-art technologies and unify them into applications that served their avocation.

The most well-known but equally mysterious advocate for Cypherpunk values is the cypherpunk messiah and bitcoin's creator, Satoshi Nakamoto. Statements Satoshi made demonstrated qualities shared with cypherpunks, even if nobody had spoken with Satoshi directly. We can learn by the virtual community Satoshi kept, though.

One such individual was Hal Finney. He fit the profile as a Californian cyberpunk. He was young and well-educated, intelligent, and well-versed in technology, although he was also married and held down day gigs. Finney lived in a comfortable home in the suburbs with a wife and two children. But, he also had a corner of his home from which he could crank up his laptop and log into his loose network of others who shared his computer interests.

While perusing an online bulletin board for like-minded cypherpunks, Finney came across someone who was self-labeled Satoshi Nakamoto. If one were to probe more deeply, that name might have seemed a bit odd because someone of Japanese descent may reverse the order of the surname and given name. It also mattered little whether Satoshi was male or female, although a male in his twenties or early thirties is more likely. But, in the virtual world, such subtleties are unimportant. Instead, Finney was interested in Satoshi's idea of a virtual currency called bitcoin.

Satoshi had been discussing various digital currency ideas within the electronic bulletin board world, but nobody other than Hal Finney showed much interest. Finney had suggested to Satoshi that concepts for digital cash that interested Satoshi could be best described if Satoshi could write some code to demonstrate how it would work. Part of the cypherpunk credo is that code speaks louder than words.

In fact, Hal Finney had already been working on ways to protect private communications, so Satoshi's articulated concern for transaction privacy was appealing. In his spare time outside of gigs as a software developer, Finney had collaborated on work initiated by the computer scientist David Chaum to protect communications by combining a public key to gain entry to a communications forum and a private key to then convert to meaningful communications what would otherwise appear to be random gibberish. He also found employment with an antinuclear activist and computer scientist named Phillip Zimmerman who was developing software called Pretty Good Privacy (PGP) that could encrypt emails.

Later, Zimmerman would articulate a law that explains his motivation, in which he states "The natural flow of technology tends to move in the direction of making surveillance easier." As a corollary to his law, he stated "The ability of computers to track us doubles every eighteen months,"[3] as a play on Intel founder Gordon Moore's prediction of the doubling rate of computer processors. The inevitability of threats to our privacy concerned Satoshi and Finney.

The First Digital Coins

Finney's knowledge of cryptography from his work on PGP and the shared value with those who subscribed to *The Cypherpunk Manifesto* had a few years earlier led him to propose a new digital currency. Called CRASH (for Crypto Cash), Hal was following in the wake of innovators such as David Chaum, who had also tried to popularize an Internet-based digital currency called *DigiCash*. This alternative digital currency had some followers, but suffered from the need of some sort of moderator to authenticate transactions. Most were skeptical that such a digital currency was any better than currency obtained at a bank. Cypherpunks were concerned that one still had to trust an organization to authenticate transactions. In cypherpunks' minds, institutions can be corrupted and can't be trusted.

Meanwhile, even the institution of institutions announced their willingness, or at least their tolerance, of a digital currency. In a speech by then Federal Reserve Chairman, the enigmatic Ayn Rand apostle[4] Alan Greenspan made a speech in 1996 (to be discussed in more detail later) that signaled he would accept as inevitable the creation of a digital currency that permitted

---

[3] https://en.wikipedia.org/wiki/Phil_Zimmermann, retrieved March 2, 2022.
[4] https://www.vanityfair.com/culture/2000/12/hitchens-200012, retrieved March 7, 2022.

online transactions. This suggestion that an innovation would not automatically result in resistance from the Federal Reserve spurred accelerated interest in cryptocurrencies. Soon thereafter, a British computer scientist named Adam Back developed *hashcash* that would protect transactions using encryption from an increasingly appreciated NSA innovation called a hash function.

Such a function, to be described later, is a technique that converts a series of transactions into a summary number. This hash process is hard to calculate and reverse engineer but easy to verify once solved. This way, a transaction could be wrapped within a puzzle and encoded so that a bank of computers working for years would be necessary to break the code, but once solved, the solution is easy to verify. The idea was to make it so costly to break the code that the reward at the end was not worth the energy to break it.

> **The First Definition of Proof of Work and Early Examples of Digital Currencies**
> The term for this type of encryption was labeled Proof of Work by Markus Jakobsson and Ari Juels (1999). Those who were working on encryption that is expensive to break was innovative in the 1990s and 2000s. David Chaum's original digital coin concept was subsequently improved by others, including Nick Szabo's bit gold and Wie Dai's b-money. Each subsequent concept was a bit more refined than the last. They all hoped to permit subscribers to transact in a digital coin safely and privately, but none had figured out a way to remove a referee from the validation process that ensured people actually owned the currency they proffered. Should one figure out that part of the puzzle, such digital coin could permit us to transact without banks or on credit cards and avoid their various transaction and merchant fees.

Satoshi observed bulletin board discussions of the various digital coins that were developed and failed in fits and starts, primarily over concerns about the need for some sort of trusted authenticating institution. The Satoshi persona appeared out of the blue in an email asking Adam Back if he'd look over a concept Satoshi had developed. Satoshi did not receive much interest from this correspondence, but continued to develop a new concept and shared it on a bulletin board devoted to cryptography discussion. Satoshi began "I've been working on a new electronic cash system that's fully peer-to-peer, with no trusted third party."[5] This statement may not have meant much to most people, perhaps even among a generation that had benefitted from other peer-to-peer exchanges over the 1990s to exchange music and videos on Napster

---

[5] https://nakamotoinstitute.org/, retrieved March 7, 2022.

and other user connection services. But, what caught the eye of cypherpunks was the reference to "with no trusted party."

A New Electronic Cash System That's Fully Peer-to-Peer

Satoshi's innovation, described more fully in a nine-page document posted in October of 2008, garnered scant interest at first. A week after it was posted, Hal Finney responded to Satoshi and made some thoughtful recommendations on Satoshi's presentation. The gist of Finney's comments was that Satoshi's concept would be more meaningful if code could be provided to see if the concepts could be translated into functionality. This was productive, given that most who responded to Satoshi noted that similar efforts were tried in the 1990s but failed. Finney was more constructive.

Satoshi accepted Finney's challenge and forwarded some prototype software ideas over which Finney and Satoshi bantered back and forth over the remainder of the year. Then, in January of 2009 Satoshi posted to a new bitcoin listserv and to Finney working code ready to install on computers of those willing to help develop the software. It allowed transactions to be memorialized in a public ledger of subsequent blocks of data, much like a large spreadsheet that added a worksheet tab every ten minutes. We shall describe this technique later. For now, though, Satoshi's new bitcoin seemed to work, even if it appeared that Finney was its only beta tester.

The next few chapters will more fully describe Satoshi's protocol and the various ingredients that allowed it to succeed when others failed. At first, Satoshi and Hal were the only true believers running the software. Finney could run Satoshi's software on his personal computer when he otherwise did not need to rely on its processing power. He expressed concern that running his computer day and night to generate bitcoin every ten minutes for a potential reward of 50 new bitcoin was not productive given that bitcoin had no intrinsic value. Hal knew that such *bitcoin mining* was costly in both electricity expense and the carbon-spewing that electricity generation produces.[6]

It would take some time before additional disciples would join Satoshi and Finney. For a good part of a year, though, the new bitcoin software was churning away and encoding essentially nothing, in exchange for 50 bitcoin every ten minutes, 300 coin an hour, 7,200 a day, and 2.628 million per year,

---

[6] Popper (2015, pp. 27).

much of it by and for Satoshi. To then, though, bitcoin had yet found any following, and hence had no value.

What was already clear was the passion for these early developers of cryptocurrency. They were motivated not by profit but by service to the cypherpunk community that was ideologically preoccupied with privacy and transacting in a virtual market. This is illustrated by the necessary investment in electricity to "mine" bitcoin using Satoshi's protocol, if only perhaps at a California cost of a couple of dollars a day, to generate digital tokens of no apparent value. In fact, it would take more than a year and a half before bitcoin developed any value at all. This was a pursuit that is not uncommon among idealists. They are little concerned about a modicum of electricity and myriad hours of effort in their pursuit of intellectual curiosity and an ideology. We shall see this genius at work next.

2

The Creator

Some among us are driven to create, without thought of personal gain, or for that matter whether the value of their creations will be recognized by others. These individuals take profound ownership in concepts they create and guard the intrinsic beauty of their works with the pride of an artist. Stories abound of artists who destroy their works rather than have them coopted and warped by others, just as the protagonists in the Ayn Rand novels inspired many cypherpunks. Satoshi stated, "The nature of Bitcoin is such that once version 0.1 was released, the core design was set in stone for the rest of its lifetime."[1]

One often cannot immediately know at the time whether such pride of ownership is warranted. With the passing of time, we find that, once in a rare while, humanity encounters something of such beauty or perfection that humans often attribute the genesis of its creation to divine and otherworldly forces. The Mona Lisa or Van Gogh's Starry Night, Einstein's creation of four new and completely revolutionary concepts in physics, all in one year, or Satoshi's design of bitcoin, are all examples of works that one marvels at how they could be created by mere mortals. Many good ideas and works abound, but few are so exceptional and moving that our interest turns beyond the thing of beauty and to the person whose inspiration created it.

Coders and computer scientists now admire a piece of work developed in 2008 by someone who called himself or herself Satoshi. It seems likely now

---

[1] https://bitcointalk.org/index.php?topic=195.msg1611#msg1611, accessed April 19, 2022.

that the name forever attached to the invention of bitcoin is not the inventor's or the inventors' true name(s).

> **On the Nature of Genius**
>
> Einstein's Annus Mirabilis of 1905 did not occur in a vacuum, and nor did the white paper that first described a peer-to-peer financial transaction method that would become bitcoin. In Einstein's case, his "On a Heuristic Point of View Concerning the Production and Transformation of Light" proposed that light consists of discrete packets, or quanta, rather than propagated as continuous waves. In creating wave-particle duality, he was also an originator of quantum mechanics, which gave him discomfort for the rest of his theoretical life.
>
> In his "On the Movement of Small Particles Suspended in Stationary Liquids Required by the Molecular-Kinetic Theory of Heat," he deduced that the movement of tiny particles under a microscope may be influenced by the momentum of an invisible particle we now call atoms. In his "On the Electrodynamics of Moving Bodies," Einstein took paradoxes suggested by Hertz, Maxwell, Mach, Michelson, and Morley before him and resolved these unanswered questions into his "Special Theory of Relativity" that rewrote Newtonian mechanics which had by then stood as law for three centuries.
>
> Finally, in his "Does the Inertia of a Body Depend on its Energy Content?," Einstein left us with perhaps the most beautiful and dangerous equation in all of science, $E = mc^2$. Each of these were so groundbreaking in new fields of discovery that any of them deserved the award of a Nobel Prize, something that cannot be given to one person in one field more than once in a lifetime. Einstein won his Nobel not for the first theory of relativity, but rather for the photoelectric effect that flowed from the first paper discussed above. Nonetheless, each of these papers, in their compactness and ingenuity, deserved the prize.

The Computer Science Equivalent of a Nobel Prize

There is no Nobel for computer science, but the Association for Computing Machinery Turing Award is recognized as the top award for a contribution of lasting and major technical importance to the computer field. Like the Nobel Prize, it follows recognized innovations for many years to be certain of its permanent and prominent place in computing. For instance, in 1968, it was awarded to Richard Hamming for his work in coding data to be better able to detect and correct errors that may arise from its propagation, while Edgar F. Codd won in 1981 for his contributions to the theory of database management systems, and Manuel Blum won in 1995, Andrew Yao in 2000, Ron Rivest, Adi Shamir, and Leonard Adleman in 2002, and Whitfield Diffie and Martin Hellman in 2015, also for their work in cryptography, among other related contributions.

These awards are currently valued in the neighborhood of $1 million U.S. and recognize the many fold value the innovations create for society. Each of these are awarded to a known person or group of people. Because of the mystery surrounding Satoshi, there have been no such awards presented to the creator of bitcoin, despite Satoshi's invention of a concept that has given rise to a trillion-dollar industry.

Little is known about Satoshi, but much speculation abounds. The person or people first made a mark in a 2008 white paper that described a method to allow the exchange of a digital currency between peers that is decentralized and hence not under the auspices of a monetary institution or authority. The white paper, entitled "A Peer-to-Peer Electronic Cash System," appeared on a new website with the address Bitcoin.org by an author Satoshi Nakamoto, with an email address satoshin@gmx.com.

In the previous decade, peer-to-peer networks had been used to exchange music and other copyrighted materials in a way that avoided institutions and hence detection and prosecution. Satoshi shared this mistrust of overseers, especially if it resulted in the possibility that such institutions could co-opt, corrupt, or restrict a new alternative to cash. Satoshi's method combined the concept of a blockchain to link sequences of transactions in a subsequently immutable way, entrusted to a broad and decentralized network of machines and computer power to prevent some minority from corrupting the exchange system. This method will be described in greater detail in a subsequent chapter, but I begin with the motivating paragraph from Satoshi's original paper:

> "What is needed is an electronic payment system based on cryptographic proof instead of trust, allowing any two willing parties to transact directly with each other without the need for a trusted third party. Transactions that are computationally impractical to reverse would protect sellers from fraud, and routine escrow mechanisms could easily be implemented to protect buyers. In this paper, we propose a solution to the double-spending problem using a peer-to-peer distributed timestamp server to generate computational proof of the chronological order of transactions. The system is secure as long as honest nodes collectively control more CPU power than any cooperating group of attacker nodes."[2] - Satoshi Nakamoto

---

[2] https://nakamotoinstitute.org/bitcoin/, accessed April 26, 2022.

> **A Dissection of Satoshi's Writings**
>
> The wording of Satoshi's writings is important for a couple of reasons. First, the grammar appears to be generated by one whose native language is likely English. The excerpt is from Satoshi's original white paper, published on a web page of Satoshi's creation rather than as a product of peer review and multiple edits and revisions. Yet, the grammar and writing quality suggests the author had good command of the English language. Given the use of "We propose" rather than "I propose" or "It is proposed that," the English may well be the Commonwealth rather than the American English variety. Other observers have noted that Satoshi references "grey," "colour," and "flat" rather than "gray, "color," or "apartment," among numerous other Commonwealth English references.
>
> Second, the Swiss software engineer Stefan Thomas observed that posts from Satoshi were almost never time-stamped during the midafternoon or early evening hours in Japan, which seemed to suggest an author who resided in the Eastern Americas or Western Europe, at least if one assumes Satoshi kept regular daylight hours.[3]

Computer scientists and cryptographers have speculated that any one of half a dozen people could have employed the Satoshi pseudonym. These include Hal Finney, the first person to run new bitcoin mining software and make bug reports, or Dorian Prentice Satoshi Nakamoto, a Japanese-American California Polytechnic physicist who worked as a computer engineer and worked with cryptography and financial technologies. All of these individuals deny they are the Satoshi in question.

The Australian academic Craig Steven Wright once claimed to be Satoshi, but the proof he proffers remains unconvincing to experts in the bitcoin field. Nick Szabo, an enthusiastic advocate for the Proof of Work technique Satoshi proposed, is most often associated with Satoshi. However, Szabo also denies the association, and there remains no conclusive evidence that he is the author of the 2008 white paper.

The World's Most Mysterious Multi-Billionaire

The mystery could be due to one of two reasons. It is possible that Satoshi was indeed of Japanese descent, but was educated and lived in the Americas or Europe, and perhaps died or otherwise disassociated his or herself from the bitcoin concept shortly after its development. However, to leave no further traces following such a separation seems implausible.

---

[3] https://www.nytimes.com/2021/01/1, accessed March 18, 2022.

There is another explanation for Satoshi's virtual disappearance. Satoshi had a libertarian streak and a distrust of institutions, and found him or herself the owner of roughly 1 million bitcoin. A recent valuation would place the true Satoshi within the top twenty wealthiest people in the world. With that wealth creation would come a tax liability of upwards of tens of billions of dollars U.S., and all the notoriety and lack of privacy incredible wealth would induce. Certainly, to protect a quarter to a half of one's wealth valued at upwards of $50 billion U.S. would be incentive enough to maintain secrecy, especially if that wealth can be maintained in ways that defy discovery by tax authorities. One might imagine a relatively introverted and private genius somewhere quietly enjoying the quality of life that great wealth can provide, without any of the distractions usually associated with such wealth, and without an ego that would overpower the advantages of anonymity. However, the wealth Satoshi created as the first bitcoin miner remains untapped.

This genius may be one of those candidates already mentioned, but for the observation that some of these individuals welcome attention, and none live with the accoutrements of one of the world's wealthiest individuals. It is conceivable that the wealth was lost, due to a failed hard drive, or some other error. But, one who owns such wealth would have likely and redundantly guarded the unique private keys that unlock bitcoin wealth. Perhaps Wei Dai, whom the journalist Nathaniel Popper (2015) described as an intensely private computer scientist, is the most likely of candidates. He is a University of Washington graduate who developed many concepts that were precursors of bitcoin. Similarly, recall the British computer scientist Adam Back who also developed early versions of digital currencies that depended a hash function, the central technology employed by bitcoin. Again, neither of these early cryptocurrency developers make any claim to Satoshi's identity, nor the wealth bitcoin provided to its creator.

The mystery associated with Satoshi merely amplifies the same fascination and mystique enjoyed and suffered by Albert Einstein. A person who has captivated such attention often attracts intense interest and, at times, spawns conspiracy theories that mere mortals never endure. For instance, Einstein's innovations had roots in paradoxes or ideas of others who came before him, but Einstein took the leap and viewed these apparent paradoxes within a new paradigm.[4] With no knowledge of any personal aspects of Satoshi's life, such comparisons gain little traction.

---

[4] Some conspiracy theorists have argued that his first wife, a brilliant and more serious Serbian student of physics and mathematics named Mileva Marić, was the true originator of some of the greatest genius attributed to Einstein.

Life abounds with minor mysteries. Few have made the discoveries or must bear the scrutiny of Einstein or Satoshi. It is our mortal amazement at these geniuses that gives rise to such intense interest. Perhaps we are interested in the backstory because the brilliance of their work seems so otherworldly that we seek some divine explanation. Perhaps the human foibles that give rise to conspiracy theories are easier for laypeople to understand than the profound theories themselves. Or, perhaps we want to feel greater intimacy and understanding of those whose work has made such profound influence on our world.

Perhaps it doesn't matter, though. The brilliance behind the Mona Lisa, the Theory of Relativity, or the flawed beauty of bitcoin really does not change their reality nor the utility and fascination that flows from them.

There remain some questions I would ask, had I the opportunity to meet Satoshi. I would demonstrate *The Bitcoin Dilemma* that shows bitcoin mining necessarily requires greater and greater global power consumption as the coin grows in popularity and price. Could one have imagined in 2008 that this coin alone would place its electricity consumption in the planet's thirty largest countries? Would this almost fatal flaw have been enough to induce Satoshi to propose a different scheme to protect the immutability of the digital currency? Was global warming such a nascent concern then that the immense power consumption this coin commands be less obvious then than it is today? Did Satoshi realize that improvements in cost or energy efficiency of mining would merely exacerbate *The Bitcoin Dilemma*? Or, did Satoshi never realize the potential for growth for the currency, or the incredible wealth as the owner of a million such digital coin? These are questions we will address, but, if perhaps for no reason other than intellectual curiosity, it would have been most interesting to hear Satoshi's thoughts on these and myriad other subjects.

3

The Disciples

The pioneers of cryptocurrency share a number of interests and attributes. A good measure of the culture shared among these early pioneers can be characterized by Marshall McLuhan's famous statement that "the medium is the message." We shall even see that Satoshi included in bitcoin's first block, known as the *Genesis Block,* a statement that taunted the Bank of England. In doing so, Satoshi made a declaration to all those who will follow the coin.

Before the first bitcoin was mined on Satoshi's computer, a white paper was issued to the Cypherpunk community. On October 31, 2008, Satoshi opened the statement with a summary of an approach that had eluded other digital coin inventors. Satoshi wrote, "We have proposed a system for electronic transactions without relying on trust. We started with the usual framework of coins made from digital signatures, which provides strong control of ownership, but is incomplete without a way to prevent double-spending. To solve this, we proposed a peer-to-peer network using Proof of work to record a public history of transactions that quickly becomes computationally impractical for an attacker to change if honest nodes control a majority of CPU proof-of-work."[1]

While perhaps cryptic to the uninitiated, Satoshi's solution was profound and prophetic, if not perhaps still a bit ahead of its time. Only a handful of virtual colleagues followed up with Satoshi at first, but the elegance of a

---

[1] https://nakamotoinstitute.org/bitcoin/, accessed April 19, 2022.

solution to a viable digital currency was slowly recognized by the Cypherpunk community.

These pioneers and early champions of bitcoin were disaffected Gen X cypherpunks who perennially suffered in the shadow of the baby boomers that monopolized management of most institutions, from corporate America to government, our non-profits, and our universities. Their generation was post-Watergate and held little confidence in what they saw as the corruptibility of existing institutions, or their ability to make change from within.

They were bright, creative, well-trained, and resourceful. They had a far better grasp of technologies that were becoming ubiquitous as they were exposed to nascent technologies through their formative years a decade earlier. Compared to the sizeable but technologically sleepy generation of the 1960s and 1970s, young people of that era shaped and used technology like no generation before them. They were idealists, but not without a sense of social responsibility. They gave rise to an industry, Silicon Valley, but also a mindset and culture.

> **The Friedman Doctrine**
>
> In 1970, Milton Friedman, the most prominent economist of his day, wrote an influential editorial for the New York Times that could be a manifesto for the generation that followed the Woodstock generation. Entitled "A Friedman Doctrine – The Social Responsibility of Business Is to Increase Its Profits," this superficial appeal to the allure of capitalism seemed to shrug off corporate social responsibility. Likewise, in a simplistic ode to Friedman and to the unbridled pursuit of money and power, Michael Douglas uttered the "Greed is Good" speech of Gordon Gekko in the 1987 movie *Wall Street*.
>
> Subscribers to such libertarian values who came of age in the 1980s and 1990s did not eschew in corporate responsibility. Rather, they believed an individual should not ponder the question too deeply. Indeed, society as a whole must shoulder social responsibility while individual members of society should be afforded all the liberty their personal constitutions grant them, so long as they do not detract from the liberty of others. This was the libertarian credo shared by many young people, especially if they choose to do good as they do well.
>
> A libertarian streak flourished in Silicon Valley (and still does), among young people who felt held back by society's rules and wished to find technological ways around such constraints. They were idealistic, not with a nostalgia for our institutions, but rather in ways for the individual to prevail in spite of institutions. They were law-abiding, but also believed minor transgressions for the greater goal of democratizing markets and exchanges is not a travesty.

The Peer-to-Peer Movement

The formative years for these individuals were frustrated by large media corporations that were getting wealthier by charging $6 for movie tickets and $15 for CDs. The Internet was coming of age at the same time, and its increased bandwidth afforded young people an opportunity to distribute digital copies of things of value between themselves and over the Internet. After all, they would argue, the creative artists see a dismal share of the wealth they create. Instead, media conglomerates held all the power and the profits. The Peer-to-Peer Movement was determined to redistribute these profits.

Their ideal of democratized sharing of creative property was realized through broadly subscribed file sharing services. At first, nodes were set up to index and thus help distribute digital media content. Napster was one such mechanism that became an instant success. It helped share information among users about where content such as music files could be found and created a connection between those who will share and those who want their content.

This facilitated peer-to-peer file sharing mechanism was shut down for copyright infringement by 2001, but the technology it helped foster was already one step ahead. A loose virtual assembly of self-professed nerds figured out ways to promote file sharing among peers without the need for central servers, through Gnutella, Kazaa, and other novel pieces of code. Cypherpunks had adapted a technology designed by the U.S. Navy to permit encrypted communications and route virtual transactions. The method called "The Onion Router" (TOR) acts as a network to directly connect like-minded file sharers.

As regulators in turn attempted to cripple such peer-to-peer exchanges, a new standard called the BitTorrent protocol formed that allowed communities to exchange content in ways that could not be pinned to a particular person. Instead, it was and remains a decentralized method for which open source enabling software is distributed widely. The protocol probes computer clients across the network around the world to provide information as to where digital copies of materials can be found and exchanged. Proponents argued that this method reduced the cost of distribution of media content, even though they admit it challenged the traditional media publisher model that paid royalties to artists.

A CBS News poll in 2003 estimated that 70% of 18- to 29-year-olds felt such file sharing was acceptable in general, at least in some circumstances.[2] A

---

[2] Poll: Young Say File Sharing OK Archived 2013-10-29 at the Wayback Machine *CBS News*, Bootie Cosgrove-Mather, September 18, 2003.

full 75% thought it was acceptable to exchange media files this way, even if it is illegal.[3]

Soon, such peer-to-peer exchanges broadened well beyond mass media. Any digital record of value could be exchanged, including Social Security numbers, secret government documents, software, and patient records. Obviously, given the ability to participate somewhat anonymously, but also instantaneously and efficiently, the methods developed for peer-to-peer exchanges that can be self-administering and maintainable had the potential for both good and evil, depending on the morals of the participants.

The Blockchain

Meanwhile, a concept called blockchain had also been in development. Blockchain is a sort of database, but without the necessity for centralization. Databases are, in essence, tables of data, while blockchains are series of blocks of data that are interconnected over time. One might think of a blockchain as a series of worksheets in one large Excel workbook, with each new worksheet a tab that is linked to the preceding tab for sake of continuity.

Each of these blocks could contain any sort of sequential information, such as a deed of ownership, additions to a medical record, the reassignment of an airline seat, weather records for the day, or perhaps even transactions of the title of items exchanged between one participant and another. By linking these blocks in the chain, one could then ensure that no block can be subsequently modified without destroying a link in the chain. Hence, the blockchain acts as a way to preserve its contents and their ownership for posterity.

Encryption adds another layer. Each block could be completely public and available for all to see, or could also be encrypted so that only those with a key can determine its contents or perhaps who transacted with whom. Whether encrypted or not, by linking each block in the chain to its adjacent blocks, the integrity of the entire chain is protected. The contents of each block are memorialized through their storage centrally or in nodes, or participating clients, across a network. In essence, any node can back up the entire system. If a voting model is superimposed on the blockchain, a majority of all nodes that maintain the blockchain must consent to add a block to the chain. Only once these peers verify or authenticate the accuracy of the addition does the block become official.

---

[3] TT/Adam Ewing. 8 June 06 09:54 CET. "Young voters back file sharing" Archived August 15, 2010 at the Wayback Machine, *The Local*.

This rather clever blockchain technology was developed in the early 1990s by two Bellcore Labs computer scientists named Stuart Haber and Scott Stornetta, as an extension of a 1982 Ph.D. thesis by cryptographer David Chaum, entitled "Computer Systems Established, Maintained, and Trusted by Mutually Suspicious Groups." Their goal was to create a system of interlinked documents that all participants could witness. In essence, a transparent democracy prevents corruptibility. Haber and Stornetta's 1990 paper, "How to Timestamp a Digital Document," published in the Journal of Cryptology, described such a process, and proposed a technique, called a hash, to authenticate each subsequent document.

I leave to the next chapter the details of how such a chain of individual blocks can be immortalized with the cryptographic technique called a hash function. But, with this additional piece of the puzzle, much of the technical detail was available by the early 2000s. The blockchain can immortalize a sequence of data, and peer-to-peer networks can both oversee the process, ensure the data is correct, and record it by consensus on the network.

The next step is for someone to combine the dual techniques of blockchain and decentralized peer-to-peer networks to create some sort of alternative to cash. That was Satoshi's mission. Heavily influenced by the previous work of Haber and Stornetta, Satoshi attributed most of the references in the seminal 2008 white paper on bitcoin to the work by the pair of authors.

By the early 2000s, blockchains were recognized as consisting of up to five parts; a hardware infrastructure, a network of nodes or clients that can propagate and verify the blockchain, a consensus or authentication method to ensure an adverse agent cannot corrupt the chain, the blocks of data themselves, and, possibly, programs or applications that act to process or present the blocks in a useful way.

Software could be designed to perform these tasks. To improve the software over time, a soft or a hard "fork" can be proposed or implemented. Such a shift changes the rules that govern the processing or authentication of blocks. A soft fork can best be described as a software update for each node which could be of the form of a minor update that enhances efficiency or utility, while a hard fork is a major update that may move the network to an entirely new approach to authentication. For instance, a completely decentralized system for the verification of each block may be hard forked to move the chain from a Proof of Work method by which all machines participate in both the recording and authentication of blocks, to a Proof of Stake model in which a few trusted machines provide the verification.

The inherent decentralization of such a peer-to-peer network using Proof of Work authentication reduces the risk that one bad actor can overpower it by rigging polling of nodes. So long as a bad actor cannot control more than 50% of the network, the blockchain's integrity is maintained. In the case of bitcoin, for instance, to command more than 50% of the network would incur a cost of both the machinery and electricity employed by more than half of the network capacity, which would likely well-exceed the value any such manipulation could benefit a malicious actor.

While the potential for a blockchain to represent an immutable public record of transactions between private individuals hidden behind protected private account numbers had become obvious to Satoshi by 2008, there are a number of other digitizations that blockchain technology can immortalize. For instance, the blockchain can represent the terms of contracts that can be approved or authenticated by various parties, and then remain immutable unless both parties agree to a subsequent modification.

Banks could use a blockchain internally to record and distribute financial transactions, loan applications, cash settlements, and asset transfers. Similar record-keeping duties required by local governments to record land transactions and titles, or stock exchanges to record asset or derivative purchases or sales. Gambling houses that record and reward bets can likewise find blockchain technology an efficient record-keeping and protection mechanism.

Even the supply chain can be enhanced by blockchain technology. Its inherent recording and time-stamping of data allow for tracking of product, even as it perhaps monitors and records temperature or product handling. Any item that must be traced from initial provider to end user could employ blockchain technology to monitor product movement and handling. Such a decentralized data network could even assist in the maintenance of the efficiency and reliability of the electric grid by providing a single location by which power companies can monitor and exchange electric capacity.

Given these important qualities of time-stamping, tracking, and data integrity authentication, and the flexibility to perform these functions in either a public or private (encrypted) way, with a broad network itself performing these functions in Proof of Work, or one or a few trusted entities doing so in Proof of Stake, it is no wonder that so many entities are exploiting and exploring the blockchain technology. In 2008, it was merely a matter of time before someone proposed these methods for the exchange of purchasing power itself.

Before we continue with how bitcoin and similar Proof of Work applications of blockchain technology are designed, let us for a moment differentiate between the blockchain itself and the philosophy of peer-to-peer transactions. Blockchain is no more ideological than a linked ledger or a spreadsheet.

Rather, the innovation is in the democratization of block authentication. The ideology of decentralization and institutionless peer-to-peer transactions is rooted in either a belief that such a decentralization is more efficient or is perhaps less controllable, transparent, or regulatable by potentially corruptible institutions. The Proof of Work concept replaces trust in institutions with a system based on a decentralized and democratized network that shapes a technology. Blockchain is apolitical, but peer-to-peer networks had their roots in a desire to circumvent traditional ways in which value is created or transferred.

This philosophical distinction is an essential element in the foundations of the cryptocurrency movement. The techniques are not designed to make traditional pathways for commerce substantially more efficient. Rather, the techniques reroute these pathways to bypass traditional institutions completely. The reasons can be as benign as a desire to improve system redundancy, but are more likely articulated in a desire to make obsolete traditional institutions, as we shall soon see when we more carefully parse Satoshi's motivating statement in the seminal white paper and analyze the first *Genesis Block* of bitcoin. Much of this emotional and intellectual energy is rooted in a desire to support a way to interact beyond the influence and control of traditional institutions, that may include nations' central banks, but also Facebook and Google as they strive to monopolize the Web to create a new world of virtual commerce.

A Reinvention of Global Commerce and Communications

The World Wide Web has evolved since the inception of Web 1.0 in 1991. These more primitive websites were static sources of content without significant interactivity. In 2004, Web 2.0 was developed. It spawned burgeoning forms of social media in which consumers of content also became producers. This was the era in which MySpace, Friendster, and Facebook thrived. People could communicate through encrypted channels that bypassed telecommunications companies through Instagram, WhatsApp, etc., and skateboard singing, dog dancing, and recipe producing talents could be shared instantly through TikTok and YouTube.

The term Web3 was popularized by Gavin Wood, a co-founder of the cryptocurrency protocol Ethereum. In 2014, he envisioned a decentralized online ecosystem based on blockchain technology in which one can freely transact and use tokens protected by the blockchain to verify identity and define ownership of content. By using blockchain technology, the concept presumes we own our data and can maintain our privacy or anonymity without having to rely on or trust companies like large telecommunications companies, Google, Facebook, or its most recent reincarnation, Meta. Proponents of this somewhat vague concept, beyond its obvious utility in its adoption of cryptocurrencies over central bank-sponsored and commercial bank-distributed fiat currencies, argue that the World Wide Web would not need to be regulated if it became decentralized. An alternate proposition would be that it could not be regulated if it were decentralized.

Under such a decentralization, society would not rely on Facebook or Twitter to oversee and regulate hate speech, cyberbullying, or cybercrime, or the circulation of child pornography. On the other hand, this hyper-individualism and decentralization of the Internet are consistent with the strong libertarian views that typically underpin these and similar Cypherpunk-inspired developments since the mid-1990s. While they characterize their goals within terms such as decentralization and personal empowerment, the opposite side of that coin is an intense distrust of large corporations, government, and similar monolithic institutions.

The Dystopian Ideal of Web 3.0

Jack Dorsey, the co-founder of Twitter, saw through the empowerment veneer of Web 3.0 proponents. He observed that such a movement merely shifts power away from traditional non-digital institutions, only to eventually be captured by sophisticated digital institutions such as Facebook.[4] Indeed, Mark Zuckerberg's reinvention of Facebook as Meta and its investment in Artificial Reality software and hardware are designed to create for his company even more toeholds into its clients in such a Web3. By expanding its reach beyond traditional consumer-developed content, Meta expected to draw participants into their world of virtual reality, through their purchase of the Oculus headset company, so one could install their virtual reality hardware and presumably be connected at work, travel, and play into an endlessly broadening Internet experience that encompasses almost all of our waking lives, and perhaps someday beyond that as well, with each element owned and controlled by Meta. The hope is that we would interact and transact solely within a Metaverse. In turn, a Cypherpunk ideal becomes corrupted and corporatized in a way that makes an institution wealthy by owning our personal data even if they claim to do so on our behalf.

Ironically, in, or perhaps under such a dystopian world, we do not become less intertwined with large institutions, but more so. The Meta world could

---

[4] Vlad Savov (December 21, 2021). "Jack Dorsey Stirs Uproar by Dismissing Web3 as a Venture Capitalists' Plaything". *Bloomberg*, retrieved February 5, 2022.

be a clever way to co-opt Web 3.0 rather than offer an alternative to it. Certainly, in such a blockchain and cryptocurrency world, the traditional roles of banks, government, Visa, Mastercard, and American Express, central banks and treasuries, and other institutions will be diluted or irrelevant, but Google and Meta may take their place. Indeed, Facebook was developing its own cryptocurrency, Libra, which it claims to have abandoned under the resistance of regulators and their concern that Libra would become, in essence, a virtual bank for a privatized virtual economy, all conducted through scrip on the company store. Libra may be gone for now, but the new day it promises is not likely forgotten. The belief that private individuals or new mega- (Meta-?) institutions can be more trusted than government-run or government-sponsored institutions remains questionable.

4

The Genesis Block

Recall Satoshi's motivation for the need of a Proof of Work cryptocurrency. Satoshi advocated for a digital payment system that would allow direct transactions between parties without the intervention of a "trusted third party." These transactions can be memorialized in perpetuity by raising the cost of corrupting the system of transactions to an impracticably expensive level. The security of the system is ensured if there are a sufficient number of honest, independent and uncontrolled nodes with more collective processing power than any possible coalition of those who would try to corrupt it.

Satoshi strove to prevent the corruption of blocks in the chain. Benjamin Franklin once said that a secret could be kept between three people only if two of them are dead. Satoshi's concern was that any third party that required trust could be corruptible. The innovation was to make such corruption impractically expensive. Satoshi proposed, "What is needed is an electronic payment system based on cryptographic proof instead of trust, allowing any two willing parties to transact directly with each other without the need for a trusted third party. Transactions that are computationally impractical to reverse would protect sellers from fraud, and routine escrow mechanisms could easily be implemented to protect buyers."[1]

Satoshi's method employed a blockchain verified using a standard hash function called SHA-256. This hash function is an algorithm of the SHA-256 family that converts the contents of a block of data into a value that is 256

---

[1] https://nakamotoinstitute.org/bitcoin/, accessed April 19, 2022.

binary bits long, and hence capable of representing 2^{256} values, equivalent to 1.158×10^{77} different combinations. To put its scale in perspective, this 256-bit number is large enough to count almost all the atoms in the entire known universe.[2]

Such hash functions were designed by the U.S. National Security Agency in 2001 and patented by the National Institute of Standards and Technology (NIST), a federal agency responsible for standardized measures. The algorithms were patented as royalty-free, which allows anybody to employ them. This open access patent ensured that no entity could monopolize and hence limits its utility. Like the TOR network developed by the U.S. Navy, these hash functions provided by the NIST proved useful to cypherpunks.

The unique aspect of the hash algorithm is that it can translate any alphanumeric sequence that constitutes a block into a single number such that even the slightest change in the contents of the block will yield a dramatically different encoding number. For instance, for the previous sentence without the period, the SHA-256 hash output would be (in the more compact 16-bit hexadecimal form, and hence a quarter the length of the binary equivalent):

392c7bcd5ba339b465907e17d4df4b7586daa3443530e8e81c6ed4497e2e32e0

If I merely include a period at the end of the sentence, the hash output changes dramatically:

40f611798a37449e564715c777f6c8e7323b7a80ff0f7c2837c7c777044dbe81

The important properties of such a hash function are its incredible sensitivity of the output to even the slightest change of the input, and the output that can assume an almost unfathomable number of combinations, each which appears as a random number.

The Genesis Block

Satoshi employed this readily calculable hash function to ensure no link in a block chain can be subsequently modified without changing the block's

---

[2] https://www.liverpoolmuseums.org.uk/stories/which-greater-number-of-atoms-universe-or-number-of-chess-moves, retrieved February 5, 2022.

identifying code. To see how this is done, let us consider first Satoshi's *Genesis Block*[3] (underlining emphasis added) below:

> **Raw Code for the Genesis Block**
> 01000000
> 0000000000000000000000000000000000000000000000000000000000000000
> 3ba3edfd7a7b12b27ac72c3e67768f617fc81bc3888a51323a9fb8aa4b1e5e4a
> 29ab5f49
> ffff001d
> 1dac2b7c
> 01
> 01000000
> 01
> 0000000000000000000000000000000000000000000000000000000000000000
> ffffffff
> 4d
> <u>04Ffff001d0104455468652054696d65732030332f4a616e2f323030392043686</u>
> <u>16e63656c6c6f72206f6e206272696e6b206f66207365636f6e64206261696c6f</u>
> <u>757420666f722062616e6b73</u>
> ffffffff
> 01
> 00f2052a01000000
> 43
> 4104678afdb0fe5548271967f1a67130b7105cd6a828e03909a67962e0ea1f
> 61deb649f6bc3f4cef38c4f35504e51ec112de5c384df7ba0b8d578a4c702b6
> bf11d5fac

The underlined string above, when inserted into a hexadecimal to text converter, yields[4]:

The Times 03/Jan/2009 Chancellor on brink of second bailout for banks

This first block appeared at 6:15 PM UTC on January 3, 2009, a few months after Satoshi published the white paper on bitcoin design on October 31, 2008. It contained but one transaction, the payment of 50 bitcoin as a reward to the first miner who could successfully encode the block, and recorded to an address that has never been drawn down. It also contained the text series that restates a headline from the London-based Times Newspaper: "Chancellor on brink of second bailout for banks."

The block was recorded to show the following creation of bitcoin:

---

[3] https://bitcointalk.org/index.php?topic=52706, retrieved February 26, 2022.
[4] http://www.unit-conversion.info/texttools/hexadecimal/, accessed April 19, 2022.

> **Block Transaction 0[5]**
>
> Fee.
> Btc
> Hash.
> 4a5e1e4baab89f3a32518a88c31bc87f618f76673e2cc77ab2127
> b7afdeda33b 2009–01-03 13:15
> To: COINBASE (Newly Generated Coins).
> The Times 03/Jan/2009 Chancellor on brink of second bailout for banks.
> 1A1zP1eP5QGefi2DMPTfTL5SLmv7DivfNa
> Btc

Satoshi's choice of content in the block narrative telegraphs a profound mistrust in traditional financial institutions, a sentiment widely shared among cybergeeks of that era, and beyond. In 2008 there was growing mistrust of banks and other large institutions too-big-to-fail, and their central bank co-conspirators, that many blamed for the *Great Recession*.

The Genesis Block is important because, as the first link in the chain, it cannot yet contain any reference to a previous link. However, beyond the content of recorded transactions, each block since the Genesis Block also contains a randomly generated 256-bit number that a computer processing the bitcoin protocol inserts into the new block. This content and the randomly generated number, called a "nonce" for "number used once," are then run through the SHA-256 algorithm to generate a new 256-bit number.

Such an output from a hash of this next block can be considered a random number too, albeit a very long one that could also take on any of its 1.158×10^{77} possible values. The odds that this calculated hash is less than a certain threshold then depend on the size of the threshold. Specification of a narrow threshold amounts to a limit of the share of hashes that could meet the threshold requirement. Satoshi defined such a threshold as a requisite series of leading zeroes at the beginning of the hash code output. The greater number of these leading zeroes specifies a tighter range for a hash code to match a tolerance the bitcoin protocol specifies. Such a threshold limits the number of candidates that are permitted to successfully calculate the block.

---

[5] https://www.blockchain.com/btc/block/0, accessed April 19, 2022.

The Difficulty Threshold

Early on, this difficulty threshold was very loose since personal computers in Satoshi's day were not able to calculate as many hashes each second as processors commonly perform now. Satoshi also built into the protocol the automatic adjustment of this threshold so that there could be but one successful hash every ten minutes, on average, even as network hashing power rises. Indeed, for this very first run of the SHA-256 algorithm on the Genesis Block, Satoshi defined a tolerance to be such a wide margin that a single personal computer (usually Satoshi's) could successfully calculate on average one successful hash every ten minutes. Beyond that, should more processing power become available, the tolerance would automatically become narrower so matches still occur only about every ten minutes on average.

The next link in the chain following the Genesis Block was not actually processed for another six days. After a series of runs, a sufficiently successful hash included the 256-bit output from the SHA-256 hash of the Genesis Block, another mining reward, and another guessed nonce, but still with no transactions. It was run through the SHA-256 algorithm once again and one fortunate output was deemed sufficiently within tolerances to justify its reward, worth nothing at that time because there was nobody yet with whom to exchange these interesting digital coins. Once the various nodes, or collection of clients, on the network verify and vote in affirmation of the match, the various accounts can be credited and debited through a system of private wallets, and the process moves on to the next block.

A Brief Primer on How a Bitcoin Hash Works

You can now see how block integrity is maintained. Every block contains a 256-bit number that uniquely represents the contents of the previous block, and a series of transactions, each identified by an account number paid from, an amount paid, and an account number to which the bitcoin is paid out. Finally, it includes a unique nonce inserted by the mining processor. The miner then runs all the data through the hash function to generate an output that is hopefully "close enough" to the tolerance required by bitcoin's ever-evolving difficulty tolerance. Since any processor running the SHA-256 bit algorithm can quickly confirm whether a miner claiming success produced a hash within the required tolerance, any miner on the network can vote to affirm a claim of matching success. In other words, the block is difficult to encode within

> the required tolerance over the specified ten-minute period, but easy to verify after a node on the network claims a hashing success.

This technique ensures that one could not go back and reinvent history. To do so on even a single block would require command of the equivalent of the majority of the combined processing power of the entire network. Such a corruption of a single block would result in a new hash output that would not match the inserted code recorded in the next block. A potential corruptor of the system would have to recalculate the block, and also all the blocks that occurred since then. As the network grows, so does the relative impossibility of network corruption in this manner. Satoshi was eager to grow the network so that it becomes less corruptible and more resilient to malicious attackers.

Private Wallets Augment the Public Ledger

We now see how raw processing power takes publicly observable data shared among the nodes to link each block, with each neighboring block acting as links that align and protect the immortality of the transactions across links of the blockchain. We must also provide a series of "wallets" that obscure and protect each individual owner by making observable only a public account number without revealing its owner. Such accounts are credited and debited accordingly once the block is authenticated. These wallets are encrypted so that, if one cannot steal directly from the blockchain, nor would it be easy to try to steal from individual account owners.

This protection is done in two ways. First, every account has its public key that can be seen within the authenticated block. Each wallet also has a private key which must be highly protected in the early coin on a private hard drive or a thumb drive, now on in a digital wallet through an organized exchange. The public face of any account can be debited or credited, but the transfer of tokens remains incomplete without knowledge of the associated private key. This associated network of wallets is now typically housed in large cryptocurrency institutions such as Coinbase, or Gemini, founded by the Winklevoss Twins of Facebook founding fame, that act in some ways act like banks, as I describe later, but, in Satoshi's time were held on local hard or thumb drives.

Rewards to Miners that Maintain the Blockchain

The final piece of the puzzle is the reward offered to the processors, called miners, that do the computational work in inserting nonces and running hashes. This reward, in the form of bitcoin, is at the root of *The Bitcoin Dilemma*.

The initial reward level in 2009 was set to 50 bitcoin for each successful block encoded every ten minutes. At that time, the value of a bitcoin was essentially zero. More than a year later, on May 22, 2010, the first bitcoin transaction of 10,000 coin purchased two pizzas. It was not until two years later, in February of 2012, that the value of a bitcoin rose to $1 U.S. More recently, in November of 2021, the price rose to almost $70,000.

Bitcoin was designed to add to its supply 50 new coin initially as the miner reward every ten minutes on average. The bitcoin algorithm was designed to eventually converges to a fixed supply of coin maintained by miners rewarded through transaction fees. But, leading up to the phasing out of transaction fees, Satoshi designed this reward structure to halve every four years after the mining of 210,000 blocks. When halving is taken into consideration, by 2140 the current supply of 19,000,000 bitcoin outstanding will have risen only slightly, from its level today to 21,000,000 bitcoin. Beyond 2140, further encoding would be done by miners that compete for transaction fees built into each transaction rather than for a fixed but declining block reward.

Of the 19,000,000 coin mined so far, Satoshi successfully mined about 1 million of them in those early years. An estimated 2.78 million and 3.79 million bitcoin have been lost.[6] Much of this loss of coin arose because people forgot their 256-bit private address, its 64-character hexadecimal equivalent, or a critical sequence of words that act as their private key to allow them access to their funds.

> **Coins Lost Will Benefit All Others**
>
> In one notorious case, an early miner, James Howells, earned 7,500 bitcoin by mining using his personal gaming computer. When he cleaned out his office years later, he realized that the hard drive containing his private key was likely lost to a landfill in a Newport, Wales. He has raised millions of dollars to try to excavate the landfill, which may hold the key to a wealth that has a value approaching $500 million.[7]

---

[6] https://www.coindesk.com/tech/2021/12/08/bitcoins-lost-coins-are-worth-the-price/, retrieved February 5, 2022.

> Such a loss of coin acts much like the destruction of money. With each such loss, the remaining coins become more scarce and valuable, just as occurs with a monetary deflation. On the other hand, the increased supply of bitcoin from mining every ten minutes dilutes the coin already in circulation, and hence acts like an inflation, with current bitcoin holders ultimately paying the price. Satoshi noted, "Lost coins only make everyone else's coins worth slightly more. Think of it as a donation to everyone."[8]

Clearly, with a current mining reward of 6.25 coin after three halvings, but with the price of bitcoin rising to approach $70,000, mining of bitcoin can be very lucrative, so long as the value of bitcoin rises faster than the halving of the number of bitcoin rewarded per block. For the first few years of bitcoin mining, the rewards were tiny, and hence, it is easy to understand how coin can be inadvertently lost. However, we shall show that the price of bitcoin has always increased faster than the coin rewarded halved, so the reward structure, while not lucrative in 2009, became so years later. I will discuss the implications of six-digit reward payouts in a later chapter, and at the same time describe more fully *The Bitcoin Dilemma*. Next, though, I contrast this reward structure to other possible ways to sustainably reward the effort to maintain blockchain integrity.

---

[7] https://www.newyorker.com/magazine/2021/12/13/half-a-billion-in-bitcoin-lost-in-the-dump, retrieved March 7, 2022.

[8] https://bitcointalk.org/index.php?topic=198.msg1647#msg1647, accessed May 2, 2022.

Part II

Cryptocurrency Corporatization

I next describe how the growth of bitcoin demand relative to its relatively fixed supply spawned a corporatization of the coin and created huge profits for a few highly capitalized miners. Instead of a democratized coin that could bring banking to the masses, and make obsolete the financial monoliths Satoshi mistrusted, new financial monoliths were created and more wealth was concentrated, often with funding from the same financial institutions Satoshi lamented were too-big-to-fail.

This conversion of the Gospel of Satoshi to a new Gospel of Profits could have, in retrospect, been predicted. One should never underestimate the ability of the free market to capitalize on any social phenomenon, even if it corrupts the original purpose of a new technology. MySpace and Facebook were created to allow people to share pictures of their family, friends, and cats. But Facebook quickly became a tool that allowed rogue players to undermine democracy while it made Facebook's creator one of the world's richest people. Einstein created perhaps the most succinct and beautiful equation in physics' history, $E=mc^2$, only to see it used to build nuclear bombs. Sometimes the road to hell is paved with good intentions. This section documents how the inherent design of bitcoin had implications Satoshi could not have imagined that frustrated the purity of the messiah's visions.

This is not an indictment of capitalism. Indeed, as Milton Friedman argued, a corporation's responsibility within a capitalist system is to seek out opportunities to profit and hence create value, hopefully by not harming others more than the corporation benefits. Those who profit can then use their new wealth to do good in society. This ideal has been tarnished in the years since *The Cypherpunk Manifesto*, and it opens up an avenue for regulation to return bitcoin back toward Satoshi's vision.

I describe how bitcoin arose out of discussions and theories in computer science circles, especially around encryption, and from some early attempts to develop a blockchain system that is difficult to corrupt. From these beginnings, Satoshi assembled strands from cryptography and blockchain and interjected a personal philosophy regarding a digital currency that could replace institutions overseeing our transactions with a peer-to-peer network that rewards entities called miners willing to oversee transactions in a way that makes corruption difficult.

I trace the early innovators and the ideas that Satoshi put in place for the first bitcoin protocol. We shall see that, at first, Satoshi worked with a handful of collaborators, with the bitcoin client released in 2009 employed by only a small number of committed hobbyists. Satoshi believed that bitcoin would either fail or succeed spectacularly, but over the period Satoshi was involved, until 2011, it was difficult to imagine which outcome would prevail.

What really accelerated bitcoin mining was not only the hype and increased acceptance the digital coin started to enjoy by 2013, but also innovations that brought to mining significantly more powerful and specialized processors. Bitcoin soon went from a nascent hobbyist stage into a corporate phase, beginning mid-2016, with the invention of highly specialized processors that were priced out of reach of hobbyists, but not of corporations with access to venture capital funds.

At that point, the trivial economics of the industry became big money. I will show that mining activity is determined by the bitcoin price, as is the equilibrium amount of processing power and electricity consumed. We shall see that the economic model predicts very well the vast increase in electricity consumption once Satoshi's beloved decentralized network became institutionalized. Indeed, I show that electricity consumption for mining has already reached an incredible level and will rise at roughly the pace of bitcoin price increases over time. This *Bitcoin Dilemma* presents an important public policy problem once the electricity consumption from mining bitcoin begins to rival the consumption of major countries. I will also show that the profits arising from mining come at the expense of others who consume electricity and the holders of bitcoin themselves.

Various researchers have commented on the dynamics of the bitcoin market, but none have produced a well-specified model of market dynamics until now. A number of researchers have honed our intuition, though. For instance, Okorie (2020) observed that a bitcoin that experiences consistently increasing demand will generate returns that attract investors and miners. The increasing number of miners will translate into greater electricity consumption, which, in turn, naturally generates more greenhouse gases. He recommended development of greener electricity and regulation to mitigate these effects. However, I will show that such intuitive policy recommendations actually fail to deliver reduced industry energy consumption

Gonzales-Barahona (2021) produced the most complete analysis to date by including a number of intertwined factors. Energy consumption should depend on the reward offered to miners, in the form of the bitcoin price, the number of bitcoin minted per block, and any transaction fees awarded miners. These revenues are exhausted through the purchase of electricity at whatever energy price a miner may obtain, mining machine costs that are amortized over the life of a miner, and profits accruing to the operator of a mining farm. He noted that public policy can be used to influence these various prices and costs. However, the model is relatively incomplete in the description of these factors. I am able to extend his simple "Bitcoin Energy Factors Formula" to tease out some strong policy implications that a more complete model permits.

A few authors have noted that energy costs cannot exceed mining rewards and hence are able to calculate a theoretical upper bound of energy costs that permit profitable mining of bitcoin. For instance, Sedlmeir et al. (2020) correctly observed that this upper bound of energy costs is given by the sum of mining rewards and transaction fees. They were one of the first to correctly note that long run energy costs may not decline with improvements in mining efficiency, but argue that these costs may decline in the short run. Since their model is somewhat incomplete in its description of market equilibrium, they do not explore the implications of significant bitcoin price increases, but they do note the effect of reward halving in reducing energy consumption.

Finally, Alsabah and Capponi (2020) develop an interesting game-theoretic Research and Development (R&D) race in which manufacturers race to produce the most innovative mining machines. They note that, in such an R&D race, firms are unable to capture the full benefits of their investment in more innovative designs because competition degenerates into an aggressive and wasteful arms race. They also determine that the mining industry is thus prone to centralization, in stark contrast to the fundamental ideology of Satoshi and the founders of early cryptocurrencies.

The move from the hobby room to the corporate boardroom with the dramatic run-up in the price of bitcoin produces some unintended consequences that should now come as no surprise if we consider bitcoin's computer science roots. Böhme et al. (2015) note that the development of bitcoin was from a software engineering perspective, without the perspective of lawyers, economists, or regulators. Unlike conventional payment systems, bitcoin does not have institutional overview. One of the most influential in the cryptocurrency world, Marc Andreessen, noted in 2014 that "(Bitcoin) gives us, for the first time, a way for one Internet user to transfer a unique piece of digital property to another Internet user, such that the transfer is guaranteed to be safe and secure, everyone knows that the transfer has taken place, and nobody can challenge the legitimacy of the transfer… that does not rely upon a central intermediary like a bank or broker."[1] The lack of an intermediary makes unintended risks difficult to manage, though. It also begs the question—Are there alternate and less resource-intensive ways to accomplish the same goal? The answer is yes.

Bohme et al observe that the irreversibility of bitcoin creates transaction risk of mistakes in transfers that cannot be reversed, operational risk (of a 51% attack, for instance), and legal and regulatory risk. We shall document how this irreversibility enables bitcoin-specific crimes such as money laundering, and the facilitation of illicit activities. The lack of consumer protection mechanisms challenges regulators to reduce these risks. Indeed, the authors also note that central banks cannot tailor monetary growth of digital currencies in even the most basic way. For instance, the cryptocurrency does not merely implement a Friedman k-percent rule for annual growth of the currency supply as used in well-managed paper currencies to prevent inflation, but instead creates a risk of a deflation that occurs when coin is lost. On the other hand, we shall see that the issuance of new bitcoin every ten minutes dilutes the value of existing bitcoin much like printing too much money can induce an inflation. They conclude by noting that there exist coins with superior qualities when compared with bitcoin, such as lower latency or reduced electrical burden, but that the momentum bitcoin developed places it in a more enviable and dominant position.

In the next section, more formal descriptions of both the reward structure and market equilibrium are developed. This full formulation allows us to draw some fascinating and surprising conclusions about the nature of bitcoin mining. By the end of the section, we will have at hand both a model based on economic theory, and a test of the model that explains the observed run-up of

---

[1] https://breakthrough.unglobalcompact.org/disruptive-technologies/blockchain/, accessed March 22, 2022.

mining capacity and energy consumption as the price of bitcoin rises, despite huge improvements in miner efficiency. This result is something that Satoshi appears to have not fully contemplated in the formulation of the Bitcoin Proof of Work protocol.

5

A New Testament

Bitcoin was certainly no overnight success. Following the mining of the first block on January 3, 2009, it was not until six days later, on January 9, 2009, that the source code to run a bitcoin node was released to SourceForge, a site that functions as a clearing house for digital innovators. From then on, Satoshi was hashing blocks regularly and earning 50 bitcoin with every additional linked block in the chain, even though no transactions had occurred. It would take more than a year for a single purchase to be made with bitcoin, and two years before bitcoin attained a value above one dollar.

On release day, programmer Hal Finney downloaded and ran the software to encode the first block processed by someone other than Satoshi. In the first linked block that actually included a transaction, Block 170 contained the previous block's hash, a nonce, inserted by the miner, the mining reward, and a gift of 10 bitcoin from Satoshi's public key to Finney's public key as a gesture of appreciation for Finney's interest in Satoshi's new digital coin (Fig. 5.1).

If Satoshi was the original alpha tester, Finney was its beta tester. Over the next few days, Finney and Satoshi kept mining and maintained email exchanges critiquing the software. The feedback allowed Satoshi to continuously improve bitcoin's design until the algorithm could run essentially uninterrupted and stably so. The difficulty target was so low that one or two machines could easily proceess enough hashes in ten minutes to satisfy the bitcoin protocol in those early days.

While Finney harbored some of the strident libertarianism which many programmers shared at that time, his business partner noted that Finney was quite normal, without the antisocial or socially uncomfortable attributes many of his interested colleagues in his field shared. A collaborator of Finney, Phillip Zimmerman noted that "Sometimes people pay some price for being extremely smart - they are deficient in some emotional quality. Hal was not like that."[1]

Nonetheless, Finney was drawn to digital currencies that could skirt the scrutiny of government and banks. He experimented himself with early digital currencies and hence quickly realized the internal beauty of Satoshi's approach. He continued to help support bitcoin's development, even while bedridden in the advanced state of Lou Gehrig's Disease by employing devices that permitted him to edit software using equipment that tracked his eye movement.

Satoshi's star sunset as quickly as it rose. Satoshi's last public posting on the bitcoin forum was December 12, 2010, when the price of bitcoin was $0.23. The last private correspondence to collaborators was April 26, 2011, when bitcoin remained at $1.56. Satoshi passed the baton and was not heard from since. Mike Hearn, one of the virtual colleagues who noted Satoshi's passing, wrote "He communicated with a few of the core developers before leaving.

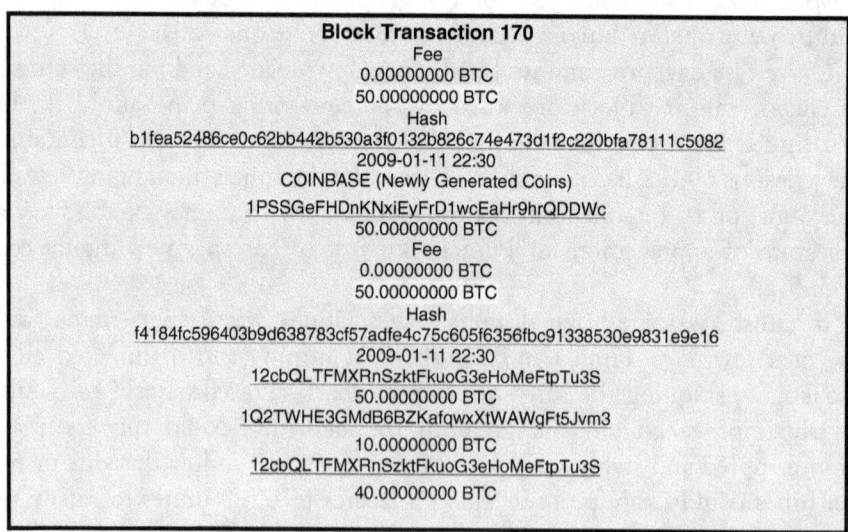

Fig. 5.1 The first bitcoin transaction gifted 10 bitcoin to Hal Finney

---

[1] https://www.nytimes.com/2014/08/31/business/hal-finney-cryptographer-and-bitcoin-pioneer-dies-at-58.html, accessed March 21, 2022.

He told myself and Gavin that he had moved on to other things and that the project was in good hands."[2]

Finney had also moved on, but checked in some time later to discover his reward earnings, and his gift from Satoshi, was still recorded for immortality in the blockchain. At that time, bitcoin aficionados held their private keys that unlocked their public transactions in the bitcoin blockchain on hard drives or thumb drives. This private key is represented by a code only the owner knew that could open up the wallet by anybody presenting the proper private key. Since bitcoin was almost worthless in these early days, people did not think much about wallet security.

Unfortunately, Finney's diagnosis of Amyotrophic Lateral Sclerosis took his life on August 28, 2014. On the day he died, the price of bitcoin was $507.82, and 19,862,000 coin had changed hands. Given that there was well less than that amount regularly in circulation, some people were already valuing the coin not for transacting but also for speculation.

Some of Finney's savings in bitcoin went to pay his hospital expenses. Hopefully, he was also able to leave his family a legacy. In his obituary following his death in August of 2014, Finney noted that his life work was dedicated to "making Big Brother obsolete" and explained his motivation in the development of cryptographic technology was motivated by his concern about the ability of corporations and governments to spy on citizens.[3]

Even before Finney's passing, by mid-2010, Satoshi's involvement in bitcoin had also tapered off. The bitcoin creator's main concern was to ensure that the network was sufficiently populated by active miners so that no one miner, or a coalition of miners, could dominate the network and vote to fork the bitcoin algorithm in a direction that would violate Satoshi's ideals. Satoshi ultimately left oversight of bitcoin to the non-profit *Bitcoin Foundation* that continued to develop and support the currency until a series of disagreements forced dissolution of the foundation in 2015.

Over 2010, the bitcoin protocol continued to be refined. It was discovered, for instance, that a high total sum of transactions that exceeded 2^{64}, or about a trillion coin, could cause overflows that allowed a transactor to transfer 92 billion bitcoin to two addresses presumably associated with the person who exploited the flaw. The flaw was fixed and the software was forked to prevent such an exploitation in the future. By consensus agreement of the nodes mining bitcoin at that time, the network also invalidated that exploitative transaction. No serious bugs have emerged ever since.

---

[2] https://bitcointalk.org/in108047dex.php?topic=145850.20;wap2, accessed April 26, 2022.
[3] https://www.nytimes.com/2014/08/31/business/hal-finney-cryptographer-and-bitcoin-pioneer-dies-at-58.html?_r=1, retrieved February 5, 2022.

Early Mining Technology

Mining in 2010 remained small-scale until April of 2010. To then, mining relied on Central Processor Units (CPUs) at the heart of any personal computer, with a difficulty target that ran from 1 for all of 2009 to about 8000 by the end of 2011. A unity difficulty factor of one would allow a successful hash once in a ten-minute period when only Satoshi was mining, while a number of 8000 would pare the odds down to 1 in 8000 to ensure but one of perhaps 8,000 PCs running Satoshi's software, or one machine 8,000 times more powerful than Satoshi's PC, would succeed every ten minutes.

Recall that a hash function will produce a dramatically different output for the most minor change in its inputs. The nonce inserted each time a miner hashes a block is a random number. The output of the algorithm it then runs appears random in that even minor changes in the block acts as a seed to generate an almost entirely unique 256-bit output. If that number which can span all possible values is sufficiently close to zero, as defined by the difficulty factor tolerance, the miner that first meets the criterion wins the reward, subject to verification by the other nodes on the network. Such a verification is a quick and simple matter. Any successive run of the algorithm with the same input will produce the same reproducible output.

> **What's in a Block?**
> While the term blockchain sounds exotic and complicated, it is actually quite simple and clever. Inside each link or block in a chain can be any sort of information. For bitcoin, it is a set of transactions, with the public half of the address (account number) of a sender, address of a receiver, and the amount of bitcoin transferred. There is also the public address of the miner that wins the block encoding lottery every ten minutes and the amount of bitcoin rewarded. The block can also contain a message, as Satoshi included about central banks in the first (Genesis) block.
>
> These specified public addresses all take the form of a 64-character long hexadecimal string, consisting of numbers 0 to 9 and characters A through F. Each character then assumes one of 16 possible values, and the entire string can then assume 16^{64} possible unique combinations. Since 16 is equal to 2^4, that same address could also be represented in binary code that is $(2^4)^{64}$ bits long, or 2^{256}, where a bit can be either a 0 or a 1. Such a 256-bit long string of 0s and 1s gives the algorithm that summarizes a block the name of a "Secure Hash Algorithm" SHA-256 hash function.
>
> Two more strings must also be included. One is the unique hash output of a 256-bit or 16 hexadecimal string hashed from the previous block, except for the Genesis Block, of course. The other is a 256-bit random number the successful miner inserts as an essential part of the puzzle solved every ten minutes to receive the block reward. A modern miner can take all these public addresses,

transactions over the last ten minutes, any notations, the allowed block reward coming to the miner's address, the previous block's hash code, and the miner's inserted code and runs it through the miner's hash processor at a rate today of more than a hundred trillion times per second. Every miner then creates a new 256-bit hash output many trillions of times a second, for 600 seconds in every ten minute block. That's a lot of possible blocks encoded and summary 256-bit hash outputs generated, by millions of miners at a time.

Of all these outputs, each of which can take on one of 2^{256}, or 1.1579×10^{79} possible values, but the network requires this summary output from the hash function to be sufficiently small that it is below a threshold adjusted to ensure only one such calculation is successful every ten minutes. Such a lottery is not particularly high tech or computationally taxing. It requires but one thing for each mining machine competing on the network—lots of electricity to perform this one calculation over and over again on the same block of data, with a different random number (called a nonce) inserted and hence different hash outputs each time. Only one machine emerges with the output that meets the tolerance. To be sure there is no cheating, the other miners check the successful miner's work by running its same random number to ensure a match. They then vote to approve the miner's reward, and the network moves on to the next block of another new set of transactions, with the hash from the successful block acting as a new seed to be combined with a new set of transactions and a new random nonce.

Each block in the chain is not exotic or particularly high tech. It is typically not even encrypted. Anybody can view every block in the history of bitcoin by referring to any number of online block viewers. But, each block is secure because any subsequent tampering would prevent a block from matching up with the previous block and the next one, and would require incredible computing power to finagle.

For the first couple of years, much of the successful mining was done by Satoshi and a small group of dedicated hobbyists who generated far more in electric bills than in anything yet of value. The difficulty target remained so low that almost any nonce inserted into the input block result in a hash output that fell within the difficulty tolerance range. The reward was a relatively large quantity of coin, but the value of each coin was trivial. There was very little incentive to have many cybergeeks mining away day and night, and perhaps generating heat and imposing wear and tear on their expensive home personal computers.

These processors relied on the Central Processing Units (CPUs) primarily made by Intel, with Advanced Micro Devices (AMD) also emerging in the mix. A CPU is a jack-of-all-trades. It is able to process a complex instruction set, which translates into reasonable efficiency at any sort of calculation one could throw at it, from word processing to number crunching. It shuttles information between its CPU and a very modest amount of memory on its chip, called a cache, and a larger bank of specialized memory for the bigger tasks. Neither memory is particularly quick, by today's standards, while the speed of the processor is defined by the product of the number of tasks it can handle at a given time and the clock speed of the processor that defines how many such cycles it can handle per second.

If CPUs are the workhorses of computers, Graphics Processing Units, or GPUs, are the racehorses. They run at high clock speeds, and they typically employ faster memory that is collocated very near the processing chip. To process graphics, one does not need to consider incredibly large numbers, given that one 24-bit number can represent almost 17 million colors, shades, and intensities. While 17 million is not a large number for a spreadsheet or scientific number crunching, it is fine for graphics. In addition, three-dimensional graphics requires the ability to rotate perspectives, which results in a large array of these smaller-bit representations to be assembled and then translated and viewed from different angles. As such, a GPU performs less complex but more specialized tasks. They do so in a way that requires reduced-instruction-set processors to work quickly and very closely with dedicated and fast memory, which allows gamers to view an evolving scene with many frames per second.

Satoshi was actually opposed to GPU mining. In a statement in 2009, Satoshi wrote:

> We should have a gentleman's agreement to postpone the GPU arms race as long as we can for the good of the network. It's much easier to get new users up to speed if they don't have to worry about GPU drivers and compatibility. It's nice how anyone with just a CPU can compete fairly equally right now.[4]

The GPU and FPGA Mining Revolution

Nonetheless, in April of 2010, Laszlo Hanyecz developed the necessary code, written in a language used to control GPU cards called OpenCL, that allowed him to much more efficiently mine bitcoin, just as Satoshi had feared. These GPUs are much more suited to the necessary register shifts used to process the SHA-256 and other cryptographic algorithms. The algorithm Hanyecz developed was able to divert bitcoin processing to these more specialized Graphics Processor Units, with a significant increase in processing ability. Also, by then, more hobbyists were becoming interested in the novelty of bitcoin.

---

[4] https://bitcoin.stackexchange.com/questions/3572/when-was-the-first-gpu-miner-made-available-publicly, retrieved March 7, 2022.

> **The First Bitcoin Transaction 16 Months After Bitcoin's Release**
> Well before the departure of Satoshi and Finney, bitcoin was indeed beginning to garner attention and use. The first real transaction of bitcoin for a retail transaction, beyond the gift Satoshi provided Finney early on, was an offer of 10,000 mined bitcoin for two pizzas from a Florida Papa John's restaurant, on May 22, 2010, valued at $25. This first bitcoin transaction imparted an imputed price for bitcoin of $0.0025, or a quarter of a penny per bitcoin. An enthusiast who had been generating significant rewards himself posted a proposal on a shared bulletin board for anyone who would deliver him two pizzas to his Florida residence. Someone took the bait, and Laszlo Hanyecz happily completed the first purchase using bitcoin.[5] Each pizza would be worth about $35 million at bitcoin's price peak.

However, while Hanyecz and another GPU coding pioneer who went by the screen name ArtForz could have easily monopolized the code they developed for bitcoin mining and hence corner the bitcoin mining market for themselves, they did something aligned with Satoshi's ideology. Rather than profit personally from their creation, ArtForz made this new software publicly available so that others too could help expand the network. The increased processing productivity was the force that likewise increased the difficulty factor for miners, from 1 in 2009-2010 to 8000 by 2011. It was becoming much harder and more competitive to win what was still a prize of 50 bitcoin. Certainly, in today's age, such an innovation would be privatized and capitalized for great wealth. In 2010 and 2011, though, the Cypherpunk ideal of information sharing for the common good remained strong.

Greater interest in bitcoin was also starting to pay dividends around this era. With a growing value as each bitcoin rose, there was a proportional increase in activity within the growing bitcoin community.

The final innovation that began the transition away from home gaming computers to highly specialized equipment was the experimentation, by mid-2011, with Field Programmable Gate Arrays (FPGA). These devices are reduced-instruction-set collections of processors on a single board, with their associated memory, that can quickly be reconfigured to adapt to different needs. They allowed a programmer to pick and choose the best combination of processors and memory, and configure them in the best balance to suit the processing demands of the problem to which they are assigned.

---

[5] https://www.coindesk.com/markets/2020/05/22/10-years-after-laszlo-hanyecz-bought-pizza-with-10k-bitcoin-he-has-no-regrets/, retrieved March 7, 2022.

These programmable arrays were configured to optimize the Bitcoin SHA-256 algorithm and hence could run much more efficiently than either CPUs or GPUs.

This technical innovation constituted the beginning of the end of CPU-based and PC-based mining. The FPGA initiated a wave of special purpose miners that would soon make PC mining obsolete.

By 2011, imitators and innovators began to appear in the cryptocurrency space. A year later, bitcoin was going more mainstream, with such examples of national attention, including an episode of The Good Wife based on a bitcoin transaction, with cable television business show host Jim Cramer playing himself. The Bitcoin Foundation was also helping to accelerate the standardization, protection, and growth of the coin. By the end of 2012, more than 1,000 merchants were accepting the coin, which had grown in value to about $13, from 30 cents since the beginning of 2011.

In 2013, the upstart San Francisco, U.S.-based bitcoin exchange Coinbase was enabling bitcoin transactions valued at $1 million U.S. per month at a price averaging $22. The first bitcoin automated teller machine (ATM) was set up, in Vancouver, Canada, to service a downtown coffee shop. But, also by late in 2013, the People's Bank of China prohibited Chinese financial institutions from facilitating bitcoin transactions over concerns its use facilitated money laundering or undermined capital movement restrictions. Meanwhile, reminiscent of the famous "Irrational Exuberance" speech by Alan Greenspan in Japan in 1999, Greenspan issued a controversial warning about bitcoin, on December 4, 2013, once again for fear of an asset bubble. A few months later, Warren Buffet labeled bitcoin a financial mirage. To emerging *Crypto Bros*, there is no such thing as bad publicity, while *Cypherpunks* viewed rejection of such a traditional financial institution as Warren Buffet to be a badge of honor.

The ASIC Revolution

By 2014, more and more companies were beginning to accept bitcoin. Mid-2014 saw the hash processing capacity of the network hit 100 petahashes per second. This dramatic increase in the number of hashes per second the network could muster is mostly attributed to the development of Application Specific Integrated Circuits (ASICs) designed solely to process the bitcoin hash functions. By 2016, sixty-three such chips wave-soldered to a board, and with three boards in each miner resulted in the most dramatic explosion of processing power in the industry (Fig. 5.2).

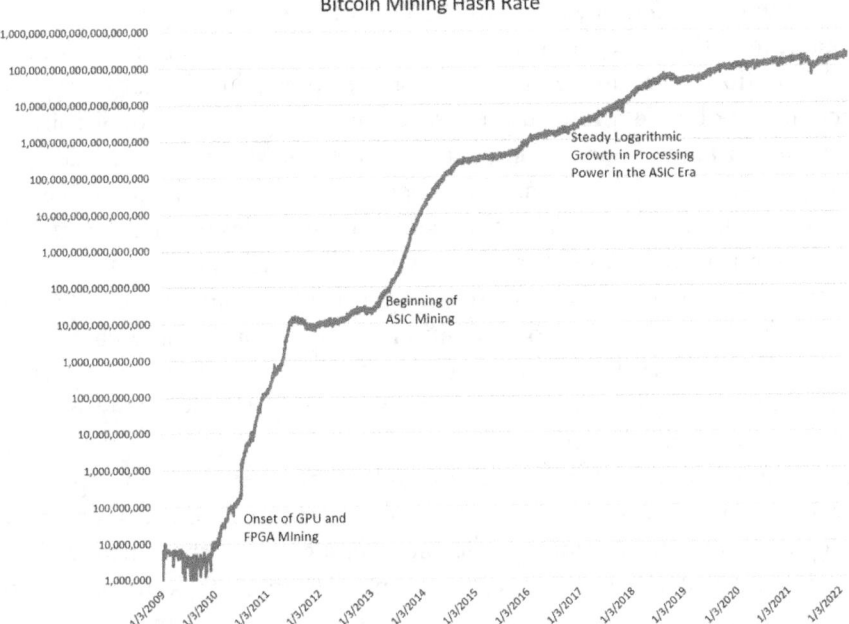

Fig. 5.2 The Evolution of the bitcoin Hash Rate with Improved Technologies

Since early 2013, when the first 130 nm ASIC chip was designed and built for specialized mining, the ASIC chip was able to shrink in size, to 16 nm silicon transistor spacing, a 100 times greater density on an integrated circuit by 2016. These new state-of-the-art Antminer S9 mining machines were designed and manufactured by the Chinese company Bitmain. With each such successive improvement came an enhancement in processing speed but not at the incredible rate of innovation and processing capacity that occurred with the initial introduction of FPGAs and ASICs, with their concomitant dramatic increase in processing power between 2013 and 2015.

ASIC's Continuous Improvement and the Beginning of the Corporate Era

Since this era of rapid growth over the first two years of ASIC development, subsequent improvements have been more evolutionary rather than revolutionary. Future efficiency gains will likely not be as dramatic, but, as we shall see, increases in bitcoin prices will continue to fuel more if not significantly better machines, and greater energy consumption. The amazing increases in bitcoin processing power in a few short years to 100 billion times, or 10^{11}

times the processing power across the industry since mining first began is a testament to the success of the coin's technology, utility, and innovation.

Innovations were also occurring outside of the technological front. With each month of 2014, more businesses were accepting payment in bitcoin, and new bitcoin-based financial products were developed. These included swaps and other financial instruments called derivatives, that derive their value from bitcoin. Soon, financial markets were developing tradeable instruments with all the sophistication and innovation that is Wall Street's hallmark.

By 2015, almost 100,000 merchants accepted bitcoin, and coin clearing and wallet companies expanded significantly. Numerous small exchanges and clearing houses also went bankrupt, sometimes driven by theft or scandal, while large pools for miners and exchange houses for their earnings were developing as stable businesses.

By the end of 2015, bitcoin was poised for a big breakthrough in processor power, number of miners, and profitability in this new era of bitcoin acceptance and production. While bitcoin's algorithm that enables digital transactions was relatively static, pools and exchanges arose to support the industry through the processing and protection of private keys.[6]

Today bitcoin has been mined for barely a dozen years, but dominates the digital currency industry. Yet, recent digital coins, such as ether based on the Ethereum 1.0 protocol, benefited by Satoshi's innovation and had adopted some of its principles while avoiding some of its flaws. Bitcoin's development has not been completely frozen, though. Proposed improvement that can gain consensus approval of its installed and decentralized base can culminate in a successful upgrade. Taproot is one such improvement.

A Bitcoin 2.0?

In 2022, the bitcoin network accepted this Taproot upgrade designed to increase anonymity and improve mining efficiency. There have been other proposed updates that have not been accepted and have resulted in new forks that have not succeeded, such as the creation of Bitcoin Cash. Taproot was accepted by the network because it allowed transactions to be streamlined, processing speed improved slightly, and processing cost likewise improved. In doing so, the upgrade was the most significant since the beginning of bitcoin's corporate era.

The upgrade processes transactions in a block so that multiple transactions by the same address can be sorted together to allow for more streamlined authentication and assist in confirmation of available funds for each address.

---

[6] https://www.nytimes.com/2014/08/31/business/hal-finney-cryptographer-and-bitcoin-pioneer-dies-at-58.html?_r=1m retrieved February 5, 2022.

In previous iterations, verification of a transaction required each digital signature to be validated individually. Multiple signatures across the block meant multiple such validation confirmations simultaneously. The Taproot upgrade streamlines this process into a single verification.

Aggregating addresses not only makes it easier to confirm transactions, but it also speeds up confirmation. More transactions can then be processed, which would presumably reduce the cost of verification. Taproot also improves privacy by disguising multi-signature transactions into an aggregated single signature transaction.

Taproot also took a step toward implementing a greater ability to support smart contracts, for which Ethereum had been the leader of the two digital currencies, and is being enhanced far further with the Ethereum 2.0 protocol. As a result, depending on the success of implementation of smart contracts into the bitcoin protocol, bitcoin may be able to play a greater role in Decentralized Finance (DeFi) as discussed in a later chapter.

These enhancements in efficiency and speed will permit bitcoin to be more competitive with cryptocurrencies of more recent vintage. By increasing the functionality of bitcoin, it is hoped that bitcoin market share can expand and command a higher market price and capitalization. However, bitcoin still suffers from smaller block size compared to its main competitor and remains hampered by a block duration of ten minutes. In comparison, Ethereum supports a block size of four to eight megabytes and a block duration of fifteen seconds, which is 1/40th the latency of bitcoin. These are substantial advantages if a digital currency is to process the volume of transactions that greater retail use demands, and with the speed that consumers will tolerate.

There remain inherent flaws in the bitcoin protocol that limits its potential, though. In Chapter 8, I derive *The Bitcoin Dilemma* that shows improvements in efficiency, reductions in processing costs, and an increase in the value of a bitcoin will have the perverse effect of accelerating the miner arms race still further, and increase the already immense amount of electricity consumed. In addition, competing digital currencies support even greater smart contract functionality, larger block size, and reduced latency which bitcoin cannot match. Various digital coins that employ Proof of Stake mining are much more readily amenable to still further enhancements. Satoshi's benevolence was designed to increase the accessibility of the new digital coin but the net result in practice was a coin few can afford to transact.

We know just a few highly trusted machines can take care of all processing needs of any digital currency. Indeed, with the same block size and latency, Satoshi's home CPU performed much of the mining necessary to maintain the blockchain in its nascent years. Presumably, Satoshi could have corrupted the blockchain when just a few enthusiasts dominated bitcoin mining. The way Satoshi designed the coin resulted in larger mining rewards as the price of bitcoin rises to levels we see today. As such, the Satoshi's design ensured there was a high cost of blockchain corruption that has indeed become proportionally more expensive as bitcoin is transacted in greater volume and at a higher price. This increased incentive has induced a vast increase in mining nodes and clients that do not rely on the trust of any central authority. One cannot roll that clock back, but it may nonetheless be theoretically possible to move to trusted authentication for bitcoin, but for the thousands of nodes and millions of clients that would refuse to approve such a move toward their collective irrelevance.

6

Public Ledgers, Private Wallets, and Crypto Vulnerabilities

Bitcoin was designed from the onset so that each new set of transactions to be mined across a peer-to-peer network could be processed over the Internet with no institutional intervention or oversight necessary. In doing so, it had to establish a mechanism of self-policing in which participating nodes on a network would do the work necessary to maintain the bitcoin protocol, possibly improve upon it over time by proposing enhancements to the protocol through a democratic vote of all nodes, and perform the grunt work every ten minutes to ensure the most recent set of transactions in the digital currency are legitimate. Satoshi's design was based on the following premise:

> We consider the scenario of an attacker trying to generate an alternate chain faster than the honest chain. Even if this is accomplished, it does not throw the system open to arbitrary changes, such as creating value out of thin air or taking money that never belonged to the attacker. Nodes are not going to accept an invalid transaction as payment, and honest nodes will never accept a block containing them. An attacker can only try to change one of his own transactions to take back money he recently spent.[1]

In such a self-policing mechanism, the network must collectively verify the accuracy of the work performed. If mining is verified broadly across all nodes, the miners must be rewarded for their efforts. This method of verification to

---

[1] https://nakamotoinstitute.org/bitcoin/, accessed April 19, 2022.

sustain the integrity of the system is appropriately called Proof of Work, as coined by Ari Juels and Markus Jakobsson (1999). By doing its part, each miner in the maintenance and application of the Bitcoin Protocol is rewarded in proportion to the amount of processing work they perform.

Computer scientists have have invented a number of techniques to ensure data integrity. Indeed, the processing or transmission of data is potentially fraught with errors. If protocols did not build into their framework some sort of way to track and correct errors as they crop up, such errors would propagate exponentially with each successive stage of data processing. When the stakes are low, we can trust protocols and programs themselves to self-correct. When the processes represent our transactions and the wealth we own, the prevention of error propagation becomes more critical, especially when bad actors constantly attempt to corrupt a process to steal wealth from others.

The Various Methods of Authentication

President Ronald Reagan popularized a saying "trust, but verify." From a Russian slogan, "Doveryay, no proveryay," an American scholar named Suzanne Massie introduced the saying to the President, who, in turn, used it as a strategy in his disarmament negotiations with the Soviet Union.[2] Certainly, we must accept as a matter of faith that the Bitcoin Protocol Satoshi invented works as intended. However, with billions of dollars on the line, it is also important to verify at each step that the process has not been hijacked.

We all must trust on a regular basis. A safe and leisurely drive down the road depends on our trust that drivers moving in the opposite direction do not veer into our lane. Every transaction with a credit card requires us to trust that the merchant and the participating banks properly debit our account by no more than the purchase. Indeed, we must trust institutions many times each day to protect our interests even if they could profit, at least in the short run, by violating our trust.

Cypherpunks and Satoshi were of the belief that trust is best assured if we can collectively and democratically monitor the accuracy of transactions, and the machines responsible for processing transactions for us will do so because their interests are aligned with ours. Proof of Work bitcoin mining

---

[2] https://en.wikipedia.org/wiki/Trust,_but_verify, retrieved March 7, 2022.

accomplishes that goal and maintains integrity in a network that is capitalized at a level approaching a trillion dollars. The stakes are high.

The Proof of Work method bitcoin employs is a simple and effective way to oversee digital coin transaction processing, but it is by no means the only mechanism. In fact, there are other mechanisms that are far more efficient to implement, but also require a greater degree of trust on our part.

For instance, the most common alternative to Proof of Work, in which myriad participants in the processing network oversee, authenticate, and vote on the accuracy of each other's work, is the Proof of Stake model. It is helpful to distinguish between these various authentication techniques, especially as the Ethereum protocol, which processes the second most popular digital currency, named ether, has transitioned from Proof of Work to Proof of Stake.

The Proof of Work method Satoshi adopted requires miners to successfully solve a cryptographic puzzle and reveal their proof to others on the network in a way that others can easily verify. The Proof of Work method has been employed by almost a hundred other digital coins.

A version of Proof of Work was first developed as an early digital transaction method by Dwork and Naor (1993) as a method to prevent junk mail. You are familiar with puzzles used as a challenge we might confront to gain entry to a website. We may be asked to slide a piece of a jigsaw puzzle to its appropriate spot or identify cells which contain pictures of buses or boats. Completing the puzzle is somewhat time consuming to perform, and can't easily be replicated automatically by a robot, but is easy to verify once the puzzle is solved. This is a flavor of Proof of Work called Challenge-Response. Another alternative is Solution-Verification as used by bitcoin. In fact, a variety of possible puzzle protocols can be employed so long as each commands non-trivial resources, in processing power, memory demands, or network bandwidth.

The Proof of Work method is based on a design asymmetry. The work itself to properly authenticate and then encode a bitcoin block to ensure it remains immutable is expensive in processing power and electricity. But verification of successful work is cheap. The verification of a proposed solution to the cryptographic puzzle that can take ten minutes for the network to solve can be verified in nanoseconds, given that a state-of-the-art miner today can verify 140 trillion such candidates on one second.

In the most common alternative to Proof of Work, Proof of Stake, a number of coin owners are required to stake their digital wealth as collateral if they are to participate as validators of an authentication proposal. The pool of validators is randomly chosen to validate a given block in proportion to their stake. In the new Ethereum 2.0 protocol, for instance, this stake will require 32 ETH coin to be anted to become a validator, and multiple validators will be polled before a block is accepted. Various Proof of Stake models use different validation methods, with the common feature that the stake in collateral is lost if validators attempt to corrupt the block for their own benefit. In this way, a finite number of validators are trusted because they are staking their collateral as a measure of their collective integrity.

Delegated Proof of Stake is a variation of Proof of Stake that relies on a pool of those willing to sufficiently stake, or collateralize, their authority to vote for a series of delegates chosen to authenticate a new block. Another technique called Proof of Capacity requires puzzles to be solved across many devices so that it would be costly to replicate the collective solution in a way that could corrupt the system.

Proof of Elapsed Time distributes processing power randomly across potential validators based on the amount of time they have stood in a queue awaiting their opportunity. Proof of Identity requires validators to, in essence, validate themselves by providing a private key that will stake a specific transaction. A similar method, called Proof of Authority, uses a potential validator's true identity as the collateral to be provided to prevent corruption. In essence, validators' reputation acts as their stake. Finally, Proof of Activity is a combination of Proof of Work and Proof of Stake in which a validators are chosen at random from a pool willing to offer a stake, with larger stakes earning a proportionately larger likelihood of being chosen for the authentication group. The group collectively authenticate and sign a validated block candidate. If a block remains unsigned by some of the members of the group, the block is rejected. The reward for an accepted block is divided among the group according to their relative stakes.

Private Keys

Proof of Work and Proof of Stake represent the vast majority of authentication and verification methods, with Proof of Stake increasingly employed by new coins unwilling to repeat the inefficiencies constraining bitcoin. Each of these methods establish consenses in different ways, but they all meet the needs of blockchain immortalization. All of these alternative mechanisms perform more efficiently than Proof of Work with regard to the amount of actual resources, primarily electricity and processing power, that must be employed to authenticate and validate a block in the blockchain. Only Proof

6 Public Ledgers, Private Wallets, and Crypto Vulnerabilities

of Work enlists millions of miners committing to millions of times the effort and cost compared to the other methods. And, with ether transitioned to Proof of Stake, bitcoin represents 95% of the market capitalization of all Proof of Work coins. It is now essentially bitcoin and its Proof of Work algorithm versus the rest of the cryptocurrency world.

We saw how Satoshi's bitcoin algorithm can take a 256-bit output that uniquely identifies the previous block, includes a new block of the last ten minutes of transactions between accounts, inserts a nonce, and then runs the sequence of numbers through its SHA-256 hash function to generate a new 256-bit number that, hopefully for the miner, comes close enough to zero to satisfy the difficulty tolerance. Given the guessed nonce, every part of this process can be replicated and hence verified by any machine capable of running the SHA-256 algorithm, and all the data is freely available for the entire network, and the public to see.

Anonymity in transactions does not come from some ability to hide the contents of the block in some sort of encrypted way. For this reason, the term cryptocurrency is a bit misleading, although there are cryptocurrencies that further protect the anonymity of every transaction. Instead, with bitcoin, protection comes in the difficulty of associating an account number with its owner. This aspect of bitcoin arises from another layer of protection. While the public account number can be observed, to discern the source of the owner also requires a private key that only the owner knows. If this complex key is lost, so goes the bitcoin associated with it.

Such a mechanism does indeed have its origins in cryptography. You know from the secret decoding pin Ralphie prized in "A Christmas Story" that a private key allows one to transform a message we can all observe, but appears as random gibberish, into a private message that only the authorized recipient can read.

A hash works with public keys. Every miner has the same candidate information for a block and the same encoding algorithm. We can think of the public key that all can see in a given block as just one part of an individual's account number. For instance, Satoshi employed many public addresses and private keys. Satoshi's first public address (in hexadecimal form) was:

1A1zP1eP5QGefi2DMPTfTL5SLmv7DivfNa.[3]

---

[3] https://bitcoinke.io/2022/01/bitcoin-turns-13/, accessed April 12, 2022.

In public-key cryptography, the transaction is incomplete until a private key can be paired with the public key to reveal the parties to the transaction.[4] The secrecy of this private key is essential to maintain the integrity and anonymity of the actual movements of bitcoin funds.

These private keys are also 256 bits long or the equivalent to a 64-digit hexadecimal code. They can also take the much more easily represented QR code or a unique series of words called a mnemonic phrase. At 256 bits, there are the same number of possible combinations, 1.158×10^{77} that we saw earlier in the discussion of the SHA-256 algorithm.

When a transaction is proposed to bitcoin, the transactors behind their public keys remain hidden. The transaction is thus protected by the institution that represents you and holds your digital wallet. These essential private keys that were once maintained by their owners on scraps of paper or a hard drive are now typically held for us by custodians on Internet cryptocurrency exchanges that owners join. Users never physically hold their cryptocurrency since it resides in perpetuity within blocks authenticated by the SHA-256 algorithm and recorded in the cloud. Ownership of the wealth associated with a private key comes from the fact that only the owners and their custodians have access to the private key and hence can unlock that value, transact with it, or convert it to traditional cash. In other words, the locally held private keys, or these custodian wallets, are the other half of the bitcoin methodology.

The Weakest Link

The most obvious place to steal cryptocurrency is at these exchanges which hold our balances. When asked why famed American criminal Willie Sutton robbed banks, he responded famously, "Because that's where the money is."[5] An exchange is entrusted by its depositors to administer their private keys to authorize purchases using bitcoin, but must also promptly permit its accountholders to transfer cash and move cryptocurrency to cash, or vice-versa. Just as a bank holds some of its assets in the form of cash should a customer make a withdrawal, an exchange must also hold cash and digital coin in the form of a float that it can quickly transfer back and forth across the Internet to a customer's brick-and-mortar bank account.

---

[4] Actually, to receive funds, all one would need is a public key, under the assumption that nobody would be opposed to receiving funds. But, to retrieve these funds, one must present to some entity the private key owned solely by them.

[5] https://www.fbi.gov/history/famous-cases/willie-sutton#:~:text=When%20asked%20why%20he%20robbed,bank%20early%20in%20the%20morning, retrieved February 6, 2022.

Much of the theft risk in bitcoin comes not from diverting blocks themselves, but from the exchanges that guard our wallets. In 2021, crypto criminals stole $3.2 billion U.S. in other people's cryptocurrency.[6] These thefts arise in a number of ways. For instance, on December 4, 2021, a large exchange named BitMart revealed that the equivalent of $150 million was stolen from the bank's hot wallets. Such wallets are accounts containing reserves of various cryptocurrencies and cash that are attached to the network and allow the exchange to rapidly move money when necessary. To understand how theft can occur, we must delve deeper into the inner workings of digital currency exchanges.

Unlike banks, in the relatively unregulated and free-wheeling world of cryptocurrency, these bank-like institutions are not required to carry depository insurance to protect the accounts of their clients. Nor are they monitored by a central bank for adequacy of reserves and safeguards from theft. The implications of this lack of regulation will be discussed more fully later, but this lack of oversight makes exchanges the weakest link in the security of cryptocurrency transactions.

The second vulnerability comes from hacking of individual personal computers. On our personal computers there reside private keys that unlock our ability to withdraw funds or make cryptocurrency transactions. If one were to discover our private key, they may be able to falsely represent themselves as us and authorize a transaction to move cryptocurrency from our wallets to theirs. Short of having access to our hard drive to search for such keys, they may instead employ a keystroke-reporting application that one may inadvertently open from an innocent-looking email purportedly from a friend asking us if we remember people in an attached picture, for instance, only to open a link that instead surreptitiously installs spy software on our computer.

Such phishing and malware schemes abound to interject malicious software on our machines. It is then just a matter of time and patience before an observer sees the passwords and userids we commonly use, and either randomly, or by observing our queries to an exchange, eventually find an exchange that accepts our userid and password. We may discourage such theft by employing new and more elaborate authentication schemes, such as Two-Factor Authentication (2FA), which requires a second step for authentication, such as a response to a text message, or a biometric authentication such as a fingerprint to stymie attacks and theft of one's crypto.

---

[6] https://theconversation.com/crypto-theft-is-on-the-rise-heres-how-the-crimes-are-committed-and-how-you-can-protect-yourself-176027, retrieved February 6, 2022.

Of course, various such phishing attacks are only lucrative if the phisher finds a foolish bitcoin owner who does not take sufficiently careful precautions to protect such valuable information. The more direct route to steal larger amounts of cash is to directly attack the exchanges themselves, using the same sort of techniques against which banks and traditional financial institutions must guard against.

One can protect accounts at exchanges by transferring their assets to hardware wallets. However, that merely shifts the target of attacks. In addition, access to accounts could still be discovered by infiltrating the weaker security a local machine may maintain. Such local maintenance of account balances is also vulnerable to failure of local hardware.

To combat such thefts of the contents of uninsured accounts, one could immediately transfer digital assets to cash and then into traditional bank accounts. A crypto customer may not want to take this step for a number of reasons, though. First, while the transaction cost to move currency from one form to another is small, it is not insignificant. Second, such a conversion may create a taxable event for which the customer may owe capital gains tax. Third, the customer may be holding the cryptocurrency for speculative purposes and hence may not wish to convert to cash and miss out on future capital gains.

Governments in nations with strong regulatory mechanisms are increasingly licensing and overseeing exchanges that hold cash and cryptocurrency for transactional and speculative purposes. However, most nations have been slow to fully oversee and regulate a technologically sophisticated sector which many fail to understand, including its potential regulators. With a patchwork of incomplete oversight, and the ability to easily transact across jurisdictional boundaries over the Internet, exchanges can easily find jurisdictions with lax regulations that fail to protect accountholders. Such regulatory challenges will be covered in Part VI.

Suffice it to say that the integrity of the bitcoin network to act as a safe and storable medium of exchange between willing individuals requires adherence to a number of security measures that will likely increase in complexity as the potential value of theft via the Internet increases over time. With bad actors needing only some ingenuity and an Internet connection, and with dramatic failures resulting if malicious actors succeed only once, while the industry must successfully protect us every single time, the risks are larger in this sector than in other financial sectors—by far.

These exchanges that hold our crypto keys are where much of the money is now made through fees charged to their clients. Not only do they maintain our accounts, but they collectively earn various crypto banking fees that dwarf even the profits of mining. These new institutions, which did not even exist a decade ago, are now as large and monolithic as the banks Satoshi hoped to replace. Surely such a concentration of wealth and power would cause Satoshi to roll over in a virtual grave.

Other Vulnerabilities

Satoshi was concerned about security. In designing a bitcoin protocol that was completely decentralized, poor design would leave myriad entry points for corruption of its blocks. Satoshi's solution to this challenge was to design a system that depends on polling its nodes to ensure the majority approve any proposed candidate for a successful block, and, for that matter, changes in the protocol over time.

The brilliance of the design Satoshi implemented was the extreme cost to corrupt the network by requiring a malicious agent to command at least half the miners on the network and pay at least half the electricity cost of encoding a block, which can run into many hundreds of thousands of dollars over a ten-minute period.

Finally, even if such an attack could be pulled off, the most the attacker could accomplish is to spend multiple times in one block their account balance recorded on the network. Safeguards effectively deter a potential attack by making it almost impossible to be profitable. And, if an attack was initially successful, a subsequent fork agreed upon by the network could negate that block probably well before false transactions are confirmed.

Satoshi designed bitcoin to be immutable by such an assurance of a network of nodes or clients that monitor proposed codification of each block based on client peer voting. Just as with any voting system, if 51% of the votes are controlled by a single party or coalition, they could elect to endorse a block that includes fraudulent transactions. In doing so, the sheer brute force of the coalition could theoretically override other protections designed to agree to only authorized transactions.

There have been such "51% attacks" in lesser coins that employ networks not as broad as are found in bitcoin. For instance, in August of 2021, a bitcoin offshoot called Bitcoin SV lost 5% of its value following such an attack, while another bitcoin fork, Bitcoin Gold was subjected to a 51% attack in 2019. A version of ether, called Ethereum Classic, also suffered such an attack in 2019. To date, though, bitcoin itself has remained free of successful attacks.

A coin that uses the Proof of Work method inherently depends on network consensus for approval. In essence, the significant amount and expense for Proof of Work is an impediment to the purchase of sufficient capacity and electric power to mount such an attack. As a further deterrent, the benefactors of such an attack would be plain to see, even if some forensic accounting would be necessary to root out the individual(s) behind such an attack. One need only follow the money.

In the economic model presented in Chapter 8, I include an analysis of the case of miner rentals. Indeed, the bitcoin mining sector offers many such opportunities to rent mining capacity and pay the electric costs of mining, without the requisite purchase of machines. If mining rentals constitute a significant portion of all mining activity, it may be theoretically possible for an individual to rent the capacity necessary to mount a 51% attack. The extent of current bitcoin miner rental markets does not pose such a threat, although other alternative coins have much larger rental markets that approach the majority of mining capacity of those coins.

The Digital Currency Initiative sponsored by the M.I.T. Media Lab has conducted research on instances in which blocks of other cryptocurrencies have been retroactively modified to permit the double spending of cryptocurrency described above. They found that, since the launch of their tracker in June of 2019, forty such reorganizations of blocks retroactively, six or more blocks deep, have occurred, invariably in lesser coins with extensive miner rental markets.[7]

The form of any successful attack, as Satoshi surmised, would likely come from double spending. When a block is authenticated, the network checks a file to be sure that the account to be debited has sufficient funds. Within the block, a rogue coalition could propose to spend these funds multiple times. Authentication typically prevents such multiple spending of the same coin within a block, unless a 51% attack enabled such double spending.

However, a 51% attacker could not cover its tracks. Were a block subsequently manipulated, the attacker would have to match or replace the nonce contained in the block and then ensure that a run of the block through the SHA-256 algorithm would result in an output below the difficulty threshold. An entire network can manage such a feat once every ten minutes, so a huge amount of processing power would have to be commandeered to do so. Should a malicious actor manage to succeed, recall that the hash output must be close enough to zero to match the tolerance defined by the difficulty target, but the output code is also included in the subsequent block. Any such

---

[7] https://dci.mit.edu/51-attacks, accessed February 7, 2022.

attempt to retroactively modify even a single block and double spend some of its content would be easy to detect and correct since the block and those that follow will no longer link up properly. Such attempts are simply too expensive and insufficiently profitable in a well-decentralized bitcoin network since the cost of covering the tracks of a malicious attack would be formidable.

A second deterrent is the inevitable drop in price if coin users become averse to using the digital currency subject to the attack. If a currency cannot be trusted, it loses a significant amount of value as a consequence of what economists call "Gresham's Law." Such an aversion to one coin can induce a contagion across many coins as consumers find it difficult to distinguish between good and bad coins. Indeed, past successful attacks of other coins or of exchanges resulted in a reverberating effect across all coins.

> **Non-Fungible Tokens (NFTs) and the Biggest Heist of Them All**
>
> In April of 2022, the largest heist of digital currencies was reported by the U.S. Treasury. They alleged that the Lazarus Group, a notorious assembly of hackers purportedly assembled by North Korean dictator Kim II Jun, broke into the servers of Ronin. This Axie Infinity-associated bridge allows their game, Sky Mavis, to sell non-fungible tokens to be used in gaming as ways to differentiate their users and allow trades of tokens. These tokens are paid using ether and a Stablecoin called USDC.
>
> These digital currencies were diverted to accounts owned by the attackers. The value of the diversion was $625 million at the time. To prevent future such attacks, the Treasury Department implored the cryptocurrency industry to implement safeguards that prevent the type of laundering cryptocurrency networks tolerate so that future attempts to hack exchanges and bridges cannot continue to divert funds to terrorist organizations.[8]

Large coins such as bitcoin and ether are less vulnerable to such attacks because of the breadth of their networks. However, the miners especially running the bitcoin network are almost invariably designed and built in one country, and, until recently, most of the mining capacity and pools were housed there too. If 51% of manufacturing and mining capacity all fall within one political jurisdiction, logic suggests that this could create a vulnerability. Such a vulnerability has never come to fruition for bitcoin.

If all miners are built by just a handful of companies, most all which reside in one nation, experts have been concerned about the possibility of backdoor attacks. For instance, Huawei telecommunications equipment purchases were banned in the United States because the Trump Administration believed

---

[8] https://www.coindesk.com/policy/2022/04/14/us-officials-tie-north-korean-hacker-group-to-axies-ronin-exploit/, accessed April 19, 2022.

that the Chinese government may have either infiltrated or otherwise forced Huawei to include in their smartphone, router, and network equipment a provision that allows an entity to surreptitiously observe or manipulate traffic on the network. Such facilities may allow hackers or government agents to perform a backdoor attack on a network.

Often, these backdoor entry points are engineered for an appropriate, if perhaps misguided purpose. Such an entry point may allow a customer service representative to take control of your personal computer on your behalf to repair settings that has been corrupted. Backdoors to enter the electronics of a space satellite may allow engineers to repair the satellite when no rebooting or regular pathways may have worked. Of course, any such backdoor is a closely guarded secret, for the obvious reason to not invite attackers into equipment. It is then difficult to know if backdoors exist. Even a hacker who discovers such a backdoor would be loath to share such information, at least without a reward payment, because the backdoor may have value to the hacker at some future date.

A Balance Between Security and Innovation

While many nations have laws against hacking, the novelty of bitcoin and its rapid development pace typically means that regulators are far behind the innovators and hackers. Laws do not prevent a single owner from amassing more than 50% of mining capacity, and hence, few safeguards are in place. In 2013, just six mining pools, most of which were run out of China, controlled 75% of all bitcoin processing power. A year later, a single mining pool named Ghash.io controlled 51% of the networks processing power. Since then, the pool industry agreed among themselves that no single pool can represent more than 39.99% of hashing power.

Jurisdictional problems also exist with such a global digital currency. The nature of public account keys that also have a corresponding private key element makes tracing of transgressors difficult. Wallets could be held anywhere, including in jurisdictions with weak oversight and few extradition treaties. Oversight of wallets remains weak worldwide and is often left to individual states or localities, given the inability, unwillingness, or ignorance of national governments to promulgate effective regulation.

Likely the greatest protection against any such commandeering of bitcoin comes from the bitcoin community itself. A study of the history of bitcoin demonstrates the tremendous intelligence, creativity, and genius of its pioneers, especially the mysterious Satoshi. These cypherpunks were consistently suspicious of those who might try to institutionalize their coin. Their inherent distrust of institutions was the impetus for bitcoin in the first place, a mechanism that allows and facilitates transactions across borders almost instantaneously, and, in doing so, completely bypasses traditional banks and monetary authorities. More likely are attacks that take advantage of vulnerabilities in wallets held by large exchanges instead of the mining and authentication network. Techniques may even be employed to attack cold storage wallets which are not directly linked to external bank accounts.

As with their Cypherpunk brethren, the bitcoin pioneers did not trust government to refrain from manipulating their currency or monitoring its users. Their trust came from verification and network decentralization. To inject such features as backdoors or the ability of institutions or governments to somehow coopt their coin would be sacrilegious to bitcoin's pioneers and would threaten the profits of their modern corporate equivalent. Millions of miners translate into millions of eyes to ensure the network remains transparent and is not coopted. Sunlight is the best disinfectant.

These factors combine to ensure that bitcoin will likely not be compromised, even if lesser digital coins may be. Some still continue to foster more bitcoin protocol innovation. There have been attempts at forks toward new versions of bitcoin that overcome some of its limitations such as a limit to a block size of one megabyte, or block durations of ten minutes on average. While it is true that potential forks would make bitcoin more amenable to more frequent and more abundant transactions, each such fork has failed to attain any sort of success or scale as enjoyed by the original bitcoin.

In fact, such forks in other digital currencies have shown their vulnerability in ways that the vastness of bitcoin prevents. Were some nodes knocked out by accident or by poor design, the bitcoin network is quickly able to replace these nodes as a crab may replace a lost limb. The simplicity, limited scope, compactness, and ability to expand and replicate all ensure that nodes can be knocked down but never out. These qualities of extreme robustness also ensure that any attempt to constrain bitcoin, either physically at each node, or collectively over the Internet, are bound to fail as clients can pop up again anywhere there is household current and an Internet connection. When combined with an ability to harbor myriad small-scale operations, bitcoin defies attempts to limit its scope.

Finally, while the coin itself is transparent and robust, mining operators are often opaque and misleading. When they come to town, they rarely do so with precise announcements of their intentions and scope. This secretive quality and mistrust of government is ingrained in the decentralized, and some may even argue, anarchistic tendencies of bitcoin pioneers. Such qualities result in a robust coin that confounds regulation at the local, state, national, and global levels, and is described in more detail in Section III.

7

Bitcoin Goes Corporate

Satoshi could not have imagined the corporatization of bitcoin mining and the vast exchanges that now hold our accounts. In the early days while Satoshi was active, private keys still resided on hard drive as large coin exchanges did not yet exist. Satoshi's primary hope was for orderly expansion in the number of people subscribing to bitcoin. Too rapid growth and unnecessary attention, such as occurred when Wikileaks stated it would take donations in bitcoin, could derail the steady growth that would keep bitcoin manageable, while insufficient growth would doom the coin. Late in 2010, Satoshi expressed the concern, "It would have been nice to get this attention in any other context. Wikileaks has kicked the hornet's nest, and the swarm is heading towards us."[1]

Satoshi did not lack confidence in the network's ability to process the blockchain, though. Rather, Satoshi viewed bitcoin as the people's coin and was wary of mining and transacting becoming corporatized or institutionalized.

Despite Satoshi's concerns, by 2013 and 2014, bitcoin mining was increasingly becoming an industry. The era in which a hobby miner who had a personal computer or two toiled away mostly out of fascination and small rewards was mostly over. Application Specific Integrated Circuits (ASICs) had entered into the mix.

---

[1] https://bitcointalk.org/index.php?topic=2216.msg29280#msg29280, accessed April 19, 2022.

The first widely available ASIC machine was developed by a nation well-equipped for rapid product development that quickly transitioned into efficient product manufacturing and deployment. A Chinese company named Bitmain was interested in bitcoin mining, but also in manufacturing newer, faster, and more specialized mining machines based on the ASIC-based hash boards. These new miners could process the SHA-256 algorithm so much faster and without consuming the same amount of electricity per hash as would personal computers, even those equipped with state-of-the-art graphics processing units. The earliest ASIC machines made the decentralized network of hobby miners obsolete almost overnight.

> **The Early History of Processor Electronics**
>
> The electronics industry is more than a century old. It began with the development of the first device used to control the movement of electrons, the Fleming valve, patented in Britain in 1904. This simple diode could act as a one-way switch to turn electric current on or off, or it could allow current to flow only in one direction, from a cathode to an anode in a tube evacuated of air.
>
> A couple of years later, American electrical engineer Lee de Forest inserted another element called a grid between a cathode and an anode to better permit regulation of the flow of electrons between the two elements in a *triode* vacuum tube. In doing so, a small signal, for instance from a microphone, could then control a much more powerful flow of electricity between a cathode and anode to form an analog amplifier.
>
> This process of vacuum tube amplification in Lee de Forest's Audion was perfected over the ensuing decades to allow stereo amplifiers that many audiophiles still prefer to use today. An audio signal limited in frequency to perhaps 20,000 Hertz, or oscillations per second, could also modulate a much more rapidly oscillating radio frequency signal that may be measured in millions of hertz, or megahertz. Such devices heralded in the era of high frequency wireless radio that has since been extended to very-high frequency (VHF), ultra-high frequency (UHF), and beyond. With the Manhattan Project determined to design and engineer the world's first nuclear bombs, these vacuum tubes were soon enlisted to run one of the world's first digital computers.

The ability to control a signal to an almost infinitesimal level of finesse allowed simple circuits of vacuum tubes and then transistors to act as early analog computers to add, subtract, multiply, and divide signals, as read out by dials. Such analog computers were application specific. In other words, to derive the desired result, a circuit generally had to be designed to model a particular purpose as represented by a schematic diagram that shows how the various components must be connected.

The greatest utility for such devices, up to World War II, was for communications. These devices could convert voice signals to radio frequencies perhaps a thousand times higher, which could propagate through the atmosphere, and even bounce back and forth between the earth and the ionosphere to travel great distances. The radio frequency signal could then be converted back to audio. Television worked on the same principle, at least until recently.

During World War II, two pressing needs directed such vacuum tube technology in a dramatically new direction. While analog computers could be helpful for some calculations necessary in designing the nuclear bomb as part of the Manhattan Project, one of the project's scientists, John von Neumann, a Jewish emigre who escaped Nazi Germany's clutch over his nation of Hungary, needed a machine to process more elaborate calculations. He proposed a digital computer that would work quickly on binary numbers, which are merely representations of our traditional base-10 numbers in base-2, or two states, one perhaps with a vacuum tube switched on, and another off.

Vacuum tubes could easily perform this function, although they were finicky. Each tube required a heat source to warm a cathode sufficiently for it to eject electrons. These heating coils tended to burn out just like the resistance elements in light bulbs. And, the rate a vacuum tube could turn on and off was somewhat finite, which would limit the computing speed of John von Neumann's machines.

The programmable ENIAC computer was built with 18,000 6SNT dual triode and other vacuum tubes, mammoth cooling to keep them from burning up, and a new way to control the collection of vacuum tubes. These first computers assisted in the design of the nuclear bomb while, on the other side of the Atlantic Ocean, a British engineer and early Nazi code cracker named Alan Turing was using the same sort of devices to try to decode encrypted German war messages.

Both pioneers realized that their machines were most successful when they could be easily reprogrammed. In other words, the application specific nature of traditional circuits was not ideal if a quick change in function or style of calculation was necessary. Instead, Neumann and Turing separately invented methods to make large banks of generic vacuum tubes perform in particular ways through programming. This technique required the construction of algorithms that specify a particular way to command a bank of vacuum tubes. Various algorithms could then be assembled in a library and drawn upon to reprogram these early computers as required for the next set of calculations.

This method moved computing from application specific to generalized processing power, with the true processing residing in the software algorithms that instruct the processing units how to behave, rather than the hardware itself. Such an approach may be more complicated and less specialized, but the benefit was that these devices were much more versatile.

The emphasis then shifted to the development and assembly of algorithms, contained in libraries of instruction sets, and programming languages that can properly coordinate the employment of these instruction sets. Still, to do the same sort of calculations that the simplest of calculators can now perform required a large building full of very hot and relatively unreliable vacuum tube processors.

The next big innovations were in the development of the semiconductor diode by Russell Ohl in 1939, and the transistor by John Bardeen, Walter Brattain and William Shockley of Bell Labs in 1947. These devices were far faster, more energy efficient, smaller, and more reliable than their vacuum tube counterparts. The innovation allowed the size of an early computer to shrink from requiring a building to a small room, but they too were either specialized or programmable circuits. At this point, all attention went into optimizing programs and shrinking electronics.

The revolution that allowed computers to develop to the point we know today was the invention of integrated circuits. Transistors could be assembled first in the tens and hundreds, and now in the billions, on a single wafer of specially prepared silicon. The silicon can be configured to act as transistors, diodes, resistors, and capacitors, all the essential components of electronic devices. These circuits are all integrated many times over on a silicon wafer, which can then be divided into individual chips of silicon. One such small chip could soon perform the functions that an entire room of circuits required just a decade earlier.

Today integrated circuits abound, even though there remain uses for individual diodes and transistors. Often, these are Application Specific Integrated Circuits (ASICs) designed to perform a set of functions without programming. Indeed, the shortages of vehicles in the COVID-19 era of 2020 to 2022 arose because even the windshield wipers on our cars required such application specific integrated circuits which worked so well for decades that they were rarely redesigned. They were simple but not very efficient. With supply chain shortages, it made more sense to devote precious chip plants to the highest use, which was not the more primitive device that operates our vehicle wipers and became in short supply during the COVID-19 era.

In 1971, Intel released an alternative to ASICs. The first popular microprocessor they designed was a programmable integrated circuit that employed 2,300 transistors. While only $1/8^{th}$ the number of processing elements of the original ENIAC computer, this integrated circuit could operate more than seven times faster, synchronized 750,000 times per second (750 kHz). Some microprocessors had also been developed around that same time to control operations for the American F-14 fighter jet, but the versatility of Intel's 4004 spawned many simple digital computers and was the impetus to the design of the 8008 in 1972, and the venerable 8080 in 1974. This latter Intel Central Processing Unit (CPU) could process 0.290 Million Instructions per second (MIPS) using a synchronizing clock frequency of 2 MHz to coordinate operations and employed 4,500 transistors spaced 6,000 nm apart, or a millionth the density of modern integrated circuits.

ASICs Spawn the Corporatization of Bitcoin

For many years, these versatile microprocessors and their successors ruled the day because of their low cost and their flexibility. However, their versatility is also their limiting factor. They are not highly specialized to perform just one task because of the needs to sacrifice specialization for their superior versatility.

Some ASICs continued to be designed and built, but they were not needed in the great volume microprocessors commanded. Hence, the ASIC designs were either expensive or proved to be less refined than other state-of-the-art devices as time passes. These ASICs remained a niche market item until cryptocurrency came along.

When the first ASICs for bitcoin mining came to market, the complexion of bitcoin mining changed almost overnight. Canaan Creative was the first manufacturer to realize it is more lucrative to supply miners with specialized machines than mining itself. Just as outfitters became wealthier than the gold miners they supplied in the Klondike Gold Rush, Canaan Creative cornered the market for the first ASICs used in bitcoin mining and became almost as lucrative than mining itself

Canaan Creative was established in 2013 by Nangeng Zhang. He had completed his master's degree in software engineering from Beihang University and was studying for his doctorate. While he never completed his Ph.D., Zhang instead focused on designing and building specialized processors optimally designed to run the SHA-256 algorithm for bitcoin mining. At the same time, Bitmain and MicroBT were two other exploring ASIC manufacturing and nipping at Canaan's heels.

These first ASIC miners were based on transistor spacing of 130 nm on wafers of silicon, which is 1/50th the distance between transistors as the groundbreaking Intel 8080 processor, and hence 2,500 times their two-dimensional density. The race was then on, in both attempts to place more transistors on a given piece of silicon and to make the ASICs run at a faster clock speed.

In the integrated circuit world of silicon, real estate is money. Chips are not built one at a time, but are rather etched by the hundreds or thousands onto a large silicon wafer, and then cut into individual chips. The ability to shrink chips by reducing transistor spacing quickly translates into lower costs by placing more chips on a wafer. In addition, the decreased distances on a more compact chip allow electrons to navigate the chips more quickly, given the finite speed electro-magnetic signals can propagate on silicon. A smaller chip also runs cooler since silicon has resistance that generates heat with the transmission of electrons, and resistance multiplies with distance.

Following that first year of 2013, chips had shrunk to 28 nm spacing and halved again to 14 nm spacing by mid-2016. Also, by 2016, the popularity and price of bitcoin was burgeoning. That was when bitcoin's destiny moved from hobby rooms to board rooms.

Bitmain was founded by technologist Micree Zhan and entrepreneur Jihan Wu in 2013, at the same time Canaan was designing their groundbreaking machines. Zhan had formed a startup for set top boxes that would allow streaming content to be played on a television, while Wu was a manager of a private equity firm. Their first product, the Antminer S1, was able to process the bitcoin hash algorithm at a rate of 180 GH/s, or 180,000,000,000 SHA-256 hashes per second, using less power than would be consumed by a typical home personal computer mining bitcoin. Not only were they consuming much less power, but they were processing at a far faster rate. Mid-2016, Bitmain released its Antminer S9 mining machine that quickly became the industry standard. Bitmain Technologies remains a privately held company based in Beijing that designed and built the ASIC mining machines that fueled much of the industry's rapid growth.

When bitcoin was devised, early CPU-based processing might attain perhaps a million hashes per second, or 1 MH/s. If the S1 could process 180 GH/s, or 180,000 times faster, one such ASIC miner could replace 180,000 personal computers and use less power than a single personal computer. The production of just a dozen miners could outswamp the entire bitcoin network and would create such a performance advantage that no personal computer stood a chance of receiving rewards. This marked the beginning of the bitcoin miner arms race, with electricity the ammunition, and the corporatization of mining.

Bitmain immediately emerged as a gigantic force in the industry. The company also serviced networks of miners by constructing mining pools. By joining a pool, a single miner need not wait until it was the fortunate machine to successfully authenticate a block. While each miner could by then solve the hash puzzle many billions of times per second, that rate remains insignificant compared to the overall processing capability of all miners combined worldwide. Instead, operators would register their individual mining machines in a pool, just as staff in an office may pool their lottery tickets when the pot rises, to increase their odds of winning. However, they must also share those winnings with more people. Joining a pool allows a miner to more evenly secure a rewards flow over time.

> **Bitmain Abandons Mining**
>
> Bitmain eventually suffered major financial losses, not because they were not producing popular and powerful mining machines. Certainly, their mining pool profits were relatively easy money since they had to invest only in cloud technology to coordinate the mining of millions of member miners. They also earned a steady commission with little overhead. Their a miner research and development (R&D) spawned a miner arms race that was producing increasingly powerful and energy-efficient machines at increasingly competitive prices. Bitmain also made the unsustainable decision of trying to compete in mining directly. Just as outfitters could earn a steady and profitable income at the expense of gold fever-inflicted miners in the Klondike Gold Rush, profits were very good for miner designers until the R&D arms race made this sector increasingly competitive. As China cooled to bitcoin mining, farms sought cheap electricity elsewhere and Bitmain focused on its core businesses of manufacturing and mining pools.

Bitmain realized it could then make far more money by building and selling machines than by mining itself, and by charging a small commission on any winnings of miners in their pools. Bitmain also operated its own mining farms in China and took advantage of favorable hydroelectric and coal power rates offered by the Chinese government to confer a competitive advantage for Chinese companies. Years later, Bitmain abandoned much of its mining activity in favor of upstream production of miners and downstream maintenance of mining pools.

The Current State of ASIC Mining

By 2022, ASICs are primarily produced by Bitmain and MicroBT, although Canaan and others also serve the industry. Recently, Intel entered the fray with the promise of a new ASIC Bonanza chip that is reported to generate 137 gigahertz per second (GH/s) using only 2.5 watts. Most such machines operating today aggregate hundreds to upward of a thousand such mining chips in a miner that consumes about three kilowatts of power so they can readily run off of a 240-V line on less than fifteen amperes of current. As Intel enters the market with hash boards containing chips assembled to a typical power level, their machines would attain a speed of approximately 137 terahashes/second (TH/s) while they generate a manageable amount of heat equivalent to about two home space heaters you might employ to warm your toes under your desk. Intel also pledged to halve the cost of a miner to better compete with other state-of-the-art miners.

Other machines currently available include the Antminer S19, priced at approximately $10,000 per machine, and capable of 110 TH/s while consuming 3,250 watts, the Canaan AvalonMiner 1246 able to process at 90 TH/s and consume 3.43 KW, for about $5,000, while the Whatsminer M30S will process 112 TH/s for about the same power consumption.

These new and state-of-the-art machines certainly improve the economics of the industry. The first mainstream corporate miner, the Antminer S9, processed the hash function at less than a tenth the rate of the proposed Intel miner, but still consumed half its power. The ubiquitous S9 machine is thus only about a fifth as efficient in watts per terahash/second. As of early February, 2022, Blockchain.com estimates total operating mining capacity has ballooned to 200 million terahashes each second[2] with Antminer S9 machines representing a market share that has fallen to about 25%, from about 75% just a few years earlier. Even at 25% market share, this translates into approximately 2,250,000 operating S9 machines, with the industry collectively processing at a rate approaching the equivalent of between ten and twenty million S9 machines.

The subject of miner economics begs a few questions. How many miners can the industry support, when is it profitable to purchase a new miner, and when is it no longer profitable to operate an older miner such as an S9? This is the economics of the industry, and its analysis will produce a very surprising result. I next analyze the economic implications of mining and miner design. I first describe the unique aspects of the economics that drive the corporatization of bitcoin, I then explore the degree to which increased concentration of wealth can make vulnerable some digital coins that are designed to be robust and democratic.

---

[2] https://www.blockchain.com/charts/hash-rate, accessed February 6, 2022.

8

The Fundamental Flaw of Bitcoin

For the reader interested in the economic theory behind bitcoin mining, this chapter describes the industry dynamics. Those less interested in the mathematics of the industry may prefer to skip to Chapter 9. With some understanding of the economics of the industry at hand, I next complete the economic picture. First, notice that industry dynamics are unique in that the supply of bitcoin is essentially fixed and will expand by only about 5% over the next 118 years. Economists call this supply inelastic because supply varies little, regardless of price and the level of demand. Indeed, when private keys are lost, or coins owned by Satoshi go unspent, supply actually declines in the bitcoin model. Just as in a deflation, the unit of digital currency becomes more valuable. But, when mining is rewarded through new coin, the value of existing bitcoin balances declines just as the economy suffers in a monetary inflation.

Satoshi understood an essential aspect of the economics of bitcoin mining, even if the price of bitcoin, and its effect on mining, was likely not fully contemplated. Satoshi wrote, "The price of any commodity tends to gravitate toward the production cost. If the price is below cost, then production slows down. If the price is above cost, profit can be made by generating and selling more. At the same time, the increased production would increase the difficulty, pushing the cost of generating towards the price."[1] Satoshi added:

---

[1] https://bitcointalk.org/index.php?topic=721.msg8114#msg8114, accessed April 19, 2022.

It's the same situation as gold and gold mining. The marginal cost of gold mining tends to stay near the price of gold. Gold mining is a waste, but that waste is far less than the utility of having gold available as a medium of exchange. I think the case will be the same for bitcoin. The utility of the exchanges made possible by bitcoin will far exceed the cost of electricity used. Therefore, not having bitcoin would be the net waste.[2]

To better understand the cause of *The Bitcoin Dilemma*, I next model how bitcoin and other Proof of Work cryptocurrency algorithms reward miners. While I will use the example of bitcoin, and resort, for simplicity, to a standardized miner, the approach is easily generalized. I will do so once we tease some important results from the economic analysis. Readers uninterested in the economic details may prefer to jump to the discussion in the next section.

Satoshi knew that one single miner could have easily satisfied the basic encoding function that successfully links blocks to prevent subsequent tampering. Indeed, Satoshi defined the ten-minute block interval to be long enough for personal computers at the time to perform the necessary encoding. However, Satoshi also chose to build into the algorithm a feature that would provide an incentive for other miners to take up a task Satoshi performed for the first year or two of mining. That way, many decentralized machines could do the encoding and the verification necessary to ensure the network remains democratically decentralized and coordinated by majority vote of the nodes to ensure the digital coin is almost impossible to compromise.

Satoshi ensured a sufficient number of miners could be supported by defining a reward structure that encourages more miners and makes it unlikely that any miner or coalition could monopolize and corrupt the network. At first, the Bitcoin Protocol provided a reward of 50 bitcoin for the first miner to successfully encode a given block, followed by verification of its peers. The automatically adjustable difficult factor ensures that successful encoding occurs only once every ten minutes on average, while the reward for mining also declines over time.

Let us define the amount of electric power M^* that miners in the network consume in equilibrium, measured in kilowatts, to power enough miners to encode at a rate that ensures six block mining successes every hour. The total processing power for the entire network of standardized miners is then equal to M^* times the processor speed of miners per kilowatt of power.

The total processing power of all miners is currently approximately 200 million terahashes per second. I next determine how this collective processing

---

[2] https://bitcointalk.org/index.php?topic=721.msg8114#msg8114, accessed April 19, 2022.

rate and its electricity consumption is affected by the price of bitcoin and its growth rate, the cost of electricity and miners, the reward rate and the rate rewards halve, and improvements in miner efficiency.

The Assumptions

Let this equilibrium power consumption of standardized miners operating simultaneously be given by M^*. At the current collective processing rate, the Difficulty Factor D must adjust to ensure that one miner, on average, successfully mints new coins every ten minutes. For instance, with the equivalent of twenty million idealized miners operating in early 2022, this difficulty factor must be one in twenty million over ten minutes. Within such a vast network, even a very large mining farm, consisting of upwards of 100,000 such miners would represent but 0.5% of industry capacity and mining success.

The interesting aspect of mining is that the overall success is stochastic. In other words, while the bitcoin algorithm revises its difficulty target to ensure, on average, that a successful block solution arrives every ten minutes, this process has a random element.

To better understand how to model this randomness, consider the analogy to a shuttle bus fleet that brings people between an airport and a nearby hotel. Assume that the goal of the operators is to have a bus arrive at either the airport or the hotel every ten minutes, and let's assume the round-trip time is about ten minutes. We would need six shuttle buses to handle this route.

When the service begins in the morning, each bus departs in a staggered manner, with one bus leaving precisely every ten minutes. By the end of the day, delays for one driver, or light loads for another mean that, while all six buses are still transporting passengers, and an average all six buses complete the loop every hour, the time of arrival is no longer precisely every ten minutes. It has become randomized according to a stochastic pattern called a Poisson process. On average, the arrival rate remains six per hour, and hence the average arrival duration is every ten minutes, but these rates and durations have become random numbers that follow a Poisson distribution.

Under such a Poisson process, the average delay is simply the reciprocal of the rate of potential solution arrivals. If solutions would arrive on average six times per hour, based on the difficulty target and industry processing capacity, the average arrival rate translates into the requisite ten minutes.

This equilibrium Poisson arrival rate λ per hour of bitcoin mining is then equal to:

$$\lambda = 6M/D, \tag{8.1}$$

where D is adjusted by the bitcoin protocol to result in an average mining success rate of one machine every ten minutes. We can define D to be the necessary processing power or the corresponding network-wide electricity consumption necessary to ensure an average ten minute blockchain coding success rate.

> **How is Mining Rewarded?**
>
> Satoshi designed a fixed reward structure that has resulted in 19 million bitcoins mined to date, and another 328,500 to be added in 2022, based on the current reward of 6.25 bitcoin every ten minutes. With the next halving in 2024, the annual addition shall drop to 164,250 new bitcoin. Such discrete halving every four years complicates the reward mathematics somewhat. I can simplify our calculations by assuming instead that the reward structure halves every four years, but on a continuous rather than discrete basis. In doing so, I treat the value of the reward in terms of a half-life, with the half-life in this case the four-year halving period.
>
> As the coin reward halves in quantity every four years, the network shall add only two million additional bitcoin over the next 118 years. The increase in supply amounts to about 10% over the next 118 years, while the annual increase falls to a rate of 0.8% by 2024. In economics, there are few, if any, examples of such restricted and fixed supply. Note that this supply is completely disconnected from demand.
>
> With the price of one bitcoin in late 2021 approached $70,000 U.S., an estimate of the monetary reward every ten minutes to those conducting roughly 10^{23} hashes each block period is approximately $400,000. Since all hashes are identical, each miner, on average, shares in that reward. The only way to improve one's odds is to generate more hashes than other miners per kilowatt-hour of energy consumed, or by finding a larger energy allocation to run more miners.

Here, we can see the advantage of participation in a mining pool. In one year, with the equivalent of millions of these standardized miners in competition, but with only 52,560 blocks rewarded each year, one would need hundreds of miners operating full time to secure a single reward each year on average. By extracting a small transaction fee of usually around 1%, a pool ensures that such rewards are divided up according to one's contribution to the pool, and rewarded daily, but in the form of dollars per miner per day rather than many hundreds of thousands of dollars very rarely, if ever.

I next model in our analysis the cost of mining machines. For instance, in early 2022, a state-of-the-art Intel Bonanza miner that can produce 140 TH/s was able to generate revenue of approximately $1,200 per month. An investment of $5,000 would pay off in well less than half a year. Indeed, mining machines are typically ranked by the number of days of revenue necessary to purchase a given machine. Historically, this payback period has consistently been less than one year, and often profitable within 100 days. If these machines can operate reliably through adequate heat dissipation, the capital cost of purchase of mining machines is relatively insignificant, especially when one compares rules of thumb payback periods for other investments that typically are around five years (Fig. 8.1).

The maintenance costs of such devices are also likewise reasonably low. Should a ubiquitous Antminer S9 fail, it can be dismantled and reassembled with a replacement circuit board in five minutes. An Antminer S9 has but four such boards, and one power supply that is even easier to replace. Since one large room may house 10,000 such miners in a large operation, one low-skill security guard can oversee an entire operation and conduct any necessary repairs or machine substitutions.

Such facility and labor costs are insignificant compared to tens of millions of dollars of revenue per year that a large mining farm can earn given the bitcoin prices seen in 2021. I will ignore these labor and facility costs and pool commissions, for sake of simplicity, given their trivial scale. I treat later the capital costs of machines, but will demonstrate the single most significant cost will be for the purchase of electricity.

Each miner uses a significant amount of electricity, almost all of which is dispersed as heat. In fact, the greatest challenge of mining is heat dissipation.

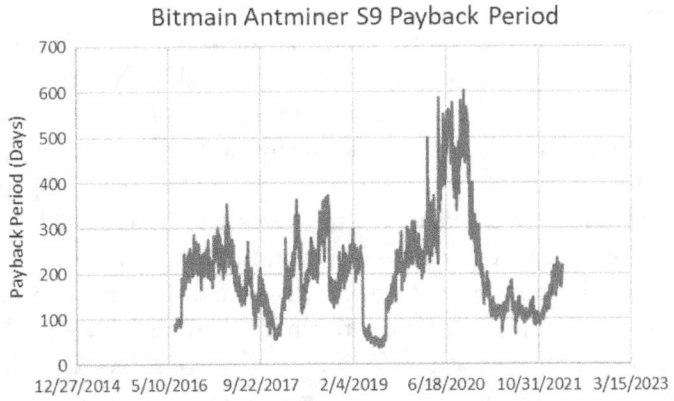

Fig. 8.1 The payback period for a typical miner

Imagine the equivalent of 10,000 space heaters running in a building the size of a small box store of perhaps 10,000 square feet of floor space. Large heat dissipating fans must line the ceiling and walls to circulate a sufficient amount of fresh air to cool a commercial space that is hot and noisy and consumes perhaps twice the power as a medium-sized factory. This industry prefers to compare itself to data centers that might power a cloud operation, but a data center typically consumes less electricity and generates much less heat and noise. Meanwhile, data centers devote upwards of 15% of its revenue to employ workers, mostly of higher skill level, than a typical mining farm of the same electricity consumption, while bitcoin mining farms employ very few people.

To now, I have characterized an industry with negligible labor and facility costs, as a share of revenue, equipment costs that can represent less than a year's share of revenue, and an electricity cost that falls with increased miner efficiency, on a terahash per second basis. These investments, primarily in two factors of production, miners and electricity, are compared to the revenues that are straightforward to calculate given the amount of bitcoin rewarded to mining is known and proportional to the hashrate of miners. In addition, current bitcoin prices are known, and future prices can be extrapolated based on various assumptions.

Given these market characteristics, one can apply economic theory to characterize the nature of equilibrium as the bitcoin price changes and mining technologies improve. I indicated earlier that the design and production of miners is likely best described as an oligopoly or perhaps monopolistic competition. I shall discuss later the implications of this portion of the industry. However, mining itself is decidedly competitive. In fact, one could not imagine an industry that better fits the assumptions of the perfectly competitive model.

A branch of economics called Industrial Organization describes how an industry will perform based on its structure and the ways in which its competitors interact. Under such a Structure, Conduct, Performance (SCP) paradigm, the mining industry is decidedly perfectly competitive. Capital costs are relatively low, when compared to gross profits, and no operator has a significant advantage in accessing existing or new technologies. The delivered cost of a miner is essentially the same worldwide. Every miner with access to electricity and the Internet produces the same product, the processing of SHA-256 hashes, even if they are differentiated by their speed. There is no ability of any operation to affect the supply of bitcoin since a predetermined number of new bitcoin will be mined every ten minutes, regardless of the actions of any operator. Further, the product is distributed over the Internet, again with no ability of any mining operation to affect the nature of supply and demand.

> **Intuition of *The Bitcoin Dilemma***
>
> Proof of Work mining has two aspects by design that have troubling implications. The method it employs to prevent the network of blockchain authenticators from corrupting the chain is to require an effort that is financially onerous. As the benefit from corruption, in the form of multiple spending of the same account within one block, increases with the value of bitcoin, the cost, in electricity and miners increases proportionately. The largest and only significant ongoing cost is electricity, so amortized miner purchases, profits, and other minor and insignificant costs can be priced at the unit of account of the price of electricity.
>
> For successful mining using the ubiquitous Antminer S9, the breakeven electricity cost that begins to yield profits hovers around $0.10 per kilowatt-hour. More efficient miners, such as the S19, can profitably operate at much higher electricity costs. As the bitcoin price rises, so does the breakeven electricity cost. This permits more miners to affordably plug in and network processing power increases accordingly, as does electricity consumption.
>
> This mechanism designed into Bitcoin's Proof of Work protocol was benign in Satoshi's day when the price of bitcoin was under a dollar and the block reward for a successful miner every ten minutes was less than $50. In such a case, an insubstantial $300 of electricity might be consumed in an hour. More recently, the price of bitcoin has increased this competition for miner profits ever higher, to the point that upwards of $60 million in electricity can be consumed in a day. As the price of bitcoin rises, so does this electricity consumption.
>
> More efficient miners that are less costly to purchase per kilowatt-hour consumed only makes matters worse. These more efficient miners actually cause an increase in electricity consumption as miner capital costs come down and profits are hence even more dependent on low electricity costs. In the end, mining farms are in a race for cheap power.
>
> A simple example shows why an improvement in miner technology does not improve this dismal Bitcoin Dilemma. For simplicity, assume all miners are identical and a costless miner firmware upgrade becomes available that increases processing power with no increase in electricity consumption. The first few miners to upgrade will gain a temporary advantage in having a larger effective share of processing with no increases in costs, and hence their probability of successfully mining a block increases. But once all miners upgrade, their profit advantage ends and the industry is left with the same number of miners consuming the same amount of power, but with greater combined processing power. If the innovation also results in cheaper miners, less of the costs go to miner capital, the breakeven electricity cost rises, more miners can afford to compete, and electricity consumption actually rises.

In addition, mining is essentially unregulated worldwide. The only differentiating factor, as we shall see, is the cost of electricity. Accordingly, I next model revenue and substantial costs in this industry. In doing so, I will contrast the long run equilibrium and the short run the forces that may induce a miner to enter or depart the industry. I will do so by making some simplifying assumptions that do not affect the nature of equilibrium, and then relax these assumptions in turn to better understand the dynamics of the industry.

The Model

I take as given the time path of bitcoin prices, which I define as P, and assume, as discussed, the decline of bitcoin Q rewarded for successful mining. This reward decays continuously at a constant rate which yields the requisite halving every four years, in the case of bitcoin.

For simplicity, I assume that mining machines are rented or financed and amortized in a competitive market at a rate proportional to their mining efficiency. This is a simplifying assumption only, for three reasons. First, capital costs are relatively insignificant. The cost of machines is low relative to the revenue they create. Second, a robust market exists for used machines, and these machines do not depreciate significantly, especially within the short payback period. Finally, the assumption that machines are amortized or rented does not at all restrict the degree to which the price of these machines is determined in their separate product market. The advantage in treating capital as an ongoing variable cost is that it readily allows us to explore how equilibrium will evolve as miner pricing changes. Note, though, that while such miner rental or amortized costs are relevant in the decision to begin mining, once the investment is sunk, they are irrelevant. To continue mining only requires rewards that at least cover electricity costs.

Based on these assumptions, revenue and expenses in the industry can be modeled in continuous time. I begin with revenue. The flow of industry revenue for each block mined every ten minutes is then given by:

$$\text{Revenue} = P_0 Q_0 e^{(g-f)t}, \qquad (8.2)$$

where P_0 is the initial price of bitcoin, Q_0 is its initial reward to a successful miner, g is the bitcoin price growth rate while f is the reward decay rate, and t is the period of time measured since the initial price and quantity. For a four-year reward halving rate, the decay rate f is equal to 17.3% annually.

On the expense side, I begin with machine costs, which are rented at a cost r per unit of time for a miner of average processing capacity. Given the assumed miner standardization, this capacity is modeled based on energy consumption M. This technical distinction does not affect our conclusions.

Based on these parameters, the profit function for the industry per hour is given by:

$$\text{Profit} \prod(c) = bP_0 Q_0 e^{(g-f)t} - M(c+r), \qquad (8.3)$$

where I denote b as the number of blocks solved per hour, c is the electricity cost per kilowatt-hour, and r is the hourly rental rate for a miner of average efficiency. For the bitcoin algorithm, this block rate b parameter is equal to six, but such a generalization allows application to other Proof of Work cryptocurrencies that process blocks at a faster rate.

I can now make some initial observations before I characterize equilibrium and the way equilibrium may evolve as parameters change. Based on the Structure, Conduct, Performance paradigm that predicts the free entry of new miners will dissipate any excess profits, profits given in (8.3) converge to zero at least for the marginal miner that can operate at the breakeven electricity cost point c^*. Note that this does not imply all participants earn zero profits. It merely characterizes the point at which it is no longer profitable for a new entrant to purchase a miner in the expectation of positive long-term profits at the breakeven electricity price c^*, measured per kilowatt-hour. Then, the free-entry equilibrium is defined by:

$$0 = bP_0 Q_0 e^{(g-f)t} - M^*(c^* + r) \qquad (8.4)$$

The equilibrium amount of electricity M^* consumed depends primarily on the amount of available power. All else equal, miners will migrate toward the least expensive power, and hence fill all available power opportunities up to the point c* where it is no longer profitable to mine. If this cumulative distribution of available electricity M is given, I can determine the total energy consumption M^* in equilibrium.

What is not immediately apparent in the zero profit, free entry condition is the nature of the difficulty target D. Indeed, the label of *The Bitcoin Dilemma* arises because of the way the difficulty target interacts to determine equilibrium. The difficulty target is set to adjust every 2,016 blocks, or every two weeks, to ensure that necessary mining capacity must evolve so that but one successful block match occurs per requisite period. By definition, D adjusts to ensure that the market mining capacity M obtains the correct block encryption rate.

From these conditions, I can derive the following free entry equilibrium result rather easily:

Total Industry Electricity Consumption $M^*(t) = bP_0Q_0e^{(g-f)t}/(c^* + r)$.
(8.5)

I am able to draw some immediate conclusions from Eq. (8.5). Note that, all else equal, total industry mining capacity in equilibrium $M^*(t)$ rises in proportion to the increase in bitcoin price. This verifies the primary conclusion of *The Bitcoin Dilemma*. As the bitcoin price rises, it is dissipated through the entry of new miners, which increases mining capacity and the difficulty target. Mining capacity also rises as mining machine rental costs r fall. As mining machines become less expensive, mining capacity increases, as does the difficulty target and total electricity consumption.

The next result arises because of the effect of improvements in machine energy efficiency or reductions in energy costs. Either effect reduces expenses in the denominator of (8.15) and hence increases the level of mining capacity. To further explore the net result in an improvement in energy costs or energy efficiency, let us rearrange (8.5) to give the following expression for the free entry condition:

$$M^*(t)(c + r) = bP_0Q_0e^{(g-f)t} \qquad (8.6)$$

Since mining revenue on the right hand side of (8.6) is fixed, then:

$$-d\ln(M^*(t))/d\ln(c+r) = 1 \qquad (8.7)$$

Equation (8.7) reveals that a 1% fall in electricity consumption and capital rental costs results in an equal 1% rise in the total industry mining capacity and electricity consumption. However,

$$d\ln(c + r) = (dc + dr)/(c + r) < 1 \qquad (8.8)$$

for a rise in electricity cost c or rental rate r.

Then,

$$-d\ln(M^*(t))/d\ln(c) < 1 \text{ and } -d\ln(M^*(t))/d\ln(r) < -1 \qquad (8.9)$$

and $-d\ln(M^*(t))/d\ln(c + r)$ approaches -1 as capital costs r become irrelevant. This result shows that a proportional fall in electricity costs dc/c results in a slightly smaller than proportional rise in electricity consumption. This proportional change converges to unity as miner capital costs decrease in relative significance.

This Eq. (8.9) shows that equilibrium energy consumption rises as the cost of electricity and miner rental costs fall equally, and rises at a slightly lower rate than electricity costs fall. This characterization of *The Bitcoin Dilemma* is particularly profound. It demonstrates that reductions in miner or electricity costs or increases in miner efficiency actually induces an increase in total mining capacity by an amount roughly proportional to the fall in these costs. As a consequence, total energy consumption rises with increased availability of low-cost power or less expensive miners, despite industry claims otherwise. Innovation and less expensive energy translate into greater energy consumption.

Note also that a miner will remain online so long as the revenue it receives at least covers the electricity it consumes, if one neglects other costs that remain essentially fixed or trivial. Let us continue to assume for simplicity that all miners are of equal efficiency. The maximum energy price for mining machines to remain profitable;

$$\text{Cutoff energy cost } c^* = b P_0 Q_0 e^{(g-f)t} / M^* \qquad (8.10)$$

Those with energy costs below c^* then divert electricity savings directly to pure profit. In other words, profits arise solely because of electricity advantages. Offering a concession of a share of total energy at a lower cost c simply grants these operators a profit of $(c^* - c)$ for each kilowatt-hour they consume.

Of course, by diverting power to such operations results in higher electricity prices paid by the remainder of ratepayers, at a rate even larger than miners' profits since utilities must replace inexpensive power diverted to miners with more expensive power at its marginal cost. This is often in the form of coal-fired power plants or natural gas-fired peak power plants. Such plants have high marginal costs, but comparatively low fixed costs when compared to the high upfront costs of solar and wind, but with almost zero marginal costs.

In other words, if the utility must purchase additional energy at an effective retail price higher than the cutoff energy cost c^*, ratepayers pay an additional burden and hence significantly subsidize miners. This theoretical result has recently been verified by Benetton et al. (2021) who show that diversion of cheap power for bitcoin mining resulted in an annual $244 million increase in residential and business ratepayer electricity charges in Upstate New York following the arrival of mining, and $1 billion of increases across the nation. Ratepayers in essence pay for the profits miners receive.

It is now straightforward to determine the effect of improved miner energy efficiency to disprove the common industry assertion that more efficient miners will result in lower energy consumption. Let a new miner process the hash function at a multiple $\gamma > 1$ of the industry average. For instance, the next generation of miners produced approximately 500% the rate of hashes as the ubiquitous S9 miner per dollar of electricity. This improvement yields a $\gamma = 5$, which I assume is also accompanied by a commensurately higher miner rental rate γr proportional to its higher return. Then,

$$\text{Total Industry Miners } M^*(t) = \gamma b P_0 Q_0 e^{(g-f)t}/(c^* + \gamma r)$$
$$= b P_0 Q_0 e^{(g-f)t}/(c^*/\gamma + r) \qquad (8.11)$$

Equation (8.11) immediately implies conclusions regarding *The Bitcoin Dilemma*. We see the additional profit arising from a more innovative miner yields:

$$\Delta \pi(c) = (\gamma - 1)\left(b P_0 Q_0 e^{(g-f)t} - r\right) > 0. \qquad (8.12)$$

This result shows that a new higher performance miner will offer the same increment to profits by replacing a miner at any available power. In addition, the differentiation of (8.12) gives:

$$dM^*(t) = \left(M^*/(c^*/\gamma + r)\right)\left(c^*/\gamma^2\right)d\gamma \qquad (8.13)$$

Rearranging (8.13) gives:

$$[dM^*(t)/M^*(t)]/[d\gamma/\gamma] = (c^*/\gamma)/(c^*/\gamma + r) < 1 \qquad (8.14)$$

This result shows that a 1% improvement in miner performance results in a positive but less than 1% increase in total energy consumed. However, once all miners are eventually replaced with state-of-the-art machines, the performance advantage of state-of-the-art miners converges to unity, and energy consumption reverts to the previous value, dependent primarily on the path of the bitcoin price rise.

In other words, benefits that arise from mining efficiency improvements are temporary. Innovation allows better miners to win the battle but we all eventually lose the war in the mining arms race. This relationship is worsened if more efficient miners are also less expensive per unit of processing power. Such a fall in mining machine capital costs r may then increase the total mining capacity and hence worsen energy consumption still further.

Total industry profits can also be determined. Mining is fueled by the conversion of electricity savings vis-à-vis the maximum profitable cost c^* into profits. If $m(c)$ is the amount of electricity available and devoted to mining, in kilowatts, between the lowest available source at c_{min} and the highest feasible price c^*, then profits are given by:

$$\text{Total Profits} = \int_{c_{min}}^{c^*} m(c)(c^* - c)dc. \qquad (8.15)$$

The economic model for bitcoin is a simple one. <u>Savings in electricity costs translates directly into miner profits but at an equal or greater expense to ratepayers once one considers that displaced ratepayers must obtain replacement power at a rate greater than c^*</u>. The bitcoin model predicts that the level of energy consumption from bitcoin mining will rise in proportion to the excess of its price increase, net of its half-life decay. In addition, periods of innovation will temporarily increase energy consumption still more while miners with a lower processing rate are replaced with more efficient miners.

The Theory Is Put to the Test

To test the predictions of the model, I compare the logarithm of energy consumption over time relative to the logarithm of the bitcoin price. Should the theory above prove true over a period of continuous and substantial mining efficiency improvement, we should expect a coefficient between mining rewards and electricity consumption to be slightly less than one. The difference from unity occurs because of the temporary savings from energy-efficiency innovations until long run equilibrium is reestablished. If so, these theoretical results explain a phenomenon that has remained unexplained to date.

A graphical comparison of the bitcoin price superimposed over mining capacity and energy consumption should reveal a strong correlation. If one graphs these quantities since the new era in bitcoin mining in 2017, we should see both a pronounced increase in the price of bitcoin as a consequence of steadily growing demand, but also a correspondingly dramatic increase in energy consumption, despite significant improvements in miner efficiency of an order of magnitude over the same period. Recall that the bitcoin price is a demand driven phenomenon, given the deterministic and inelastic nature of its supply. The upward and significant march of the price of bitcoin is simply a measure of its popularity, or anticipation of future price increases. It has nothing to do with the cost of mining, its machine costs or efficiency, or electricity costs.

To see the relationship between bitcoin mining reward and electricity consumption based on our theory of perfect competition within the Structure, Conduct, Performance paradigm, I next graph the product of the price of bitcoin and the block reward level versus mining energy consumption over the corporate era, with price on the left vertical axis and electricity consumption on the right vertical axis. I use the logarithmic scale for these measures so that I can more easily explore the percentage sensitivity of movements in price to electricity consumption (Fig. 8.2).

While the bitcoin price data is available from a number of sources, there are a couple of commonly employed estimates for energy consumption. The mining industry is loath to share data on its energy footprint or profits, but their consumption can be inferred by a couple of methods. The research

Fig. 8.2 Relationship between bitcoin hourly block reward and annual energy consumption

group Diginomics publishes an estimate of total energy consumption based on the value of bitcoin in proportion to the amount of reward revenue generated. This estimate should then be considered the upper bound of electricity expended. In addition, another group publishes the Cambridge Bitcoin Electricity Consumption Index that monitors the total processing power in the bitcoin mining network at a given time, as published by the various pools. From there, the researchers assign first the processor power to the industry's most efficient and profitable miners, and round off the processing power by allocating it to such miners as the Antminer S9 until the total industry processing limit is reached. The group knows the energy consumption of these various miners and hence can then provide an estimate of total electricity consumed to produce the industry processing power. For the purposes of the graph in Fig. 8.3 and the empirical comparisons, I use the more conservative estimate (Fig. 8.4).

Fig. 8.3 Relationship between level of bitcoin rewards and energy consumption

SUMMARY OUTPUT

Regression Statistics	
Multiple R	0.868526
R Square	0.754338
Adjusted R Square	0.754208
Standard Error	0.346083
Observations	1887

ANOVA

	df	SS	MS	F	Significance F
Regression	1	693.2659	693.2659	5788.139879	0
Residual	1885	225.7731	0.119774		
Total	1886	919.039			

	Coefficients	Standard Error	t Stat	P-value	Lower 95%	Upper 95%
Intercept	-4.45292	0.109733	-40.5796	2.7281E-259	-4.66813596	-4.23771
X Variable 1	0.726745	0.009552	76.07983	0	0.70801061	0.745479

Fig. 8.4 Regression Analysis Between the Logs of Bitcoin Block Reward and Energy Consumption

Over the years of the new era since 2017, we have seen a steady increase in the price of bitcoin. In continuous time, bitcoin halving every four years is equivalent to an annual reward decay rate of -17.3%. Over the same period, the annualized rate of increase of the price of bitcoin has been 137%, which far offsets the modest reward decay rate. Indeed, over the past two years, the bitcoin price has risen by an annualized rate of 165%, with 242% in the last year alone. Figure 8.3 shows that this dramatic increase in bitcoin price, net of the eventual decay in reward quantity resulted in increased energy consumption. This example of *The Bitcoin Dilemma* occurred over a period in which mining efficiency improved by an order of magnitude in terahashes per kilowatt.

These observations can be verified by conducting a simple regression analysis of the bitcoin reward as a determinant of energy consumption. Using the logarithmic form for data allows us to immediately compare the elasticity of energy consumption arising from a 1% change in bitcoin reward. Over the period from January 1, 2017, I compare 1,887 samples of these variables.

The regression data is easily accessible. Bitcoin prices are quoted daily, and the data are readily available for download. The Diginomics think tank that generates their Bitcoin Energy Index estimates energy consumption based on their observed mix of mining machines and total mining capacity. I compare the logarithm of these two data sets as the basis for a linear regression that explains the relationship between mining rewards and electricity consumption. This log/log regression yields an R^2 of 0.75, which is highly significant, especially when one considers that the equation models only a single explanatory variable. Likewise, the F-statistic measure of overall fit is also highly significant. The t-statistic for the explanatory bitcoin price variable is also highly significant, with a value of 76.08. These statistics verify that the bitcoin price and reward determines mining industry electricity consumption.

The coefficient for the dependent electricity consumption variable compared to the independent bitcoin price variable shows that a 1% increase in the reward for bitcoin mining translates into a 0.73% increase in the quantity of energy consumed. As predicted by *The Bitcoin Dilemma* theory, increases in the price of bitcoin induce increased energy consumption at a rate slightly lower than unity in the short. Over a time horizon of five years, and a period of significant miner efficiency improvements, mining electricity consumption nonetheless increased statistically and substantially. By no means does energy-efficiency improvements result in decreased consumption over time, contrary to the assertion of mining advocates. The steady growth of energy consumption proportional to the growth of bitcoin prices, and further increased by the growth of energy efficiency provides a shocking prophecy for an industry that already represents global electricity consumption that exceeds 1% of global energy consumption alone.

9

The Bitcoin Dilemma

Bitcoin security was based on the premise that a sufficiently large miner base would make the commandeering of more than 50% of the network expensive and not feasible. Satoshi predicted, "I anticipate there will never be more than 100 K nodes, probably less. It will reach an equilibrium where it's not worth it for more nodes to join in. The rest will be lightweight clients, which could be millions."[1]

Once again, Satoshi was most prophetic. Indeed, there are many nodes, but many millions more power-hungry miners, assembled in mining farms and consuming more power than the lightweight, power-sipping clients that Satoshi had imagined.

What Satoshi could not have imagined is the incredible jump in processing power over time and the miner arms race that ensued as the price of bitcoin skyrocketed to astronomical levels. Since electricity is the ammunition of the bitcoin arms race, the mining industry's power consumption is many orders of magnitude larger than Satoshi envisioned. Instead of using a reasonable amount of electricity that is still sufficient to up the ante of any potential coin corrupter, the power consumption is immense, and still growing dramatically.

The Bitcoin Dilemma is likely an unintended consequence of a principle Satoshi espoused. Satoshi believed that trust in the integrity of a cryptocurrency blockchain arose from a combination of network transparency and validation consensus. These protected blocks are transparent in that each

---

[1] https://bitcointalk.org/index.php?topic=286.msg2947#msg2947, accessed April 26, 2022.

node can see the 256-bit hash output from the previous block, the set of transactions, the inserted nonce in the new block, and the current difficulty target. Every miner could then run this data through their SHA-256 algorithm and confirm that any claimed successful output is within the tolerance the difficulty target permits. This new and verified hash output then becomes the seed for the next block.

Only if a majority of the nodes agree to the proposed immortalization of the block does this verification become formal. The system cannot be hijacked to fraudulently double-spend accounts owned by those with malicious intentions unless those with malice command at least 51% of the nodes. To try to organize a coalition would ultimately constitute wire fraud. To purchase one's way into controlling half the nodes would be prohibitively expensive, not only in the purchase of machines, but also in the electricity to serve them. It is these prohibitive barriers in investment that Satoshi believed constituted a hurdle that would prevent a criminal thwarting of the bitcoin network.

Satoshi's notion of the beauty of such a self-enforcing peer-to-peer transaction network was brilliant in its conception and consistent with a great faith in decentralized systems over institutions. The system worked well for a couple of years when the price of bitcoin, and hence the rewards, were low, and Satoshi was one of the few active miners. Satoshi believed that, as the stakes rise with a higher bitcoin price and hence a greater number of nodes, the system design would become even more decentralized. Instead, it became more corporatized.

It is unlikely Satoshi imagined that the reward system, when combined with the adjustable difficulty target that keeps the mean authentication delay to approximately ten minutes, would create a *Bitcoin Dilemma* that would consume almost inconceivable amounts of power. Satoshi would have likely been surprised if the network will someday demand electricity valued at more than $2 million in a year, much less an excess of $2 million generated by mining each hour as we see today.

Based on our modeling of the economic structure of bitcoin authentication in this almost perfectly competitive industry, I find that the unintended effect of Satoshi's model is that, while raw computing power and electricity consumption is precisely the force Satoshi believed world protect network integrity, the incredible rise in the price of bitcoin translates almost immediately into greater power consumption until the majority, perhaps even the vast majority of mining revenue in a seemingly ever-expanding concept and network, goes to electricity purchases in the long run.

9 The Bitcoin Dilemma

The implications of the modeling of this *Bitcoin Dilemma* are profound:

a. The amount of bitcoin rewarded for successful mining decays constantly, at an annualized rate of 17.3%, which is small in comparison to the three figure annual percentage increase in bitcoin over its life, and certainly since the new era of ASIC and corporate mining beginning in 2017.
b. *The Bitcoin Dilemma* economic model demonstrates conclusively that bitcoin price run-ups in excess of quantity of coin reward decay inevitably results in a proportional increase in energy consumption.
c. While mining advocates argue that increasingly powerful or energy-efficient mining machines, by measure of processing power per dollar of purchase or rental price or per dollar of energy consumption, should ameliorate the increased power consumption result, *The Bitcoin Dilemma* demonstrates the opposite. Industry cost improvements actually cause mining capacity to grow with these efficiency improvements, which actually exacerbates *The Bitcoin Dilemma* energy consumption conclusion.
d. The intuition behind this result is easy to see. Let us assume that the industry is constituted by a single miner type, for instance, the ubiquitous Antminer S9. The industry is in equilibrium in that no new machines can enter the market and earn a non-negative profit. Consider a firmware improvement of the sort the industry as seen with S9 machines. The firmware improvement will consume x% more electricity, but mine at a proportionally greater rate y%. This sets up a *Prisoner's Dilemma* for the industry. Miners will be put at a competitive disadvantage if they do not install the upgrade. But, once all miners install the efficiency update, energy consumption remains at its previous level. The increase in total mining capacity is usurped by a necessary increase in the difficulty target.
e. Similarly, as new miners become available at lower capital costs relative to capacity and lower power consumption, such initial savings are eventually consumed through expanded mining capacity and increased energy usage. As a consequence, the new wave of more cost-efficient Intel Bonanza miners makes electricity consumption worse. This is because more efficient machines are actually less costly per unit of miner processing capacity. The rental or amortized purchase price of mining has been falling since the first S9 machines just four years earlier. With free entry, this results in greater revenue exhausted for electricity purchases rather than machine costs, and hence greater electricity demand as the difficulty target continues to accelerate upward with increased mining capacity. Innovation is not an antidote to *The Bitcoin Dilemma*. Indeed, the arrival of powerful Intel miners at half the price of other state-of-the-art miners

will merely worsen energy consumption that is especially compounded as other mining machines likewise drop in price to compete

f. In the short run, the production of power is fixed, with excess demand accommodated by restarting natural gas fueled peak power plants. Such increased demand is the highest cost energy provider. If other sectors of the economy do not decrease their power consumption by the same amount of increased power consumption according to *The Bitcoin Dilemma*, increased power demand will result in higher electricity prices for all ratepayers who do not contract for a specific rate. In other words, ratepayers pay the higher costs arising from *The Bitcoin Dilemma*. In the long run, coal-fired plants are either brought online or are not decommissioned as planned to accommodate the greater electricity demand.

g. In these scenarios, the emissions of greenhouse gasses rise more than proportionately than the increase in energy demand since the energy supply response rests solely with high-cost fossil fuel plants.

h. These results of *The Bitcoin Dilemma* occur even if mining operations are able to secure inexpensive or sustainable energy. Unless their demand is met with their own supply in equal measure, installed and paid entirely by the mining operations, their increased competition for a fixed supply from the electric grid requires all ratepayers to incur additional costs for their power in an amount equal to or greater than the profits earned by miners.

i. The result is driven by efforts of cryptoentrepreneurs to constantly seek profitable opportunities for new power that is perhaps five or ten cents less expensive per kilowatt-hour than that paid by the average consumer. Such savings, multiplied by ten million miners translates directly into immense profits for operators that are ultimately borne by ratepayers.

j. In addition, as operators scour locations for less expensive power contracts, the average power cost declines, which, based on free entry of new miners, results in increased power consumption. Again, this is at the expense of other energy users as cheap power is diverted to mining.

k. Cambridge Center for Alternative Finance constructs a *Cambridge Bitcoin Electricity Consumption Index* that makes a best estimate of total worldwide energy consumption based on its research of the mix of mining machines manufactured and employed in the industry. They estimate that the industry consumes at an annualized rate of 142.4 terawatt-hours in 2022.[2] This total is equivalent to the annual electricity consumption of Sweden.

---

[2] https://ccaf.io/cbeci/index, retrieved March 7, 2022.

1. This electricity consumption is equivalent to 41 medium-sized coal power plants, each which produces an average of 3.5 terawatt-hours of electricity each year. Globally, there are about 8,500 coal plants, and they collectively produce about a third of the world's electricity and a fifth of human-made greenhouse gasses.[3] Coal plants generate 9,440 terawatt-hours of electricity per year representing 40% of global electricity production, and creates 10.1 gigatonnes of carbon dioxide emissions.[4] At a rate of 1.07 megatonnes of carbon dioxide emissions per terawatt-hour of electricity produced, the carbon dioxide emissions that could be avoided from a reduction of the entire 142.4 terawatt-hours of electricity devoted to bitcoin production represents a carbon footprint of 142 million metric tons of carbon dioxide. This annual energy consumption is exceeded by less than 30 nations in the world (out of 218 nations),[5] and exceeds the 52.5 TWh annual power consumption of New York City by a factor of three.

Note that the analysis modeled the point at which new miners find it unprofitable to enter the market. The competitive position of various miners and operations are easy to calculate. Such calculators abound on the Internet that are able to determine mining profitability for a given miner processing rate and electricity cost, given the current price of bitcoin.[6]

The vast increase in electricity consumption that arose with the recent run-up in the bitcoin price occurred over a period of unprecedented miner efficiency improvement, by an order of magnitude in processing power in terahashes per second (TH/s), while the electricity consumption per machine approximately doubled. Hence, the ability of a state-of-the-art miner to process per kilowatt-hour of electricity consumed increased by a factor approaching five. Despite these huge efficiency improvements, electricity consumption has actually been increasing, with each 1% increase in the bitcoin price translating into a 0.73% increase in electricity consumed.

---

[3] https://en.wikipedia.org/wiki/Coal-fired_power_station, accessed February 13, 2022.
[4] https://www.iea.org/reports/global-energy-co2-status-report-2019/emissions, accessed February 13, 2022.
[5] https://en.wikipedia.org/wiki/List_of_countries_by_electricity_consumption, accessed February 7, 2022.
[6] https://www.cryptocompare.com/mining/calculator/btc?HashingPower=14&HashingUnit=TH%2Fs&PowerConsumption=1300&CostPerkWh=0.0&MiningPoolFee=1, accessed February 7, 2022.

Part III

Cryptocurrency Consequences

Part II developed an economic model that explains the continuous rise in electricity consumption from bitcoin mining, even in light of significant improvements in miner processing power. It shows that cheaper sustainable electricity and more cost-effective mining processing network increase electricity consumption. I explore later the ramifications of such electricity consumption on the environment and global warming. First, though, I describe other unintended societal and industry vulnerabilities of bitcoin mining as the industry footprint extends well beyond what Satoshi could have prophesized.

This section treats a number of such unintended consequences of mining. Economists lump these detrimental effect on others who are affected by bitcoin mining but are not miners themselves as externalities.

In such cases, one can internalize the externality by requiring miners to pay the full cost of their actions as they would any other factor of production. Alternately, when the internalization of externalities is not possible, regulation can be imposed on the industry to ensure that it acts in a way that promotes the common good. This part describes some of the effects of bitcoin mining on other entities.

First, I explore the effects of mining on local, state, and national governments. I also illustrate how bitcoin mining has affected other sectors in computing and other cryptocurrencies. Finally, I look at recent innovations in bitcoin and other cryptocurrencies that may ameliorate some of these industry concerns, if not perhaps local, state, and national nuisances or concerns.

Foley et al. (2019) significantly further our understanding by chronicling the nature of bitcoin transactions themselves. Their groundbreaking research began with the construction of a database of all bitcoin transactions since the Genesis Block. From that database they develop a classification system to determine whether transactions are speculative or enable illicit and legal transactions. From their innovative forensic methods, they conclude that 46% of bitcoin transactions are for illegal exchanges, worth approximately $76 billion annually, comparable to all illegal transactions in drugs annually in the U.S. and Europe. While even more opaque cryptocurrencies and an acceleration of bitcoin speculation is expected to reduce this share, bitcoin has been a boon for Dark e-commerce.

Werbach (2022) offers further support for the conclusions of Foley et al. They cite a 2019 study that showed 95% of volume in lightly regulated cryptocurrency exchanges arose because of artificial wash sales designed to conceal gains from ballooning asset prices, purchases of Non-Fungible Token transactions, and money laundering. Fortunately, McIntosh (2019) observes that problems of money laundering through complex wash sales are less prevalent in exchanges located in more highly regulated nations such as the United States. I will describe these phenomena in a later chapter.

Bitcoin enables international crime and knows no borders. Benner (2022) reports on the largest seizure of bitcoin wealth arising from illegal activity. U.S. officials retrieved bitcoin valued at $3.6 billion six years after a breach of Hong Kong-based Bitfinex in 2016. Other abuses of bitcoin are rising as well. Richter (2021) adds that more than $400 million was paid out in cryptocurrency ransom in 2020, up by 337% over the previous year.

Bitcoin also affects some communities more than others, especially communities blessed with inexpensive power. When confronted with other unintended consequences of bitcoin on cities and towns, some localities fare better than others. Greenberg et al. (2019) tracked the City of Chelan, Washington moratorium in 2014 to address how it attempted in an orderly way the consideration of the backlog of applications for 220 MW of their hydroelectric power. The moratorium allowed the city to ration their power to high-density users that would also be responsible for the costs of additional infrastructure and power costs. They quoted a city councilor at the time who, fairly or unfairly, articulated a common view that crypto miners are "fly-by-the-night-money launderers … selling fake Rolexes out of the back of a pickup."

The authors also argued that such concerns and stigma about bitcoin legitimacy may be tied to a lack of understanding of the technology and concerns about digital coin mining decentralization. They rely on work by Freudenburg (2006) to conclude that environmental degradation that can affect local communities arises from uneven access to energy resources that allows some entities to abuse electric power in ways that degrade the environment without sufficient regard for the costs they impart on others.

For instance, diversion of power can increase global reliance on fossil fuels as bitcoin mining depletes a significant amount of sustainable energy. Yet, some states still vie for the economic activity mining may bring. As an example, the State of Montana valued the crypto industry to the degree they offered the industry a $416,000 job creation grant in 2017. Monroe (2022) added that Texas Governor Abbott has invited in cryptocurrency mining to his state out of a belief that the additional demand will induce the utility industry to invest in more capacity. She quotes experts who believe that Texas will by 2023 represent 25% of global bitcoin mining, even though the predicted electricity generation capacity has failed to materialize. Moss (2021) quotes Lee Bratcher, President of the Texas Blockchain Council, that bitcoin mining should add upwards of five gigawatts of power demand by 2023, on top of the .5 to 1 gigawatt already diverted to mining.[1] Yet, the state also generates 72.5% of electricity from fossil fuels,[2] which will require a large increase in greenhouse gas emissions if production must be expanded to accommodate greater demand

Perhaps one of the biggest challenges arises when sustainable electricity is diverted to bitcoin and hence is unavailable to other consumers. Using data from 2018 to 2019, Benetton et al. (2021) show how cryptocurrency mining in upstate New York resulted in an estimated increase in electricity costs of $79 million annually for small businesses and $165 million for residents. They estimate the national cost of such power diversion in the U.S. to be $1 billion.

Some of these losses were mitigated by modest increases in business taxes, which partially explains why some communities welcome cryptocurrency mining, even when these positive spillover effects are well-outswamped by higher electricity costs. Meanwhile, we also see states begin to compete for mining farms. Namcios (2022) reports that two bills in Georgia and Illinois propose to offer tax incentives by including mining operations in the favorable treatment offered data centers if they invest at least $250 million and generate 20 jobs in Illinois, for instance.

---

[1] https://www.datacenterdynamics.com/en/news/texas-could-add-5000mw-of-cryptocurrency-mining-data-centers-by-2023-even-as-ercot-warns-of-grid-vulnerability/, retrieved March 10, 2022.
[2] For instance, see https://www.electricrate.com/data-center/electricity-sources-by-state/, retrieved February 28, 2022.

Communities and states are not the only stakeholders. In 1996, then-Federal Reserve Chairman Alan Greenspan noted in a speech that:

> From today's presumably far more sophisticated view of such matters, we may look askance at what we have often dismissed as "wildcat banking." But it should not escape our notice that, as the international financial system becomes ever more complex, we, in our regulatory roles, are being driven increasingly toward reliance on private market self-regulation similar to what emerged in more primitive forms in the 1850s in the United States.... As financial systems become more complex, detailed rules and standards have become both burdensome and ineffective, if not counterproductive. If we wish to foster financial innovation, we must be careful not to impose rules that inhibit it. I am especially concerned that we not attempt to impede unduly our newest innovation, electronic money, or more generally, our increasingly broad electronic payments system.

Yet, he also offered a cautionary note:

> As Professor Nathan Rosenberg of Stanford has pointed out, even relatively mature technologies can develop in wholly unanticipated ways...Our optimum financial system is one of free and broad competition that is presumed to calibrate appropriately the changing value of products to consumers so that the risk-adjusted rate of return on equity measures the success in providing what people want to buy... This has turned out to be broadly true in practice and supplied regulators with some sense of which products were serving consumers most effectively. This signal may not be so readily evident in the case of electronic money. The problem is seigniorage, that is, the income one obtains from being able to induce market participants to employ one's liabilities as a money. Such income reflects the return on interest-bearing assets that are financed by the issuance of currency, which pays no interest, or at most a below-market rate, to the holder... Historically when private currency was widespread, banks garnered seigniorage profits. This seigniorage increasingly shifted to the federal government following the National Bank Act, when the federal government imposed federal regulation on bank note issuance, taxed state bank notes, and ultimately became the sole issuer of currency... Today, there continue to be incentives for private businesses to recapture seigniorage from the federal government. Seigniorage profits are likely to be part of the business calculation for issuers of prepaid payment instruments, such as prepaid cards, as well as for traditional instruments like travelers' checks. As a result, in the short term, it may be difficult for us to determine whether profitable and popular new products are actually efficient alternatives to official paper currency or simply a diversion of seigniorage from the government to the private sector.

Greenspan concluded:

> … electronic money is likely to spread only gradually and play a much smaller role in our economy than private currency did historically. Nonetheless, the earlier period affords certain insights on the way markets behaved when government rules were much less pervasive. These insights, I submit, should be considered very carefully as we endeavor to understand and engage the new private currency markets of the twenty-first century.

Greenspan recognized both the potential and peril of cryptocurrencies, as I do here. Concerns go far beyond borders. Researchers increasingly find that there are international consequences to bitcoin mining as well. Handagama (2022) documents Sweden's petition of the European Union to adopt a ban on mining in the wake of China's 2021 crackdown, which is, at least in part, a response to the need to phase out coal power production.

Isaac and Browning (2022) report that some believe the crypto craze has gone too far, and now often resemble digital Ponzi schemes with prices for such things at Non-Fungible Tokens that escalate artificially in excess of their value. The gamer community is upset that game studios are now trying to push NFTs on gamers. Gamer and YouTuber Mutahar Anas believes they are "trying to sell you snake oil" as game publishers try to make a cash grab to sell unwitting gamers such tokens to exchange among themselves. For example, such microtransactions may be in the form of a set of armor for a game character's horse for a fee of $2.50. One platform through popular game maker Ubisoft, called Quartz, has issued 10,000 wallets, while Ubisoft has already minted its first 3000 such NFTs that it intends to sell to gamers.

In the upcoming section, I document such unintended and cascading consequences that, ironically enough, erode the trust in a cryptocurrency that Satoshi created to avoid the necessity of trust.

10

Towns and Cities Against Noise and Power Hogs

By 2016, the Application Specific Integrated Circuit-based Bitcoin Antminer S9s became available. Earlier machines were no match for the S9 miners that appeared en masse in 2016. They represented a huge increase in mining efficiency that moved bitcoin beyond hobby mining to corporate mining.

The bitcoin mining Arms Race had begun. Any ASIC miner could compete with another, but someone with ten or twenty million dollars could afford to purchase upwards of 10,000–12,000 ASIC machines in 2016 and become one of the biggest players in the industry. Such an investment would instantly command a market share of approximately 8% of all bitcoin processing. And, with the reward still set at 25 coin every ten minutes, and soon to halve to 12.5 coin on July 9, 2016, but with prices beginning to rise rapidly, to around $1,000 by the end of 2016, an 8% market share earned the miner upwards of ten million dollars of profit every month (Fig. 10.1).

Such an operator started up in Plattsburgh, New York with an estimated 10,000 new Antminer S9 machines. By the summer of 2016, CoinMint was already establishing itself in Plattsburgh. It chose a location carefully. As noted earlier, the essential ingredient is cheap and abundant power. Such an operation in support of upwards of 10,000 machines would need around 12 megawatts of reliable power. Time is money, and these operations run 24 hours a day, 7 days a week. With a revenue run of upwards of $10 million per month, just a few days without power results in a revenue loss of a million dollars.

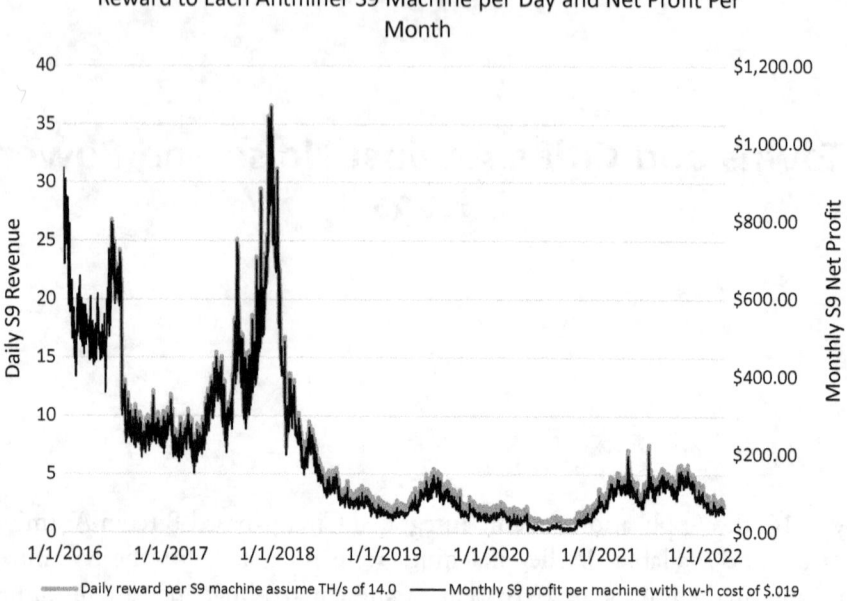

Fig. 10.1 Antminer S9 profits per month in Plattsburgh, New York

Until they migrated toward an even larger power allotment of 435 megawatts in another New York State community, this mining farm was the city's most profitable enterprise, by far. The key to such profits was inexpensive electricity, and perhaps neighbors that were not too nosey. The location CoinMint found was near a substation in an abandoned dollar store at the edge of a strip mall.

This operation did not come to that strip mall by coincidence. By early 2017, as I began my four-year term as Mayor of the City of Plattsburgh, bitcoin miners from all over the world were inquiring about the city's power availability. The first and only questions they had was how much power we could offer and at what price. They were not interested in any other public infrastructure, the quality of schools for their employees, the property tax rate or quality of our first responder network in Plattsburgh. It was only the price and quantity of power that interested them

Our city has one of the lowest industrial prices in the world. At 1.9 cents per kilowatt-hour as the industrial rate, Plattsburgh offered inexpensive power in an effort to attract job-generating industry. Its competitive advantage was a long-term municipal contract for inexpensive hydroelectric power from the Niagara Power Authority that dated back decades from the original site of large-scale power generation in the world, back when Nikola Tesla won out over Thomas Edison in Tesla's idea of alternating current generation.

There were some other municipalities in Plattsburgh's association of municipalities that had equally inexpensive power as well, but our city had a large quota, or at least we thought. On a given day the city was afforded about 120 megawatts of power, which was twice as much as we would need on a nice spring day, and just about what we need on cold winter nights as households cranked up the electric heat ratepayers universally used in the winter.

Plattsburgh has a few other large electricity consumers. A plastics factory uses about five megawatts, and the city has a major hospital and a campus in the State University of New York system. But, even the residential and commercial rate for our customers, at about 4.5 cents per kilowatt-hour, is so low that almost nobody finds it economical to heat with natural gas or heating oil. Practically everybody warmed with electric resistance heat, usually in the form of electric baseboards lining each room, with thermostats on the wall or floor. For spot heat, one might employ a small space heater which, coincidentally enough, was about the size of, consumed the same amount of power of, and generated the same amount of heat as the ubiquitous Antminer S9 machines that began to crop up in Plattsburgh and everywhere in 2016.

Because almost all residents and businesses heat with electricity, the city would exceed its quota on the occasional very cold winter night. But that overage event was relatively rare, and might not occur at all some years. When it does occur, I had our city purchase forward renewable energy credits to ensure we could meet our power needs but still remain 100% renewable.

The Problem

The economic complexion of this picturesque city on Lake Champlain changed quickly. By 2017, the former dollar store had sprouted fans across its roof and down its walls. These big industrial fans were quite loud as they sucked air through every nook and cranny into the mining room and then expelled the hot air outside. For miners, heat is their enemy, and the colder the incoming air, the better. Adjoining shops were not so keen on the cold air suddenly dragged under their doors and through small cracks in their window frames. Tenants complained that they could have their heat on full and yet be unable to hold their storefronts above 50 degrees Fahrenheit.

The owners of these machines run them 24/7, and the colder the weather the better. Apart from the complaints of noise suffered by neighboring residents, the biggest complaint was from residential ratepayers who suddenly saw their electricity bill rise. The city had anticipated some quota overages in the middle of winter, and the energy forward contracts were usually sufficient to keep our electricity bills predictable. But, once mining began in earnest, the city forced to buy extra and much more expensive power, while everybody shared in that cost.

> **The Transition from Carhartts to Pinstripe Suits**
>
> In 2017, municipal leaders observed that more and more operators arrived every month requesting power for their new "data centers." In the parlance of regional economic developers, data centers are welcome. They are relatively high tech and staffed by engineers. They build or purchase their buildings, and hence pay property taxes, as do their employees. Their operations are clean and quiet, and these invest enough for the community to know they aren't going anywhere. About 15% of their revenues go toward employing staff, compared to an estimated 1% in a mining farm such as the one that opened in Plattsburgh.
>
> Soon, when potential operators appeared in the Mayor's Office, they were increasingly wearing business suits and backed by venture capital money. It was recently reported that 20% of all bitcoin mining is through publicly listed corporations, up from just 3% the previous year.[1] An industry that can generate more than a hundred million dollars of revenue a year using the space of a dollar store, with perhaps half a dozen employees to make sure the fuses don't blow or nosey neighbors don't come to inspect, is certainly worthy of serious Wall Street money. Of course, if you ask too many questions, in their minds you clearly just don't understand their business model, or are an anti-technology Luddite.
>
> As a physics major who also studied graduate level electrical engineering in cryptography, and with a law degree, a Master's of Accountancy in Taxation and an MBA, and a Ph.D. in economics and finance, I had no problem at all understanding their business plan. We just did not have any more power to sell them, especially if our residents would end up paying the overages on those days our quota was exceeded. In a month we could have sold to bitcoin operators lining up at our door enough power to exceed our quota many times over. If we had, not only would our residents be irate at huge increases in their electric bills, but our bitcoin miners could disappear just as quickly as they came, as we once saw when the largest operation reduced their Plattsburgh footprint by a half once it was promised even more power in a nearby municipality.

Plattsburgh was not the only community experiencing such inundations of "data processing centers." Chehalis in Washington State also had cheap hydroelectric power to sell. However, while the bitcoin industry is very well-organized, with experienced lawyers, slick sales pitches, and well-honed

---

[1] https://decrypt.co/97003/dominance-public-bitcoin-miners-jumps-nearly-sixfold-15-months, accessed April 7, 2022.

talking points written by K-Street and Madison Avenue experts, most municipalities rarely know what hit them. Municipalities can sell some power, at cost, but none would see any significant share of the huge profits generated at that time, given the industry's preference to rent and not own facilities, and to avoid paying property taxes. Mining farms also hired very few employees at relatively low wages consistent with the low skills requirement for their plug and play miners.

The Local Solution

By early 2018, the city of Plattsburgh realized we had to do something. Our resident ratepayers were fed up over rising electricity bills. The crypto media outlet reported, "The city council unanimously approved an 18-month moratorium on crypto mining activity in Plattsburgh. The idea of a moratorium was first introduced by Mayor Colin Read in January after residents reported inflated electricity bills."[2]

A moratorium on large-scale power installations afforded the City some time to construct solutions to emerging problems. During the next six months, we tackled a few problems.

First, I petitioned the New York State Public Service Commission for a rate structure that ensured a large and energy-dense industry which forced municipalities to purchase extra and more expensive power must pay for these cost overages. The resulting Rider A protected our residents and businesses alike from overages unrelated to their traditional electricity needs. Rather than sharing the expected cost overages by averaging them across all ratepayers, the mining farms were required to pay the additional marginal costs of their overages.

To protect our workers, we applied an Occupational Safety and Health Administration (OSHA) standard for acceptable levels of heat and duration in a working environment. We also adopted a noise code that is not unusual for cities and which protects residents living near industrial sites.

Out of concern for our firefighters who may go to fight a fire without realizing that a mining operation is located on the other side of exterior walls, we required operations to install facilities that allow firefighters to shut down power from outside, and fire extinguishing systems that are designed for electrical fires, which is not the usual water-based mode of fire suppression contained by our tanker trucks and fire hydrants.

---

[2] https://cointelegraph.com/news/us-plattsburgh-ny-introduces-temporary-ban-on-new-crypto-mining-operations, accessed April 26, 2022.

We took no longer to put these reasonable standards in place than necessary, and were actually able to remove the moratorium earlier than expected, but not without a series of hearings with a great deal of very upset and vocal residents in attendance, and a few bitcoin industry representatives and *Crypto Bros* trying to explain to irate residents what they just did not understand—the dubious claim that mining afforded cities and towns to be on the leading edge of global high technology and engineering. However, one additional provision, which seems quite reasonable, but has not been replicated elsewhere to my knowledge, was a requirement that on those days when we expect to begin drawing more electricity for seasonal heating, mining operations must recycle a portion of their heat rather than disperse it into the atmosphere.

This responsible level of recycling, on occasion, was not onerous. Our idea was that perhaps half the heat mining farms generate on such days could be used to warm a nearby school gymnasium or field house. By doing so, as miners consumed more energy, some other users could consume less. Hence, a locality could collectively minimize the need to demand a greater amount of energy. The details of the code provisions for the City of Plattsburgh can be found in the Appendix.

We quickly learned that miners prefer jurisdictions with abundant cheap power but without regulation. The fewer the conditions, and the greater locals' faith in false promises of abundant jobs, the better the civic environment is for mining. Of course, such a mentality is consistent with the libertarian nature of an industry that was formed to challenge rather than embrace existing institutions, especially when they view onerous government as bent on curtailing their profits. At times, this reactionary spirit becomes counterproductive, especially since there are certainly enough profits to go around, and, with a bit of tweaking of the model, everybody can benefit, at least if we can work together to solve some serious environmental problems.

Over this period, Plattsburgh's predicament certainly caught the attention of national and international media. Meanwhile, mystery about bitcoin remained. Few people understand the extent of *The Bitcoin Dilemma*. Municipalities across the country are independently coping with what we experienced, but without the benefit of our experiences. It is certainly compelling to picture the creation of all the jobs promised, but never delivered, especially in rural areas such as ours that have a difficult time retaining the population and property values we enjoy. As mythical Pandora pulls demons from her box, war and pestilence, sickness and death, it is hope always lingering on the bottom of that box. Bitcoin mining offered hope for jobs and economic activity that invariably fail to materialize.

11

No More Duffel Bags Full of Cash

There are certainly legitimate needs for the privacy that so concerned cypherpunks. There is also no doubt that anonymity obscures illegal transactions. Satoshi recognized a potential seedy underbelly to anonymity, but was not willing to throw the baby out with the bathwater. Satoshi noted, "Users either don't want the spouse to see it on the bill or don't trust giving their number to 'porn guys.'"[1]

Perhaps one of the oddest experiences I share is the sudden loss of asset forfeiture money that at one time afforded our local police force to fund training and equipment that it could otherwise not afford. Plattsburgh, New York's nearest city by travel time is in Canada. Contraband crosses the nearby St. Lawrence River and finds its way to the first U.S. city. There was a time when police officers would regularly seize duffel bags full of cash from trunks of cars carrying drugs. All of a sudden, while crime and drug smuggling was getting worse, cash seizures completely dried up. The criminal element discovered a much safer, more difficult to detect, and impossible to seize, medium of exchange.

A border city may typically seize the equivalent of tens or hundreds of thousands of dollars of cash in the pre-bitcoin days. While not huge sums, that does not imply the stakes are low. The first recorded U.S. seizure of bitcoin instead of cash in the U.S. occurred in 2013 when a number of agencies coordinated by the Drug Enforcement Administration seized 11.02

---

[1] https://bitcointalk.org/index.php?topic=671.msg13844#msg13844, accessed April 19, 2022.

bitcoin in a drug bust, which was still worth little at that time.[2] Later that year other U.S. law enforcement agencies seized 385,000 bitcoin. On August 27, 2013 Cornelius Jan Slomp was arrested by the U.S. government Immigration and Customs Enforcement agency and its associated Homeland Security Investigations branch. Slomp, then a 21-year-old computer programmer, ran a broad drug distribution ring, through the postal and package delivery system, bought and paid for on the notorious haven for illegal trade over the Internet, the Silk Road.

As part of his plea, Slomp implicated Ross William Ulbricht, the operator of the Silk Road Internet site, which resulted in the seizure of another 144,000 bitcoin and the closure of the underground Silk Road that sold contraband over the Internet globally.[3]

However, in monetary terms, the largest seizure was in February of 2022, when the United States Justice Department announced the arrest of Ilya Lichtenstein and his wife, Heather Morgan, and the seizure of bitcoin valued at $3.6 billion U.S. That seizure arose from suspected proceeds from the Hong Kong based Bitfinex cryptocurrency exchange heist, which was hacked in 2016, with 119,754 bitcoin stolen. The entire theft was not fully recovered. Had it been, the current value would have been $4.5 billion.[4]

Following that attack, the value of bitcoin plunged by approximately 20% as some questioned the security of crypto in general. This was the beginning of the Great Crypto Crash of 2022. The arrested couple Lichtenstein and Morgan employed a variety of techniques to obscure their movement of bitcoin, such as "tumbling" and "wash sales." Tumbling is a generic term for techniques of laundering methods designed to obscure holdings and transactions over time, while wash sales occur when a user is both the sender and receiver of the same funds transferred, often multiple times, between multiple accounts. There are organizations that act as intermediaries to allow users to engage in tumbling to confuse the destination of transfers, for a small commission in the order of 5 to 10%. If the intermediaries are known, or if law enforcement officials recognize fixed and sizable commissions being paid in bitcoin, their forensics alert them to the possibility of such crypto laundering.

---

[2] https://www.theverge.com/2013/6/26/4468302/drug-enforcement-agency-seizes-11-bitcoins-in-south-carolina-bust-silk-road, accessed March 21, 2022.

[3] https://www.forbes.com/sites/andygreenberg/2013/10/25/fbi-says-its-seized-20-million-in-bitcoins-from-ross-ulbricht-alleged-owner-of-silk-road/?sh=367293392765, accessed March 21, 2022.

[4] https://www.cbsnews.com/news/heather-morgan-ilya-lichtenstein-bitcoin-scheme-separated-trial/, accessed March 21, 2022.

An Accounting of Illegality

In fact, there are a number of characteristics of illegal activity that allow law enforcement officials to track illegal activity, despite the limited anonymity most coins provide. In addition, the pattern of transactions allows researchers to estimate the degree of criminal activity within a cryptocurrency such as bitcoin.

In a brilliant piece of research by Foley et al. (2019), the authors not only describe what law enforcement officials may look for in tracking transfers of bitcoin, but they also provide estimates for the extent the network is used for illegal activity. Their indictment of the techniques employed to obscure identity and harbor illicit trade, money laundering, and ransom payments, and the inability of the cryptocurrency industry to police itself, not only reveals the extent of the illicit transaction problem. It also explains why regulators remain reticent to encourage and hence oversee an industry that, by its nature and philosophy, is designed to avoid monitoring and frustrate established authorities.

A discussion of the methods employed by Foley et al. is illustrative as it offers a window to the ways the bitcoin network is used in support of illegal activity and the "Darknet," the name for the series of sites used to conduct illegal activity using methods to hide transactions and identities. Foley et al. (2019) estimated that this Darknet spans 6 million accounts worldwide.

The nature of the blockchain means that every transaction since the coin's inception can be observed, at least between public keys, but without the private keys and account holder identities. Foley et al. created a database of all bitcoin transactions by collecting and extracting information from each block since the Genesis Block of 2009. They then organized the data in clusters that show activity sorted by public addresses. From this database, they can distinguish between likely legal and illegal transactions through observation of certain transaction characteristics.

Examples of characteristics more likely than not associated with illegal activities include the rate and value of transactions between certain public addresses. For instance, transactions for speculative purposes are typically of larger amounts, with transactions representing a buy for point and a sell at a later point in time. Or, sex workers may be paid an identical amount a number of transactions timed at predictable hours.

The rate of illegal transactions is also correlated with increased activity on the Darknet, and may be increasingly denominated in bitcoin when other alternative coins with even greater anonymity, such as Monero and Zencash, depreciate in value. When bitcoin is experiencing a period of increased

Internet and media hype, the authors observe that more transactions are speculative, and, hence, a smaller share of transactions are for other activities. Finally, the authors can detect public addresses that tend to churn through tumbling and wash sales, which suggests the owners of the addresses are attempting to obscure their transactions, likely because they represent illegal activity.

Indeed, Foley et al. found that illegal transactions tend to be much more concentrated and follow predictable patterns of trade among themselves compared to the more random nature of transactions for legitimate purposes. The networks that facilitate trade can be likened to methods for transacting legal goods and services, such as eBay and PayPal.[5] Bitcoin and the Darknet allow the digitization of what would have otherwise been cash transactions, and, in doing so, easily span borders and promote anonymity.

> **The Darknet**
>
> Various Darknet sites, such as the infamous Silk Road, will even rank sellers based on user ratings much like eBay users would rank sellers, to lend confidence in their reliability. Such ratings are essential, given the anonymity these illegal activities command. Users can then use encrypting services to ensure that their contract details are not recoverable, which allows bitcoin accounting forensics to attempt to trace transactions.
>
> Aspects of transactions on the Darknet have other identifiable characteristics. For instance, criminals recognize they are dealing with criminals, so they cannot rely on trust or responsive customer service departments. Instead, Darknet purchases typically constitute transactions of deposits of a certain percentage, followed by balance paid in full upon receipt of the illegal goods or services such as drugs, child pornography, stolen items, or sex or human trafficking. The equivalent of escrow accounts through intermediaries can also be used, which has identifying characteristics by identical amounts moved into and out of accounts, perhaps less a fixed percentage commission.
>
> As had cypherpunks through their adaption of TOR networks, the Darknet too employed anonymous networks to obscure identity or blur the Internet Protocol (IP) paths employed in transactions. Between obfuscated contracts, secure networks, and bitcoin semi-anonymity, the Darknet has flourished, even if various elements, such as the Silk Road, have been shut down. Like the game of Whack-a-Mole, when one is shut down, another magically appears, to the point that Matthews et al. (2017) observe steady growth in both venues and participants over time. One such site, AlphaBay, as a tribute to eBay, had 350,000 illegal items for sale in 2017.

---

[5] It is likely that eBay also facilitates the exchange of stolen property, typically without the knowledge of buyers.

Forensic accounting of illegal activity over the Internet has developed significantly of late. Early methods include the observation of transactions in the blockchain originating from IP addresses associated with identifiable personal computers. In the past, identities have been revealed in this way by seeking subpoenas to obtain records from Internet providers regarding their clients and the IP pathway these clients employ. Some cryptocurrencies remain more amenable to such tracing, which may result in shuttling between various cryptocurrencies based on their perceived anonymity of the ability of these currencies to maintain value.

Finally, seizures related to investigations often reveal a great deal of transactions and Internet addresses that further improves the ability of policing and regulatory authorities to expand their scope and detection of illegal activities. As we saw, the arrest of Slomp in 2013 allowed authorities to arrest and seize the cryptocurrency assets of Ross Ulbricht, later that year, and shut down the expansive Silk Road site that pedaled illicit goods and services online.

Foley et al. applied their various techniques to analyze the millions of transactions since 2009. They were able to narrow potential candidates for illicit transactions by removing a great deal of transactions that represent proceeds from mining, transactions with known legal entities, and commissions or transaction fees paid. They also ruled out transactions that follow patterns associated with speculative purchases and sales. For the remainder of transactions, they employed algorithms to detect laundering techniques related to tumbling and wash sales. They traced approximately 6 million addresses associated with Darknet activity or participation in Darknet forums.

The Level of Illegal Activity Through Bitcoin

When Foley et al. apply analyzed their a sample of 606 million bitcoin transactions that represent $1.6 trillion in value, they discovered clusters and patterns of transactions and were able to discern differences in transaction modes between legal and illegal activity are identified through Detection-Controlled Estimation (DCE). Through their combination of techniques, they reveal some profound conclusions.

The authors find that total activity in bitcoin began to increase significantly in 2012, with illegal activity leading the way. In other words, criminals were early adopters of the bitcoin technology, by three to four years. They estimated that, in 2017, the beginning of the bitcoin corporate era, there were 27 million illegal users of bitcoin making 37 million transactions annually. Based on the price of bitcoin at that point in time, it represented annual transactions of about $76 billion, with about $7 billion held by criminals at any given time. Notably, unlike legal users and speculators, illegal users typically do not wish to hold their currency long in hopes of speculative gains. They transact in bitcoin and plow their revenue into expanded illegal activities, but do not invest in the coin to the same extent as speculators.

Foley et al. conclude that approximately 26% of all users, and 46% of all bitcoin transactions are related to illicit activity. This represented 23% of the dollar value of all transactions, and 49% of all bitcoin holdings. They note, though, that while illicit transactions are on the rise in absolute terms, their share of transaction value has declined relative to the increase in speculative activity.

It is fair to conclude from their observations that speculation and illicit activity represent the bulk of bitcoin transactions and ultimately give the fiat digital currency its value. The supply of bitcoin is essentially fixed, while demand for both speculation and illicit activity continues to grow. These are the necessary elements for an increasing bitcoin price, which has, over the corporate era, averaged an annualized growth rate of 72%. In a later section, I will look at various market analyses that forecast the expected future price path of bitcoin.

An increasingly common, but still comparatively small, form of illicit activity is to pay ransom, often to hackers who threaten to destroy commandeered corporate or municipal computer networks. Such successful ransom payments are reported, and the values in bitcoin known and typically are round numbers paid from known addresses. At first, hackers would exploit vulnerabilities in a corporate Information Technology (IT) network to freeze and encrypt their data. By paying a ransom, the corporation would be provided with a key to unlock their network.

More recently, there have been a number of instances of hackers infiltrating corporate networks not by attacking individual networks but instead by attacking the providers of services to corporate networks. By injecting code into a program employed by corporate networks, hackers create Trojan Horses that allow their creators to enter potentially thousands of such networks.

For instance, Richter (2021) reported that a popular IT network management program designed and sold by the U.S. software developer Kaseya allowed hackers to institute a ransomware attack on up to 1,500 businesses that used their software.[6] Small businesses worldwide were paralyzed and held for ransom for a reported $70 million U.S. In 2020, corporate victims paid

---

[6] https://www.statista.com/chart/25245/total-value-of-cryptocurrency-received-by-known-ransomware-addresses/, accessed February 9, 2022.

more than $400 million in ransom, up by 337% from the previous year. Invariably, such ransom is paid through bitcoin.

Of course, cash has also been used for illegal transactions. However, cash must be moved physically, which is risky and prone to seizure, and can be more easily tracked if financial institutions are employed. Regulatory agencies have honed their skills in tracking these traditional movements, and in monitoring the various ways in which such cash can be laundered so they may enter the financial system disguised as legitimate transactions. These attempts to evade are both expensive and risky.

By its very design, bitcoin especially, but other Proof of Work currencies as well, permits anonymity and movement of large sums across borders at almost no cost and with a great deal more difficulty to detect. As more digital coins are popularized, typically using Proof of Stake as the authentication method, and as the Ethereum protocol completes its transition to Proof of Stake, illicit activity may actually migrate to the even more decentralized bitcoin under the perception that the dispersed and democratic Proof of Work coin may protect anonymity more than a closely-held Proof of Stake coin administered by a central trusted and subpoena-able authority.

12

States and Bitcoin

While a number of aspects of bitcoin mining affect local jurisdictions, states have also been drawn into controversies. Local issues arise because bitcoin produces minor and limited local benefits, primarily in the form of a few jobs created, but with substantial local nuisances. States stand to assist local governments in internalizing such externalities because they typically have at their disposal a greater array of policy tools. However, state governments are also a step removed from the problems that mining can create.

Satoshi's perspective aligned with the distinct libertarian philosophy of cypherpunks. Technologists often fail to appreciate some of the socio-economic consequences of their creations. Satoshi commented on bitcoin, "It's very attractive to the libertarian viewpoint if we can explain it properly. I'm better with code than with words though."[1] Nonetheless, the economy must deal effectively with the unanticipated effects of bitcoin mining.

Economists define an externality as a benefit or cost incurred by a production or consumption activity on individuals not associated with the activity. A positive externality may occur if my consumption of 1960s music is also enjoyed by my neighbor. On the other hand, that same activity could be a negative externality if my neighbor detests The Doors.

While positive externalities are rare, and become an issue only from the perspective that we would like to encourage, and perhaps even subsidize such activities, negative externalities abound. Unlike positive externalities in which

---

[1] https://satoshi.nakamotoinstitute.org/emails/cryptography/12/, accessed April 19, 2022.

the creator of such an activity has an incentive to internalize the externality by constructing mechanisms for others to subsidize their activity, negative externalities are typically much more difficult to treat. Because correction of the externality typically requires a cost to be imposed on the externality producer, the producer has an incentive to hide the activity or shirk its responsibility.

The classic example of a negative externality is pollution. In the absence of mechanisms to require producers to pay for the damage they induce on the environment, producers are able to manufacture their products without paying the full cost of the resources they employ. Certainly electricity, materials and supplies, equipment rental, labor and other costs are borne by the producer, but their consumption of clean air, or the equivalent production of dirty air, is unpriced. Producers then have an incentive to pollute clean air without bound, especially if it allows them to economize on other factors of production such as more expensive but less polluting manufacturing technologies.

In our previous discussion of local issues that arise from bitcoin mining, noise, an unsafe level of heat endured by workers, and dangerous conditions created for firefighters are all negative externalities that the City of Plattsburgh remedied through revised building and nuisance codes. Heat dissipation into the atmosphere may be offensive from an environmental perspective, but it is unlikely to cause significant local harm. Indeed, the heat coming off a bitcoin operation in Plattsburgh was credited with keeping an adjoining parking lot snow free in winter, which, oddly enough, may translate into a positive externality for some.

To address the noise issue, and to better prevent overheating of equipment, some miners are adopting liquid cooling for their machines. Such liquid cooling does not at all reduce the amount of heat that must be dissipated, but it improves the effectiveness of heat removal, which translates into lower maintenance costs for miners, and quieter heat dissipation fans to benefit neighbors concerned about noise. Data processing centers have used lake or sea water to dissipate that heat, and miners are exploring similar opportunities. In doing so, though, they may induce lake warming that imbalances the water ecosystem and creates algae blooms, reduces fish and other aquatic populations, and can even cause harm to humans.

A Role for State Regulators

Emissions into the atmosphere and waterways are typically permitted either by state or federal governments. Hence, there is a legitimate role for state regulation for which there is no local regulatory authority. In addition, state and county governments are concerned about job creation to a greater extent than local authorities because jobs often generate income tax revenue and property taxes beyond the town in which a mining farm is located.

States are also able to promulgate model building codes that can apply to all localities within its borders. This is generally a very slow process compared to the ability of local jurisdictions to act. States relatively carefully and slowly consider those changes they wish to apply broadly across all constituents in a process that must navigate multiple committee consideration before coming to a vote by a legislative body. Hence, states rarely weigh in on issues of perhaps intense but isolated local concern.

We see states place their imprint on an issue such as bitcoin when they believe another level, for instance a federal government, ought to act but has not, or when a few localities can mount sufficient pressure to force statewide consideration.

Just a few local jurisdictions have managed to stay ahead of the negative externalities mining farms can impose, states have also been loath to engage. Since the beginning of the corporate era in mining, especially with bitcoin, owners of mining farms have become increasingly organized and have developed sophisticated playbooks and talking points based on what they find has worked in various places. Mining advocates employ terms such as "data centers," conflate construction with permanent jobs, promise to support local public infrastructure through donations, and assure citizens that miners will buy carbon credits to offset their extensive carbon footprint. These techniques have been effective in convincing localities to offer mining operators the benefit of any doubt. Of course, once permits are issued or operations commence, subsequent changes to building codes are difficult as existing operations are typically "grandfathered in," at least until the point that an operation proposes major modifications. Various other promises made can be easily forgotten.

The cryptocurrency mining industry has also invested heavily in lobbying efforts for state and federal legislators and has of late produced expensive advertising campaigns with top flight media stars and major ad buys, such as for the 2022 Superbowl. They have named a major league sports arena, and have planted opinion pieces likening their contribution to society to such innovations as the first flight of the Wright brothers. They work to marginalize those who oppose expansion of their industry as Luddites afraid of change. Yet, very little discussion is devoted either to any actual benefits of blockchain technology or digital currencies to society, or the amelioration of their various negative externalities.

Some states have been most supportive of the industry in the hopes of local job and wealth creation. They have not gone so far as offering considerable inducements as a state may for a new automobile factory. These states may believe they have power to spare, are receptive to campaign and civic donations, and have created favorable climates for mining facility investments.

The most significant avenues for state regulation have been in ratepayer and in financial consumer protections. To afford some protection, New York State's Public Service Commission approved a rate structure that applied to any industry that concentrates more energy than 250 kilowatt-hours per square foot of floor space per year. This category of industrial user is considered high energy density because ultimately such an intensity generates significant concentrated heat, with its attendant dangers. In New York State. The resulting Rider A required any such industrial operator to pay the costs of extra power that must be purchased to ameliorate any additional burden on other ratepayers if a municipality exceeds its power allotment.

In fact, the only industry that would likely exceed such a high energy density threshold is cryptocurrency mining, regardless of whether it is air or liquid cooled. Note, though, that this New York State provision only applies to communities that face a power quota. If communities do not face such a quota, but nonetheless find themselves purchasing more power, at naturally a higher cost to the electric grid as demand expands, those increased costs are spread across ratepayers. This is an example in which a local jurisdiction would not have the authority to impose such a rate structure, but a state regulatory agency can step in on its behalf.

The Various Hidden Costs of Bitcoin Mining

The Bitcoin Dilemma theory shows that residential ratepayers pay a significant additional burden of alternate power purchases if miners are able to divert or are offered power at a subsidized industrial rate. This was verified in New York State, where Benetton et al. (2021) found that bitcoin mining resulted in increased costs to residential consumers of $165 million annually in their electricity bills, while commercial users had to pay an additional $79 million in annual electricity. The authors determine that, across the United States, ratepayers suffer increased annual energy costs of $1 billion per year, based on 2018 and 2019 data.

The subsidization of industrial power by commercial and residential ratepayers is one of the most significant hidden costs of large-scale Proof of Work mining. However, the additional costs which were captured by Benetton (2021) include the implications of employment of more expensive peaker power to accommodate increased electricity demand, Goodkind (2020)

> analyzed the health consequences of mining, given the fossil fuel generation mix in the United States, and the dilution of value of existing bitcoin as more bitcoin are added to supply every ten minutes. He found that for every $1.00 of bitcoin mined, the U.S. pays $0.49 in environmental and health costs.

Another frequent dimension of state regulation is in consumer protection, at least in those rare states that closely oversee financial markets. Significant state regulations and measures to protect consumers are relatively rare because financial markets tend to be regulated by multiple federal agencies. However, a state like New York, with its significant financial sector, has greater than average financial regulation sophistication and hence imposed financial regulations relatively early on in the development of the bitcoin industry.

The reasons why a state may regulate is not solely for consumer protection, though. If a cryptocurrency is bought and sold, it becomes a traded financial asset, with attendant capital gains tax implications. Cryptocurrency exchanges have been subject to oversight and regulation to ensure accurate capital gains reporting in New York State, for instance, well before federal agencies became engaged.

Transactions themselves are difficult to monitor, though, until coin to currency conversions occur. Up to that point, transfers and transactions made in the original digital currency defy monitoring and transparency, as discussed in other chapters. Indeed, mining machines themselves are typically purchased in bitcoin, and there are examples of payment to workers or property owners in bitcoin as well, which causes reporting for tax purposes to be an exercise in trust rather than verification.

These large cryptocurrency exchanges are where the money resides, in more than their obvious capacity as holders of clients' digital wealth. About $7.5 billion of gold is mined each year, but Gold.org reports that $183 billion of gold is transacted daily. Similarly, about $15 billion of bitcoin is mined each year, but $5.4 trillion is transacted, three to seven bitcoin per second, with approximately 100,000,000 transactions in 2021.[2] A miniscule commission on such transactions can generate far more revenue that does mining, and immensely more profit. Bitcoin exchanges also engage in lending idle funds under their control. Such Decentralized Finance (DeFi) is described in more detail in Chapter 18. The cryptocurrency industry is begging for regulation,

---

[2] To place this annual transaction rate in perspective, the Visa and Mastercard networks process that number of transactions in about two hours. https://www.blockdata.tech/blog/general/bitcoin-volume-mastercard-visa, accessed April 12, 2022.

if for no other reason than to protect the deposits of customers and vulnerable institutions from the blockchain industry.

Other examples of potential state engagement in regulation are through the channels of various departments of environmental conservation, or the permitting of power plants that are increasingly purchased to supply consistent power at subsidized industrial rates to very large mining operations. These power facilities are typically obsolete coal-fired plants, or natural gas-fired peak plants, both of which require air and water discharge permits. By purchasing an entire fossil fuel generating plant, a massive mining farm can generate power upwards of 500–1000 megawatts, in the case of a typical coal-fired power plant.

> **The New York Attorney General and the State Assembly**
>
> I document in Chapter 17 the efforts of the New York State Attorney General to protect consumers from false or misleading statements by purveyors of new crypto exchanges or instruments. Because New York City is a major global financial hub, in the absence of federal oversight, some state attorneys general step in.
>
> The United States currently hosts the most bitcoin mining capacity and, within the fifty states, the one of the largest concentrations of mining is in New York State. Much of the new corporate mining involves purchases of electricity generation capacity, often at a cost of ten or hundreds of millions of venture capital-funded dollars. These purchases are typically of obsolete coal or peaker natural gas-fired plants. In 2022, a moratorium on operating permits of such conversions passed the New York State Assembly and Senate. The bill was then moved to await the Governor's consideration.[3]

Venture capitalists typically purchase existing air and water discharge permits that could be decades old and hence fall short of more recent standards, so long as the operation does not expand previous discharge limits. By purchasing this magnitude of electricity generating capacity, in one fell swoop an operator can obtain sufficient power to command a 2% market share in bitcoin mining capacity, worth upwards of $400 million in annual mining revenue in 2021.

With such revenue potential, and with obsolete coal and natural gas generation plants available at very low cost after decommissioning over concerns for global warming, the economics of massively large mining improves significantly. The ready supply of electricity, of 400 to 500 megawatts at a time, has proven so advantageous that a number of such conversions have occurred

---

[3] https://observer.com/2022/05/exclusive-it-is-so-modest-inside-new-yorks-bitcoin-mining-moratorium/, accessed May 2, 2022.

in various U.S. states, including New York, Montana, Pennsylvania, and elsewhere.

Obviously, such large investments and commensurate expectations of significant revenue flows require a great deal of financial sophistication. Wall Street and Silicon Valley venture capital firms have increasingly converged on cryptocurrency mining, especially ASIC bitcoin mining, since the dawn of the corporate era. Venture capital funds are especially attracted to those seeking huge returns from an industry that generates $15 billion in mining rewards each year. Controlling such investments and revenue flows commands an innovator's energy and resources to a far greater degree than the regulators who may oversee such an industry, or the politicians willing to take advantage of their largesse. Much of these financial flows to purchase influence are at the federal level, though, which is the next topic of discussion.

13

National Policy and Bitcoin

Satoshi harbored great skepticism about large financial institutions, especially in the wake of the artificial mortgage-backed securities-fueled asset bubble of 2007 and the ensuing financial meltdown that led to the Great Recession. The failure to sufficiently regulate banks and insurance companies too-big-to-fail cost Wall Street and required significant taxpayer-funded bailouts. But while Wall Street was saved, and these same institutions soon grew even larger, Main Street suffered. Ineffective regulation that fell far short of rapid innovation in the financial sector left citizens picking up the pieces and plunged economies worldwide into the worst recession since the Great Depression. Satoshi was part of a movement that harbored a healthy amount of justifiable skepticism about large institutions, but perhaps before our attention shifted much more toward global warming and global pandemics.

National policies toward cryptocurrencies are typically designed to protect citizens or the environment, but, in some circumstances, are formulated to generate jobs or create a substitute monetary base that may be less prone to inflation or monetary tool manipulation. As discussed at the state and local levels, the hope that cryptocurrency will create a broader tax base or significant employment is destined for disappointment. Indeed, given the difficulty of directly monitoring bitcoin mining or transactions, economic activity from traditional industry is a safer proposition.

In addition, the share of invested capital in mining is small relative to its difficult-to-track revenues, and capital is notoriously mobile. For instance, when China recently banned bitcoin mining, miners were packaged and shipped abroad almost overnight to the United States, Kazakhstan, and anywhere else operators could find cheap power and lax regulation. Since then, industry has learned the lesson, and now often installs miners in shipping containers to allow quick relocation should lower electricity and less regulation be obtained elsewhere.

This leaves us to rely on national policy that is more typically designed to prevent harm than create jobs. There are some nations, such as Kazakhstan until recently, that have fostered a national policy to encourage mining. Likewise, El Salvador recently tried to shift reliance on bitcoin as a national currency rather than the U.S. dollar, a frequent reserve currency in nations unable to control inflation, and Portugal sought to become a tax haven for the cryptorich. These examples tend to be misguided and are likely to fail, for the myriad reasons discussed in subsequent chapters. This leaves the primary goal of bitcoin and cryptocurrency regulation—to mitigate harms or foster positive aspects of the blockchain for which national agencies can control.

The challenge to traditional regulation is that bitcoin and other Proof of Work cryptocurrencies defy oversight by design, and challenge regulatory agencies loath to endorse or oversee such digital currencies. However, the benefits of digital currencies and the blockchain are potentially significant, and the profits for mining immense. Many of these activities will occur regardless, somehow and somewhere. The challenge, then, is to develop policies that permit us to enjoy digital currencies' benefits as we ameliorate their harm.

China's Experience

China has been on the forefront of oversight of the digital currency mining industry before any other nation. Its incredible entrepreneurs developed the first mass marketed miners early in the ASIC era and created a cottage mining industry that grew substantially to take advantage of inexpensive hydroelectric power at subsidized rates. Until recently, China commanded more than half the bitcoin mining worldwide, most of the bitcoin exchanges, and almost all the mining machine production. China understood before any other nation the breadth of this industry. It also has an economic system that can move with speed and resolve when it deems necessary.

On December 5, 2013, China was the first major nation to prohibit banks from transacting in bitcoin over fears of money laundering, illicit transactions, capital flight, and tax evasion. At the same time, China warned residents about the risk of transacting in bitcoin. And, in 2021, China moved from bitcoin mining market leader to fully banning the cryptocurrency.

China is certainly not the only country to ban cryptocurrency. A number of Muslim nations have also done so, while many others have restricted the ability of their banks to deal in digital currencies or cryptocurrency exchanges. About a quarter of the world's nations have limited cryptocurrencies to some degree.

Nations' regulatory motivations differ. Many are concerned about the ability to engage in illicit activities protected by the relative anonymity of cryptocurrencies. Others are concerned about destabilization of or substitution for their domestic currency, with its attendant effects to be described in a later chapter. Still others are concerned about energy consumption from Proof of Work mining of coin such as bitcoin, while some regulators express concerns about the general lack of oversight and regulation in a freewheeling "Wild West" mentality that is sometimes associated with cryptocurrency mining and *Crypto Bros*, rightly or wrongly. But no other nation banned cryptocurrency mining with the same resolution as had China.

China is significant because it was the world leader in bitcoin mining and machine manufacturing when it imposed bitcoin bans. It also represented a good share of transactions, especially considering it is also the world's second largest economy. Their regulatory clampdown created significant bitcoin volatility, although a complete understanding of the way bitcoin works should lead one to conclude that there is not, and almost cannot, be any detrimental effects from the bitcoin supply side arising from such a change in regulatory regimes. Perhaps the greatest threat of cryptocurrency corrupt is an attempt to manipulate the blockchain. As we know from Satoshi's mining early on, a single miner can successfully maintain and extend the bitcoin blockchain, albeit with greater risk for a malicious 51% attack. Concentration of mining in one autocratic nation also increases such a risk.

Gyrations in bitcoin prices following China's moves were, at least theoretically, based solely on concern about reduced demand from participants in the world's second largest economy than from any sort of supply distortion. There was also concern that China would create its own Stablecoin, and hence potentially reduce demand for bitcoin. However, our previous discussion demonstrate that much of the demand for bitcoin is not for the type of legal transactions that might migrate to a Stablecoin. Indeed, the bitcoin algorithm authenticates transactions relatively slowly, with an average blockchain duration of ten minutes, followed by another ten minutes of encoding delay. Such latency is unsatisfactory for most day-to-day transactions but suffices for illegal or speculative transactions. In addition, bitcoin is limited to blocks that do not exceed one to two megabyte in size, which is a tiny fraction of the size and rate that the Visa network clears transactions, for instance.

Rather, China was concerned about money laundering and the energy intensity of Proof of Work mining, as we will discuss in greater detail in a later chapter. With the mining network consuming the equivalent of 41 medium-sized coal power plants, and with the world critical of China's reliance on coal, especially in light of the Paris Accord and the recent Glasgow summit on global warming, China could easily reduce demand for a couple dozen coal power plants in one fell swoop as they shed their share of the total global bitcoin hash rate that had dramatically risen by 2021.[1]

The September 2021 cryptocurrency ban in China also allowed their central bank to promulgate its own digital currency to both stem capital flight and to limit their national government's concern about money laundering and illicit activity transacted through cryptocurrency. China has historically limited capital flight by imposing a $50,000 cap on foreign currency purchased annually by Chinese nationals. Evading these capital flight limits has become a cottage industry for wealthy Chinese nationals who wish to purchase property in Vancouver, Canada, London, England, Sydney, Australia, or other similar English-speaking countries with strong ties to Hong Kong. Bitcoin made such wealth transfers much easier, and did not require the imaginative techniques typically employed, through creative invoicing of goods and services sold across their borders.

As noted, China initially banned transactions in bitcoin in 2013, and operation of cryptocurrency exchanges within its borders in 2017. China outright banned cryptocurrency ownership in 2021. These policies were designed to retain capital within China, and within the oversight of the People's Bank of China. Authorities were also concerned about a greater subscription by Chinese nationals in Tender, a Stablecoin tied to the U.S. dollar, for those interested in transacting rather than speculating in digital currencies. While one can understand China's concern about retention of domestic capital as it attempts to maintain the 6% to 8% gross domestic product growth, and concerns over recent deflations of some of China's asset bubbles, especially in real estate, China's monetary authorities will be hard pressed to stem that tide simply by banning bitcoin.

---

[1] https://www.coindesk.com/policy/2022/02/09/crypto-advocates-push-back-on-swedens-call-for-eu-mining-ban/, accessed February 9, 2022.

Global Regulatory Considerations

More recently, Sweden petitioned the European Union to ban cryptocurrency mining. Their concern is that too much public power is being diverted unnecessarily to Proof of Work mining, which either requires additional new capacity, or prevents countries from mothballing obsolete coal powered plants. Increased demand, for whatever reason, also increases electricity prices. This has been galling to some when miners are able to secure preferential electricity rates, especially from sustainable sources, which translates into even higher rates for everybody else.

The EU is the first major entity proposing action solely for energy consumption reasons, but others will follow, given the nature of *The Bitcoin Dilemma* presented earlier. It is important to distinguish, though, between cryptocurrency mining broadly, and mining as Proof of Work. Other authentication methods do not have the same energy intensity or carbon footprint, but can still provide even greater blockchain and digital currency advantages.

The United States is much less coordinated in its consideration of regulation. The U.S. government is unable to legislate so quickly as can China's more monolithic Communist Party. As of 2022, the U.S. Congress and Senate are conducting hearings through their various committees, from mandates such as securities regulation, monetary regulation, environmental stewardship, and banking regulation, among other perspectives. However, these hearing are conducted in relative isolation, the categories of oversight overlap very little, and Congress is unable to speedily promulgate sweeping legislation.

Recent hearings by these committees of the US House and Senate highlight the difficulty of successful regulation. Committees hear testimony from witnesses who are either glowing proponents of all things crypto, or those gravely concerned about crypto's various risks. Such a strategy should not be surprising that our elected officials, many of whom are lawyers by training, are most comfortable with a system that probes key questions by appealing to the testimony of advocates on one side or the other of an issue. This adversarial system is the underpinning of the system of common law in the United States.

However, in reality, both sides can cite compelling facts from each individual perspective that bolster their side but do not offer a broad economic picture. Blockchain is a fantastic technology that has the ability to streamline and memorialize transactions for which we already engage. In addition, our society is experiencing a cultural shift, with traditional institutions such as commercial banks, mortgages, savings, and lending, replaced by financial technologies (fintech) embodied in decentralized finances (DeFi), at least in the hopes of a younger tech-savvy generation that best relates to worlds that can be presented to them on a smart phone screen.

For these reasons, fintech and blockchain are inevitable technologies. It is unproductive to turn the discussion into one of either unbridled or unregulated fintech innovation versus maintenance of our status quo institutions for fear of risks from the unknown. Instead, we must take as a basic assumption that blockchain and digital currency technologies are here to stay, and shall continue to innovate, either above or below regulatory radar screens. From that perspective, it is less helpful to hear from crypto advocates wishing to preserve and accelerate the pace of their industry, and more helpful to hear potential solutions that can address obvious risks and uncover less obvious ones.

This book is based on the fundamental assumptions of both the tremendous potential of new financial technologies and an acknowledgment of the risks, to the environment, to unsophisticated consumers of financial products, to the integrity and reliability of markets, and to our ability to successfully regulate in such a complex environment. The United States has been relatively slow to absorb the complexities of what is admittedly very complex subject matter, and to move at least as quickly in its oversight and regulation as the cryptocurrency industry evolves.

One should not underestimate the cryptocurrency mining industry's motivation to innovate and expand. At the end of 2021, bitcoin mining was generating rewards of approximately $20 billion annually and manufacturing new equipment valued at upwards of $5 billion annually. Bitcoin itself represents a capitalized value that has exceeded a trillion dollars and new financial monoliths are earning a good share of commissions from that spectacular growth. With the banning of bitcoin by China, much of that activity is finding its way to the United States. The potential for profits is significant, and *Crypto Bros* are vying for their slice of these incredibly large pies regardless of the state of regulation.

While legislators are often slow to absorb the implications of *The Bitcoin Dilemma*, the dynamic nature of the industry will power ahead without delay, and shall not wait-and-see and risk losing opportunities to others. Rather, knowing the incredible level of financial motivations within the cryptocurrency industry, and the value and potential of blockchain in particular and fintech in general, there should instead be a strident call to get regulation right before regulation-too-late becomes irrelevant. The cryptocurrency industry is too significant to the economy for nations to fail to regulate effectively and in a balanced way. This could result in either an industry and innovation that is stifled, or an industry that harms itself and our economy because of overzealous and unrestrained growth without sufficient regard for its inherent risks if left unattended.

Anyone who has witnessed the quality of discussion between those who have staked their careers and future on the success of bitcoin, and those who still wonder how the movement of electrons across the Internet can possibly represent a store of value realize that the information gulf between potential regulators and those who may be regulated is wide. And yet, the crypto sector moves so quickly that regulators are challenged to stake sufficient time to become fully educated on all the various aspects of such novel technologies. It does not further the dialog that one side most associates with the status quo while the other embraces a culture of Web 3.0 that is determined to make the status quo irrelevant. Little of the discussion seems to acknowledge that we are ultimately all in this together, and we must be able to meet somewhere in the middle, if for no other reason but for the sake of successful development of these industries.

> **The Ups and Downs of Bitcoin Havens**
>
> Meanwhile, we should be aware that countries such as Portugal and, until recently, Kazakhstan, and U.S. states, such as Texas and Georgia, are determined to market themselves as havens for the development and advancement of such technologies, and have created levels of cryptocurrency and mining deregulation or lack of regulation consistent with their policy goals. More recently, representatives of nations such as Mexico have also proposed to make bitcoin a legal tender,[2] while they also propose to sponsor their own government-backed digital currency by 2024.[3] Other nations such as India have redoubled their efforts to ban or heavily tax bitcoin usage or mining, while they also indicate they are on track to develop their own government sponsored digital currency.[4] These national goals were consistent with the vision Satoshi articulated: "I would be surprised if 10 years from now we're not using electronic currency in some way, now that we know a way to do it that won't inevitably get dumbed down when the trusted third party gets cold feet."[5]

---

[2] https://cointelegraph.com/news/mexican-senator-to-propose-crypto-law-we-need-bitcoin-as-legal-tender, accessed April 19, 2022.

[3] https://cointelegraph.com/news/mexico-confirms-plans-to-roll-out-cbdcs-in-2024, accessed April 19, 2022.

[4] https://fortune.com/2022/02/02/india-crypto-ban-plans-develop-digital-currency-taxes-regulation-bitcoin/#:~:text=India%20has%20had%20a%20hot,the%20restriction%20in%20March%202020., accessed April 19, 2022.

[5] https://www.metzdowd.com/pipermail/cryptography/2009-January/015014.html, accessed April 19, 2022.

We may need to view this issue from a game-theoretic perspective that acknowledges our codependences in these far-reaching technologies and consciously strives to neither stifle innovation nor engage in races to the bottom.

Finally, international affairs affect prospects for international regulation. Economic sanctions recently imposed on Russia following its invasion of Ukraine resulted in an international effort to limit Russia's access to the network of major global banks. Instead, Russian traders and oligarchs increasingly shifted to bitcoin to move and launder large sums of money. Without collective global oversight, such transactions are difficult to detect and deter.

As an epilogue, Kazakhstan followed the path of many other states. The promise of bitcoin mining to bring great wealth to some and jobs for all was quickly shattered. By 2021, the country realized it had mortgaged its energy future on bitcoin, and just as rapidly as they were welcomed, bitcoin miners saw the red carpet rolled up. Surcharges on their energy consumption induced miners to box up their machines and move, mostly in the second wave of miners to the U.S., and in the wake of the mining exodus from China, to the U.S. that same year.

14

The Rise of Ethereum and Hobby Mining

The subject of this book is *The Bitcoin Dilemma*, a result derived in Chapter 8 that demonstrates mining energy consumption is proportional to and bound by the price of bitcoin and can even accelerate with miner efficiency with electricity cost improvements. Should bitcoin remain popular and demand continue to increase, so will long run electricity consumption. Indeed, as miners secure for themselves less expensive power contracts, the additional price burden is borne by other ratepayers. When the industry touts its allocation of additional sustainable energy to mining, it forces consumers and commercial users toward higher priced greenhouse gas-emitting power. Access to inexpensive renewable power merely compounds the problem as cheaper electricity induces more mining and hence greater energy consumption.

These dismal prophecies generally apply to Proof of Work mining. In this chapter, the scope of Proof of Work mining by other currencies is explored. We will see that, like bitcoin, each of these alternative Proof of Work digital coins consume significant amounts of electricity. Indeed, to optimize the efficiency of processing and profits among various potential coins, there exist software programs that automatically shift processing power to alternative Proof of Work mining opportunities. These shifts can occur quickly as market conditions warrant, and can be optimized multiple times per day.

© The Author(s), under exclusive license to Springer Nature
Switzerland AG 2022
C. L. Read, *The Bitcoin Dilemma*,
https://doi.org/10.1007/978-3-031-09138-4_14

The Last Vestiges of GPU Mining

The use of such software and the existence of networks such as Nicehash allow a streamlined path into Proof of Work mining for small scale and hobby miners without the expensive investment in purpose-built Application Specific Integrated Circuit (ASIC) miners. Originally, as with bitcoin, such mining could be conducted using basic Central Processor Unit (CPU) personal computers. As Proof of Work mining competition increased, successful and economically efficient hobby mining migrated to Graphics Processing Unit (GPU) cards. The software to run these graphics cards, and indeed the processing power of these cards, improved dramatically over the 2010s to the point that a good graphics card contained more transistors and often more and faster memory, and ran at faster processing speeds, than the host CPUs that remained the backbone of a personal computer.

Satoshi expressed concerns over the onslaught of GPU mining and the now-realized fear that it would induce an arms race in bitcoin mining. Satoshi noted in the summer of 2013, "We should have a gentleman's agreement to postpone the GPU arms race as long as we can for the good of the network. It's much easier to get new users up to speed if they don't have to worry about GPU drivers and compatibility. It's nice how anyone with just a CPU can compete fairly equally right now."[1]

But, like all arms races, individual self-interest often overcomes the greater good. Not only did this mining arms race accelerate *The Bitcoin Dilemma*, but it also diverted a technology once devoted to gamers into a profit machine for miners.

The rapid development of these GPU cards was initially inspired by the needs of gamers to process the vast amounts of information contained on each frame of a modern video game, and run at sometimes more than a hundred such frames each second. The calculations and translations, and the memory capacity and speed, were optimized at first for games, but soon clever developers modified the software that ran these cards to meet the needs of Proof of Work mining. Very quickly, this tail was wagging the dog, with the graphics card manufacturers Nvidia and AMD increasingly also optimizing their hardware and software for mining purposes as well as gaming. Eventually, the demand for these cards for mining pushed card prices beyond the reach and access of many gamers, to the point that most such cards were diverted to mining, with lesser cards that are not as easily adaptable to mining left for the gamers.

---

[1] https://bitcointalk.org/index.php?topic=284212.40, accessed April 19, 2022.

While I initially label this share of Proof of Work mining by the name hobby mining, GPU mining has been corporatized as well. For now, I describe how gaming cards are used to perform the mining functions of certain cryptocurrencies. Such a diversion of GPU cards to mining rather than gaming is not technically an externality because the price system moderates these competing demands. Gamers may nonetheless consider diversion of GPU cards to mining to be a nuisance.

These sophisticated gaming cards have grown to be so powerful that that they are now used as the primary processors in some of the world's fastest supercomputers. They are reasonably priced too, especially given their prodigious processing power, at $400 to $700, although demand for mining has pushed the market prices up by upwards of a factor of two or three, depending on the prevailing price of bitcoin and ether, the number two coin.

A personal computer typically has two to six slots for additional cards to run various functions. The graphics cards used for mining typically take up twice the space of a simpler card perhaps designed for a wireless connection or something more mundane. In addition, they generate more heat than other personal computer components, so, in reality, a state-of-the-art motherboard for the best personal computers cannot accommodate more than a couple, or upwards of three such graphics cards. Even so, the power consumed by such cards is comparatively high, at around 125 to 200 watts per board, and hence a personal computer built for such mining will also need a larger and more reliable power supply.

Otherwise, these personal computers appear just like your common PC, albeit usually in a slightly larger case to accommodate the size of the graphics cards and additional cooling needs. While specialized, they are not ASICs, and nor do they consume the same amount of power as a specialized bitcoin miner may. Their combined power consumption will be somewhere between 500 and 1,000 watts, compared to the 1,400 watts for an Antminer S9 bitcoin miner, or upwards of 3,250 watts for the largest and fastest bitcoin miners. These GPU-based miners are also quite a bit larger than an ASIC, and hence are rarely operated in a way that requires the power and heat dissipation of bitcoin mining.

As such, a small hobby GPU-based mining operation that includes a few such machines, usually assembled from individual components by the hobby miner, can be concentrated in one rather warm room without extraordinary power or cooling needs. They cannot efficiently mine bitcoin, but such a hobby mine can generate perhaps five to ten dollars a day mining other digital coins, with comparatively lower power costs, and could generate much more per day in the early days before more coins migrated to Proof of Stake and corporate mining began to take over. The cost of one such PC-based hobby mine is comparable or may even exceed the cost of an ASIC in 2017, and a collection of a few such hobby machines approach the cost of a modern ASIC, but without either the same revenue potential or power consumption.

Since mini mining farms also permit gaming and other computing uses, the dual-purpose aspect of these machines often justified the economics. The problem is that, like many hobbies, such mining often takes on a life of its own such that these personal computers are almost always mining rather than gaming so that the revenue they can potentially generate is not sacrificed.

Recall bitcoin started as a hobby mining coin itself in the early days before ASICs. Likewise, some traditional hobby mining coins such as ether also became sufficiently competitive to warrant the development of new ASICs to mine efficiently. As such, hobby mining is no longer particularly lucrative, but it remains an interesting and constructive hobby that provides some return that can pay for its investment and energy consumption over time and provide some heat to warm a small room.

These hobby miners consume a fraction of the energy, as a share of revenue, as does bitcoin mining. Indeed, the primary driving force for *The Bitcoin Dilemma* is that a good share of long-term revenue from bitcoin mining is devoted to electricity purchases, while hobby mining must direct more of their returns to relatively higher equipment capital costs. Unlike bitcoin mining using ASICs, with a payback period for the miners in the order of 100–200 days, and typically less than a year, a CPU-based miner may take many years to pay back its capital investment, while GPU-based mining will often take between one or two years, up from levels that were once comparable to bitcoin just a few years ago.

Corporate Mining in Altcoins

The corporate era in cryptocurrency mining arose from the simultaneous availability of fast ASIC mining machines for bitcoin and the realization that the combination of low energy prices and significant market share for large mining farms translated into eight and nine figure revenues and eight figure profits. The bitcoin industry led the way, with deep pockets and venture capital funds migrating toward the lowest energy costs they can find. As *The Bitcoin Dilemma* demonstrates, the difference between electricity at eight cents per kilowatt-hour and two cents per kilowatt-hour, once a hundred or couple of hundred days had paid for their machines, translated into three times the profits. Cheap electricity was and remains the paramount economic factor.

The economics of mining digital currencies other than bitcoin were marginally more challenging. Miners for these subsectors, especially in the mining of ether using the Ethereum protocol, were more expensive, not because of any sort of monopolization in the manufacturing of mining equipment, but in their limited supply. Recall that bitcoin mining machine manufacturing is best treated as a monopolistically competitive industry. Yet, the miner arms race often ensured that miner manufacturing was not exceedingly lucrative, given the constant need to improve miner designs to remain competitive. Bitmain remained profitable by vertically integrating its manufacturing of machines that supplied their own mines, and by pooling processing power of their mining farms and others on their own pooling network. They were also able to provide in-house design of ASICs and contract with Chinese chip fabricators to wring out every bit of possible cost efficiency.

This economic model worked well, but each of these sectors was quite competitive. The design of new machines was particularly difficult because Research and Development costs are high, as is the expense of securing chip manufacturing capacity. In an increasingly competitive miner manufacturing industry, gross profit margins had to cover these innovation costs. For Bitmain, once Chinese regional governments began removing subsidies it offered miners, profits were eroded to the point that Bitmain required a reorganization of their business model.

Such competitiveness in manufacturing of ASICS was partly a product of mining dynamics. If the price of an ASIC was too high in an attempt to extract more profits to manufacturers rather than miners, only the very most efficient mining operations with the lowest electricity costs would purchase them. Manufacturers recognized they could make more on volume than by artificially restricting supply.

While manufacturers could not extract significant profits in the ASIC market for bitcoin, the market dynamics in ether mining was even more peculiar. Gaming GPU manufacturing had traditionally been very competitive, with the two manufacturers AMD and Nvidia attempting to outperform each other in both processing power and price. The industry was not designed for the scale that mining would require, though. There was far more mining interest than gaming demand, and, with corporatization, this demand took off dramatically.

> **The Economics of Hobby Mining**
>
> At first, one GPU could earn tens of dollars per day and pay for itself in perhaps a hundred days. Given the ease of conversion from gaming to mining, the initial profitability, and the already strong customer base, profit incentives were once high. Mining of ether and other GPU-mined coins does not require significant CPU power, so rigs were designed that could run six to sixteen or more GPUs from a single motherboard and a CPU of only modest capability. Good cooling and multiple power supplies to provide about 150 watts per GPU was all that was necessary to scale up.
>
> The limiting factor with this dramatic scalability was the availability of GPUs. However, GPU manufacturers did not ramp up sufficiently, for two reasons. To expand sufficiently would be costly if mining went the direction of bitcoin toward ASICs. In addition, GPU design was a matter of constant innovation, primarily designed to the long-term gaming market, although both major manufacturers were willing to distribute software optimized for mining rather than gaming.
>
> Given these strategic decisions, a perennial supply shortage occurred. A GPU with a Manufacturer's Suggested Retail Price of $600 would subsequently be resold at twice the price. To ensure they did not frustrate their gaming base, manufacturers also attempted to impose conditions such as one GPU per customer policies, and voided warranties of GPUs modified or used for mining. These conditions merely exacerbated the shortages, especially once venture capitalist funded corporations attempted to procure thousands such GPUs at a time.

Mining is hard on GPUs, which were never designed for the level of concentration of heat per unit of volume, nor the continuous 24/7 operation. A GPU warranted for two years assuming an hour or two per day of gaming use will exceed that usage in only a few months of continuous running, especially when cooling and power supplies are not ideal. Manufacturers would face greater return rates at such a high utilization rate typical in mining. This was not a fork in the road that AMD and Nvidia found particularly appealing from a long-term marketing perspective.

The corporate GPU miners were most sophisticated. They could run banks of thousands of GPUs from central control stations that could be located anywhere in the world. To maximize GPU life, they improved cooling, with some miners designing liquid immersion cooling methods with a much-improved heat transfer rate than traditional fans and their airflow could provide. Special liquids used to distribute heat in high voltage power transformers but which were not electrically conductive allowed miners to strip their GPUs of fans and any moving parts and move heat away under immersion cooling to be dissipated through large radiators.

By employing these techniques, corporate miners could reduce the costs of running and cooling GPU miners, allow the miners to operate at a higher speed without generating more heat than they could dissipate, and at the same time improve reliability. These various economies of scale allowed corporate miners to enjoy a scale and cost advantage compared to hobby miners. Unlike bitcoin mining, hobby mining and the more efficient corporate mining could nonetheless survive side by side, with the corporate miners obtaining a better return by shifting on the fly to mining the most profitable coin at any given time.

The End of GPU and Hobby Mining

These GPU mines were not the noisy, dirty, and potentially hazardous operations that mined bitcoin. But, nor could they scale up enough for long enough to produce the same consistent level of profits as found in corporate bitcoin mining. Finally, since GPUs required a greater investment per unit of revenue, but were more energy efficient, at least at first, the economics differed. Once ASICs were developed for ether mining, and discussions began by 2018 to move the Ethereum protocol to 2.0, with Proof of Stake mining and larger, faster, and more interconnected and sophisticated blocks, further investment in corporate or hobby GPU mining began to decline. In a sector with such an expensive present and uncertain future, consistent growth never materialized to the same extent for the mining of typical Proof of Work coins.

With these uncertainties and the greater capital needs of GPU mining, most Proof of Work activity was directed toward bitcoin. Recall that more than 95% of all mining activity was either bitcoin or ether and, now that the Ethereum Protocol has converted to Proof of Stake, 94% of all Proof of Work mining will be in bitcoin. A co-founder of Ethereum, and one of the most influential advocates for responsible cryptocurrency development, Vitalik Buterin, recently wrote, "I don't believe in proof of work!"[2] Even some of the lesser coins, such as ZenCash and Litecoin converted to ASIC mining. With a sunset in ether mining under the Proof of Stake model, and such an installed base of GPU machines able to convert from one to another coin, the movement to Ethereum 2.0 protocol essentially leaves all these GPUs vying for market that has been decreasing with each passing year.

While the salvage value of GPUs is higher than the zero value of an obsolete ASIC, the huge demand and partially-met supply has created such an imbalance that GPUs once used for mining will likely have a salvage value of perhaps twenty-five cents on the dollar, compared to the premium prices

---

[2] https://twitter.com/vitalikbuterin/status/1077548790272405504?lang=en, accessed February 17, 2022.

at which these GPUs once sold. Over the GPU mining era, the venerable AMD 470s and 570s, and the NVidia GTX 1070s and 1080s are competent gaming machines but no longer state of the art, given research and development over the ensuing half dozen years. Manufacturers have also increasingly designed newer and more powerful GPUs so that they cannot be used for mining.

Cryptoslate.com currently reports 359 Proof of Work coins in circulation today.[3] Of these coins, there is very little mining activity in some, and others have readily available ASICs that make GPU mining uneconomical. Still other digital assets can be mined using GPUs. If the two most popular coins are now processed using ASICs, as are many of the top ten, GPU mining activity is quickly declining. The market capitalization of the two top Proof of Work coins sums to $1.25 trillion US, compared to a total Proof of Work sector capitalization of $1.31 trillion. In other words, the vast majority of Proof of Work mining is now done by ASICs, in the case of bitcoin, or increasingly by ASICs, in the case of ether.

The fundamental nature of *The Bitcoin Dilemma* is that bitcoin will likely always remain Proof of Work and continue to rely on the broad network Satoshi envisioned, albeit in a much grander and more corporatized manner. There is simply too much invested in the decentralized and democratic bitcoin network for the network to agree to move to any sort of alternative fork in the protocol. Ethereum is a superior protocol, is the next best prospect, and is actually a better blockchain coin in every dimension, including block latency, at fifteen seconds, and size and sophistication of what a block can perform. It is also controlled in such a way that facilitates soon-to-be-completed transition away from Proof of Work and into Proof of Stake. It shall require a shrinkingly small miner network to authenticate blocks. As Proof of Stake is fully integrated into the Ethereum 2.0 protocol, many investments in Ethereum ASICs will have little residual scrap value, while personal computers with graphics cards can still be used for gaming and scientific calculations.

As the Ethereum protocol abandons Proof of Work mining, the next largest coin in market capitalization, Dogecoin, has a much smaller market capitalization of about $21 billion, compared with bitcoin at $871 billion in early 2022.[4] GPU-based hobby mining and any Proof of Work mining but bitcoin are fast becoming an endangered species.

---

[3] https://cryptoslate.com/cryptos/Proof/of/work/, accessed February 9, 2022.

[4] https://cryptoslate.com/cryptos/Proof/of/work/, accessed February 9, 2022.

Build It New and Better

With the arrival on July 30, 2015 of the new ether coin, six years after bitcoin's slow rollout, its designers were able to include in its blockchain a number of features that bitcoin did not anticipate. In a recent interview, Ethereum co-founder Vitalik Buterin stated that he doesn't regret starting ether under the Proof of Work model, but noted that as the coin matures, evolution toward a more environmentally efficient and feature expanding version is natural.[5] As he laid out a timeline for the transition, Buterin noted that Proof of Work had its place as an authentication method, especially in the early days when one could not imagine the much larger, more frequent, and feature-rich protocols necessary to allow a digital coin to provide a great deal more in services to the public.

For instance, one can deploy decentralized applications through Ethereum, which enables a number of new applications related to Decentralized Finance (DeFi), to be covered in more detail later. This allows the platform to act as a superior vehicle for features such as Non-Fungible Tokens (NFT) that verify ownership of property, as a forum to exchange titles of items of value, tangible or digital, beyond merely a coin, and applications to provide services that would otherwise be provided through intermediaries, such as purchase and sale of stocks and bonds, including lending and borrowing provisions.

Indeed, Buterin suggested that bitcoin might have been better served to announce it would operate for the first five years as a Proof of Work, with a transition to eventual Proof of Stake stated in advance. The issue shall be that, given bitcoin could not fork in this way by receiving the consensus necessary in that protocol, will there be only bitcoin left eventually as Proof of Work? And, if so, will it continue to cultivate a clientele less interested in a feature-rich coin, and more interested in its ability to support anonymous transactions for speculative, illicit, and some traditional purposes?

The lesson is that the once promising GPU mining of coins counted in the hundreds will soon vanish, even though bitcoin may never die down. Most new coins never move beyond marketing hype, and those that do have learned the lesson that times have changed since bitcoin. The economic model works well for bitcoin, energy consumption and environmental issues aside, but does not work to the same degree for other coins. Proof of Work mining is not sufficiently adaptable or scalable and remains energy inefficient and expensive. Most new coins are designed without such a commitment to Proof of Work mining, and either start out as Proof of Work without any long-term guarantee, or adopt another authentication method such as Proof of Stake at the onset.

---

[5] https://cryptoslate.com/vitalik-buterin-doesnt-regret-starting-ethereum-as-a-pow-consensus/, accessed February 9, 2022.

Part IV

Born-Again *Crypto Bros* and the Gospel of Profits

Bitcoin can serve a greater good according to Satoshi's vision of finances and bank-like functions that can be brought to the unbanked through digital technologies. I contrast this value for all with the profit-seeking mantra of the new breed of *Crypto Bros*. Bitcoin mining has proven to be lucrative to those able to secure financing and access to inexpensive power or the backing to start new coins or exchanges. I leave until a later section the description of a fissure that is growing within the *Crypto Bros* family.

Bitcoin mining in particular has bred an evangelical following of those seeking their share of annual crypto revenues tallied in the tens of billions of dollars. These *Crypto Bros* have emerged to praise the glory of almost unbridled profits. The institutions they create or employ would have surprised and disappointed Satoshi, whose dream was to bypass large and deep pocketed institutions, not to create monolithic new financial powerhouses of a different stripe and fantastic wealth for a few, at the expense of all others. Satoshi was a true believer in an ideal that was designed to benefit everybody and toiled selflessly to bring the bitcoin concept to fruition. Left untapped is the immense wealth Satoshi's own mining created. Equally unspent is the human capital Satoshi fomented through bitcoin and its successors. Satoshi walked away from the movement early on, and certainly before one could comment on how an innovation for the common good could be metamorphized into a movement fueled by hunger for profits.

A cryptocurrency on behalf of the common good was the core value in its creation. In Dupont, editor (2017), Professor Golumbia discussed the role of bitcoin within the context of other stores of value. The author recognizes the fervent defense of bitcoin's place among other stores of value. He quoted Jon Matonis (2012) that:

> Just as the Second Amendment in the United State, as its core, remains the final right of a free people to prevent their ultimate political repression, a powerful instrument is needed to prevent a corresponding repression – State monetary supremacy.[1]

The analysis recognizes the importance of the "store of value" nature of currencies, and laments its volatility. Golumbia notes that economists have an interest in reducing risk arising from such volatility. However, most non-economists miss an important point. Economists view the money supply not as a right protected by free expression but as a tool to regulate the banking system to maintain solvency and as a mechanism to balance the economy on the knife edge between deflation and inflation. Monetary experts rarely advocate for the regulation of other stores of value, but have concern that effective monetary policy and the technically complicated theories behind it depend on a regulated currency that remains the primary unit of account in an economy.

Just how far have we departed from Satoshi's ideals? Satoshi's digital currency has moved from a medium of exchange with low transactions costs to an ideal vehicle for speculation, because of its volatility, that is also now very costly to exchange, if not to the transactors, certainly to the economy. The mystique of bitcoin clouds its comprehension and a well-informed policy discussion. For instance, Sharma (2021) reported in a CNBC story that about a third of 750 crypto investors knew very little about their investment. The reporter asked "What happens to these people when they lose big?" She quotes Peter Klein, a cognitive-behavioral psychotherapist, who observed an "increase in the severity of the crypto addiction symptoms that people are experiencing."

Sharma also interviewed Hashim Yasir, 19, who lost significantly in a bitcoin price decline, Yasir related that it had affected his mental health for some time. Even those who bet against bitcoin experience stress. She quotes Sandip Das, 27, who stated "I've also started developing pain at the back of my neck and shoulders due to high levels of stress… Crypto will wreck you emotionally and physically… You will get scarred for life."

---

[1] Matonis, Jon, "Bitcoin Prevents Monetary Tyranny", Forbes, 4 October 2012, http://www.forbes.com/sites/jonmatonis/2012/10/04/bitcoin-prevents-monetary-tyranny/, retrieved February 28, 2022.

Another interviewee claimed he is addicted to crypto and has lost £110,000. He adds, "Mentally, it's sickening, because I have not been able to even share this with my wife… I'm in a poor state financially and it isn't the state I want to be in. It's ruined my world and my mental health… I've reached a point of attempting to commit suicide."

These concerns are countered by celebrated *Crypto Bro* Adam Smith, who runs an advice forum called The Crypto Advisor. He suggests such recovering *Crypto Bros* "take a deep breath, have diamond hands, and HODL. The near future for bitcoin, and the crypto market as a whole, is likely to continue to be turbulent while a number of global and regulatory decisions remain unresolved." This mantra to *Hold on for Dear Life* is an industry credo to buy but never sell in a way that could cause the price of bitcoin to decline. *Crypto Bros* want to ensure nobody rains on their parade, no matter what.

This cryptoevangalism has been spawned by a coalition of digital coin pioneers. Venkataramakrishnan et al. (2021) are concerned that bitcoin is dominated by an unusual assemblage of hardcore libertarians, bank-hating left-wingers, and cypherpunks, a group of privacy-obsessed coders. They quote Stephen Diehl, a crypto-skeptic software engineer,

> Crypto is essentially an economic cult that taps into very base human instincts of fear, greed, and tribalism, combined with economic illiteracy as a means to recruit more greater fools to pile money into what looks like a weird, novel digital variant of a pyramid scheme…Although, it's all very strange because it's truly difficult to see where the self-aware scams, true believers and performance art begin and end. Crypto is a bizarre synthesis of all three.

"Neil," a pseudonym out of concern for his reputation, added "I think nerdy types like me got fooled because bitcoin made us feel cool, like a Revenge of the Nerds type thing, so we were incentivized to not ask ourselves hard questions. And then, the non-technical people got fooled because they didn't understand the technology,… So, it created a powerful pair of blinders."

Venkataramakrishnan et al. (2021) also note that such a virtual cult is unusual in that it has no physical presence. Its online nature distinguishes it from traditional cults that rely on physical proximity to reinforce adherence to the cult's vision. Nor do bitcoin speculators have a single charismatic leader. Diehl notes "(Bitcoin has a) doctrine passed down by a mysterious unknown founder, puzzle-solving, and internet meme culture and lots of predictions about politics/economics that are completely unfalsifiable… (Followers are) rooted in this ideology that claims to oppose a common enemy: corruption and untrustworthy intermediaries, and both see the internet as the way to finally eradicate those problems in some great apocalyptic event."[2]

Like some cults, the original cypherpunks shared among its membership a sincere concern for anonymity and fear of market manipulation by monolithic and wealthy financial institutions and government, as stated in *The Cypherpunk Manifesto*. Indeed, the messiah Satoshi was the most virtual and anonymous of them all. Korhonen and Rantala (2021) added to this theme when they identify the hacker ethics of "information wants to be free" and "mistrust authority," and strive to "remove any barriers between people and the use and understanding of any technology, no matter how large, complex, dangerous, labyrinthine, proprietary, or powerful." They assert that bitcoin grew out of anger over the financial crisis, with bitcoin "a crusade in the costume of a currency," but without a full understanding by cypherpunks of the potential for cryptocurrencies to become coopted by monolithic institutions that were the bane of bitcoin's founder and encouraged unbridled speculation. They conclude that such classification of motives is ultimately not helpful. Rather, the description of sustainability principles, perhaps sponsored by the United Nations, may be more productive.

Similarly, David Golumbia (2017) asserted that "Most cults affect a few hundreds or thousand people…This really is much more widespread and affects many more, which makes it much harder to find out how to resist it." Golumbia quotes Dogecoin founder Jackson Palmer, who stated upon his departure from the movement that "After years of studying it, I believe that cryptocurrency is an inherently rightwing, hyper-capitalistic technology built primarily to amplify the wealth of its proponents through a combination of tax avoidance, diminished regulatory oversight and artificially enforced scarcity… These days even the most modest critique of cryptocurrency will draw smears from the powerful figures in control of the industry and the ire of retail investors who they've sold the false promise of one day being a fellow billionaire…. Good-faith debate is near impossible."

Another critic, Jorge Stolfi, Professor of Computer Science at the State University of Campinas, lamented how he was targeted by *Crypto Bros* after he wrote a letter to the Securities and Exchange Commission in response to proposed rulemaking to regulate the burgeoning cryptocurrency market.

---

[2] Venkataramakrishnan, Siddharth and Robin Wigglesworth (2021), "Inside the Cult of Crypto," Financial Times, https://www.ft.com/content/9e787670-6aa7-4479-934f-f4a9fedf4829, accessed March 7, 2022.

A fake account purportedly authored by him signed up to sadomasochist forums and published false and embarrassing material. He noted, "I get all kinds of insults," he says. "Every time I criticise cryptocurrencies, they tell me you are defending fiat because you are an employee of the government, you want to continue the scam of national currencies which are Ponzi schemes, you work for an entity which extorts money from people with guns." Neil, the previously quoted former Coinbase exchange employee, noted "(for some potential critics) Their career depends on them being right, their financial stability may depend on them being right—because they hold their wealth in crypto—their friendships may depend on them being right," he says. "To admit they are wrong would be literally life-changing." The backlash for some who have been critical have included labels such as "CIA shill."

Observers note that there is an army of social media commentators that follow a virtual campaign to quash any dissent that might detract from the continuous climb of bitcoin and the speculative profits it shall generate for *Crypto Bros*. DeRose (2017) observed, "There's a large swath of internet neurotics that take it upon themselves to homogenise the herd by chastising the deviants in their midst." He adds "I think when the final retrospective on this space is written, we'll come to find a kind of 'History never repeats itself, but it does often rhyme' story, with a specific kind of rhyming here, to the story of the 'South Sea Bubble'."[3]

> **Thoughts of Nobel Prize Winners** A number of Nobel Prize laureates are perhaps even more critical. Puiu (2021) quotes Nobel Prize-winning economist Paul Krugman who, in 2018, wrote of cryptocurrencies "Their value depends entirely on self-fulfilling expectations — which means that total collapse is a real possibility. If speculators were to have a collective moment of doubt, suddenly fearing that bitcoins were worthless, well, bitcoins would become worthless." He added later in Twitter, "Its value rests on the perception that it's a technologically sophisticated way to protect yourself from the inevitable collapse of fiat money, which is coming one of these days, or maybe one of these centuries. Or, as I say, libertarian derp plus technobabble."
>
> Puiu notes the mantra of *Crypto Bros* to only share positive news and that all should be done to ensure the value of bitcoin is always upward. He refers to comments by Rachel Kranton and her interview with the Nobel-prize winning economist, George Akerlof. They invoke the concept of identity economics as an explanation of why people may behave in a way that defies rationality. Akerlof ponders whether the crypto enthusiasts will be able to

---

[3] DeRose, Chris (2017), "Investment Cues from the South Sea Bubble," Coindesk, https://www.coindesk.com/markets/2017/04/16/cryptocurrency-investment-cues-from-the-south-sea-bubble/, accessed March 9, 2022.

> HODL, and noted that there are "quite a few Lambos," references to the mantra "Hold On for Dear Life" and the term "When Lambo" that affirms the belief adherence to bitcoin will eventually place one in a life of luxury.
>
> Finally, Truby (2018) adds to the chorus of Nobel Prize laureates the concern of Joseph Stiglitz. He commented to Bloomberg that "Bitcoin is successful only because of its potential for circumvention, lack of oversight. … So it seems to me it ought to be outlawed. It doesn't serve any socially useful function."[4]

It is important to differentiate between cypherpunks and *Crypto Bros*. *The Cypherpunk Manifesto* stated a set of altruistic values designed to protect society from their perceived threats to our privacy and liberty. They celebrated information and communications, and took issues with their perceived greed of monolithic institutions—banks, central banks, government, and perhaps even international institutions. On the other hand, *Crypto Bros* wish to tamp down dissent and strive to preserve and promote profits for some individuals at the expense of all others who are not members of the brotherhood. This is a Gospel of Profit, not the Gospel of Satoshi.

Martin et al. (2022) provide a study in the psychology of *Crypto Bros* that points to fundamentally different motivations than their Cypherpunk brethren. The authors study the subset of investors who are primarily interested in cryptocurrency speculation. Among these individuals, the authors identify a strong association with the Dark Tetrad traits of Machiavellianism, higher levels of narcissism, sadism, and psychopathy. These speculators are motivated by a fear of missing out (FOMO), a strong sense of optimism in their abilities, and, consistent with many of their Cypherpunk predecessors, a suspicion of government.

Indeed, many *Crypto Bros* likely are unaware of *The Cypherpunk Manifesto*. Instead, they realize that preservation and expansion of profits to some require a continual new flow of new crypto bros to invest in crypto and increase its price, much like a pyramid scheme, but with an almost religious zeal. I next treat this struggle between ideology and reality to try to forge a common ground of understanding and hopefully a common vocabulary.

I also explore the fork in the bitcoin philosophy from one dedicated to the democratization and accessibility of transactions and financial markets

---

[4] See Caughill, Patrick (2017), "Nobel Prize-Winning Economist Says Bitcoin "Ought to be Outlawed"" "https://futurism.com/nobel-prize-winning-economist-says-bitcoin-ought-outlawed, Nov. 30, 2017, retrieved February 28, 2022.

for the common good to a new mantra based on profit and speculation, with little regard for the damage the sector might render to the economy or the environment.

15

A Hard Fork in the Bitcoin Philosophy

One's self-identity is a filter which affects the way we relate to others. We each view the world through our individual eyes, filtered by a combination of our experiences and desires. Given the myriad ways various people can judge differently the same circumstances, this ability to filter our environment based on our own world view creates self-coherence and offers a simpler path to navigate life. So long as our world view is not overly obtuse or threatening to others, people can then understand, or at least tolerate, the wide variety of perspectives contained in the human condition.

Cults take a distorted world view to the extreme and, perhaps for self-protection or for convenience, respond through a hardening of positions, and a contempt for the positions of others. The greater the gap between their own goals and the goals of others, the greater the separation.

Yet, we all must function within the same socio-economic system. Some paper over disharmony by focusing on telling others what others want to hear, or what they believe others should hear to best advance their own interests, rather than by telling the unvarnished truth. Truths become filtered, and hence the dialog becomes cynical.

This dichotomy of interests and the gulfs they create are not uncommon. Especially within the modern-day isolation induced by social media, in which we can now virtually cultivate community globally and instantaneously, we become increasingly self-assured of our own positions. Many now, in essence, live within virtual cults of like-minded people who feel oppressed by the other-minded that don't share their perceptions. Our virtual worlds are self-reinforcing, and present to us filters and mantras, perspectives and talking points, that advance our interests without regard, understanding, or concern of other hostile perspectives. This is the nature of cults, virtual, or not.

Such cultish thinking in which we, and those with whom we associate, tend to think very much alike. The resulting polarization widens the gulf between groups in society. We sometimes try to fill this gap by tossing out pearls of wisdom for which we might all agree, even if these pearls do nothing to narrow the chasm between us.

From these definitions, many modern advocates of cryptocurrency have become a cryptocult that substitutes the Gospel of Profit for the idealism of *The Cypherpunks Manifesto* and the Gospel of Satoshi.

Cryptocurrency is a term that perhaps inadvertently results in an insincere attempt to paper over genuine concerns. Of course, cryptographic techniques are highly innovative. We all wish to protect our privacy in conducting our personal affairs as *The Cypherpunk Manifesto* asserts. If cryptography can protect the anonymity of our digital transactions much like cash (but without the serial numbers) and can protect the privacy of our legal transactions, that sounds like a good thing. And, currency as a method to act as a store of value and a medium of exchange that solves our double coincidence of wants is also a good thing. Certainly, the economy thrives through the use of efficient currencies. Finally, if all this is done using fascinating new technologies, well, over what could we disagree?

In fact, cryptocurrency does not necessarily hide our transactions, at least in bitcoin and most other digital coins. Our transactions are no more private than the large institutions that safekeep our private keys on their servers. Nor do cryptocurrencies act like other traditional currencies as a reliable store of value, as the volatility of bitcoin demonstrates. Finally, while the blockchain is a fascinating technology, and the perfection and efficiency of mining machines are indeed high technology, mining itself is not high technology. Rather, miners are noisy black boxes that convert electricity into heat, new coins, and immense profit.

It is important to recognize the significant differences between the cults of cypherpunks with their legitimate concerns over privacy, authority, and institutions, and the *Crypto Bros* who rarely invoke the privacy ideology of the cypherpunks. These new cryptoevangelists pursue speculative or mining profits, and in the process, create a cultish divide whenever disparate groups assemble to discuss the future of cryptocurrency, in our city, country, or planet. On one side is a group advocating for cryptocurrency, with the hope and expectation of significant profits. Another side is concerned about privacy aspects of cryptocurrency beyond the intrinsic beauty and elegance of the blockchain.

A third side is concerned about the environmental consequences of bitcoin mining, while a fourth group laments the instability of financial markets and the suffering of naïve investors.

Crypto Bros rarely squarely address these concerns and instead retort that environmentalists are luddites opposed to progress. For instance, Martin et al. (2021) interviewed crypto mining advocate Max Boonen, who argues he is unconcerned about environmental degradation among his colleagues. He asserts, "Anyone in this market feels comfortable enough about the environmental costs. If you think it is a problem, you don't participate." He adds he donates to charity to effect his altruism, in a way that Milton Friedman justified in his classic 1970 essay.

These inconvenient truths prevent effective dialog. Groups are not speaking with each other, but rather are shouting over each other, and to their base. Satoshi's ideology of decentralized and affordable financial transactions for the collective good has instead been transformed into speculation and the creation of wealth of a few at the expense and frustration of the many. Their response is to entice as many new true believers as they can into their *Crypto Bros* ranks.

Our attempts to air these disagreements to try to construct a platform upon which we can all agree invariably fail. In public hearings, each side describes ts own perspectives. Faced with challenges to their perspectives, each side often speaks louder to emphasize their positions. Consensus positions are rarely forged.

For instance, we should by now all agree that the blockchain is a useful technology that may well affect how we transact and maybe even interact someday. Likewise, digital currencies will allow us to lower the transactions costs of transferring money between smartphones or across the world. We can already do those things, but with digital currencies we have the potential to perform such functions cheaper and faster, and concentrate these savings between us rather than within large institutions like the Visa network, ATMs, or banks too-big-to-fail, at least until new monolithic financial exchanges divert our gains to their profits. As digital currencies mature, we may eventually tease out another percentage point of gross domestic product. These are not the revolutionary advances we gain by discovering a cure for cancer or heart disease, solving world poverty, ensuring equal access to education, or investing in sustainable energy technology, despite the vast sums spent on and capitalized now to the tune of trillions of dollars in a crypto industry that was barely born a dozen years ago.

The huge capitalization in digital coins, two of which constitute 95% of all crypto value, and the creation of networks of mining machines that represent more computing power than all the world's supercomputers combined, have no ability to discover new drugs, predict the weather, or design the next generation of almost limitless power. This huge investment is as precarious as the next innovation that may replace it.

How, then, has a fascinating evolutionary technology, but with limited potential compared to some truly transformational technologies, come to captivate the imagination of so many and consternation of others and attain a market capitalization of almost three trillion dollars? It is because the proponents of cryptocurrency act like a cult that goes far beyond mere advocacy.

If we can for a moment accept that cryptocurrency is fascinating and worth pursuing, but is not transformational when compared with other investments and innovations our economy may make, such as a cure for cancer, and we can agree that technologies exist that allow all the advantages of cryptocurrency without huge electricity demands and environmental degradation, then what else is frustrating our cooperation in realizing these goals? It is the cult of profit that has replaced the altruistic manifesto of Cypherpunks.

We have already seen that Proof of Stake or other authentication methods can meet the needs of a superior cryptocurrency. Indeed, the new Ethereum 2.0 protocol will allow the number two currency to function far better than bitcoin in every dimension. Its blocks can contain up to eight times the amount of information, and these blocks will permit many more features than simple currency transfers, such as apps to approve loans, solicit savings, immortalize title transfers, and track smart contracts, at fifty times the rate of bitcoin block verification. It will do so without the need for a great number of mining machines that consume amounts of power comparable to that of entire developed nations.

If we have that discussion of the inefficiencies of bitcoin mining with *Crypto Bros*, many quickly pivot to critics' fear of technology and the American Way. *Crypto Bros* are preserving huge institutions designed to rebalance, and perhaps aspire to replace the power of investment and commercial banks and regulators and to concentrate wealth from existing institutions to a new set of institutions centered around bitcoin mining and speculation, and with the expectation of significant transaction fee generation What started as an anarchist and libertarian movement with the express goal to undermine monolithic banks and central banks is now trying to preserve new trillion-dollar institutions that are making many miners, speculators, and new financial monoliths wealthy.

15 A Hard Fork in the Bitcoin Philosophy

There is a gulf in testimony as well. Often, *Crypto Bros* prefer to avoid a discussion of the wealth this sector creates for them, but instead pivot to our shared desire to advance technology, and improve the efficiency of financial markets. By wrapping themselves in the free market principles, they avoid dealing with the energy problem, something we can easily solve together, but which results in little or no income left for Proof of Work mining.

Some now label these born-again bitcoin evangelists a cult of greed. Of course, we have learned to accept that to advance one's personal interests is part of the human condition. It only becomes a cult when, in an almost blindingly intense pursuit of profit, we lose sight of our ultimate goal and of the welfare of others. This concerned Satoshi, who wrote "I don't mean to sound like a socialist. I don't care if wealth is concentrated, but for now, we get more growth by giving that money to 100% of the people than giving it to 20%."[1] Satoshi felt that broad-based small scale bitcoin mining would democratize the digital currency and ensure it was less likely to be corrupted by the greed that caused cypherpunks to reject the large financial institutions too-big-to-fail.

> **From Satoshi's Own Words**
>
> We can compare the Gospel According to Satoshi to the degree to which motivations have devolved into a Gospel of Profit. Consider these quotes that Satoshi made, mostly on cryptocurrency forums, in a couple of short years between the birth of a white paper and Satoshi's metaphoric death among the crypto community.
>
> "The root problem with conventional currency is all the trust that's required to make it work. The central bank must be trusted not to debase the currency, but the history of fiat currencies is full of breaches of that trust."[2]
>
> "The Times 03/Jan/2009 Chancellor on brink of second bailout for banks."[3]
>
> "It might make sense just to get some in case it catches on. If enough people think the same way, that becomes a self-fulfilling prophecy."[4]
>
> "I've developed a new open-source P2P e-cash system called bitcoin. It's completely decentralized, with no central server or trusted parties, because everything is based on crypto proof instead of trust."[5]
>
> "It's very attractive to the libertarian viewpoint if we can explain it properly. I'm better with code than with words though."[6]

---

[1] https://www.bitcoin.com/satoshi-archive/emails/laszlo-hanec/1/, accessed April 19, 2022.
[2] https://news.bitcoin.com/the-satoshi-revolution-a-revolution-of-rising-expectations-, accessed April 19, 2022.

> "Banks must be trusted to hold our money and transfer it electronically, but they lend it out in waves of credit bubbles with barely a fraction in reserve. We have to trust them with our privacy, trust them not to let identity thieves drain our accounts. Their massive overhead costs make micropayments impossible."[7]
>
> "What is needed is an electronic payment system based on cryptographic proof instead of trust, allowing any two willing parties to transact directly with each other without the need for a trusted third party. Transactions that are computationally impractical to reverse would protect sellers from fraud, and routine escrow mechanisms could easily be implemented to protect buyers. In this paper, we propose a solution to the double-spending problem using a peer-to-peer distributed timestamp server to generate computational proof of the chronological order of transactions. The system is secure as long as honest nodes collectively control more CPU power than any cooperating group of attacker nodes."—Satoshi Nakamoto[8]

It is interesting that Satoshi never alluded to personal profit, and indeed left an immense wealth untouched. We have since seen the replacement of one set of monolithic financial institutions Satoshi abhorred with another that concentrates wealth even more, and shows little sensitivity to the environment. The debate among the born-again *Crypto Bros* is more aligned with Gordon Gekko's "Greed is Good" speech in the 1987 movie Wall Street, than even Milton Friedman's essay "A Friedman doctrine– The Social Responsibility of Business Is to Increase Its Profits."[9]

Friedman's famous essay is today misunderstood. On the surface its perhaps overly provocative title suggests that the pursuit of profits is a legitimate goal in its own right, indeed perhaps even an obligation, and should not be conflated with social irresponsibility. He actually clarifies in his essay that the profits capitalism can create permits the owners of a corporation, the shareholders, to have the tools and capacity to pursue their human obligation for social responsibility. However, he was not advocating for economic institutions that act as a negative sum game. The profits of miners should not come at the expense of our collective social responsibility, increasingly to mitigate the damage to the earth from climate change.

---

[3] https://www.investopedia.com/news/what-genesis-block-bitcoin-terms/, accessed April 29, 2022.
[4] https://satoshi.nakamotoinstitute.org/emails/cryptography/17/, accessed April 19, 2022.
[5] https://satoshi.nakamotoinstitute.org/posts/p2pfoundation/1/, accessed April 19, 2022.
[6] https://satoshi.nakamotoinstitute.org/emails/cryptography/12/, accessed April 19, 2022.
[7] https://satoshi.nakamotoinstitute.org/quotes/banks/, accessed April 19, 2022.
[8] https://www.irs.gov/pub/irs-utl/2018ntf-bitcoin-cryptocurrency-an-introduction-and-tax-consequences.pdf, accessed April 19, 2022.
[9] https://www.nytimes.com/1970/09/13/archives/a-friedman-doctrine-the-social-responsibility-of-business-is-to.html, accessed February 11, 2022.

15 A Hard Fork in the Bitcoin Philosophy

On the other hand, Gordon Gekko's speech in the movie "Wall Street" is a greater rationalization of greed as a great disruptor[10]:

> I am not a destroyer of companies. I am a liberator of them! The point is, ladies and gentleman, that greed -- for lack of a better word -- is good. Greed is right. Greed works. Greed clarifies, cuts through, and captures the essence of the evolutionary spirit. Greed, in all of its forms -- greed for life, for money, for love, knowledge -- has marked the upward surge of mankind.[11]

If one accepts this position, and likely most miners would, Gekko is referring to the initial disruption of traditional financial transaction mechanisms, not in the immense wealth and electricity it diverts to itself by commanding cheaper power sources for itself. Meanwhile, ratepayers face higher cost electricity, while existing owners of bitcoins suffer dilution of their wealth, while all of us suffer damage to the environment.

Economics is the study of discovering greater efficiencies. The analogy is the promotion of a larger economic pie. Satoshi did that, if we accept the realized and potential value the blockchain and digital currencies create. Now that the pie has been expanded, we don't want to see this expansion dissipated through increased electric power consumption from coal-fired power plants, nor increased power concentrated in new financial monoliths.

In other words, we've both realized Gekko's and Satoshi's prophecy of disruptive economic evolution. Now, we are decreasing the size of the economic pie by engaging in a needless arms race of mining machines that consume ever increasing amounts of power simply to make some miners very wealthy. Our pie is contracting as the mining industry fights over its pieces. This displaced economic energy diverts our efforts from something more productive. This is not what Adam Smith or Gordon Gekko, or Satoshi advocated.

However, to hang their hats on the Gospel of Profit rather than the Gospel of Satoshi, self-serving bitcoin advocates are cleverly distorting the dialog through obfuscation and tokenism. I later document the efforts by some, including the founder of Ripple, to bridge the growing gulf between cryptocurrency purists and those who merely see a profit opportunity.

---

[10] https://www.imdb.com/title/tt0094291/quotes/qt0393950, accessed April 29, 2022.
[11] https://www.americanrhetoric.com/MovieSpeeches/moviespeechwallstreet.html, accessed February 17, 2022.

16

The First Crypto Bros Millionaires

Bitcoin has become a lure that fosters a pyramid investment scheme in which something becomes more valuable only because more people are induced to purchase it, rather than for the intrinsic enjoyment or value it can create. Bitcoin speculation is both enticing and dangerous for unsophisticated investors. Some people are easily swayed by promises of easy money, especially if there is an element of hip to it, as witnessed by the flocking of inexperienced investors to the Robin Hood investment platform aimed at young people, or the attempts to manipulate the price of Game Stop, a popular electronic games software retailer that was on the verge of bankruptcy.

Some were induced to believe that their investment in these opportunities was cool, even though stories abound of large sums lost, at least to those who were manipulated. For instance, many such unsophisticated investors likely lost millions collectively in their valiant attempts to prop up the price of Game Stop. A few sophisticated investors pocketed the losses of myriad others.[1] Such profiteering concerned Satoshi, who stated very early on in bitcoin's development that "When someone tries to buy all the world's supply of a scarce asset, the more they buy the higher the price goes."[2]

The same get-rich-quick mentality is employed in shilling cryptocurrencies. Successful shilling convinces people who understand the digital world that they have an advantage in investment in such markets because traditional

---

[1] https://abcnews.go.com/Business/gamestop-timeline-closer-saga-upended-wall-street/story?id=75617315, accessed April 7, 2022.
[2] https://satoshi.nakamotoinstitute.org/quotes/economics/, accessed April 19, 2022.

© The Author(s), under exclusive license to Springer Nature Switzerland AG 2022
C. L. Read, *The Bitcoin Dilemma*,
https://doi.org/10.1007/978-3-031-09138-4_16

money just doesn't get it. Some people are given the sense they have insider information, and if they just invest everything they can, and hold on as long as they can, their superior knowledge and understanding will eventually make them rich. One random cryptocultist exclaimed:

> If you can't flaunt your wealth because it's criminally obtained, then what's the point? Literally, why become a billionaire if you have to have a middle-class house and eat at Applebee's and drive a Toyota? It's almost like crime doesn't pay, and even if it does, you can't spend it.[3]

Fortune Favors the Young?

The cryptocurrency hype industry has even produced its own vocabulary, with *Crypto Bros* bandying the term "*When Lambo*," which expresses the sentiment that it is not if cryptocurrency speculation will make the bold few rich enough to buy a Lamborghini, but merely a matter of when. A barrage of articles such as "This 25-year-old says he's a millionaire after investing early in ether and bitcoin"[4] constantly fuels this belief. Each article that shows, often by anecdote rather than proof, anyone with a few thousand dollars can translate their investment into millions, and a ticket to the good life, without any particular expertise except that they are young and hip, makes every hipster wonder if they too can be the next Lambo cryptomillionaire. But, when they were doubling down and borrowing as much as they could as bitcoin approached $70,000 late in 2021, only to then see it subsequently fall by 70%, tens of thousands, and maybe a lot more, *Crypto Bros* lost significantly. They may now be wondering "When Yugo" instead "When Lambo."

Hedge funds were hyped in similar ways in the 1990s. A bull market that lasts long enough will inevitably make many people wealthy, at least on paper and until investors collectively try to cash in and convert their cryptocurrency wealth to hard currency. The euphoria that arises when one's finances temporarily perform fantastically instills a certain sense of investor invulnerability. In a rising market it is difficult not to make money, consistently almost day in and day out. Paper millionaires abound and hedge funds compete with each other to demonstrate the largest triple digit returns. Everybody is a

---

[3] https://arstechnica.com/information-technology/2022/02/3-6-billion-bitcoin-seizure-shows-how-hard-it-is-to-launder-cryptocurrency/?comments=1, accessed February 12, 2022.
[4] https://www.cnbc.com/2021/05/21/how-crypto-investor-bought-btc-eth-early-used-defi.html, accessed February 12, 2022.

winner, and nobody who somehow loses in such an environment will be very public about their losses.

When the inevitable market adjustment occurs, billions in paper losses follow, and once high-flying hedge funds evaporate. The nouveau riche who were so generous with structured donations that earn them publicity when their paper wealth was at its peak quickly disappear, along with their contributions, during the market turndown. Within the hedge fund literature, researchers understand the survivor effect. If one were to measure the profitability of hedge funds by looking at the spectacular returns of existing funds, but do not dig deeper into the many bankruptcies of lesser hedge funds that have long since disappeared, such isolated successes give the impression of greater profitability than really exists. Certainly, if we saw an equal number of articles about how someone lost their shirt in cryptocurrency investing, we might have a truer and more realistic sense of the returns to speculation. However, while *Crypto Bros* demonstrate their conspicuous consumption as a display of their wealth at any opportunity, those who lose everything are reluctant to discuss their embarrassing losses. The market can also avoid judgment day so long as hype can keep the market growing.

Prominent *Crypto Bros* Liken Crypto to a Ponzi Scheme

Perhaps one of the most prominent of all crypto advocates is the founder of FTX, one of the world's largest crypto exchanges. When asked about yield farming, a practice that allows speculators to temporarily lend out funds they are not using to other speculators in need, and garner a small return, Sam Bankman-Fried made a larger statement on crypto institutions and platforms in general. He stated: "You start with a company that builds a box and maybe for now actually ignore what it does or pretend it does literally nothing... pour another $300 million in the box and you get a psych and then it goes to infinity...then everyone makes money." The surprised commentator Matt Levine exclaimed "(You just said) – I'm in the Ponzi business and it's pretty good."[5]

In the article reported in The Post, the journalist Greg Barker observed that, unlike most other investments, crypto is not a positive sum game, and is even at best a zero-sum game, as is gambling. Profit often occurs only if prices rise, under the "greater fool theory" that characterizes Ponzi schemes. Dogecoin founder Jackson Palmer has made remarks of concern for the industry. At the bitcoin 2022 Conference in Miami in April of 2022, well-known crypto investor Mike Novogratz also described bitcoin investment in terms usually reserved for pyramid schemes. He noted, "I come from a long line of storytellers, I was a macro investor my whole life, we try to see around corners, we try to understand the trends of the world, put big bets on them, and then tell stories, so my role has been telling stories–trying to pull people into the tent... and as

> more people get comfortable, the tent grows and fills–I look at the tent today, and it's double the size of last year... If we keep growing at this pace... watch out!"[6]

These various biases toward the illusion of success for hipsters in digital currency speculation have fueled an asset bubble in securities that defy oversight and regulation to protect the young and invincible. Recall that cryptocurrency is a fiat asset. There is no real commodity such as gold that is backing it, although I discuss in the next chapter Stablecoin that attempt to back such digital currencies. Maintenance of value of a cryptocurrency depends on steadily increasing demand, just as any pyramid scheme. Experienced investors know this and prefer to invest in instruments that have an underlying intrinsic value as a backstop.

It is sometimes argued that the financial markets in which sophisticated investors participate in, such as futures trading, do not require much regulation because sophisticated investors know what they are doing and are smart enough to not mortgage their future on bad bets today. These are the reasons why we must protect inexperienced investors by providing more complete information through various consumer protections. Such policy goals are not designed to concentrate profits within established institutions, but to ensure inexperienced investors do not suffer long-term consequences for financial decisions made early in life. Our economy is much better served when we instill the value in earning a living through valuable work rather than winning a living by betting one is a bit smarter than the next guy. The economy will come crashing down if we all spent the day gambling rather than producing.

Yet, one can't turn on the television nowadays without a shill trying to turn you on to the next crypto play. Numerous Superbowl commercials, actor Matt Damon comparing the boldness of investing in digital currencies to the courage of the Wright Brothers by claiming "Fortune Favors the Brave,"[7] and a basketball arena named for a cryptocurrency exchange makes one wonder if the investment world has more marketing dollars than sense. They are shilling an investment that produces no tangible good but the possibility of trimming a few basis points off transactions costs, at least up to the point that new crypto exchanges extract these efficiency gains for themselves. But, like

---

[5] https://unherd.com/thepost/is-crypto-just-one-big-ponzi-scheme/, accessed April 30, 2022.

[6] https://coingeek.com/bitcoin-2022-miami-mike-novogratz-likens-btc-holdings-to-pyramid-scheme/, accessed April 30, 2022.

[7] https://news.bitcoin.com/matt-damon-stars-global-crypto-ad-fortune-favours-the-brave-air-in-20-countries/, accessed March 7, 2022.

any pyramid scheme, those on the top maintain and expand their wealth by constantly recruiting more on the bottom. This model is vastly different from goods and services production that creates new items for which we can both invest and consume.

The Baby and the Bathwater

Digital currencies of some form will be of some benefit to society. Most of us won't transact with them until they are a steady store of value, like the dollar, so we won't have to worry whether we can pay the rent in a month when bitcoin drops by 70%. These gut-wrenching gyrations are what one would expect from penny mining stocks or the currencies of corrupt dictators.

Unfortunately, so much of crypto is cryptic. It touts itself as something that will revolutionize commerce, even if it is vague about how. Indeed, Stablecoin that pegs its value to the dollar may be helpful for those who don't have access to an ATM or a credit card. Perhaps someday it will help the great unbanked, but it won't revolutionize commerce.

Decentralized Finance (DeFi) may be transformational for some transactions. Bitcoin won't be that vehicle, for various technical reasons, but the second largest coin, ether, may well be. Built into the Ethereum 2.0 Protocol is the ability to operate smart contracts that are applications which may someday allow you to receive a car loan approval in 30 seconds, buy stocks or bonds, or confirm a paperless airplane ticket, among other opportunities that a decentralized financial system may provide. The market must mature, and regulators must learn to oversee crypto before smart contracts are ready for prime time, but in the not-too-distant future, access to near-banking may change significantly. With these innovations will come profits for the institutions that pioneer DeFi, but downstream savings to consumers will likely be modest, but for a greater measure of convenience.

We must also deal squarely with the environmental legacies suffered because of crypto, mostly from bitcoin. Fortunately, bitcoin is the exception rather than the rule in its carbon footprint. Unfortunately, bitcoin is also the biggest digital currency by far. The challenge is to foment a dialog in an immature industry. Satoshi, the mysterious creator of bitcoin until the disappearance a decade ago, had a vision to decentralize finance that could bring banking to the masses. But some *Crypto Bros* who ride on Satoshi's cape are often profiteers at best and charlatans at worst, motivated far more by greed than the desire to make the world a better place.

Consumer Protections for Unsophisticated Investors?

Good regulation is not designed to punish us or prevent us from doing what we want to do. It should protect us, often from ourselves, and perhaps give us a bit of rope, but not too much that we hang ourselves. Crypto has become fantastically lucrative and the industry can afford to throw tens and hundreds of millions of dollars on arenas, Superbowl ads, and Madison Avenue shillers, paid from bitcoin profits without a real product that proportionately benefits society, at least the non-speculating and legal part of it.

> **Buffett's Blunt Bitcoin Prognosis**
>
> Warren Buffett, the "Wizard of Omaha" and one of the world's most astute and successful investors, is most blunt[8]: "If you said... for a 1% interest in all the farmland in the United States, pay our group $25 billion, I'll write you a check this afternoon," "[For] $25 billion I now own 1% of the farmland. [If] you offer me 1% of all the apartment houses in the country and you want another $25 billion, I'll write you a check, it's very simple. Now if you told me you own all of the bitcoin in the world and you offered it to me for $25 I wouldn't take it because what would I do with it? I'd have to sell it back to you one way or another. It isn't going to do anything. The apartments are going to produce rent and the farms are going to produce food." At a speech at his recent annual meeting of Berkshire Hathaway, he added, "In my life, I try and avoid things that are stupid and evil and make me look bad in comparison to somebody else – and bitcoin does all three," Charlie Munger, Berkshire Hathaway's Chief Executive Officer, also chimed in, "In the first place, it's stupid because it's still likely to go to zero. It's evil because it undermines the Federal Reserve System... and third, it makes us look foolish compared to the Communist leader in China. He was smart enough to ban bitcoin in China."

Regulation regularly lags behind even slow-moving social phenomena and way behind something moving as quickly and as opaquely as crypto. Lagging regulation combined with the ability to grease the skids a bit to be sure the regulation doesn't go in a direction that stops the party and cause the industry to suffer makes for a dangerous investment environment.

Bitcoin generates fortunes for *Crypto Bros* in a few ways. First, miners maintain the blockchain and, in return earn rewards upwards of $2.4 million in new bitcoin every hour. Second, speculators earn profits by guessing how volatility in demand, given inelastic supply, will translate into changes in the price of bitcoin. Sometimes, bitcoin miners are speculators too, but they

---

[8] https://www.cnbc.com/2022/04/30/warren-buffett-gives-his-most-expansive-explanation-for-why-he-doesnt-believe-in-bitcoin.html, accessed May 1, 2022.

also have electricity and machines to buy so they can expand their crypto holding. Third, exchanges charge commissions when they enable both groups to convert their cash into bitcoin and back again.

But, miners with wads of cash in their pockets and bitcoin on their smartphones are no longer the biggest income earners in the industry. Now it is owners of exchanges who wear pinstripe suits and have Manhattan offices. Like brokers, crypto exchanges earn a perhaps the steadiest and sizeable profits by charging their clients commissions on digital currency exchanges, and can lend out unused client funds just as a bank may lend out my deposits to earn an interest rate margins on their loans. Unlike banks, cryptocurrency exchanges could do so without the same level of oversight regulators impose on depository institutions.

> **Is Bitcoin Gold?**
> Exchanges cater to speculators hoping simply to profit from the volatility of bitcoin by buying low and selling high, or shorting, which is borrowing bitcoin that they then sell with the expectation the price will soon drop, and then later repurchasing the coin to replace the amount they borrowed. Now, just as with stocks, one can buy and sell options to make subsequent purchases or sales of bitcoin to speculate at low cost. These options can subsequently be traded, and rarely the option to buy or sell is even exercised. Such speculation represents bets on bitcoin. Intense speculation translates into fluctuations in the price of bitcoin, and has produced three periods of intense price run-ups, followed by gut retching pullbacks. This investment is perhaps likened to the buying and selling of gold or day trading of stock, but on steroids.
>
> The comparison of bitcoin to gold is imperfect, though. It is true that both are scarce in supply. High gold prices result in a faster pace of exploration and supply increases, while bitcoin supply is expanded by a formula that is baked into its design, with expansion actually occurring at a decreasing rate until the coin is frozen in supply in 2140. Gold is also transacted for uses other than speculation. Gold's intrinsic demand comes from industrial and commercial uses, while bitcoin's intrinsic demand comes from the need for a growing share of its owners to speculate and fuel greater demand. Also, unlike gold, bitcoin competes with hundreds of other digital currencies in practice, and thousands of others in theory, with someone shilling a new coin almost daily.

Movements in bitcoin are driven to a much greater degree on market news or intentional hyping. In fact, the speculative activity in bitcoin was found by Foley et al. (2019) to be closely correlated with the degree of market hype, as measured by news stories and social media messages. There even exist hype indices that bitcoin speculators follow to allow them to better time their speculative investment. To further fuel such speculation, large investors are able to leverage their positions by borrowing upwards a hundred dollars from others for each dollar of their own. Such leverage ratios of 100:1 exceeds the 30:1 or 40:1 leverage of speculation with mostly borrowed money in major hedge funds.

Speculation especially fuels price run-ups when investment success is almost a sure thing, but results in equally spectacular selloffs once such asset bubbles pop and speculators are forced to sell quickly to ensure they retain enough capital to pay the loans that fueled their crypto purchases. Bitcoin speculators use the techniques of hedge fund managers and day traders.

Much more so than other securities, cryptocurrency trades on news, sometimes real but also often manufactured. Fortunes are lost when naysayers cast question marks or skepticism. Dogecoin plunged 34% within minutes after Elon Musk made an off-the-cuff joke about the coin. Typically, transgressors that frustrate *Crypto Bros'* mantra of only positive raves are swiftly met with rebuttals, trolling, and runs through the wringer on Reddit. The ensuing discussion is not meant to be civil. Rather, it is designed to deter anybody from taking away the punch bowl or pricking their asset bubble.

The world is awakening to grave problems with global warming and the ways Proof of Work mining contributes to them. This growing consternation has even occurred without the benefit of a full understanding of *The Bitcoin Dilemma* presented above that shows only the price of bitcoin can limit the almost unbounded demand for electricity that Proof of Work mining requires. Bad news that could possibly induce investors to instead explore Proof of Stake cryptocurrency instruments can potentially destroy hundreds of billions of dollars in speculative bitcoin holdings as investors move toward other coin without the global warming dilemma. The stakes are extremely high.

The reason that even the catastrophic prediction of an energy dilemma is insufficient to permanently destroy bitcoin value is that electricity costs are supply side. Yes, a decrease in the price of bitcoin by 1% will reduce mining activity and energy consumption by almost the same amount in the long run. As the market adjusts to the bitcoin energy dilemma, the vehicle still services its primary roles of speculation, illicit, and legal transactions. Speculators do not need to dwell on the underlying economics of the currency. Speculation only needs a coin that offers sufficient volatility to fluctuate regularly in price so that buy and sell opportunities are continuously created.

Conspicuous Consumption Fueled by Bitcoin Profits

Crypto Bros use their bitcoin wealth to also shuttle spending into other digital currencies or assets such as Non-Fungible Tokens. The ups and downs of bitcoin induces sideways movements into and out of substitute assets, so long as the overall interest in bitcoin can be continually hyped and shilled. Now that bitcoin has gone corporate, tens of millions of dollars are spent on major advertising buys, sponsorship of sports arenas, and even investment in major media companies, all with the express hope of maintaining and expanding the interest and subscription in cryptocurrencies in general, but especially bitcoin, while the industry also hopes to dissuade regulators from closer scrutiny.

The exchanges themselves invest in media hype campaigns as they stand to gain the most with every trade, whether markets rise or fall. They sponsor the primary crypto media outlets. Well-placed articles, a plethora of books written to celebrate the glories of crypto, but with little discussion of the challenges, and media campaigns are meant to fill the newsfeeds with positive stories and promises of strong returns to the point that they drown out criticism. Increasingly, pressure on legislators, using campaign contributions as leverage, is designed to prevent regulations that could have any ability to dampen speculation. The *Crypto Bros* believe no regulator is a good regulator, at least in their arenas.

The problem of shilling and media placements, false or not, to artificially influence security prices is certainly not new with bitcoin. When this occurs in traditional financial securities, the Securities and Exchange Commission (SEC) investigates such market manipulation. However, hyping and digital bulletin board rumor-mongering in bitcoin and other cryptocurrencies often occur through underground message boards, with the occasional tweet for good measure. Yet, to now, the SEC does not oversee crypto securities. Speculative sector remains the Wild West, with little law governing their actions, just as we saw in the hyping of U.S securities markets in the Roaring Twenties.

> **When Is Shilling Illegal?**
>
> A lot of money has been made and lost in cryptocurrency investing. At times, markets such as commodity or options exchanges on the Chicago Board of Trade are left more lightly regulated by the Commodity Futures Trading Commission than other retail markets such as the trading of public companies on major exchanges. For these more retail and broadly subscribed marketing of securities, the Securities and Exchange Commission plays a significant role in oversight.
>
> Such oversight is designed to ensure consumers are fully informed with regard to their prospects for investment. Such provisions as full disclosures or the listing of trades by directors of boards are designed to prevent insider trading or the use of pump-and-dump to artificially generated interest in a security to drive up its price so insiders behind the shilling can profit from and then abandon a security at its peak.
>
> There is little protection in the crypto world for hyping of securities and similar price manipulation. Perhaps the most notorious examples are marketing of Initial Coin Offerings (described in the next chapter), and the hyping of Non-Fungible Tokens. These tokens of title to digital content are particularly prone to pump-and-dump because there is no tangible physical product transacted and hence no tangible pricing. Hence, it is equally difficult to question claims of value, despite how exaggerated or dubious.

The *When Lambo* crowd no longer derive all their wealth primarily from mining, although those who are able to secure large allocations of cheap power at the expense of residents and businesses have become quite wealthy. Now, most wealth is created through speculation, and so are most losses, with the *Crypto Bros* who own exchanges profiting either way.

Unlike speculation in gold and commodities designed to steer new supply to the best use of these commodities and signal future demand to guide current supply decisions, speculation in bitcoin does not create a better mousetrap. Sometimes venture capitalists hit upon a new innovation, and may profit spectacularly, to compensate for the other half dozen they invest in that fail. But, without their investment, previously underfunded or identified technologies may never see the light of day. There is no such supply response to bitcoin speculation, though, as the supply of bitcoin is predetermined. *The Bitcoin Dilemma* demonstrates that all speculation accomplishes is a driving up of the bitcoin price to profit a few, and the consumption of more energy and production of greenhouse gasses. Their greater electricity consumption results in higher energy costs for the rest of us.

More correctly, speculation in something of fixed supply is worse than the zero-sum game of gambling as the world must devote more energy to its mining. And, in this gambling, for every *When Lambo* winner, there is some much quieter individual who may have lost their savings, or worse. These *Crypto Bros* are not the "Fortune Favors the Brave" of crypto commercial fame.

17

The Coin du Jour: The Rise of Initial Coin Offerings

Myriad *Crypto Bros* have concluded the path to affluence can come from the design of a new coin. Some have done so for notoriety, and still others even on a lark. A few innovators, such as Satoshi, appear motivated only to satisfy a sincere ideology to bring banking to the masses without the need to rely on institutions too-big-to-fail.

The early bitcoin purists certainly advocated for bitcoin, but also believed that the coin itself was not the best vehicle for day-to-day transactions, as even Satoshi collaborator Hal Finney noted. Actually, there is a very good reason for bitcoin-backed banks to issue their own digital cash currency, redeemable for bitcoins. Bitcoin itself cannot scale to have every single financial transaction in the world be broadcast to everyone and included in the block chain. There needs to be a secondary level of payment systems that are more efficient and with a minimal carbon footprint. Likewise, the time needed for bitcoin transactions to finalize will be impractical for medium to large value purchases.[1] There is room for new coins backed by bitcoin, just as dollars were once backed by infrequently traded gold.

An initial coin offering (ICO) is a new digital token that is created and initially funded, often in exchange for bitcoin or ether. As with any fiat currency, its success depends primarily on the confidence and attractiveness it can instill in potential users or speculators. Should a new digital coin fail to capture the imagination of the public and garner its confidence, it fails in

---

[1] https://bitcointalk.org/index.php?topic=2500.msg34211#msg34211, accessed March 27, 2022.

the same way some Initial Public Offerings (IPOs) fail. Somewhat rarely, its backer(s) manage to capture our confidence and raise the funds to create a new token of exchange.

These creators of new digital currency can even spawn new crypto exchanges, and perhaps make their new tokens a central aspect of new decentralized instruments, as we see with the COMP currency on its DeFi platform, described later. As with other more established digital currencies, new currencies fall between the regulatory cracks as agencies disagree on their nature as a security or a commodity. Given the vagueness of regulatory oversight and the competition for serious and capricious coins alike, most new coins fail within months, and others become vehicles for fraud. But, in the first half of 2018 alone, $7 billion was raised to create new ICOs.

Bitcoin was a peculiar ICO. It grew organically by creating a cohort of enthusiastic miners and transactors around a coherent and altruistic vision. Ethereum is perhaps the first digital coin that successfully raised sufficient capital to establish itself. Ether followed the earlier model of another venture capital coin called Mastercoin that went public in established in 2013, but without the interest ether garnered. The first ether tokens were sold in 2014 to successfully raise 31,000 bitcoin, worth $18.3 million at the time, and establish Vitalik Buterin as one of the first visible and successful digital token entrepreneurs. He earned that distinction in the wake of bitcoin's organic growth as a developer of a decentralized and democratic coin, not one designed to raise capital and establish an institution.

Three years after ether was established, at a time when bitcoin corporatization had overtaken the industry, new ICOs began to flourish. An ICO named Brave raised $35 million in thirty seconds. Later in 2017, $2.3 billion in ICO subscriptions occurred within the year and had already eclipsed ICO creation and subscription from the previous year by a factor of ten. By the end of the year, the previous year's total was exceeded by a factor of forty. More than two ICOs were being created every business day. By early 2018, an ICO named Filecoin raised more than a quarter billion dollars within days of its inception.

An E-Coin on a Lark

Dogecoin is an interesting example of one such ICO. Initiated by software engineers Billy Markus and Jackson Palmer, the coin was meant to make fun of the proliferation of new cryptocurrencies. Dog-E-coin was released in late 2013, and, by 2021 reached a market capitalization of $85 billion, with the help and support of high-tech entrepreneur Elon Musk, who also has an appetite for irony and slightly off-center humor. It was meant as a parody of bitcoin and other ICOs with even more grandiose and less ideological intentions.

Dogecoin, too, had growing pains through a hack of its associated exchange, Dogewallet. By accessing its filesystem and modifying its send/receive register to send all available coin to an external address, the hacker stole millions of coin on Christmas Day of 2013. The Dogecoin community crowdsourced sufficient resources to cover the loss for a coin that was only worth a fraction of a penny at that time.

After Musk's positive comments and interest, Dogecoin rose to $0.711, but when Musk joked about the coin during a Saturday Night Live monologue, he caused the coin to retreat by 34% in minutes. However, its large user base and its utility to work with the Ethereum protocol for more elaborate smart contracts than can be employed in bitcoin allowed it to retain its following. In addition, while its supply began with 100 billion coin, and was permitted to expand by five billion coin annually, co-founder Jackson Palmer stated that supply would be managed in future to prevent coin depreciation due to inflation resulting from excessive currency growth.

Dogecoin remains volatile, partly because of its capricious nature and the *Crypto Bros* attracted to a whimsical coin. Nonetheless, it has grown to the 10th largest coin, even if only a tenth the size of bitcoin. It is also quite a bit more energy efficient compared to bitcoin, although it does remain Proof of Work for now.

Typically, digital tokens perform some sort of a function. For instance, COMP is used as a medium of exchange for the various financial services offered on its decentralized finance platform. Others may represent a digital token to securitize a share of the value of an exchange, much like a traditional stock in a company. Still others might represent a share of value of some sort of a physical asset.

The fluidity of ICOs arise because there remains a debate among agencies whether such digital tokens are an instrument that derives its value from another security, such as derivatives regulated relatively loosely by the Commodity Futures Trading Commission, or whether they are securities themselves that perhaps represent a share of an exchange built around them, and hence appropriately regulated by the Securities and Exchange Commission.

Ultimately, regulators are motivated by the need to protect us from ourselves. The lack of oversight and a well-established regulatory framework, and the feature of ICOs that they are typically funded through a cryptocurrency such as bitcoin and ether, make ICOs an ideal vehicle for fraud and the eluding of oversight.[2]

---

[2] I treat elsewhere the "pump and dump" technique that shills a new digital coin innovation to raise capital and investment, only to have its creator dump a large share of the tokens at the inflated price just before the coin collapses.

Unfortunately, Gresham's Law observes that bad money, even of the digital variety, ultimately forces out the good. Indeed, major failures and frauds of prominent coins often have a depressing effect, at least temporarily, even in well-established digital coins such as bitcoin, ether, and Zencash. These and other concerns have caused some nations, most notably China in 2013, to ban all cryptocurrencies. Meanwhile, social media providers, most notably Facebook, banned the marketing of such ICOs on their platforms. Still others have expressed concerns that the frenzy around new offerings of coins may aggravate a crypto bubble that risks bringing down more established digital currencies with its sudden deflation.

Such concerns have been a strong motivating factor for regulators to take a closer look at digital currencies in general, and especially new offerings in particular. The virtual nature of cryptocurrencies, and their links to other digital currencies, in funding or in backing, defies easy regulation as would be possible with Initial Public Offerings (IPOs) of stock. In addition, the varied forms of ICOs further challenges oversight. Some ICOs are tokens that derive their value from the ability to exchange them for some sort of good or service at some point in future, not unlike a traditional stock option. Others derive their value from an actual physical commodity of value, and hence may be less speculative. Certainly, the latter is then closer to a traditional security, and as such might be regulated by the SEC, while the former is more akin to an option as regulated by the CFTC. This lack of a clear regulatory oversight mandate further complicates the potential for regulatory deadlock as agencies debate the underlying nature of the ICO.

One method to protect unwitting consumers from predatory ICOs is to have such new offerings underwritten in the same sort of way that IPOs are often underwritten by an investment banker. Such sponsorship ensures that a new financial entity is, in essence, supported by an established financial firm that ensures an ICO prospectus or its various disclosures are accurate and timely. The sponsors in effect stake their own financial backing as a guarantee or insurance policy to ensure the ICO represents value and is issued with the appropriate level of due diligence and oversight.

Regardless, initial coin offerings are an industry in themselves that begs for coherent regulation and consumer protection, if not for their own good, then for the preservation of value of other digital currencies. However, given the nature of digital currency trading over the Internet, and usually in exchange for another digital currency, regulation cannot be done piecemeal or by one nation. As with *The Bitcoin Dilemma*, global solutions must be sought for such coins that easily defy borders and challenge the ability for national regulatory bodies to perform the necessary degree of oversight to protect the entire digital currency industry and its clients.

The digital coin concept that offers the most promise holds true to Satoshi's goal of an e-coin that can facilitate our most common transactional and banking needs. The network infrastructure certainly exists, but would need modification to realize Satoshi's dream.

Can Bitcoin Be Tweaked?

The network assembled to authenticate and immortalize bitcoin is extensive indeed. The large-scale arrival of application specific integrated circuit miners in 2016 resulted in processing power just a few years later that represents the equivalent of approximately 10 million Antminer S9 machines. Each of these miners have but one purpose in life—to authenticate blocks using the SHA-256 algorithm.

> **The Bitcoin Mining Network as a Supercomputer**
>
> While CPUs in home computers perform very different functions than simply running a hash algorithm, a 2017 era home computer running a decent processor could perform perhaps 1 gigahash per second, and be capable of about 3 teraflops of single precision computations per second.[3] A single Antminer S9 machine can process hashes about 14,000 times faster, which would be equivalent to about 40 petaflops of single precision processing power. The entire bitcoin network would then represent 400,000 exaflops, which is about 100 times the combined computing power for the world's 500 most powerful supercomputers.[4] In other words, at least in the running of hash algorithms, the bitcoin network has immense processing power.[5]

The incredible ingenuity in the design of the blockchain and cryptocurrencies, the creativity of engineers in the design of faster ASICs and GPUs, and the extraordinary entrepreneurship of those who brought ideas to market are modern marvels. Imagine if this extensive network could be devoted to

---

[3] A flop is a Floating-Point Operation, a benchmark to compare CPUs and GPUs.
[4] https://en.wikipedia.org/wiki/TOP500, accessed February 13, 2022.
[5] Note, though, that such measures for supercomputers are typically based on double-precision calculations, and these supercomputers can perform many functions, not simply process hash functions.

realize Satoshi's dream of a fast and inexpensive transition to a robust and Stablecoin.

We can enjoy all these innovations, and many more to follow, without the need of Proof of Work. Indeed, if we could free up all the energy devoted to grabbing a larger piece of the economic pie, albeit with significant environmental degradation at the same time, imagine what we could do with that energy to actually expand the economic pie and improve the environment.

Unfortunately, bitcoin in its present form will prevail, though. Satoshi produced a network that has a self-preservation mind of its own, a modern version of the self-perpetuating device described in science fiction. By 2040 or 2044, after five or six additional block reward halvings, the reward for bitcoin miners will fall lower than the transaction fees offered miners. If transaction costs then rise as the price of bitcoin rises as well, the dollar amount of fees may approach current mining rewards, indefinitely into the future. As Satoshi hoped, bitcoin may well remain self-perpetuating as transaction fees replace mining rewards. At that point, continued and profitable mining will remain for the foreseeable future, if we can tolerate the greenhouse gasses that are inevitably produced when we consume power needlessly.

I say needlessly because the world's second most subscribed cryptocurrency, can do everything bitcoin can do but with three hundred and twenty times the capacity and a tiny fraction of its carbon footprint. It increasingly does so by using the alternative Proof of Stake that does not require copious amounts of power in an arms race to make network hijacking too expensive, Ethereum 2.0 promises even faster speed, greater security, and far more utility.

Non-Fungible Tokens: The New Plaything of Crypto Millionaires

Another recent innovation is in the development of Non-Fungible Tokens (NFTs). In effect, any blockchain transaction acts as a token. It establishes rights to ownership of a currency, but, as noted elsewhere, it can also document any sort of deed of ownership for any other property, real or virtual. The Ethereum protocol is especially adept at recording such ownership and transfers.

NFTs have been the darling of the crypto billionaires. It allows one to be the registered and immutable owner of the deed to a painting, a piece of digital art, even an essay or any other intellectual property one could create. Such a digital token does not give one physical possession and cannot prevent others from enjoying, viewing, or even replicating the property it represents.

An NFT is really more akin to a signed copy of a reproducible intellectual property, without any physical possession or ability to restrict subsequent reproduction.

The most expensive NFT to date is *Pak's "The Merge"* that sold on December 2, 2021 to a consortium of almost 30,000 owners for a combined bid of $91.8 million U.S. You can view the artwork for free at https://www.dexerto.com/tech/top-10-most-expensive-nfts-ever-sold-1670505/ or elsewhere for free as you wish. The token might be scarce, but the artwork is not. Amanda Marcotte of Salon Magazine, in her article "NFTs aren't art – they're just the Cult of Crypto's latest scam,"[6] interviews NFT critic Dan Olson, who narrates a damning nature of the NFT industry, and much of the self-perpetuating Ponzi-like value built into crypto in general. When asked why he is so critical of these twin industries, he notes:

> Because they're an ecosystem that exists entirely in the language of stories. That's the main thing that's being sold here. Crypto isn't functional. It doesn't do what the builders claimed it was being built to do. It has succeeded at very few of its public-facing goal. But it still transacts based on those stories, based on what it could become, based on what it intends to do, based on what it, in theory, might do in the future. It's a cultural moment that intersects with entertainment and the business of entertainment and the business of culture in a way that is just unavoidable.

These commentators describe not the lack of utility in digital currency or the potential and substantial advantages of the blockchain, but rather schemes designed to create speculative tokens of value well in excess of the benefits they accrue.

Satoshi did not predict the Non-Fungible Token explosion among *Crypto Bros*, but did articulate a digital currency that could satisfy all the needs of a paper currency, and more. It could securely store value, and it could act as a unit of account from which goods and services transactions could be priced. It could be exchanged easily with low transactions costs, and it could freely move wealth between individuals and across borders. Such a bitcoin could also provide what a government-backed currency could not—a democratized coin that would be immune to central bank tampering.

---

[6] https://www.salon.com/2022/02/16/nfts-arent-art--theyre-just-the-of-cryptos-latest-scam/, retrieved March 7, 2022.

Stablecoins to the Rescue

New ICOs in Stablecoin are meant to replicate a physical currency such as the U.S. dollar. As digital protocols move toward Proof of Stake, the stake itself may take the form of a digital currency. For instance, Ethereum 2.0 proposed to require a stake of 32 ether to vie to process its blockchain. Still others are proposed to represent regulated securities that might otherwise come under the auspices of the Securities and Exchange Commission.

Satoshi fell short of realizing a grand vision. The bitcoin creator may well still be out there, and, if so, Satoshi's stock of coin worth barely a dollar at first would make Satoshi one of the 20 wealthiest people on the planet. Rather, the coin was not expected to be a speculative asset for the *When Lambo* crowd, but a coin we could all transact, and many could mine on their personal computers.

What happened next is surely a surprise. Satoshi's coin is now dominated by speculative and illicit trades, and, like any superior speculative vehicle, is volatile in price so that profit opportunities are constantly created. In short, bitcoin is no longer a good medium of exchange with which to use to buy pizzas or pay the groceries, cover rent, get paid, and maybe even buy a home. It never realized its vision to be a substitute for a paper currency. Even for speculative purposes, it is far more like an exciting speculative growth stock such as Tesla rather than a mature stock like Toyota. Bitcoin's valuation fluctuates wildly with every piece of information that could conceivably affect its phenomenal growth. In turn, bitcoin drags along all the alternative coins (*altcoin*) that are also priced not on their current utility, but speculation on crypto in general. What Satoshi would prefer is a Stablecoin.

Stablecoins are cryptocurrencies pegged to a currency that maintains its value. These days, central banks of major nations let their national currencies float, but within a narrow band that gives no pause for concern among importers and exporters. Ironically, the central banks that so concerned Satoshi collectively act to stabilize paper currencies to which Stablecoins attach their value. Most often, the U.S. dollar, as the most universal of currencies, and the defacto currency for more nations than any other currency, is chosen to back Stablecoins. By the end of 2021, $179 billion of Stablecoin were in circulation in 74 different flavors.[7]

Central bankers maintain the value of their respective currencies in a couple of ways. First, central banks must guard against depreciation of their currencies using methods pioneered in the early 1990s by Mark Carney of the

---

[7] https://coinmarketcap.com/view/Stablecoin/, accessed February 14, 2022.

Bank of Canada and then the Bank of England, and since adopted by top central bankers worldwide. The central goal of a central bank is to control inflation with just enough of a bias to ensure that random events in the economy do not push the currency into deflation. A 1–2% inflationary target accomplishes that goal.

The second aspect is that nations maintain sufficient reserves of their own and other major currencies and coordinate their holdings so that their currencies can roughly maintain their relative values. These reserves for a currency like the U.S. dollar must be in the hundreds of billions of dollars. The central banks do not need to tap into their reserves unless exchange rates begin to veer outside a narrow band that supports predictable trade.

These reserves are not meant to satisfy all market supply and demand. If done correctly, they need only act to power steer central banks' currency goals. A Stablecoin that is somehow tied to a major currency could free-ride on the work of central banks to maintain value. Digital Stablecoin can have all the desirable qualities of a superior unit for digital exchange, but without the volatility experienced by insufficiently backed private Stablecoins.

There is no doubt that, left to their own devices, some central bank would have begun to contemplate a digital version of their paper currency someday, perhaps after a decade of market penetration from fintech companies. Certainly, the advent of stable cryptocurrencies has accelerated their efforts to the point that the Bank of China. Now, many central banks, including the Federal Reserve in the U.S., seek to fill the Stablecoin vacuum before a private coin beats them to the market.

In fact, Jerome Powell, Chairman of the U.S. Federal Reserve, noted that there would be little demand for cryptocurrencies in general if there existed a U.S. government sponsored digital currency. He probably underestimates the libertarian nature of the crypto movement, but he was correct in that many, perhaps even a majority, of Americans would transact in a suitable digital currency that had all the advantages of an ether, but without a non-pegged digital coin's volatility in value.

Crypto Bros note quite accurately that were it not for the development of private Stablecoins, governments would likely be in no hurry to develop one of their own. So long as the Federal Reserve innovates defensively, it may well never catch up. But, further utility from cryptocurrency depends on a Stablecoin to support more opportunities for decentralized finance. Such innovations, naturally tied to fintech, are developing so fast that the Federal Reserve realizes it must make progress toward a Stablecoin.

This dramatic growth in Stablecoin has regulators worried for other reasons. As a banker of last resort, the Fed had to extend its credit well beyond banks to insurance companies and the purchase of such derivatives as Mortgage-Backed Securities and other toxic assets that led to the Crash of 2008 and the Great Recession. The Federal Reserve realizes that, in the absence of federal deposit insurance, it may someday be forced to fix a failing Stablecoin just as it had to bail out banks too-big-to-fail on behalf of innocent or naïve customers. To have the ability to monitor and direct such a Stablecoin would require a full integration of Stablecoin into the commercial banking system, or develop a Stablecoin of its own, backed by the reserves of the Federal Reserve. I return to such possibilities in Chapter 23.

A Tether to the Dollar

The concept of a Stablecoin is to link its value to something of known value, such as the U.S. dollar, so that it may retain a stable value and free transactors of concerns over volatility that may drain the coin's value just before the transactor needs to spend it. Examples of Stablecoins include TrueUSD, USD Tether, and Diem. Tether (using the identifier USDT) is issued by the Hong Kong-based company Tether Limited, which is a subsidiary of the massive Bitfinex exchange. It was designed to be exchangeable for US dollars, just as the US dollar was once theoretically exchangeable for gold.

Customers and regulators discovered that their trust in the institution overseeing Tether had been violated when it was disclosed that actual U.S. dollars represented a mere 2.9% of outstanding Tether, with the bulk backed by promissory notes, and almost a quarter of the value backed only by faith in Tether, Inc.[8] The New York Attorney General's Office sued Tether for this violation of faith and disclosure and settled the suit in February, 2021 for $18.5 million. The Attorney General noted that this cash backing had been declining since sometime between 2014 and 2019, and that $850 million in financial backing has actually disappeared from Tether's books. The lack of this corporation and of the coin to follow US audit and disclosure standards placed Tether in disrepute. In addition, the corporation was accused of manipulating the price of bitcoin for corporate profit.

---

[8] https://en.wikipedia.org/wiki/Tether_(cryptocurrency), retrieved March 7, 2022.

Initial Controversies with Tether

The initial concept of Tether was to act as a currency which derived its value from the underlying value of bitcoin. In this sense, it is a derivative, or second layer currency. It evolved to derive its value from reserves in the US dollar (USTether), the Euro (EuroTether), and the Japanese Yen (YenTether). Tether's corporate owner, Bitfinex, offered trading and exchange of Tether in 2015, with the assistance of Taiwanese banks, and with Wells Fargo in the United States for the dollar side of exchanges. Tether relied primarily on bitcoin, and on bitcoin's highly liquid conversion to US dollars as its backing. In essence, it promised to offer a *token* representing ownership of US dollars through bitcoin, for instance, and by 2018 represented up to 80% of bitcoin trading volume backed by $2.8 billion US.[9]

This arrangement began to unwind when New York State Attorney General Latitia James uncovered an improperly documented relationship with a Panamanian payment processor called *Crypto Capital*. James discovered that the Panamanian entity had absconded with the promised deposit, worth $850 million. To compound their problem, Tether had deceived the Attorney General about this relationship.

In addition, it was uncovered by researchers John M. Griffin and Amin Shams (2018) that Tether's trading in bitcoin amounted to half of bitcoin's price increase in 2018. Additional research by Bloomberg reporters Matthew Leising et al. (2018) uncovered Tether's use of techniques that have been used to manipulate bitcoin prices to increase the volatility of bitcoin and manipulate its value through a bitcoin platform called the *Kraken Exchange*. Following this rocky era, Tether has reformed its practices and may well emerge as a successful private sector Stablecoin over time. Another Stablecoin, TerraUSD, suffered an even more dramatic demise. It was an algorithmic coin that claimed it could maintain value by administering a proprietary formula to further collateralize its value with another asset that relied on bitcoin's value. When bitcoin's value plummeted in the Great Crypto Crash of 2022, TerraUSD failed miserably, wiped out $60 billion in value from the coin's owners, and likely ended the financial alchemy of algorithmic collateralization.

The Next Step: Crypto Banks

A logical extension of a stable digital currency is a chartered virtual bank. A company called Kraken, and its founder, Jesse Powell, are succeeding in making this happen.

The Kraken Exchange is not without its own history of controversy. Founded by Jesse Powell in 2011 with the intention to take over the failing of the early Mt. Gox bitcoin exchange, it had grown to be a full-featured

---

[9] Larson, Erik; Leising, Matthew; Kharif, Olga (26 April 2019). "Crypto Market Roiled by New Allegations Against Tether, Bitfinex". Bloomberg. Retrieved March 7, 2022.

exchange that eventually added margin trading and facilitation for multiple currency transactions on its proprietary online platform. It enjoyed early inclusion on the Bloomberg Terminals that provide information to investors, and eventually obtained the right to do business in almost all U.S. states and worldwide.

Kraken and its founder also ran afoul of the investigations Attorney General James was conducting. Jesse Powell refused to cooperate with the investigation because he claimed crypto traders do not care about market manipulation and that crypto platforms are rampant with scams.[10] Soon thereafter, in September of 2020, Kraken had received a special purpose depository institution charter (SPDI) from the State of Wyoming and became the first bank to receive a new charter in the United States since 2006, as documented by Boot and Laskowski (2020).

The early antics of Tether and other cryptocurrencies, and the irresponsible advocacy of some, have damaged the development of Stablecoin. However, the issue still remains from a regulatory perspective. The industry prefers to have Stablecoins and their sponsors treated as a commodity, and hence under the looser oversight of the Commodity Futures Trading Commission and other commodity regulators, rather than under the much closer scrutiny to which banking is subjected. A later chapter will describe this significance of this dichotomy.

Digital currencies must gain similar legitimacy to that of a fiat currency for instance backed by the full faith and credit of the U.S. Government or its equivalent and maintained by the fractional banking system. Such a maturation will require significant additional work. Until then, though, Satoshi's hope for a stable and reliable medium of exchange to allow the multitude to access the convenience of banks remains an elusive goal.

---

[10] Cheng, Evelyn (19 April 2018). "Kraken cryptocurrency exchange says it will not comply with New York inquiry". *CNBC*. Retrieved March 7, 2022.

18

Decentralized Finance

The innovation of digital cryptocurrencies was prophesized by Satoshi to be a peer-to-peer method that may someday offer users a vast array of opportunities for digital financial transactions. On June 17 of, 2010, Satoshi posted to the bitcoin bulletin board a vision that "The design supports a tremendous variety of possible transaction types that I designed years ago. Escrow transactions, bonded contracts, third party arbitration, multi-party signature, etc. If bitcoin catches on in a big way, these are things we'll want to explore in the future, but they all had to be designed at the beginning to make sure they would be possible later."[1] Such a vision that would bring many functions of banks and near banks to one's computer or smartphone was revolutionary at the time.

Bitcoin's design and protocol is somewhat limited, especially for the volume of transactions Satoshi might have anticipated should the coin catch on. The protocol cannot support more than three to seven transactions per second, which is trivial to the 1,700 transactions per second that the Visa network averages, or the million transactions per second Amazon is designing into a proposed digital transaction platform of its own.

But, while bitcoin is much less amenable to such an expansion as a stable digital currency and smart contract platform, protocols such as Ethereum 2.0 opens up a broad new avenue for financial services. Such *decentralized finance* (DeFi) has the potential to facilitate accounts from which to save, borrow,

---

[1] https://satoshi.nakamotoinstitute.org/quotes/bitcoin-design/, accessed April 19, 2022.

or lend, to trade stocks and bonds, to auction derivatives such as options to buy or sell assets at a future point in time, or to purchase or issue insurance. Someday, likely soon, the flexibility of Ethereum 2.0 will facilitate smart contracts that allow the crypto network to offer a decentralized opportunity to engage in many of the functions for which we would currently require banks, insurance companies, stock brokers, escrow providers, and numerous other potential transactions for which we have yet imagined.

There may well be a day in which our airplane tickets, property titles, Non-Fungible Token purchases, and myriad other financial records can be secured through decentralized finance, without the need for intermediaries that necessary take their cut for services rendered.

This expansion of the blockchain well beyond the original promise of bitcoin, but without the significant brick-and-mortar investments in banks, brokers, trading floors, and all the associated salaries and overhead, can enhance efficiency and offer affordable access to anyone with a smart phone or Internet connection. It can do so without the gatekeepers that must approve our accounts, process, and record our titles to property or issue our policies. We need only a personal digital wallet to initiate these transactions that are almost instantaneously and commission-fee free. In doing so, a decentralized market makes decisions on whether to transact, independent of your financial status, race, or other factors that may have limited access to these accounts and features in the past.

These abilities are now anticipated by the new Ethereum 2.0 protocol. It is able to support *decentralized apps* (dapps) that are simple to invoke, able to link to such information as a credit report, and can provide prompt Artificial Intelligence approvals. Already, consumers in China can apply for a personal or car loans on a smartphone app and receive approval in seconds. Such flash loans can offer much greater flexibility that could be provided by a traditional bank.

Some of these features already exist in the blockchain. For instance, within one's wallet an exchange may offer you interest on your crypto or traditional currency deposits, and may offer loans, especially using the collateral of your deposits, but also match your needs with other's assets. One can trade many sorts of assets, well beyond cryptocurrencies, without the delays and commissions of brokers.

Before the public can enjoy all these benefits, there must be innovations in transactions cost transparency, especially as Ethereum 2.0 moves from Proof of Work to Proof of Scope and revises its mining reward structure. Broader adoption must also overcome the problem of thinly-traded securities with their associated volatility. Under such a decentralized regime, records necessary for tax purposes will need to be summarized and reported to tax authorities.

Decentralized Finance Apps Abound

One can imagine the possibilities and the challenges. In fact, many of these features have been available within the Ethereum protocol since 2017, with its ability to use decentralized applications and smart contracts within its blockchain. People have been borrowing and lending peer-to-peer and have been using the platform to trade in cryptocurrencies, write and sell derivatives to insure against cryptocurrency volatility, and earn an interest rate on their savings. In late 2021, the DeFi aspect of Ethereum controlled about $100 billion U.S. in assets.

Since the ability to utilize smart contracts became available in 2017, a DeFi platform called MakerDAO developed tools that use a Stablecoin to issue loans, accept loan payments, and process retirement of loans. Reliance of a Stablecoin tied to a traditional currency such as the U.S. dollar ensures that these digital platforms act much like similar services offered in the financial sector, without the speculative risk associated when one denominates transactions in bitcoin, ether, or another digital asset with a value determined by supply and demand.

Recent advances include the services provided by the Compound Finance Exchange and others for lending denominated only in cryptocurrencies but also in a new token called COMP. This token used as the denomination in the digital application (dapp) Compound is tradeable and offers sophisticated speculators the opportunity to earn arbitrage profits by taking advantage of arbitrage profits from pricing differences between pools, just as traditional foreign exchange traders may transact foreign exchange to earn arbitrage profits from slight pricing differences between markets.

Compound is certainly one of the most ambitious DeFi platforms. Started only in 2018 out of a small space near Silicon Valley in San Francisco, and backed by Silicon Valley venture capital firms Andreessen Horowitz and Coinbase Ventures, Compound's asset base quickly exceeded $20 billion, with nearly 300,000 clients, each represented by a 42-character long hexadecimal account number, with no other personal indicators, including names or nationality. The platform also offers its own cryptocurrency, the COMP, which ensures a ready market and capitalization for its shadow bank.

Such increasingly elaborate uses of DeFi that parallel transactions in traditional financial trading houses may drive upwards of two thirds of cryptocurrency price movements, according to Bloomberg, with collateral levels reaching $9 billion.[2] Various DeFi platforms are attracting noted venture capital firms such as Michael Novogratz and Andreessen Horowitz.[3] While the DeFi model continues to evolve, it remains a multi-party fight for market share, not only between traditional tech, corporate entities wishing to control their own networks but also such Web 3.0 entities as Meta, and small developers and large countries alike. This interest and next steps will inevitably engage in these new potentials cone the protocols and potential reporting can permit regulatory oversight.

> **Dapps and Exchanges Allow Financial Leverage Like Margin Accounts**
>
> Access to such feature-rich digital apps is typically through a simple browser extension such as MetaMask which allows users to access its dapp directly through ether's platform. Some DeFi platforms such as Aave has recently introduced *flash loans* that are short term uncollateralized personal loans that may be initiated and liquidated through transactions in a crypto block. These in-and-out transactions may facilitate arbitrage and collateral swaps and the unwinding of leveraged positions, using one's own balances combined with borrowed funds. For example, if a speculator invests $1000 and borrows a further $1000 to purchase a $2000 crypto asset that doubles in value to $4000, and must pay $100 interest on the borrowing, their 1:1 equity to debt leverage ratio earned the investor $2900 profits from the $1000 investment. Such easy-to-access crypto borrowing through DeFi apps allow speculators to leverage and hence magnify their earnings.

Yet another DeFi protocol is Uniswap, which functions as a *Decentralized Exchange* (DEX) that trades tokens denominated in Ethereum. Rather than relying on a physical exchange to fill orders, it incentivizes users to participate in liquidity pools and, in turn receive a share of fees collected from traders' profits earned by swapping assets into and out of a given liquidity pool. This is essentially a peer-to-peer exchange that acts somewhat like a stock exchange. The open-source software employed by their development frustrates the ability to oversee and regulates such transactions, at least during this nascent period of regulation contemplation.

---

[2] "Crypto Is Beating Gold as 2020's Top Asset So Far." Bloomberg. 22 September 2020. Retrieved 5 October 2020.

[3] "Novogratz Plows Ahead in DeFi Amid the 'Gamifying' of Crypto." Bloomberg. 29 September 2020. Retrieved 10 February 2022.

Decentralized Finance Risks

There are risks, though, from the use of these digital innovations. Human errors and hacking risks are common in this infancy of DeFi. Since Ethereum does not permit reversal of errors, there are new trading risks. One must also be able to trust the dapp within which ones interacts. A platform known as Yam Finance in 2020 raised $750 million in cash, but almost the entire amount was lost due to a coding error.[4] Since such coding is often open source, and hence can be translated into competing dapps, there remain risks of propagating errors to other similar applications.

We must also ensure that the originators of dapps are trustworthy. Various vulnerabilities make DeFi prone to hacks and unethical schemes, which begs oversight or regulation to prevent. Certainly, wide-eyed inexperienced investors are particularly vulnerable to risk associated with their lack of experience and sophistication. But, unlike investing in traditional securities that may require more experience, such as derivatives, consumer protection oversight has not yet migrated to decentralized peer-to-peer networks.

To date, much of cryptocurrency crime is concentrated in the DeFi sector.[5] Some losses are due to software and application developer incompetence, which results in irretrievably lost coin, but which then incrementally increases the value to other holders of the coin. Other opportunities for theft arise when hackers steal currency or assets from projects that have not closed all vulnerabilities. Schemes in which shillers and influencers promote a coin or dapp and then abscond with the invested funds in what the industry calls a pump-and-dump are becoming increasingly common.

Such losses in the DeFi world are not related directly to vulnerabilities in the blockchain. Instead, DeFi apps share the same vulnerabilities as do other digital applications. This included the penetration by external hackers into applications directly, or may occur when developers and their network of social media shillers raise significant funds and then abscond with the money, in what the industry calls a "rug-pull." This technique is similar to the "pump and dump" practice in which speculators will run-up the price of a coin on rumor and false information, and then dump and short-sell the coin at its price peak.

Cryptocurrency credibility will be necessary if the public is to gain confidence in the various products that already exist. The most commonly

---

[4] https://www.theblockcrypto.com/post/74810/yam-token-market-cap-collapses-by-more-than-90-flaw, retrieved February 26, 2022.
[5] https://www.cnbc.com/2021/11/19/over-10-billion-lost-to-defi-scams-and-thefts-in-2021.html, accessed March 21, 2022.

subscribed DeFi feature is the ability to earn interest on deposits by allowing the coin owner or its wallet to lend their idle cash out. Such direct and indirect lending has yielded a higher interest rate than commercial banks or money market accounts offer. DeFi dapps or wallet exchanges can also lend, with coin balances as collateral, which obviates the necessity for credit checks. This allows speculators to invest in additional purchases of a speculative coin by borrowing against existing coin collateral, and hence permits financial leverage. Such practices are what one might expect from a full-feature brokerage, but without the consumer protections and oversight afforded in traditional exchanges or brokerages.

> **Decentralized Finance Digital Apps Technicalities**
>
> The purpose of decentralized finance is to bring to other financial exchanges the same authority-less mode that transactors enjoy. That way, there is no human intervention in the approval of loans, the exchange of one crypto security for another, or the exchange of more sophisticated financial derivatives. In traditional markets, some sort of a market-maker have traditionally performed such functions. In crypto, Automated Market Makers (AMM) are algorithms that allow for such exchanges through algorithms rather than human intervention.
>
> DeFi dapps do so by forming liquidity pools and then constructing self-adjusting algorithms that dictate exchanges between the pools. For instance, if one wishes to speculate between two cryptocurrencies, for instance ETH and BTC, one would maintain some liquidity in both an Ethereum and a bitcoin pool. If x is the value of ETH, and y the value of BTC, the algorithm allows one to exchange at any rate such that $x*y = k$. As people trade in and out of the pools, the relative value of these pools change, and others can then sweep in and try to profit from these changing relative values. The constant k can then adjust over time to ensure that such trades in both directions remain roughly in balance. Other AMM algorithms are even more complex, but the general principle is that trades can be almost instantaneous, and can function at any time, with no human intervention. However, these algorithms still typically rely on the inherent strength of cryptocurrency as a whole The Great Crypto Crash of 2022 demonstrated the vulnerability when all crypto values fall.

To remain viable and expand, the industry must first assure consumers and corporations that deposits are safekept. Indeed, these near-banking is an attractive market for a number of corporations seeking an affordable pathway into fintech. BlockFi is an example of lending and borrowing platform that offers a return of 5–10% to savings, and in turn lend those funds out at higher rates. For instance, BlockFi lends to hedge funds who are able to take advantage of arbitrage in digital currency spot and future markets to earn high returns, but with commensurately high risk.

Can't Have Their Crypto and Eat It Too

Recently, a Securities and Exchange settlement of $100 million resulted from the accusation that BlockFi was acting as a purveyor of unregistered securities.[6] Such regulatory risks are magnified by the lack of oversight and of regulations that would place on DeFi institutions the same cash reserve requirements imposed on banks to enhance banking safety and limit how a platform can leverage cash deposits into loans.

In fact, BlockFi increasingly models itself as a major financial institution rather than a mere participant in the decentralized platform for bitcoin exchange as Satoshi imagined. Headquartered in Jersey City within eyeshot of Wall Street, BlockFi hopes to become the crypto version of a major bank, the same type of institution labeled too-big-to-fail at the inception of the Great Recession when Satoshi launched bitcoin. In addition to the equivalent of online savings accounts, BlockFi offers loans and a credit card, all of which primarily rely on cryptocurrency balances. It has grown to a near bank with over $10 billion in assets, almost a thousand employees and half a million clients, and uses a DeFi platform to approve loans in minutes, all without a credit check.

Others have used traditional bank charters to establish themselves. Before it obtained a bank charter, the principal of Kraken Bank leveraged $18 billion in interest-earning assets to extend loans through an automated system. To a retail customer, these accounts look very much like the digital footprint of a brick-and-mortar bank. Their individual accounts will take cash deposits, typically through a wire or other interbank transfer tool. They will also accept a number of common digital currencies. Kraken Bank is now state chartered in Wyoming and can accept deposits nationwide.

The interest rates offered on such cryptocurrency exchanges and near banks are significantly higher than offered by traditional banks, to compensate the depositor for the additional risk because these platforms are not insured as would be traditional bank deposits through the Federal Deposit Insurance Corporation. Such risks include cyberattacks, regulatory fines, volatile market conditions that may force a run on deposits, and other opaque vulnerabilities that leave depositors vulnerable.

As with other near banks, institutions such as BlockFi appear to be a bank to its customers, but with considerably more risk. Since traditional banks are chartered either nationally or by states, regulators at both the national and state levels are raising alarms. Not only do these new online institutions

---

[6] https://decrypt.co/92789/blockfi-pay-100m-penalty-stop-opening-new-high-yield-bitcoin-accounts-report, accessed February 13, 2022.

induce risks that clients may not fully grasp, major crypto institutions are already exceeding the level of assets of many large regional banks, and hence are verging on too-big-to-fail without any of the oversight or reserves that help protect the customers of traditional banks.

These shadow banks can also offer services that commercial banks typically do not. For instance, BlockFi allows its customers to borrow in dollars up to half the value of their cryptocurrency deposits. Or, a customer can earn up to an 8% interest rate on cryptocurrency deposits, which is significantly larger than the average rates offered by commercial banks. BlockFi is able to offer these high yields by lending its deposits to large investment banks, who can parlay these funds into platforms for arbitrage strategies on cryptocurrency markets, all beyond the extensive regulations a commercial bank of similar size is required to follow.

Since the lending of such a shadow bank is in proportion to the customer's deposits, it need not demand credit checks of its depositors and borrowers. Such a disconnect between banking services and good credit is especially appealing to young people who lack a history of superior credit reports. While digital near banks may appear to be one step closer to the fulfillment of Satoshi's dream to bring banking to the unbanked, the digital anonymity of banking and the lack of credit risk analyses also adds an additional level of risk to these shadow banks.

Such decentralized finance (DeFi) lending is more closely akin to margin loans through brokerage houses, or loans a pawnbroker might issue based on the collateral of the property they are offered. When BlockFi initially approached California for a banking charter, they were initially told to apply for a pawnbroker's license, until an executive from BlockFi convinced California regulators that they are distinct from pawnbrokers because their collateral is a virtual and not a physical asset. BlockFi has since successfully used such arguments to obtain licenses in more than half the states in the U.S.

Regulators still sense that this incredibly quickly moving industry is falling through regulatory cracks. Because DeFi platforms do not obtain securities licenses, they are not required to publish the various disclosures required of banks and securities dealers. For instance, clients may not be told that their deposits could be used by BlockFi to fund borrowing pools. These funds allow BlockFi to lend out idle clients' holdings to borrowers without assessing the creditworthiness of these borrowers. Rather than squarely addressing the concerns of regulators and Attorneys General in Alabama, Kentucky, Texas, and Vermont, among others, BlockFi appeals to the same retort of bitcoin evangelists, that regulators merely misunderstand the nature of their high-technology industry.

A Crowded Field of Potential Virtual Near Banks

While BlockFi is perhaps one of the best funded platforms in the DeFi space, others financial institutions, including SushiSwap, PancakeSwap, and Compound are vying for market expansion in DeFi. They share similar technologies in that they are all able to perform their functions without the need for brick-and-mortar, tellers and loan officers, or trading floors. Algorithms act as an almost costless intermediary to match lenders and borrowers in money markets and buyers and sellers for speculation. Credit reports are unnecessary, perhaps even impossible since clients are often mere wallet addresses. Artificial Intelligence technology replaces human judgment as these platforms replace many of the functions of banks, all under the illusion of decentralized and democratized markets, despite the growing size, stature, and influence of these platforms.

In fact, it is difficult to label such firms as traditional financial services providers given that their clients are mere account numbers, and their operations are computer-executed transactions. Since there are no client names, institutions have no ability to report to appropriate taxing authorities. In addition, oversight of operations is spotty or non-existent.

DeFi institutions have obvious appeal to those wishing to evade traditional regulation, oversight, or tax reporting. They also appeal to the quarter of the U.S. population that have insufficient access to banking services, a market that Walmart had once attempted to tap, unsuccessfully, as states or federal regulators refuse to permit Walmart a bank charter. By offering near-bank services to the underserved, one might argue these DeFi offer a degree of enhanced economic justice. However, this is a false justice, given the accounts of its participants do not have the protections afforded clients of traditional banks, and may well be those who most need such protections and can least afford the losses that can occur due to fraud, rug-pulling, or government shutdowns.

If You Can't Beat 'Em, Join 'Em

Regulators know that they are now trying to close the barn door when the horse is already loose. The Office of the Comptroller of the Currency (OCC) must determine how to somehow bring DeFi platforms into the fold, for clients' protection, even though the attractive elements of DeFi are that these platforms defy regulating or the revelation of personal detail of account holders.

To date, Congress has yet to determine how to proceed. As they found when they attempted to promulgate regulations that require tax reporting by cryptobrokers, such attempts produce the expected backlash from crypto industry representatives. Congress may ultimately be more effective at authorizing the Federal Reserve to compete directly by, for instance, producing a Stablecoin and by encouraging traditional banks to offer DeFi platforms for clients in these Stablecoin that would then fall under traditional OCC regulation.

Federal and state regulators recognize that the industry has sped far ahead of the regulators and are quickly becoming educated to understand the industry and its growth, and determine pathways for appropriate regulation. This will require Congress to get up to speed quickly too, within an environment of mystery, intrigue, failure to grasp the nature of the new technology, and significant industry lobbying.

Senator Elizabeth Warren has spearheaded efforts on the U.S. Senate side of the legislative branch to prevent these near banks from continuing to fall through the regulatory cracks. Her concern is that not only are cryptocurrencies much more volatile in price compared to other currencies, but they also often cater to unsophisticated consumers. She recognizes regulatory agencies inherently move more slowly than DeFi ventures. It will be a challenge merely to quickly catch up, even if the DeFi industry agreed to stand still.

The quickest avenue for regulation may be through the Securities and Exchange Commission since its autonomy and authority to regulate securities is well established. To date, the SEC has been able to reach settlements with entities such as BlockFi to regulate them as securities dealers, and hence be brought under a regulatory umbrella that was admittedly designed for vastly different financial organizations. These are the new shadow banks that offer many of the services we expect from banks, but without any of the consumer protections we expect. Recently, the SEC has proposed a broadening of the interpretation of its overview authority over financial market makers to include those who facilitate financial market transactions. They propose this broadened mission to afford them the ability to oversee emerging and expanding crypto exchanges, but are challenged by the desire of the competing Commodity Futures Trading Commission to be the lead regulatory agency for cryptocurrencies. Meanwhile, the cryptocurrency industry itself is lobbying extensively for the more lightly regulating CFTC to be the poison of choice under the belief that they will fare more unfettered under the CFTC.

While the industry remains in a period of growing pains in the implementation of DeFi, the recent improvements slated in Ethereum 2.0 protocol and a modicum of willingness to impose regulation to maintain confidence in this emerging financial sector should allow this industry to live up to its significant potential. Those that may well benefit the most are residents unable to participate in traditional financial institutions.

For instance, those who are financially unsophisticated may be intimidated by traditional financial institutions. Such an inability or aversion to have a bank account can even affect one's ability to secure a job or an apartment. Past problems with credit, even if inaccurate, can hinder one's access to borrowing, or even employment or housing. Still others may be skeptical or concerned about ways which traditional financial institutions may control or sell their financial data, and government agencies may even force banks to limit the financial products made available to a disadvantaged customer. Finally, traditional financial transactions are laden with fees to pay multiple intermediaries, and the human processing for even a simple money transfer or trading, or even something as mundane as office hours and trades to other time zones, complicates brick-and-mortar transactions and adds unnecessary costs.

We are but on the cusp of seeing what DeFi has in store for us. I treat in a subsequent chapter the need to protect customers and standardize financial contracts so we are not simply replacing one set of abusive practices with potentially yet another. Such protections are inevitable if we want to avoid Gresham's Law of bad money pushing out the good. As we do so, Satoshi's dream of decentralizing and democratizing financial markets may be realized, even if the design of the bitcoin algorithm likely means that the competing Ethereum protocol, and perhaps others, will ultimately fulfill Satoshi's prophecy.

19

The Market Prognosis for Bitcoin

Since the breakout of bitcoin prices in 2016/2017, the currency has navigated three price booms, which brought the price to a peak of $68,990.90 on November 10, 2021. The number of competing Proof of Work coins is declining, though, as some coins die off and new coins are proposed that invariably employ some sort of a Proof of Stake or similar more environmentally-benign authentication method. With the migration of Ethereum 2.0 to Proof of Stake, bitcoin dominates the Proof of Work sector, with dwindling numbers of competitors, as new cryptocurrencies now avoid Proof of Work from the onset, or specify a transition timetable to Proof of Stake.

While there will remain coin that defy moving to Proof of Stake, none have the significant advantages that will afford bitcoin to represent an increasing share of a market that is otherwise declining in size relative to Proof of Stake. This begs the question. While there are better digital coins for their ability to perform DeFi, to clear transactions more quickly, or to handle more complex transactions, none will perform better among Proof of Work coins than bitcoin for speculation and illicit purposes. So long as wallets can manage to maintain client confidentiality, bitcoin will remain the most liquid, most supply constrained, and most well-established of Proof of Work digital coins. Bitcoin performs that function very well, with no security breaches in the very robust protocol since its inception.

Where Will Bitcoin Prices Go?

Satoshi thought that bitcoin would rise in value and perhaps exceed one dollar in the time period the coin's developer remained active. Satoshi stated in early 2010, "A rational market price for something that is expected to increase in value will already reflect the present value of the expected future increases. In your head, you do a probability estimate balancing the odds that it keeps increasing."[1] At the time of Satoshi's statement, bitcoin was not yet trading and would not reach a dollar in value for another year.

This low-level trading range that bitcoin supporters observed in 2010 did not dampen Satoshi's enthusiasm, even if it may have been unimaginable that bitcoin would achieve the lofty heights observed today. What is the prognosis for bitcoin now, according to the industry? The Independent newspaper reported in early 2022 the consensus of a panel of academics and cryptocurrency market experts. Despite the 2022 price correction after hitting a high of $68,000 in late 2021, the panel of 33 fintech experts produced an average expectation for the price of bitcoin in 2022 to reach a peak of $93,171 before falling back to $76,360 by the end of the year.[2]

Looking farther forward, the experts see the value of bitcoin to rise to an average prediction of $192,800 by 2025, and $406,400 by the end of 2030. These are slight downgrades of 20–40% from predictions a year earlier, but they all still represent significant growth of the bitcoin price.

Meanwhile, JP Morgan produced the results of their research that predict the price of bitcoin shall rise to $150,000 over the longer term.[3] Similarly, Matt Hougen of Bitwise Asset Management reported to Bloomberg TV that he expects bitcoin to rise to $100,000 by the end of 2022, as did Anthony Scaramucci, heat of Skybridge Capital, and former White House Director of Communications.[4] Other experts support other long-term prospects. Most agree that bitcoin will attain a price of $100,000 within 2023, and the consensus continues to show bitcoin growth beyond that.

The basis for these steady increases in bitcoin prices is the robustness of demand for this particular coin, and a belief that there may remain additional interest from both retail and institutional investors as the potential for the

---

[1] https://bitcointalk.org/index.php?topic=57.msg415#msg415, accessed April 19, 2022.
[2] https://www.independent.co.uk/tech/bitcoin-price-prediction-2022-b2002586.html, accessed February 13, 2022.
[3] https://cryptopotato.com/jpmorgan-increases-long-term-bitcoin-price-prediction-to-150000/, accessed February 13, 2022.
[4] https://tulsaworld.com/business/investment/personal-finance/wall-street-experts-are-lining-up-to-predict-bitcoin-will-hit-100-000/article_d93f6894-33df-55a1-a095-0628be9c917b.html, accessed February 13, 2022.

blockchain as an investment vehicle is sure to improve with greater public awareness and subscription. The unusual aspect of pricing of bitcoin is its almost perfectly inelastic supply, given the reward structure baked into the protocol. Therefore, movements in the price are entirely demand-driven, with the only supply factor entering into the analysis arises from additional bitcoin mined each year. In 2022, the annual addition is 328,500 new coin adds an almost trivial amount to a base supply of more than 19,000,000. By 2024, this addition to the flow shall halve to 164,250, with another halving not occurring until 2028.

Since the market price is set based on the flow of demand for the currency relative to those willing to sell at a given time, both the stock of those potentially willing to sell and the modest flow of newly mined coin, and the flow of new demand for speculation and transactions are the determinants of bitcoin price.

Based on these market dynamics, the bitcoin analyst Plan B predicts a price of $288,000 at the coin's next peak. These peaks have been occurring on average about once every two years since the modern corporate era, with the last peak attained in November of 2021. Meanwhile, bitcoin pioneer Adam Back believes that bitcoin may reach $300,000 over the next few years, while PrimeXBT provides a summary of estimates offered by industry experts and analysts that predicts a range of $42,000–$140,000 by 2022, $63,000 to $100,000 by 2023, and between $275,000 and $500,000 by 2025.[5] Still others predict a bitcoin price that will straddle $1 million.

The reward structure offered miners for Proof of Work is not an element of these analyses. Bitcoin supply is inelastic and unrelated to the level of demand, unlike most all other commodities. However, within the category of Proof of Work coin over the long term, and given the high profile of bitcoin as the Genesis Coin, it is unlikely that any alternative Proof of Work coin will emerge over the next few years in any way that would challenge bitcoin's supremacy. While Proof of Stake will certainly be the dominant cryptocurrency class for the large market expansion in the future as cryptocurrencies go mainstream, bitcoin will be the primary safe and liquid harbor for those concerned that Proof of Stake or other authentication means will not offer the same level of anonymity that a completely decentralized cryptocurrency provides. Fear of lack of anonymity may also cause those engaged in sensitive or illicit activity to continue to rely on bitcoin mined in a decentralized network outside of the purview of regulators who oversee institutions that sponsor Proof of Stake mining. This demand for bitcoin may even accelerate

---

[5] https://primexbt.com/for-traders/bitcoin-price-prediction-forecast/, accessed February 13, 2022.

if criminal activity arising from cybercriminals such as hackers or ransomware attackers continue to outwit network managers.

In addition, bitcoin is an ideal speculative vehicle. Speculation requires sufficient volatility to produce the necessary profit opportunities. Speculators generally agree that bitcoin has sufficient market volume and liquidity and is the best opportunity for speculation. The level of market speculation in digital currencies is expected to grow in general as digital currencies increase in popularity and gain public confidence.

Finally, bitcoin offers low direct transaction fees for large and global transactions, and that market is not expected to weaken either. The recent rise in transaction volume in the wake of the imposition of banking sanctions following Russia's invasion of Ukraine is a testament to bitcoin's robustness.

In summary, while the extent of capitalization among Proof of Work cryptocurrencies may not rise significantly for the sector more broadly, there are valid reasons to expect demand and hence the price of bitcoin to grow at rates perhaps not as spectacular as some run-ups, but likely not significantly lower than what has been realized in this nascent corporate period since 2017. Using estimates from Cryptonewsz.com[6] based on recent trends, and extended to 2030, including the regular halving of the quantity of rewards in 2020, 2024, and 2028, we see a continual estimated upward trend in mining rewards from the expected increase in the price of bitcoin (Fig. 19.1).

Based on average expected closing prices, the net annual price increase exceeds the rate of bitcoin reward quantity decay. In other words, *The Bitcoin Dilemma* of increased energy consumption is expected to continue to grow in the coming years.

Indeed, according to the model, the 58% price rise beyond the end of 2021, net of one halving event in 2024, and another in 2028, shall result in a 37% increase in power consumption by 2030 alone. At an estimated current electricity consumption of 142 TWh by bitcoin miners in 2022,[7] total energy consumption shall increase to 161 TWh by 2030. Were bitcoin a country, their electricity consumption would place it in the top 30 energy consuming nations.

---

[6] https://www.cryptonewsz.com/forecast/bitcoin-price-prediction/, accessed February 26, 2022.
[7] https://ccaf.io/cbeci/index, accessed April 7, 2022.

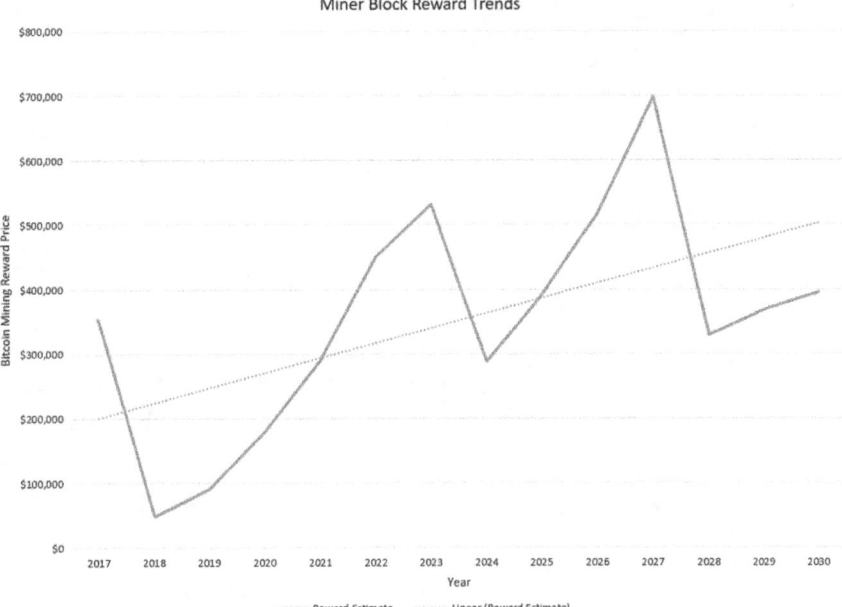

Fig. 19.1 Bitcoin mining block reward trend

Part V

Cryptocurrency and the Environment

Someday the world may have abundant sustainable power. The question is whether that day will arrive in time to avoid the cataclysmic problems associated with global warming arising from the burning of fossil fuels. Any unnecessary increase in electricity consumption merely amplifies this dismal prophecy. I explore in this part the link between electricity consumption and greenhouse gas emissions. These chapters conclude that the additional burden on energy consumption arising from bitcoin mining is already making precarious the promises made by nations to curb greenhouse gas emissions and global warming.

This book documents that the expected rise in the price of bitcoin directly translates into greater electricity demand. The energy consumption arising from bitcoin mining significantly burdens the climate and is doing so at an accelerating rate. However, crypto advocates argue the opposite. Their strategy to give the perception of environmental stewardship while simultaneously contributing heavily to environmental degradation is called *Greenwashing* and is described in this part. Most researchers agree that, if the coin is to properly internalize the consequences of mining to preserve the environment, public policies must be developed to deal directly with its environmental externalities.

A number of commentators and researchers express grave concern over the effect of Proof of Work mining on the environment, while others suggest such concerns are either overblown or addressable. Schinckus et al. (2019) register their concern about the carbon footprint and energy consumption of bitcoin mining, and assert that increased bitcoin speculation is challenging sustainability. They were one of the first to demonstrate the link between trading volume and energy consumption.

Perhaps the most publicized study appeared in Nature–Climate Change. Mora et al. (2018) asserted that, should bitcoin continue its current trend and experience the same sort of growth as other innovations, it could generate sufficient electricity consumption to contribute to a two-degree Celsius growth in the average global temperature as a result of its greenhouse gas emissions. Without the benefit of *The Bitcoin Dilemma*, the authors assert that migration of mining to less expensive (sustainable) energy can mitigate this, as could improvements in hardware and the protocol. While there may be flaws in their analysis, their concerns remain valid.

Mining Efficiency Improvements

Masanet et al. (2019) attempt to contradict the dismal prophecy of Mora et al. by claiming they insufficiently weighed improvements in miner efficiency and energy carbon dioxide footprints. Similarly, Cocco et al. (2019) also harbor hope that improvements in the bitcoin algorithm can alleviate environmental challenges. They draw parallels between bitcoin and gold mining. While these results sound intuitive, *The Bitcoin Dilemma* demonstrates that neither efficiency improvements nor diversion of sustainable power to Proof of Work mining will reverse the trend they note.

Continuing with the theme of miner efficiency as a (false) cure for the greenhouse gas externality of Proof of Work mining, O'Dwyer and Malone (2014) explore the upper bound of energy usage in the hardware Arms Race. They assert that profitability requires increasingly faster and more energy-efficient hardware, but they also fail to observe that this arms race is self-defeating, as *The Bitcoin Dilemma* describes.

Mir (2020) describes the various factors that impinge on bitcoin energy consumption and emerging ways to optimize energy use. They too assert that the reason why bitcoin does not currently consume yet more energy is that processing efficiency continues to improve. Unfortunately, they do not recognize the economics uncovered by *The Bitcoin Dilemma*. They do, however, correctly conclude that other algorithms may offer relief to the Proof of Work methodology.

Truby (2018) noted the threat to global warming from bitcoin mining and call for public policy to internalize such negative externalities. They observe that "the libertarian promise of a decentralized and secure peer-to-peer payments system have (sic) largely been substituted with the speculative pursuit of private wealth creation with little social utility." They add that the system has been designed to demand increasing energy consumption without due consideration to the environment. While Truby (2018) fails to appreciate the futility of mining efficiency improvements when there is a bitcoin miner arms race, some public policies are proffered. These include a registration or a profits charge, a maximum greenhouse gas threshold for transactions, properly priced carbon markets, and other mining taxes.

Increasingly, the mining industry is becoming aware of their environmental impact, but eschews regulation through taxation or energy efficiency standards. The fundamental Bitcoin Dilemma remains unacknowledged, as is the inevitable shift of other energy consumers to more expensive and greenhouse gas-generating fossil fuel-based electricity sources. Ultimately, environmental policies require an international approach given the ability to shift mining activity to favorable jurisdictions.

Some researchers have asserted that various other factors may hopefully but mistakenly mitigate *The Bitcoin Dilemma*. They draw this different conclusion based on the common intuition that energy efficiency improvements should normally result in reduced energy consumption. However, these statements do not explicitly model the unique nature of the bitcoin protocol and its automatic difficulty adjustment mechanism that creates the arms race to the bottom, using electricity as the ammunition. For instance, Spross (2017) questions the amount of energy bitcoin requires. He notes "Bitcoin is designed to make the computations easier as the supply of bitcoins grows." *The Bitcoin Dilemma* contradicts Spross' conclusion that bitcoin mining energy consumption declines over time, bitcoin's energy use is driven by the value of each coin. As that price rises, the return on mining bitcoin keeps rises proportionately. Nonetheless, Spross correctly observes that long and sustained declines in bitcoin's price would lower its energy consumption.

The prevailing theme debunked by *The Bitcoin Dilemma* is that there is a technological fix that will mitigate ever-growing energy consumption in bitcoin mining. Most of these optimistic researchers have relied on innovation as the energy consumption salvation. For instance, Cocco et al. (2016) document the transition of bitcoin mining technologies. They track empirically and through modeling the trajectory of bitcoin prices and note the rising necessity for improved hardware to preserve mining profits net of electricity costs. Interestingly, they also observe obsolescence of mining technology in approximately one year on average. Such obsolescence presumably results in miners of greater efficiency with each passing year. Similarly, Bondarev (2020) asserts that more efficient use of electricity resources for mining could be accomplished by an order of magnitude improvement in electricity provision qualities, improved heat handling, and other technical mechanisms,

A different approach is championed by Badea et al. (2021). They begin their analysis with advocacy for the Austrian Economic School position advocated by Friedrich August von Hayek, in his "Denationalization of Money: The Argument Refined." They argue that competition creates a superior currency. While Hayek's thesis occurred before our understanding of monetary theory in a fractional reserve system necessitates monetary oversight, the authors suggest that the 6442 cryptocurrencies in circulation (some of which live only a few days) create such a marketplace of competition for a superior digital coin.

While not a reprieve for bitcoin, others propose popularization of other cryptocurrencies. Li et al. (2019) measure the carbon footprint of the cryptocurrency Monero based on various mining technologies. They note hashing algorithms significantly affect mining efficiency and the carbon footprint. Likewise, Scheltz (2021) advocates for the differentiation between bitcoin's energy consumption and that of newer cryptocurrencies which employ more energy-efficient authentication methods.

From the environmental perspective, the authors try to salvage bitcoin mining by asserting that the economic impact of cryptocurrency is small compared to other payment systems. Consistent with other commentators, they quote Baur and Oll (2019) that technical solutions can mitigate bitcoin's carbon footprint and suggest that mining can even enhance the availability of sustainable energy, and digital currencies could save one billion trees annually. In a different approach to dilute the damage of Proof of Work mining on the environment, Baur et al. (2019) assert that bitcoin environmental consequences should be addressed not in absolute terms but rather relative to other investments. They argue that bitcoin in a diversified investment portfolio can reduce the overall portfolio carbon footprint.

The mining industry has presented a number of truisms that allow them to claim a modicum of environmental sensitivity. For instance, Walton (2022) reports that miners can earn upwards of 10% of their revenue by voluntarily participating in load-shedding agreements. Yet, he also quotes Prof. Eric Hittinger of the Rochester Institute of Technology, who states "It's complicated…It's never quite clear to me where the line is between exaggeration and fabrication… I think crypto does provide some flexibility to electricity grids. It does introduce additional demand in, maybe, some of the right places. (However) we could usually use that electricity for something that is maybe more socially valuable than mining crypto."

However, at the same time, other miners unapologetically seek cheap power with little regard for greenhouse gas emissions. Milman (2022) reports that mining is inducing a renewal of interest in fossil fuel coal plants. The Hardin coal plant in Montana is part of a wave of "zombie" fossil fuel plants repurposed for bitcoin mining, especially following China's edict to ban mining in 2021 as their way to reduce demand for their coal power plants.

These various authors assert with little proof that the industry can police itself for the greater good and consistent with accelerating environmental concern. More consistent with *The Bitcoin Dilemma* is the work by de Vries (2020), who argues that market short run dynamics and profitability may result in the employment of inefficient mining technologies. He also notes that current estimates, which do not fully incorporate long run electricity consumption trends, may actually underestimate an industry that consumes electricity at a similar scale to the 200 TWh electricity consumption of the world's data centers.

Forum Shopping

To squeeze one geography simply results in a bulge elsewhere in the balloon. A line of research explores the internationalization of bitcoin. For instance, Roberts (2022) notes that the 2022 aggression of Russia upon Ukraine has induced Ukrainian citizens to rely on bitcoin as its nation's ATM machines are depleted. Bitcoin is also employed to transfer funds to combatants, while Russia and its leaders may employ bitcoin to circumvent economic sanctions. "Like many in crypto say, the tech is agnostic." But Ethereum founder Vitalik tweeted, "Ethereum is neutral, but I am not." Roberts concludes this may be the first crypto war, but not the last.

This theme of improving mining efficiency, tapping into diverse power sources, or migrate across locations, remains a prevailing but simplistic theme. Köhler et al. (2019) outline the geographical differences in carbon footprints from bitcoin mining globally. They too assert that mining efficiency can mitigate the footprint if activity is moved to regions with a greater mix of sustainable energy. Meanwhile, Náñez et al. (2021) assert that mining sustainability can be improved by moving activity to regions that source their electricity more sustainably. They state that the China mining ban was designed in part to accomplish such a geographical displacement.

Also, along the geographical mitigation theme, Bitir-Istrate et al. (2021) provide a case study of a mining farm in Bucharest, Romania. Based on their case study, they recommend a (presumably global) protocol to develop a consistent framework to measure the net effects of mining on sustainability. They further recommend that farms employ at least 50% sustainable energy as a global policy and agree to mandates of various efficiency standards. Recently, Iran mandated a requirement for 100% renewable energy as a precondition for mining.

Others document the international mobility of bitcoin mining. Tabuchi (2022) documented that China's ban of cryptocurrency mining in 2021 resulted in an exodus of miners to Kazakhstan and the United States. This geographical shift increased industry reliance of mining from hydroelectricity to electricity derived from fossil fuels. She quotes researchers from Vrije Universiteit Amsterdam and M.I.T. that show this transition may result in the addition of 65 million megatonnes of additional carbon dioxide emissions annually, according to researcher Alex de Vries. The study relied on data from Foundry USA, a mining pool that tracks mining locations in the US.

Such nations' mining evictions displace rather than replace mining farms. Newbery (2021) observes the U.S. now represents 35% of global bitcoin mining following the China crackdown and relates that Tesla entrepreneur Elon Musk stopped taking payments in bitcoin because of environmental concerns. Newbery reports that some argue bitcoin may stimulate expansion into renewables but that two thirds of mining is from non-renewables. She correctly observed "If overall energy consumption increases in a particular state because of mining, it could push other industries to use more non-renewable energy." That states have already seen the consequences. Benetton et al. (2021) noted New York State ratepayers began to pay significantly more for energy following the arrival of large-scale bitcoin mining. Crypto's profits are ratepayers' losses.

Yet, as Newbery notes, miners continue to search for crypto-friendly regulation and cheap electricity. Such explorations have attracted them to New York for its cheap electricity, Kentucky for abundant coal and tax breaks, and Texas for crypto-friendly laws. She also notes the reopening of fossil fuel plants in Montana and Pennsylvania, and also reports on the Plattsburgh, NY experience and on the Texas blackouts exacerbated by bitcoin mining.

Despite industry claims otherwise, these environmental damages are real and pronounced. In the most detailed analysis of monetary damages, Goodkind et al. (2020) find that, for every $1 of bitcoin mined generates $0.49 in climate and health damages in the U.S. and $0.37 in China. They expect other Proof of Work cryptocurrencies to follow that similar pattern. They argue that internalizing pollution externalities are necessary to somewhat offset these problems.

Some operators wish to change the narrative. The Crypto Climate Accord (2021) is a group that offers a series of policies to reduce the negative externalities of mining, and asserts that more efficient machines and better network design, load shifting, relocation, employment of more renewables, and offsetting emissions can mitigate the damage of mining. In that same vein of internalizing such pollution externalities, Jackson (2021) discusses how the mining industry must balance "(the need to) transition to renewable energy (versus the needs of) billionaires and industry evangelists" to address the Crypto Climate Accord. He notes Ripple's participation in the Alliance, with their Proof of Stake protocol, and its use of renewable energy and improved energy efficiency. With regard to the CCA, Jackson notes:

> With the noose already tightening around the PoW protocol due to its impact on the environment, many voices supporting green crypto appear to fall into the conflicted category of self-interest and selfishness. Given the incentives and money at stake within the industry, especially as networks compete for more users and adoption, this latest attempt to self-regulate feels a little insincere… If money weren't involved or at stake, the initiative might take on a different look and feel. But given the "winner take all" attitude prevailing in today's crypto climate, the CCA might just be the edge that organizations feel is necessary to put them on a perceived higher moral plane, despite the genuine environmental concerns the industry must address.

I next explore the implications of mining on our broader physical and political environment. Ultimately, this part will conclude by noting that greenhouse gas emissions know no political boundaries.

20

Carbon Footprints

The Bitcoin Dilemma is based on an economic model of the bitcoin mining sector that demonstrates the inexorable link between the price of bitcoin and the energy its mining consumes. I further demonstrated empirically in *The Bitcoin Dilemma* from Chapter 8 that, on average, energy consumption has increased by 0.73% for every 1% price increase. This relationship proved to be both pronounced and statistically significant, even though bitcoin went through a halving event in 2020. Indeed, even with the halving in 2020, the bitcoin price actually rose at a quicker rate than the quantity of bitcoin rewarded declined in all but one year. The price of bitcoin is demand-driven and is completely disconnected from the reward offered to miners.

The incredibly high value of bitcoin dictates its energy consumption. The value of newly-mined bitcoins is essentially usurped in a combination of electricity costs and mining profits when one can secure electricity at rates below what residents and businesses pay. Electricity costs, and the heat it generates, are the prices to pay for bitcoin mining. Neither of these would be significant if bitcoin were valued at a price Satoshi observed while active. Nonetheless, both Satoshi and Finney articulated a concern for Proof of Work mining wastefulness, even at the insignificant levels in the early 2010s. Satoshi observed, "Generation is basically free anywhere that has electric heat, since your computer's heat is offsetting your baseboard electric heating. Many small flats have electric heat out of convenience."[1] The energy intensiveness observed now could scarcely be contemplated then.

---

[1] https://bitcointalk.org/index.php?topic=813.msg9454#msg9454, accessed April 19, 2022.

The dramatic increase in energy consumption since the beginning of bitcoin's corporate era, following the development of the Antminer S9 machine, spans the years in which miners increased collective processing power by a factor of ten, and three to five times the mining efficiency per kilowatt-hour of electricity consumption. Yet energy consumption continued to increase with the price of bitcoin. While bitcoin mining machines are somewhat sensitive to the price of bitcoin, and the used market especially so, the payback period for purchases of these miners nonetheless remained at less than one year typically, and sometimes significantly less. The economic environment is ideal for a free entry perfectly competitive miner arms race using electricity as the ammunition.

This bitcoin mining arms race is amplified by the nature of mining innovation. The price of miners acts as an upfront sunk cost that a new miner would have to overcome before net profits become positive. However, if such a payback period is relatively short, or if robust miner rental markets exist, miner prices do not significantly constrain mining growth. Nor are such costs relevant once a miner has already committed to mining. Miners continue to operate when revenues exceed electricity costs. If one were to abandon mining because of a lack of profitability, the salvage value of the miner would depend on whether another operation could profitably place the miner back into service. The main determinant of mining profits is not the fixed costs of machine purchases, but the variable cost of electricity.

Miners routinely appeal to online calculators that calculate the level of gross profits, net of their variable cost of electricity that one can expect at various costs of electricity. The industry well-understands that the determining factor of both profitability and energy consumption is a combination of bitcoin price, for which increases in the price raises energy consumption, and electricity costs, regardless of miner energy efficiency.

Recall gross profits from mining do not arise because of miner scarcity or an ability for the market to reach equilibrium. Instead, profits are simply a rent one receives by having access to electricity at a rate lower than the electricity price sufficient to break even in mining. A miner can be profitably operated at any electricity cost at or below the cutoff energy cost c^*:

$$\text{Cutoff energy cost } c* = b P_0 Q_0 e^{(g-f)t} / M* \qquad (20.1)$$

Those with energy costs below c^* then divert the electricity costs avoided to pure profit. In other words, profits arise solely because of electricity advantages. Offering a concession of a share of total energy at a lower cost c simply grants these operators a greater profit of (c^* − c) for each kilowatt-hour they consume. Of course, by diverting power to such operations results in higher electricity prices shared by the remainder of ratepayers, at least at a rate equal to the profits of miners, assuming the utility can obtain sufficient additional power no higher than the default rate c^*. In essence, other ratepayers pay for mining profits that arise when mining diverts cheap power to their own operations.

If, instead, the utility must purchase additional and more expensive energy at high effective retail prices than the cutoff energy cost c^*, ratepayers pay an even greater additional burden and hence subsidize miners even more. This net cost to other consumers of electricity was estimated by Benetton et al. (2021) for New York State. They determined from 2019 data that increases in electricity rates as a consequence of the bitcoin presence of $165 million for residents and $79 million for commercial users per year. Nationwide, Benetton et al. determined that ratepayers across the country pay an additional one billion dollars annually in electricity costs because of the supply that is diverted to bitcoin mining.

The discussion shows that the dynamics of mining are more nuanced than they may appear to the casual observer. Over the long run we expect the cost of mining, in both miners and electricity, to approximate their revenue. But that conclusion represents the zero-profit free entry condition, and it is defined by the most expensive energy source that can be profitably mined. For instance, the free entry condition for the most common S9 miner required a maximum electricity cost of $0.10 per kwh early in 2022. On the other hand, a state-of-the-art Antminer S19 could profitably mine at $0.30 per kilowatt-hour power cost given their greater energy efficiency by a factor of more than three, when the price of bitcoin is $45,000, net of a mining pool commission of 1%.

Put another way, the Antminer S9 machine can profitably operate in many areas of the United States. The average electricity cost is $0.1042, which would make the world's most common miner unprofitable, but the S9 is typically profitable for any region with slightly lower than average cost or if the operator is able to recycle heat generated from miners. These S9 miners would be expected to migrate to only the lower cost regions.

Let us assume a miner has excess capacity at a mining farm with access to electricity at, for example, $0.06. The operation would ensure that all its highest efficiency miners are operating. Should it also plug in any spare S9 miners? Absolutely, since the supply price is lower than the Antminer S9 breakeven price c^* of $0.10. A mining farm with surplus S9 machines that cannot operate affordably at a price higher than $0.10 ought to sell these surplus machines at whatever market price that can be obtained, unless the operator decides to retain these older devices in the hope that the bitcoin price will rise. If it does sell these units, they will be purchased by a farm that has a lower power cost than c^*, and hence could run the miners profitably.

The S9 machine is thus what economists call the marginal machine. Miners that can produce the same processing power as the S9 with less energy are then able to pocket as gross profits the energy savings per unit of processing power. If we define the number of miners as the industry capacity for S9 machines, each S19 miner would be equivalent to about three S9 machines, but at an equivalent power cost per hour of only one S9 machine. The S19 miner receives as a profit from the energy avoided of two S9 miners. Greater efficiency does not result in reduced energy consumption. Instead, it results in increased profits, at the expense of other rate payers who cannot then access low-cost electricity because of mining demand.

> **The Energy Consumption and Carbon Footprint of Bitcoin Mining**
>
> Cambridge Center for Alternative Finance constructs a *Cambridge Bitcoin Electricity Consumption Index* that makes a best estimate of total worldwide energy consumption based on its research of the mix of mining machines manufactured and employed in the industry. They estimate that the industry consumes 150 terawatt-hours annually,[2] equivalent to the annual consumption of a top-twenty five electricity consuming nation.
>
> This electricity consumption is equivalent to 41 medium-sized coal power plants, each which produces an average of 3.5 terawatt-hours of electricity each year. Globally, there are about 8,500 coal plants, and they collectively produce 9,440 terawatt-hours of electricity per year, representing 40% of global electricity production. These plants contribute 10.1 gigatonnes of carbon dioxide emissions,[3] which is equivalent to about a third of the emissions from generation of the world's electricity and a fifth of human-made greenhouse gasses.[4]
>
> Coal power plants generate one megatonne of carbon dioxide emissions per terawatt-hour of electricity produced.[5] The carbon dioxide emissions that could be avoided from a reduction of 142.4 terawatt-hours of electricity devoted to bitcoin production in April of, 2022, represents a reduced carbon footprint of 142 million metric tonnes of carbon dioxide annually.

Because each nation hosting significant bitcoin mining also operates coal-fired power plants, the diversion of sustainable energy to bitcoin production

---

[2] https://ccaf.io/cbeci/index, retrieved April 7, 2022.
[3] https://www.iea.org/reports/global-energy-co2-status-report-2019/emissions, accessed February 13, 2022.
[4] https://en.wikipedia.org/wiki/Coal-fired_power_station, accessed February 13, 2022.
[5] U.S. EPA (2019), "Greenhouse Gas Reporting Program Industrial Profile: Power Plants Sector," https://www.epa.gov/sites/default/files/2020-12/documents/power_plants_2017_industrial_profile_updated_2020.pdf, accessed April 7, 2022.

maintains demand that keeps coal production online well past the point they would have otherwise been decommissioned. Unless a bitcoin farm is totally powered by its own proprietary non-fossil fuel energy source, if it is on the grid, it is preventing nations from closing 41 coal power plants worldwide.

Once the trend in expected bitcoin prices analyzed earlier are combined with reward halving, we see a general upward trend in energy consumption that could reasonably exceed 160 terawatt-hours per year by 2030. The equivalent level of coal-fired power plants that may need to be retained to accommodate overall electricity demand as a consequence of the rise in bitcoin mining equates to fifty three coal-fired plants by 2030.

Figure 20.1 shows that expected industry projections in the price of bitcoin results in a continuous increase in global energy consumption. These calculations are based on two competing measures of mining industry electricity consumption. Diginomics typically yields a larger level of consumption, but most experts rely on the more refined Cambridge Energy Consumption Index (CECI) estimate. The latter more conservative index estimates 117.4 terawatt-hours of mining electricity consumption as of December of 2021. Based on *The Bitcoin Dilemma* model, the bitcoin price extrapolation, the reward divisions, and CECI estimates of electricity consumption, expected electricity demand is predicted to rise to 161 TWh/s by 2030, a further 37% increase in consumption. This greater energy consumption is equivalent to an additional 12 medium-sized coal power plants, based on emissions of one metric tonne of carbon dioxide per megawatt of electricity generated by coal powered generation plants, each generating an average of 3.5 TWh of electricity annually.[6,7,8]

Note also that, while the constant innovations in the industry do not decrease electricity consumption, the obsolescence of older machines also creates electronic waste of 31.57 metric tonnes per year, as documented by Digiconomist.[9]

On the contrary, Proof of Stake mining requires as few as a handful of trusted miners. Recall that blocks of bitcoin were originally mined using ordinary personal computers that could perform the hash function at a rate in the millions rather than the tens of trillions of hashes per second. Were a single trusted PC, or a modern Antminer S9 ASIC to mine blocks, one

---

[6] Generated from data from https://en.wikipedia.org/wiki/Coal_power_in_the_United_States, accessed March 9, 2022.
[7] https://www3.epa.gov/ttnchie1/conference/ei20/session5/mmittal.pdf, accessed April 7, 2022.
[8] https://www.mcginley.co.uk/news/how-much-of-each-energy-source-does-it-take-to-power-your-home/bp254/#:~:text=A%20standard%20500%20megawatt%20coal,around%204%2C750%20pounds%20of%20coal, accessed April 7, 2022.
[9] https://digiconomist.net/bitcoin-energy-consumption/, retrieved on February 26, 2022.

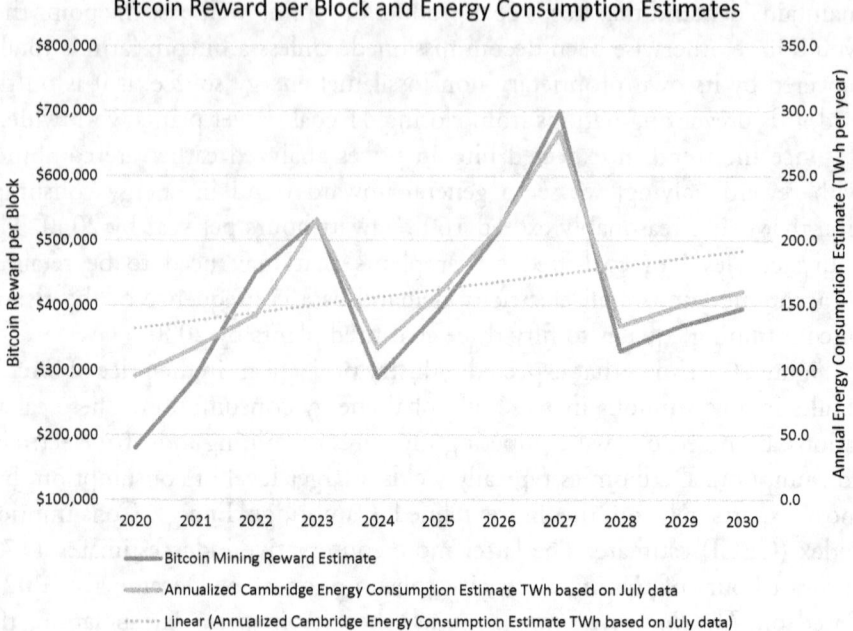

Fig. 20.1 Projections of bitcoin energy consumption

such trusted machine could easily meet all the needs of bitcoin supply. Likewise, the mining of ether using the new Ethereum Proof of Stake protocol with a block size eight times as large and block interval 50 times faster than bitcoin can be mined with but a small network of ASICs and contribute an insignificant amount to global warming.

21

Greenwashing in the Bitcoin Industry

Hal Finney was concerned about carbon dioxide emissions in the early stage of bitcoin. He commented, "Thinking about how to reduce CO2 emissions from a widespread Bitcoin implementation.[1] He understood the bitcoin mining industry inevitably and unavoidably suffers from *The Bitcoin Dilemma* that electricity consumption from mining is proportional to the price of bitcoin. The vast majority of bitcoin commentators are confident that the price of bitcoin will rise as it has in the past, at a rate much faster than the corresponding half-life decay of mining rewards in bitcoin. The result is increased electricity demand over time and increased overall carbon emissions, as described earlier. Falling miner prices merely exacerbates this trend toward greater electricity consumption. Yet, like the robot HAL that took on a mind of its own in *2001—A Space Odyssey*, so too has bitcoin proven to be resilient to attempts to modify its energy consumption intensity. Satoshi noted, "The nature of bitcoin is such that once version 0.1 was released, the core design was set in stone for the rest of its lifetime."[2]

The industry surely understands the implications of higher bitcoin prices on energy consumption, but they often offer false hope that innovations in

---

[1] https://twitter.com/halfin/status/1153096538?ref_src=twsrc%5Etfw%7Ctwcamp%5Etweetembed%7Ctwterm%5E1153096538%7Ctwgr%5E%7Ctwcon%5Es1_&ref_url=https%3A%2F%2Fwww.independent.co.uk%2Fclimate-change%2Fnews%2Fbitcoin-cryptocurrency-bad-mining-environment-b2041420.html, accessed March 26, 2022.

[2] https://bitcointalk.org/index.php?topic=195.msg1611#msg1611, retrieved February 7, 2022.

miner efficiency will result in a reduced energy consumption and carbon footprint over time. For instance, the chip making giant Intel recently promised reductions in bitcoin mining energy consumption that should result in their new design of a chip that can more efficiently mine the SHA-256 bitcoin protocol.[3] In addition, bitcoin mining advocates who recently testified to a U.S. House of Congress committee hearing made a similar claim.[4] Miner manufacturer Canaan's Senior Vice President Edward Lu recently gave a speech entitled "Clean Energy: The New Revolution Of Bitcoin Mining," in which he claimed:

> Sustainable bitcoin mining is related to the future of human society, and the key lies in the construction of more advanced energy-efficient technologies and green mining infrastructure, as well as continued increase in the proportion of renewable energy use.[5]

Such claims defy economic theory and an econometric analysis of the correlation between bitcoin prices and energy consumption. *The Bitcoin Dilemma* shows that increased miner efficiency will merely further fuel the miner arms race and will result in more miners sold, and profits for Intel, Bitmain and Canaan, but with no commensurate decrease in electricity consumption miner industry-wide. Indeed, if the advertised cost of miners fall per kilowatt of power capacity, as Intel promises, electricity consumption may actually rise.

Even if a bitcoin mine derive all its power from a proprietary solar, wind, hydro, tidal, geothermal, or nuclear source rather than from the grid with its mix that includes fossil fuel plants, consumers are deprived of these sustainable sources that could have otherwise been deployed to reduce our reliance on fossil fuels. Ultimately, every electricity user shares some responsibility for continued dependency on fossil fuels and we all must explore how we

---

[3] Senior Intel Vice President Raja Koduri stated "We are mindful that some blockchains require an enormous amount of computing power, which unfortunately translates to an immense amount of energy. Our customers are asking for scalable and sustainable solutions, which is why we are focusing our efforts on realizing the full potential of blockchain by developing the most energy-efficient computing technologies at scale." https://www.intel.com/content/www/us/en/newsroom/opinion/thoughts-blockchain-custom-compute-group.html, retrieved February 20, 2022.

[4] Expert witness Gregory Zerzan of law firm Jordan Ramis, "As the technology evolves it should be expected that the systems will become more energy efficient." Witness to HEARING ON "CLEANING UP CRYPTOCURRENCY: THE ENERGY IMPACTS OF BLOCKCHAINS," January 20, 2022, https://energycommerce.house.gov/committee-activity/hearings/hearing-on-cleaning-up-cryptocurrency-the-energy-impacts-of-blockchains, retrieved February 20, 2022.

[5] https://bitcoinmagazine.com/business/canaan-announces-a-new-bitcoin-asic-and-green-mining, accessed April 8, 2022.

can meet our electricity needs while we reduce our carbon footprint. From the perspective of crypto authentication, we must inevitably compare the efficiency of Proof of Work mining to its Proof of Stake alternative.

Smoke and Mirrors

Another argument often heard is that bitcoin farms tap energy from wind or solar power that the electric grid is unable to absorb at some times of the day. The inability of our grid to efficiently store and transport electricity is solved by a better grid and more extensive use of battery farms and pumped hydroelectric storage, not by more bitcoin mining.

Others claim that by adding a load to a grid, a bitcoin farm can somehow act as a battery for the grid. This highly misleading statement is a distortion of the opportunity for a bitcoin mine to participate in a voluntary load shedding program. Under such a program, a mining farm agrees to reduce their load when electricity demand is too high.

For instance, Mike Levitt, the Chief Executive Officer of Core Scientific, a large bitcoin mining operation that consumes roughly 500 megawatts of power, claimed that "We have arrangements with the communities and utilities wherein; when the grid needs it, we will down power…If we get a call from one of the utility companies in the geographies where we operate who need 30 megawatts available from two to five o'clock today, we put the machines into sleep mode, and it's literally a keystroke because we have a software program that manages the 160,000-plus mining rigs…Our industry really can quite legitimately, effectively and uniquely release energy utilization to the grid; it's almost as if we're acting as a battery." Levitt noted that utilities must often rely on peaker natural gas plants when electricity demand is high. He added that "Generally speaking, those peaker facilities are the old ones and the dirty ones and the expensive ones."[6]

The industry is taking credit for reduced demand for the costliest of power across the spectrum of commonly used generation facilities by claiming they may be willing to turn their miners off if need be, usually as part of a voluntary power shedding plan. They do not add that they are compensated well for their load shedding. However, there would be no need for such peaker plants had their load not been taxing the grid in the first place. To imagine that reducing a load that need not exist is somehow environmentally good is a form of greenwashing that defies logic. A mining farm willing to shed

---

[6] https://www.coindesk.com/business/2022/03/25/greener-bitcoin-mining-could-be-chinas-trillion-dollar-present-to-the-us/, accessed March 26, 2022.

load as part of a voluntary load shedding program and be paid well for that concession by the utility is preferable by the miner to involuntary brownouts without compensation. Such participation in compensated load shedding programs is not altruistic, especially since blockchain processing can be done in environmentally benign ways without the massive power consumption.

Similarly, mining farms claim that, by relying on flared methane at distant natural gas wellheads, they are reducing methane emissions. It is true that combustion of methane in diesel generators, at a thermal efficiency of about 30%, is better than emitting raw methane into the atmosphere. However, flaring is designed to convert those methane emissions to less damaging but still problematic carbon dioxide, based on the science that methane gas is between 20 and 40 times more damaging than carbon dioxide. After a number of years, methane (CH_4 molecules) combines with oxygen in the atmosphere to eventually convert to carbon dioxide and water according to:

$$CH_4 + 2O_2 \rightarrow CO_2 + 2H_2O$$

Under good conditions, flaring is of similar efficiency as natural gas combustion in a diesel generator in its conversion of methane to carbon dioxide. However, a far better alternative for stranded gas is better well technology, including reinjection of excess gas, or capping if the well is obsolete. In addition, burning a fossil fuel through flare gas conversion to electric power at a 30% efficiency remains inferior to use of the same fossil fuel in a state-of-the-art natural gas cogeneration plant that can operate at between 60% and 80% thermal efficiency, depending on the degree to which waste heat can be used by adjoining facilities. The long-term solution is improved well capping or more effective natural gas retrieval as described by Bamji (2021), not by bitcoin mining.

Carbon Credits

Finally, mining farms that employ fossil fuel based energy, either directly or indirectly through their participation on the grid, sometimes claim that their fossil fuel consumption and resulting greenhouse gas emissions are offset through the purchase of carbon credits. The concept is that, by purchasing the credit, they enable some technology that will remove an equal amount of carbon dioxide from the atmosphere. Since mining is ongoing, such credits must be constantly repurchased, not just once to make a public relations statement to appease critics.

There remains a great deal of controversy about carbon market credits. Such carbon capture may merely represent a promise not to cut or burn down a forest. The policing of carbon markets in their infancy is insufficient to ensure that the same preserved forest is not sold multiple times over or may have gone unharvested regardless of the carbon credit market. Indeed, a poorly managed forest may actually result in carbon emissions over time as over-mature trees eventually fall and decay into carbon dioxide and methane, while some carbon-based materials may remain in the soil. A forest managed for true carbon sequestration would need trees to be selectively cut before they become over-mature and die and have the lumber sequestered in the form of building materials for homes and other products.

Alternately, there are new technologies for carbon capture, perhaps pumped into underground wells, or carbon sequestration by converting the carbon into limestone or other stable materials. Or, the carbon dioxide could be converted into a green fuel that could be substituted for the extraction of fossil fuels. Regardless, the price of true carbon sequestration is currently in the neighborhood of $700 per metric tonne of carbon dioxide. The price of sequestration must fall by 90%, to a more feasible $71 per metric tonne, consistent with carbon taxes proposed by advisors to the Biden Administration, and almost half Canada's goal of a $134 per metric tonne carbon tax by 2030.[7] The resulting additional price that a fossil fuel should charge ensures that their greenhouse gas emission externality is then internalized. Such a carbon tax would cause fossil fuels to be prohibitively expensive compared to solar, wind and nuclear power, but fossil fuels could remain in demand by miners desperate for power and profits.

Satoshi designed the bitcoin protocol to ensure that the cost of corrupting the bitcoin blockchain would exceed the advantages of doing so. In Satoshi's day, a block reward was valued in pennies and reached only $0.43 when Satoshi left the public eye, and had risen to $1.56 when collaborators received no more private correspondences. The reward is measured in hundreds of thousands of dollars now, with electricity the hostage in the Prisoners' Dilemma bitcoin mining creates. The fundamental unit of account of bitcoin mining is the price of electricity in cents per kilowatt-hour, while the kilowatt-hours depend on the intensity of mining activity.

Miners understand well the breakeven electricity cost that determines whether mining is profitable. This cost is currently a bit below the national

---

[7] https://foreignpolicy.com/2021/11/29/canada-carbon-pricing-club-theory-climate-imf/#:~:text=First%20implemented%20in%202019%2C%20the,per%20metric%20ton%20by%202030., accessed March 21, 2022.

average of electricity costs to businesses and residences, which means bitcoin mining is unprofitable unless power is cheaper.

> **A Summary of Bitcoin Mining Economics**
>
> The United States now has the greatest market share of bitcoin mining worldwide, and New York State has a plurality of mining among the states. Consider the mining economics in New York State. Electricity generation by resource is shown in Fig. 21.1. The blended electricity cost per kilowatt-hour for residences and businesses at the time of writing is $0.177. This represents the average cost of electricity sufficient to cover the costs of electricity generation using various energy sources, with a fair rate of return to energy providers as approved by the state's Public Service Commission. Industrial users are offered a subsidized marginal cost of $0.065. While bitcoin miners are often able to secure even more deeply subsidized rates, let us assume that they must pay the industrial rate.
>
> As a consequence of this quirk in pricing, such bitcoin farms often receive an electricity subsidy of the difference between the average blended residential/commercial rate and the industrial rate of an amount $0.112 per kilowatt-hour. Miner rewards are approximately $0.111 per kilowatt-hour of electricity consumed, based on the current estimated mix of mining machines employed. When compared to the current value of bitcoin mining, this leaves a profit to miners of $0.046, based on the likely mix of miners in New York State. Goodkind et al. (2020) estimate environmental and health damages of $0.49 for every dollar of bitcoin mining rewards in the U.S. This converts to the equivalent premium $0.054 per kilowatt-hour of electricity consumed. When added to the electricity subsidy of $0.112, this results in total costs of $0.166 per $0.046 of gross profits garnered by miners
>
> New York State depends on natural gas peaker plants for about 15% of its power. Bitcoin currently represents about 15% of electricity demand in the state, so the additional $0.066 in extra power costs per kilowatt-hour as fossil-fueled peaker plants are kept online is paid by ratepayers, not by fixed price bitcoin mining electricity consumers. Finally, holders of bitcoin also pay for mining electricity and profits because $0.111 reward offered miners per kilowatt-hour of electricity consumed is a dilution in the value of their bitcoin holdings, just as inflation is paid by those holding any currency.
>
> The sum of these costs is then $0.343, compared to miner profits of $0.046 per kilowatt-hour diverted to bitcoin mining. Societal mining costs exceed miner profits by a ratio of 7:45 to 1. For every dollar of mining reward, others pay $7:45. The more electricity diverted, the worst the burden is on other members of the economy. Using these benchmarks, and compared to total annualized electricity consumption worldwide on April 29, 2022, of 150 TWh, bitcoin mining costs $52 billion globally. The average bitcoin transaction then costs the economy more than $500 all-in, based on 95 million transactions annually, and is paid by all members of the economy.

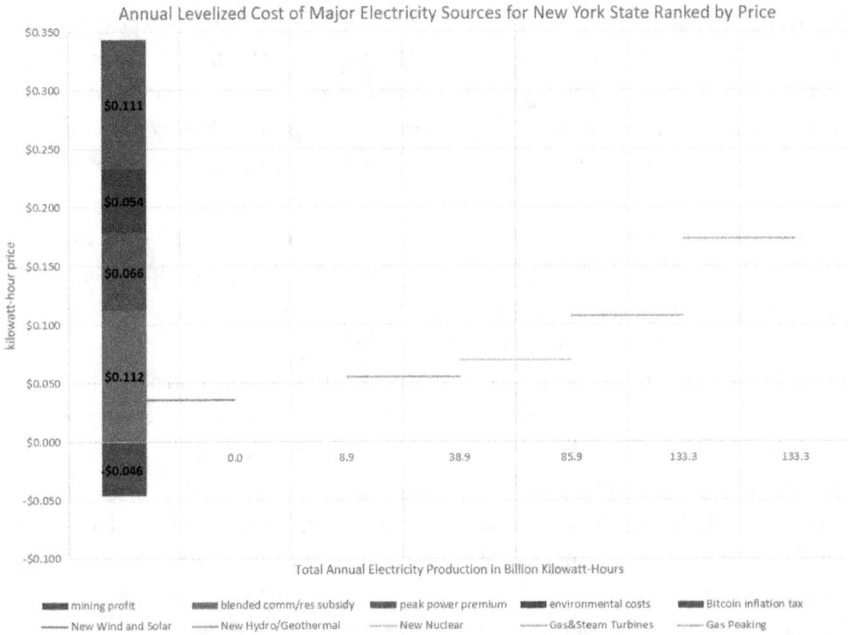

Fig. 21.1 Energy costs for various power sources in New York state, ranked by cost

The bitcoin mining industry insists that they rely more on sustainable energy than other sectors of the economy and have quoted sustainable power as fueling 40% to 75% of bitcoin activity,[8] but mining farms do so by denying other ratepayers access to such cheap and sustainable energy. This exacerbates *The Bitcoin Dilemma*.

To derive Fig. 21.1 that shows how bitcoin mining may profit in New York State compared to the costs it imposes on the economy, I used 2020 data from the Energy Information Agency of the U.S. Government and EIA data for the most extensive bitcoin mining state's electricity consumption and production patterns. The nature of the electricity industry is that there are a number of technologies. Figure 21.1 that represent new sources of power that have high initial costs but, once installed yield the lowest operating costs in the industry. These include new wind, hydroelectric, solar, and next generation nuclear plants. The industry is evolving toward investment in these technologies over time, regardless of the energy needs of any one sector. As electricity

---

[8] https://www.nytimes.com/interactive/2021/09/03/climate/bitcoin-carbon-footprint-electricity.html, retrieved March 9, 2022.

demand increases, for whatever reason, the industry is forced to expand their reliance on legacy fossil fuel plants to the right of the figure, which require construction of new natural gas plants, return online of obsolete coal plants, and the occasional use of natural gas peak power plants. Hence, new demand inevitably relies on fossil fuel power, with its commensurate high-marginal cost.

I show these ranked sources from least to most expensive, moving left to right on the graph. The graph includes these costs on the most expensive energy forms, natural gas generation, coal- fired plants, and peak power plants, adjusted for current natural gas and coal prices.

If bitcoin mining is able to extract an increasing share of renewable resources, especially from hydroelectricity or wind energy, it displaces other users who are then forced to purchase more expensive power that also create greenhouse gasses. More problematic is the lower price that mining farms secure. According to the economic model, lower negotiated electricity costs actually increased the number of miners, the industry processing capacity, and electricity consumption. In other words, less expensive renewable energy diverted to mining further accelerates the bitcoin arms race and worsens the effects of *The Bitcoin Dilemma*. The model predicts that the lower mining farm electricity rate further displaces other electricity users and results in an increase in electricity consumption from fossil fuels. If the mining industry is greener than average, the overall economy becomes substantially less green.

To the left of Fig. 21.1 is an estimate for the level of gross profits garnered by the bitcoin mining industry in New York State, expressed on the primary unit of measure for bitcoin profits, the cost and profit per kilowatt-hour of power secured. If the electricity cost offered miners is the average statewide industrial rate of $0.065 per kilowatt-hour, I calculate an average gross profit per kilowatt-hour consumed of $0.046. Note the subsidy offered to miners, calculated as the difference between the blended residential/commercial price other ratepayers pay and bitcoin miners pay, is $0.112, which is more than twice the profit rate of mining alone. In addition, about 15% of all electricity production fueled by natural gas generating plants produces the estimated amount of electricity the New York State bitcoin mining industry consumes.

Lazard publishes a regularly updated report on the levelized cost of various electricity sources. A revision of their assumption of a natural gas cost of $3.45 per Million British Thermal Units (MMBTU) and a thermal efficiency rating of 30% results in a peaker plant levelized electricity cost of $0.243, based on current natural gas prices. This results in an additional implicit subsidy of $0.066 per kilowatt-hour as states must retain obsolete plants.

Goodkind et al. (2020) determined that $0.49 of environmental and health costs are incurred in the United States for every $1.00 of bitcoin mined. This adds another $0.054 of social costs to the cost of mining. Finally, the owners of bitcoin ultimately pay for the cost of mining as well because every dollar of bitcoin mined results in a one dollar dilution in the collective value of existing bitcoin holders. This is similar to the inflation tax we all suffer when our currency is diluted through an expansion of the money supply. This cost adds another $0.111 to the cost of bitcoin mining.

When these various implicit costs are added up, they show that $0.343 is incurred by ratepayers, citizens, and bitcoin holders for every $0.046 generated in gross miner profit. Miners get rich but the economy overall is poorer by a much larger degree. If I then calculate these costs, which are estimated at over $127 million per day as a consequence of bitcoin mining, and compare them to the 254,442 total bitcoin transactions on a recent day, we find that the average bitcoin transaction incurs a cost of $503 on others. This is far in excess of the $0.44 average fee for a debit network transaction and the $25 fee for wire transfers. These bitcoin costs arise solely because of the excessive electricity consumption of Proof of Work mining as a consequence of a high-bitcoin price, as described by *The Bitcoin Dilemma*. If the price of bitcoin were $1.56 as when Satoshi left the bitcoin scene, with daily transactions then at 2,300 per day and a mining reward of 50 bitcoin, the transactions costs then were only about ten times higher than that of a debit card and environmental costs were minimal. Even so, Satoshi's primary goal was to increase transaction volume and bring down transaction costs to offer savings over debit and credit cards. At today's transaction volume, and the price of bitcoin in Satoshi's day, this cost would be less than five cents per transaction.

Using 2019 data for New York State recall that Benetton et al. (2021) calculated the cost of mining activity on residential and commercial power users to be $244 million annually because of the implicit subsidies offered miners and the necessity to secure additional power at higher costs. Ratepayers in the United States were estimated to pay an additional $1 billion annually because of bitcoin mining. Globally by 2030, I estimate that electricity demand will rise by an additional 43.1 TWh from bitcoin mining alone over 2021 values. In addition, *The Bitcoin Dilemma* model shows greenhouse gas emissions will rise by 43 million metric tonnes annually by the end of the decade.

The United States Becomes the World's Mining Haven

The United States has a greater share of fossil-fueled electricity generation compared to China. Following China's bitcoin mining ban, the industry has witnessed a dramatic migration of mining to the U.S.. According to Statistica, almost 60% of mining activity worldwide is concentrated in the U.S.[9]:

Within the U.S., Foundry USA, a mining pool employed commonly by large scale mining farms in the USA, reports the following distribution of mining activity across the states, based on statistics from their member pool[10]:

New York	Kentucky	Georgia	Texas	Nebraska	Other
19.9%	18.7%	17.3%	14.0%	10.4%	19.7%

We have seen a geographical migration by miners toward jurisdictions that offer lower electricity costs or more benign regulation as ways to expand their profits. In net, this migration has moved mining away from nations with substantial sustainable energy, most notably hydropower in China, toward nations such as Kazakhstan at first, until that nation subsequently rolled up its welcome mat. Mining also migrated to the United States that rely substantially on fossil-fueled power plants. As you recall from *The Bitcoin Dilemma* section, profits are proportional to cheap power, but once that inexpensive power is usurped, and other users displaced to higher cost power in each state, miners begin to look for the next best location that offers a combination of power and lax regulation.

Until there is abundant and almost resource-free electricity, no case can be made for the desirability of the bitcoin cryptocurrency from an environmental perspective, especially in light of the availability of competing cryptocurrencies that are environmentally benign and can perform better on every dimension but massive mining profits. Unfortunately, the way Satoshi designed the Bitcoin Protocol results in an extremely high cost for society to bear so that miners are enabled to garner their profits.

The Cost of a Bitcoin Transaction

Bitcoin mining imposes costs on the holders of the coin through dilution, equivalent to the inflation that occurs when monetary authorities print excess notes. Mining forces grids to continue to rely on peaker power, and the maintenance of fossil fuel power plants imposes additional health and environmental costs on the economy. Residential and commercial power users must pay the average

---

[9] https://www.statista.com/statistics/1200477/bitcoin-mining-by-country/, accessed March 7, 2022.
[10] https://www.cnbc.com/2021/10/09/war-to-attract-bitcoin-miners-pits-texas-against-new-york-kentucky.html, retrieved March 7, 2022.

costs of power that increases when miners secure cheaper industrial power on a marginal cost or reduced rate. These various costs were estimated in New York State to total $0.343 per kilowatt-hour consumed in mining.

When one considers the Cambridge Bitcoin Energy Index calculation of annualized mining electricity consumption worldwide of 150 Terawatt-hours per year as of April, 2022, and 92.9 million transactions annually, the total economic costs to support bitcoin mining is $52 million per year, or more than $500 per transaction. While bitcoin can successfully process three to five transactions per second, the Visa network transacts about 5,000 transactions per second in the United States.[11] The average bitcoin transaction cost of over $500 compares to $0.44 for a debit card transaction.

---

[11] https://www.cardrates.com/advice/number-of-credit-card-transactions-per-day-year/, accessed April 29, 2022.

22

Infighting in the Crypto Bros Family

Satoshi created a mechanism for decentralized exchange that yields a decreasing miner reward structure and prophesized that transaction fees will outswamp mining fees by 2040 or 2044, unless a fork is agreed upon that advances this date. Yet, so long as the bitcoin price continues to double faster than rewards halve, mining rewards will continue to be profitable. A coin for which Satoshi was barely exceed a value of $1.00 is expected by some to exceed a valuation of $1 million. For instance, ARK Invest's Cathie Wood stated in her $1 million bitcoin price prognosis that bitcoin "represents only a fraction of the value of global assets amid increasing adoption each year."[1] This valuation would lead to a bitcoin market capitalization in excess of $20 trillion. If so, bitcoin will be a huge speculative play, a vehicle for illicit purchases and a mechanism for money laundering for the world's oligarchs. Meanwhile, mining will continue, funded by fees imposed on transactions once rewards transition away and the energy consumption and global carbon footprint will continue to increase.

Proof of Stake, especially when such a protocol supports an adequate Stablecoin tethered properly to a currency like the U.S. dollar, converts an environmentally problematic methodology to one that has a minimal carbon

---

[1] "Buffet's Recent Investment Supports $1 M Bitcoin Price," *Forbes*, February 17, 2022, https://www.forbes.com/sites/danrunkevicius/2022/02/17/buffetts-shocking-bitcoin-bet-supports-1m-bitcoin-price-prediction-meanwhile-bnb-solana-cardano-xrp-and-ethereum-prices-surge/?sh=4d2571727e6b, accessed April 11, 2022.

© The Author(s), under exclusive license to Springer Nature Switzerland AG 2022
C. L. Read, *The Bitcoin Dilemma*,
https://doi.org/10.1007/978-3-031-09138-4_22

footprint. In doing so, the economy can garner the benefits and efficiencies of digital transactions without the environmental consequences.

Bitcoin remains a refuge for speculators and illicit activity, and it may be more so as other coin become regulated and bitcoin defies regulation. Even novel techniques to properly recycle heat, the other product of mining, are less efficient than other forms of electric heat, such as air-to-air or ground source heat pumps, heat recycling, or co-employment of heat from next generation nuclear power plants. In any regard, such recycling to heat homes and buildings is seasonal, but bitcoin heat production is year-round.

The various coins that use Proof of Stake and other authentication mechanisms use a tiny fraction of the electrical energy of bitcoin, and they also perform better in all important dimensions such as transaction complexity and latency. No coin serves all needs, but it is clear decentralized finance will not rely on bitcoin. The only case to be made for mining bitcoin is the huge profits it generates for miners, but at a much higher cost for the economy.

Satoshi surely could not have appreciated the environmental footprint of a coin that grew faster than anyone could have imagined in the early 2010s. Nor was the planet as aware of global warming to the same extent in 2009 as we are today. The bitcoin creator perhaps recycled part of the heat mining created to warm Satoshi's flat. But, the coin has a unique feature in that it finds its own level. Constrain the coin in one dimension will only cause it to expand in another. Satoshi noted: "Some places where generation will gravitate to (include) (1) places where it's cheapest or free, (2) people who want to help for ideological (sic) reasons, (and) (3) people who want to get some coins without the inconvenience of doing a transaction to buy them."[2]

The incredibly robustness and resistance to modification of the bitcoin protocol is an inconvenient truth for which we now see its implications. Yet, the profit motive remains powerful. Critics remain diligent in debunking the claims of bitcoin advocates that we can have bitcoin and protect the environment at the same time. I demonstrated that the technological innovations in bitcoin mining do not actually reduce the energy consumption as advocates assert. Indeed, continuous miner innovation can actually increase energy consumption. Overall, price is the primary predictor of long-term energy usage, and a price rise, on average, above 17.3% invariably overwhelms the reward halving Satoshi built into the algorithm. The rapid growth in bitcoin prices refutes the claim by Satoshi that a shrinking reward quantity would somehow moderate miner compensation that has only grown over the corporate era.

---

[2] https://bitcointalk.org/index.php?topic=813.msg9454#msg9454, accessed April 19, 2022.

We must remind ourselves too that electricity consumption of any sort represents a share of energy demand. We live in an era of prosperity that treats electricity access as a right. Most of the world's population live in nations that ensure the public is provided electricity at a reasonable cost. These nations provide electricity through a mix of generation methods. Today, sustainable energy in the form of wind and solar power is often the cheapest form once all pecuniary costs are included. Even the newest generation of nuclear power is estimated to produce at reasonably low costs. Legacy fossil fuel generation is typically the most expensive by far, especially when the cost of construction and the non-pecuniary cost of carbon dioxide and pollution are included.

However, too often we compare apples to oranges. We recognize the new investments needed for solar and wind, but the economy invests in new sustainable energy infrastructure only slowly. Instead, we remain reliant on natural gas and coal plants for which fixed investments have long since been recouped. In addition, natural gas and coal remain underpriced by their failure to include the costly greenhouse gas byproducts that they produce. It is also those fossil-fueled electricity generation plants that we must maintain past obsolescence because of the electricity demand by bitcoin miners.

There remains significant political resistance to the perceived travesty of leaving gas, oil, and coal in the ground or decommissioning functional fossil-fueled power plants. Some view this as a squandering of a resource for which they cannot afford. However, such squandering is the nature of any technology for which a backstop is available. Once the cost of using a resource, including the full cost of the environmental damage it may cause, is eclipsed by the lesser cost of a better backstop technology, resources inevitably remain stranded in the ground. This realization and the transition may be difficult for local or national economies that must reinvent themselves around sustainability. But such a transition is inevitable. It is just a matter of when.

The reality that every resource transition leaves unexploited resources in the ground is inherent in the very nature of innovation. When the automobile replaced the horse and buggy, horse farms and buggy manufacturers became obsolete and the wealth they once generated lost. When our economy moves beyond *peak oil*, at a point which new discoveries and existing extraction can no longer keep up with demand, prices rise and creative innovations substitute for oil until these fossil fuels are no longer needed and further extraction is no longer necessary. Inevitably, fossil fuels will become mostly obsolete economically someday, even though they may remain technically viable. Innovation is necessarily displacing.

Finally, if all of our consumption collectively constitutes demand, there is really no such thing as individual users purchasing green power as much as it may assuage our conscience. The electrons that we rent come from a mix of resources that supply the grid. Unless we are off the electric grid or have personally invested in solar power, we constitute part of the overall energy demand mix. And, if we secure a large amount of sustainable power on the grid, presumably in the case of bitcoin miners, at a preferred price, that simply means others do not have access to that power. Instead, coal powered plants are kept online longer than necessary to fuel the excess demand that itself may not be necessary. In such a scenario, none of us are greener than another. We are all part of the problem, and we should all strive to be part of the solution. Indeed, Benetton et al. (2021) show that, when cheap power from the grid is diverted to bitcoin mining, it raises the cost to all others.

Local Solutions

When the City of Plattsburgh, a picturesque and historic urban setting on the shore of Lake Champlain, was inundated with applications from potential bitcoin operators in 2017, it imposed a moratorium to buy some time to research how other communities dealt with various nuisances this industry imposes on its neighbors, workers, and electric providers. In my research as mayor of the City of Plattsburgh at that time, I found no examples of building or safety codes elsewhere to ameliorate these problems bitcoin mining creates. We took six months to promulgate various codes to protect the community from nuisances that arise from mining.

The two provisions that contributed to greater environmental efficiency and economic justice included the successful petition to the New York State Public Service Commission for a new rate structure, called Rider A, and a provision for heat recycling.

Residents and businesses alike in Plattsburgh heat with electricity, typically in the form of electric baseboard resistance heaters or floor space heaters. Indeed, these floor space heaters draw about 1400 watts of power and generate about 5000 British Thermal Units (BTUs) of heat each hour. This consumption of electricity and creation of heat is about the same as an Antminer S9 bitcoin mining machine. While an Antminer S9 certainly creates more noise, it is an equally efficient heat producer, per unit of electricity, as a space heater. One provision in our code was that new mining farms must somehow recycle a portion of the heat they generate that would otherwise be dissipated in the atmosphere or artificially warm a lake or stream.

More recently, a firm named Heatbit began to market home space heaters that run off small bitcoin miners. One can heat a room and have the electricity partially or fully covered by mining revenue.[3] Certainly, such an innovation would be an improvement on dissipation of the heat considered by mining farms to be a waste product. A clever Plattsburgh engineer named Ryan Brienza even designed mining farm cubes that could be placed next to a gymnasium or civic center and provide warmth that would have otherwise been provided by electric resistance heaters.[4] Such recycling would have been a good start in a city that heats with electricity anyway. I note, though, that an even better technology than bitcoin heat recycling would be the installation of heat pumps, which operate between two to three times more efficiently than the resistance heat homes invariably employ.

With a residential electricity price in Plattsburgh of only $0.045 per kilowatt-hour, the economics to convert to heat pumps is not as strong as if residents faced the national average rate of $0.104 per kilowatt-hour. Given that almost everybody heats with electricity in Plattsburgh, in the absence of heat pumps, heat recycling is a reasonable alternative. Many hobby miners heat garages or basements with an S9 machine or two. With the low cost of electricity and the current state of sector economics, homeowners generate bitcoin profits that offset their heating costs, with some profits to spare. The City of Plattsburgh's electric supply is 100% sustainable energy, but with a fixed quota, so miner heat recycling is at least a partial solution that makes more environmental sense than the various greenwashing alternatives offered up by the industry. Heat recycling is an improvement, but not a panacea, and only in the cold season when the heat is needed.

Once Plattsburgh put into place this simple code requirement of heat recycling, it no longer received applications for bitcoin mining farms. The other provision that promoted economic justice was our request for a Rider A promulgated by the State Public Service Commission. Rider A ensured that should our city demand electricity beyond Plattsburgh's fixed 120-Megawatt electricity quota because of cryptocurrency mining, or any similar very high electricity density usage, these users must pay for the cost of additional power purchases at higher spot prices made on their behalf. Before that provision was put in place, expensive energy purchases to meet residents' needs on high consumption days were shared by all ratepayers rather than by the miners that caused the phenomenon in the first place. With the support of the State

---

[3] https://heatbit.com/#preorder, March 18, 2022.
[4] https://www.northcountrypublicradio.org/news/story/40483/20200130/plattsburgh-company-tries-to-keep-cryptocurrency-industry-alive-in-the-city, retrieved March 9, 2022.

of New York Public Service Commission, the ratepayers of the City of Plattsburgh, and similar communities in New York with fixed electricity quotas who have not yet dealt with cryptocurrency mining, could be protected from increased electricity rates as a result.

> **Similar Industries Learn to Recycle Heat and Be Good Neighbors**
>
> Data centers elsewhere have successfully recycled heat, and state regulators can encourage such applications. These data centers perform an essential function without substitutes and differ substantially from bitcoin farms. They generate upwards of fifty times the jobs compared to a mining farm per megawatt of power. In addition, a number of data centers are exploring such heat recycling so they may be good neighbors in their community and good stewards of the earth. For instance, in Odense, Denmark, a Facebook data server center uses excess heat from their machines to heat the adjoining community. Their innovation allows them to heat upwards of 6,900 homes that would have traditionally used fossil fuels for their heat. Likewise, Amazon has been heating one of their corporate buildings in Seattle with excess heat from processing as well.
>
> Being green is not always easy. But it can be worthwhile and profitable, if one looks at the challenges over a longer and broader perspective. Unfortunately, bitcoin miners do not necessarily see the long and broad view in the face of substantial profits for their taking today. Regulators can provide the necessary inducements and allow the farms to capture some of the additional benefits to make it worth their while.

Of course, if one is to supply a mining farm with sustainable energy off the grid of their own construction, the only externality they induce is pecuniary. In other words, they may elevate the price of new sustainable energy construction by the solar and wind equipment for others as they divert resources to themselves. If a farm claims they are off the grid, but rely on their own coal or natural gas power plants or supplies, as venture capitalists are increasingly discovering to insulate themselves from grid dynamics and politics and ensure the steady supply of power regardless of grid condition, such an operation remains part of our fossil fuel consumption mix and our collective greenhouse gas emissions. Even this solution remains part of the problem.

The Industry Pivot

Given the nature of the Bitcoin Proof of Work industry, and the state of the environment, our inability to rid ourselves of fossil fuel power plants, and the existence of viable and superior Proof of Stake coins that are environmentally benign and of much lower transaction costs, no case can be made for bitcoin mining.

Nevertheless, the crypto industry, especially the bitcoin sector, wishes to do whatever they can to divert the discussion away from the inevitable truth described by *The Bitcoin Dilemma*. They attempt to create a sense the industry can police itself so regulators do not impose the same consumer protections and apply the regulatory tools designed to administer sound monetary policy afforded traditional currencies.

To ward off criticism and regulation proactively, a subset of those who enjoy the profits of mining have assembled the *Climate Change Accord* (CCA), in an obvious attempt to attain a modicum of the same respectability the United Nations' Climate Change Initiative has earned under U.N.'s Sustainable Development agency. Surely, any ability for the industry to self-organize and self-police is advantageous for those who wish to deflect the brunt of the public's concern over global warming. Equally certain is the ability of the industry to fund research and develop talking points on behalf of their members so they too may ward off the significant resistance when bitcoin comes to town.

However, this effort by the CCA appears defensive at best and disingenuous at worst. *The Bitcoin Dilemma* demonstrates energy consumption will continue to increase if the bitcoin price can rise faster than rewards decay for at least two more decades. Unless abundant and affordable sustainable energy for all can be developed and made broadly available before then, cheap, and even sustainable, power diverted to Proof of Work mining will result in the prophecy *The Bitcoin Dilemma* predicts. The diversion results in higher energy costs to other ratepayers, as Benetton (2021) found, while the environmental and nuisance costs of $0.49 on the dollar calculated by Goodkind et al. (2020) also burdens citizens. In addition, Fig. 21.1 shows that not only do electricity ratepayers inevitably cover the profits of bitcoin mining, but they also pay a surcharge in addition as high cost and obsolete fossil-fueled power plants are forced to return or remain online to meet mining demand.

The CCA employs a number of arguments in a format and with sufficient confidence that the casual reader may be persuaded. For instance, they note that bitcoin mining currently produces less greenhouse gasses than gold mining and the jewelry industry,[5] even though they dramatically underestimate their greenhouse gas production when compared to research by

---

[5] https://www.businessinsider.in/cryptocurrency/news/what-is-the-crypto-climate-accord/articleshow/83946286.cms, accessed March 7, 2022.

Diginomics.[6] The research group concludes that the bitcoin mining industry actually produces a similar amount of greenhouse gasses as the CCA claims is generated in gold mining and jewelry production.

Even if such a claim was true, it compares apples to oranges. Gold mining and jewelry produces stores of value that last forever and have invaluable tangible uses as well. In fact, Krause (2018) showed that gold mining generates far more product per dollar invested than bitcoin, while Cocco et al. (2019) compared bitcoin and gold mining and demonstrated that bitcoin costs far more than the value created from traditional mining in minerals such as gold.

Bitcoin mining merely encodes a number of paper (or, more correctly, virtual) transactions in a way that can easily and more efficiently be done through existing financial institutions, or, if one wishes to live up to the Cypherpunk ideology, through competing but environmentally benign Proof of Stake cryptocurrencies. Bitcoin is valued primarily because of its hype as a speculative instrument that also affords some anonymity for those transacting illicitly, as Foley (2019) demonstrate.

The CCA also compares itself to the power used in holiday lights and household appliances such as air conditioners. These are human activities to selflessly give joy to others or comfort to ourselves, rather than a method to extract profits to an industry that is incredibly lucrative for the wealthy institutions that dominate bitcoin mining. Meanwhile, other cryptocurrencies employ less costly and more environmentally benign blockchain processing technologies such as Proof of Stake.

Finally, CCA claims it has a smaller carbon footprint than the financial sector as a whole, a sector that includes those who mobilize our mortgages, manage and invest our life savings, and ensure the capital that drives our industries and creative sectors. Obviously, to compare bitcoin mining to such a broad and beneficial brick-and-mortar sector is unwarranted. Equally spurious is the CCA's claim that it uses far less energy than the world's military-industrial complex, as if national defense is an appropriate comparison.

These forty-five companies that subscribe to the CCA accord instead rely on talking points created by the CCA to deflect criticism away from Proof of Work mining, without any willingness to discuss the discontinuation of but one large Proof of Work sector in bitcoin, as Ethereum shifts to Proof of Stake.

---

[6] https://digiconomist.net/bitcoin-energy-consumption/, accessed March 7, 2022.

The CCA knows that they have a greenhouse gas emission public relations problem. They seek refuge in claims they mine only using sustainable sources, even if miners divert to their own use the sustainable energy other ratepayers enjoyed. This diversion creates greenhouse gas emitters out of other ratepayers and necessitates the continuation of fossil fuel plants we hoped to close or by the claim that they purchase carbon credits to offset the damage they cause. They raise other ratepayers' electricity rates by an amount exceeding the profits miners earn.

Indeed, the greatest value of the offsets the bitcoin industry sponsored Crypto Climate Accord (CCA) recommend to *greenwash* their industry are carbon credits. A proper offset must, *on an ongoing basis,* raise the cost of the fossil fuels they consume. Nations have come to realize that such an ongoing carbon tax is politically acceptable if in the order of $70 to $200 per metric tonne of carbon dioxide emissions. Such a carbon tax may someday be sufficient, with an improvement in technology, to truly remove or sequester the carbon emitted in the burning of fossil fuels. However, the CCA knows that to impose such a tax then makes the use of electricity from fossil fuel generation unprofitable.

Recently, *Conservation International* burst the carbon credit myth. An organization since 1987, Conservation International works to better explain to the public how we might best sustain nature and the environment for humanity. In a recent article,[7] they note that the most common carbon credit is in payments to preserve forests. They found over two decades of research that carbon credits to preserve forests could work in principle but rarely does so in practice. While well-intentioned, such a one-time purchase cannot ensure that a forest remains a carbon sink in perpetuity. Indeed, even if it could, a forest must be well-managed to offer an ongoing carbon sink.

In a recent article entitled "The Biggest Crypto Effort to End Useless Carbon Offsets is Backfiring,"[8] Bloomberg reported that while bitcoin miners often take credit for their purchases of carbon offsets, these purchases rarely fulfill their promises. For instance, the sale of a carbon credit by someone who walks to work each day does nothing to reduce the impact arising when the purchaser of the credit is enabled to continue emitting greenhouse gasses. It is impossible to ensure that these markets actually have any effect on reducing emissions.

Even if carbon credit markets functioned as promised, such management would require continual removal of carbon at the height of tree maturity to

---

[7] https://www.conservation.org/blog/3-myths-about-carbon-offsets-busted, retrieved March 7, 2022.
[8] https://www.bloomberg.com/news/articles/2022-04-07/the-biggest-crypto-effort-to-end-useless-carbon-offsets-is-backfiring, accessed April 11, 2022.

ensure that these trees do not over-mature and die, and hence release back into the air some of their carbon in the form of methane and carbon dioxide. One-time payments, perhaps pledged to influence public opinion, invariably fail to meet their promised objectives. Indeed, carbon credits may support forests that would likely have remained in their natural state even in the absence of payments. Instead, these payments seem only to insure against the threat that the forest may be cut down someday.

Many markets instead cap the amount of such offsets a company can employ to ensure that one cannot disingenuously claim that 100% of the fossil fuel emissions created, for instance, by a coal- or natural gas-fired power plant are offset in a way that makes this unnecessary generation of greenhouse gasses environmentally benign.

> **An Industry Response to Greenwashing**
>
> The narrative advanced by the alliance of large bitcoin farm owners has met with resistance within the industry. Locke (2022) reports in a recent article in Fortune, entitled "Bitcoin's Judas,"[9] about how Ripple co-founder Chris Larsen met with a strong backlash at both the issue and personal level when Larsen advocated for a movement away from Proof of Work mining in bitcoin out of a concern for the sector's environmental footprint. Larsen has collaborated with Greenpeace, the Sierra Club, and others who are mounting a campaign to reform and make credible a sector that many now realize damages the environment unnecessarily in a campaign called "Change the Code, Not the Climate."[10] Bitcoin miners object that the recommendation to move bitcoin to Proof of Stake is almost impossible given that it would require the cooperation of those who currently benefit substantially from the current protocol.
>
> Rather than applauded for his common sense, Larsen was attacked personally and accused of attempting to increase interest in Ripple products at the expense of bitcoin. Clearly, the Bitcoin Proof of Work mining sector is under increasing scrutiny for its carbon footprint and the economics of its industry. They appear to prefer to fight than switch, but advocates such as Larsen are concerned that to maintain the Proof of Work stance tarnishes the image of the entire cryptocurrency industry.

Ultimately, there is no escape from the reality of our interconnectedness. Satoshi certainly practiced an ideology of economic decentralization and a profound mistrust of large financial institutions. But such a libertarian or

---

[9] Locke, Taylor (2022), "Bitcoin's 'Judas': The Co-founder of a Rival Cryptocurrency is Pushing for a Green Revolution in Mining. It's Not Going Well," Fortune, April 2, 2022, https://fortune.com/2022/04/02/bitcoin-mining-green-campaign-chris-larsen/?queryly=related_article, accessed April 7, 2022.

[10] Kharif, Olga (2022), "Greenpeace, Crypto Billionaire Lobby to Change Bitcoin Code," Bloomberg, March 28, 2022. https://www.bloomberg.com/news/articles/2022-03-29/greenpeace-crypto-billionaire-lobby-to-change-bitcoin-s-code, retrieved April 11, 2022.

anarchistic streak does not insulate oneself from others. The legal philosopher Zechariah Chafee Jr. wrote an article in June 1919 for the Harvard Law Review with the title "Freedom of Speech in War Time." He asserted an imaginary monologue directed to a judge regarding competing rights:

> Each side takes the position of the man who was arrested for swinging his arms and hitting another in the nose, and asked the judge if he did not have a right to swing his arms in a free country. 'Your right to swing your arms ends just where the other man's nose begins.[11] (emphasis added)

We live in a market society, but one of many imperfections. One such imperfection is our failure to deal with negative externalities, often especially with regard to our actions that damage the environment and especially the generations that follow us. Any burning of hydrocarbons, by those who believe mining with energy derived from a proprietary coal or natural gas source, or from those displaced and must then collectively rely on fossil fuels, or even those miners who may do the displacing, all share in the net outcome. As an environmental and energy professor, I appreciate this interdependence and find unhelpful the folly of advocates who greenwash in a way that confuses and diverts our attention.

Someday, fusion promises to provide abundant and practically inexhaustible energy that may be inexpensive and does not produce radioactive byproducts. I recall back in 1980 when I was studying the physics of alternative energy in college that the promise of fusion was but a generation away. Fusion still remains a generation away, but there has been much interest and progress lately. Only time will tell. Hope, though, is not a solution.

Our best opportunity to combat global warming is not to hope for better technologies, but instead to evaluate the consumptive technologies we use daily and ensure that we are consuming what we need, but no more. Under that rubric, those who promote bitcoin mining to maintain and expand their own economic profits are irresponsible. Bitcoin mining is unnecessary when compared with other digital currencies that can perform better, and do so without the vast carbon footprint of bitcoin.

As this book approaches its final section, I note that there exist technologies to propel us into the digital era Satoshi envisioned, but without the environmental consequences we now well understand. The Gospel of Profit, so compelling to some, should not compel a collective irresponsibility. We can have our cake and eat it too, but perhaps without the vast profits

---

[11] https://quoteinvestigator.com/2011/10/15/liberty-fist-nose/, retrieved February 25, 2022.

earned by some who advocate for self-serving reasons to retain a technology of consequences Satoshi could not have imagined.

Part VI

The Rewriting of the Cryptocurrency Bible

The benefits of cryptocurrency usage are substantial, if not perhaps as revolutionary as Satoshi hoped. The libertarian Cypherpunk Manifesto was based on a reasonable belief that people should be free to interact and transact, so long as they do not detract from the liberty and well-being of others. The cryptocurrency industry must develop in a way that allows it to realize Satoshi's vision, but not in a way that harms others and its own aspirations in the process.

Problems arise because of the externalities inherent in the inherent design of the bitcoin algorithm, and because the financial institutions Satoshi hoped to make obsolete are replaced by new and equally wealthy and powerful institutions, but without the layer of regulations designed to protect consumers. Indeed, the traditional financial institutions and investment banks Satoshi abhorred now own a significance share of the bitcoin world. While regulation cannot isolate bitcoin, it must anticipate the regulatory needs of an entire industry that did not exist a dozen years earlier and began to burgeon just in the last few years.

Crypto regulators would be challenging enough in the best of times. The industry that is highly technical and has complicated economics, and which also earns such exorbitant profits that facilitate transactions globally. The last part of this book looks at ways to navigate the regulatory abyss and rewrite the fate of cryptocurrencies.

Commentators note that bitcoin is not a phenomenon in isolation, but is rather part of a bigger movement that is by its constitution opposed to regulation. Tiffany (2022) observes that while the Web3 movement is considered a fad by some and a scam by others, it is a structural shift away from how we traditionally interact. Obsolete are typical web platforms such as social media. They are proposed to be replaced by new proprietary ways to communicate, exchange, make payments, and store information in an incorruptible way.

The term Web3 was introduced by Ethereum co-founder Gavin Wood in a classic 2014 essay. In an interview with Wired magazine in 2021, Wood noted the short definition of Web3 is "Less trust, more truth." He added,

> I have a particular meaning of trust that's essentially faith. It's the belief that something will happen, that the world will work in a certain way, without any real evidence or rational arguments as to why it will do that. So we want less of that, and we want more truth—which what I really mean is a greater reason to believe that our expectations will be met... I think trust in itself is actually just a bad thing all around. Trust implies that you are you're placing some sort of authority in somebody else, or in some organization, and they will be able to use this authority in some arbitrary way. As soon as it becomes credible trust, it's not really trust anymore. There is a mechanism, a rationale, an argument, a logical mechanism—whatever—but in my mind, it's not trust.[1]

Tiffany chronicled the hostile reception Web3 has received in social media, but also noted the incivility of participants on such online forums as Reddit. Commentators characterize those with whom they don't agree as fools and continually strive to sanitize the bitcoin illusion by using the refrain "this is good for bitcoin" and emphasize "*Crypto Bros*' unflagging faith". She quoted Hilary Allen, an American University law professor, who observed "If (Web3 creates) a dot.com bubble, it sucks for the people who invested, but if it's (like) 2008, then we're all screwed, even those of us who aren't investing, and that's not fair." When Tiffany challenged Wood with these comments, Wood responded that people are just afraid of change, as with any major shift. "First, there's the builders, the people who are building the next generation of stuff. (Then there's a broader group of influential people who) "think quite deeply about how it is that they're living lives... (They will) largely drag along the rest of the population." Tiffany comments this "dragging along" is what people resent.

Petrik (2021) described the tendency of sites such as Reddit to heighten controversy by acting as a shill for cryptocurrencies and by removing dissenting opinions. Reddit participants call for "friends and relatives to get on board." The author professes to appreciate cryptocurrencies but laments the cult-like behavior and excessive euphoria in what is ultimately

---

[1] https://www.wired.com/story/web3-gavin-wood-interview/, accessed April 11, 2022.

a winner-takes-it-all endeavor. He advocates for more responsibility to avoid "Shitcoins."

Corbet et al. (2019) add that negative news such as bitcoin's employment in illicit activity, or bitcoin bans can cause the price of bitcoin and its altcoins to fall, as can the imposition of regulation. These challenges call into question the legitimate role of cryptocurrency as an investment asset class.

Some early cryptocurrency pioneers have since reevaluated the crypto proposition. Bambrough (2021) notes that Dogecoin founder Jackson Palmer, who created a tongue-in-cheek Dogecoin, only to find it valued at $25 billion, and within the top 15 coins, claimed the current crypto market is now "an inherently right-wing, hyper-capitalist technology built primarily to amplify the wealth of its proponents through a combination of tax avoidance, diminished regulatory oversight and artificially enforced scarcity" and

> The cryptocurrency industry leverages a network of shady business connections, bought influencers and pay-for-play media outlets to perpetuate a cult-like "get rich quick" funnel designed to extract new money from the financially desperate and naïve. Financial exploitation undoubtedly existed before cryptocurrency, but cryptocurrency is almost purpose-built to make the funnel of profiteering more efficient for those at the top and less safeguarded for the vulnerable.

This statement is certainly contrary to the Gospel of Satoshi, and the ideals of the original cypherpunks. Bambrough reports the CEO of the bitcoin and cryptocurrency exchange Coinbase retorts "crypto is simply providing an alternative for people who want more freedom" while bitcoin has "made so many people wealthy… (and has leveled) the playing field, at least to some degree." *Crypto Bros* conflate altruistic libertarianism with the individualist right to amass wealth. In addition, the leveling of the playing field occurs not from their mining wealth that makes the rest of us poorer, but also due to the rising electricity costs and greenhouse gas emissions associated with keeping online obsolete fossil-fueled power plants.

Engle (2021) observed the cult-like following of cryptocurrency is a result of speculative attempts to succeed in market timing of highly volatile instruments, with the goal to get rich quick. Dangers include high volatility and lack of intrinsic value and "Given the risks, including regulation, volatility, and valuation, it is hard to see why the cult of crypto continues to grow." He added that increased attention by the U.S. Internal Revenue Service imposes additional risk on crypto users from failure to report income.

At this juncture, we need an organized effort to save cryptocurrency from itself through thoughtful rather than reactionary regulation. Quiroz-Gutierrez (2022) reports that Egypt, Iraq, Qatar, Oman, Morocco, Algeria, Tunisia, Bangladesh, and China have explicitly banned cryptocurrency, while 42 other countries have implicitly banned them. This rate of bitcoin bans has more than doubled since 2018 and reflects a desire to stem money funneling and laundering, among other motivations. China has been most strident in its ban of cryptocurrency transactions in May of 2021, mining in June, and all cryptocurrencies in September, despite its continued role as the leader in miner manufacturing and the former leader in mining itself. It intends to popularize its own digital Yuan.[2]

Meanwhile, Horowitz (2022) documents the concerns of the Financial Stability Board, an international body representing 24 countries and jurisdictions, which stated that the "fast evolving (crypto market could become) a threat to global financial stability." The board noted "Systemically important banks and other financial institutions are increasingly willing to undertake activities in, and gain exposures to, crypto-assets (and …) If the current trajectory of growth in scale and interconnectedness of crypto-assets to these institutions were to continue, this could have implications for global financial stability."

Other nations are also doubling down. Bradstock (2022) documented Ukraine's law to allow its central bank to issue digital currency, and the rate bitcoin has been flowing into the nation that was quickly making Ukraine a cryptocurrency superpower. Ukraine is fourth on the Global Crypto Adoption Index, estimated at $8 billion cryptocurrency flow each year. Sigalos (2022) added that Portugal hopes to attract cryptocurrency wealth by imposing a 0% income tax on exchanges. She also noted that Puerto Rico is a tax haven for Americans because they can substitute a short term 37% capital gains tax rate to a 0% rate under certain conditions, and a 4% corporate tax rate rather than 21% federal tax on the mainland.

With adequate regulation, from the local to the global level, many of the financial challenges of digital currencies can be solved. Obviously, given the nature of the bitcoin sector that requires nothing but power and the Internet to thrive, global regulatory coordination is essential. The European Union, the United States, and China already represent a near majority of the world's population, and each entity recognizes the need for a coordinated regulatory response. Likely the Achilles heel of the bitcoin and Proof of Work industry remains the unnecessary energy consumption of Proof of Work mining.

---

[2] https://www.weforum.org/agenda/2022/01/what-s-behind-china-s-cryptocurrency-ban/, retrieved March 7, 2022.

Within this tension over glaring concerns begging regulation and the intrinsic mistrust in the heavy hand of government, there is little effective discussion. The final part of the book delineates the need for a sound regulatory pathway so that the benefits of cryptocurrencies and decentralized finance can be realized without their troubling consequences.

23

Central Banks Get into the Act

Satoshi shared with the cypherpunks a mistrust in large financial institutions, especially central banks. In the late 2000s, many feared both a severe inflation arising from intense run-ups in asset and commodity prices, and observed an inability of the Federal Reserve and other central banks to prevent the Great Recession. It is not difficult to harken back to fears of currency manipulation, for instance, in Weimar Republic Germany between the two world wars, or in Latin American countries in the 1970s and 1980s.

Trust was further eroded when the Federal Reserve stood helpless in 2008, at the same time Satoshi developed a coin with the express goal of making traditional central bank-backed currencies obsolete. Satoshi wrote in early 2009, "The root problem with conventional currency is all the trust that's required to make it work. The central bank must be trusted not to debase the currency, but the history of fiat currencies is full of breaches of that trust."[1]

Despite Satoshi's concerns, central banks of major nations around the world are currently exploring the possibilities in sponsoring Central Bank Digital Currencies (CBDCs). China, Canada, the European Union, and the United States have all published white papers or statements on their research of a domestic government-sponsored Stablecoin. Their common goals are to ensure public access to a digital currency tied to a nation's paper currency, develop CBDCs that are competitive with private payment networks, ensure

---

[1] http://p2pfoundation.ning.com/forum/topics/bitcoin-open-source, accessed April 19, 2022.

these digital coins are resilient and scalable, and create the ability to offer digital services to those who do not have access to traditional banking, all the while preserving privacy.

Global Central Bank Digital Currency Designs

Central banks strive to design CBDCs that meet reasonable articulated goals. China has developed a CBDC that is currently in a public trial phase, named e-CNY. The Central Bank of the Bahamas offers a Sand Dollar, while the Central Bank of Nigeria recently launched eNaira. Finally, a number of central banks have developed CBDCs in pilot stages, including DCash for the Eastern Caribbean Central Bank. Meanwhile, the Riksbank of Sweden is working on an e-krona project, and central banks within the European Union system are experimenting with various potential designs.

They also observe that the Bank for International Settlements, in combination with seven central banks, are also performing similar research toward a CBDC. Meanwhile, Amazon Web Services has formulated a Stablecoin design that can handle one million transactions per second using the sort of multiple coordinated blockchains as anticipated by the new Ethereum 2.0 protocol. Their design shares concepts for transactions processing from bitcoin, but within a model of centralized rather than decentralized trust, and with a proprietary ledger that is not and need not be publicly inspectable by users.

As a practical matter, it is anticipated that such systems can essentially replace existing networks such as debit card usage for transactions. However, one advantage of existing private networks such as Visa and Mastercard, which facilitate transactions on debit cards, is that these networks function across borders. With increased globalization and travel, a desirable system ought to be able to network with other national CBDC implementations. This would require a great deal of global collaboration at the design phase to permit ultimate global interoperability. With so much interest among central banks, but little collaboration between nations beyond Europe, the greatest challenge may be in developing suitable domestic models with international interoperability in mind.

The attention of central banks has certainly accelerated of late, after two decades below the radar screen since then-Federal Reserve chairman Alan Greenspan opened the door for digital currency inevitability. More recently, on September 22, 2021, the current Federal Reserve chair, Jerome Powell, commented, "The ultimate test we'll apply when assessing a central bank digital currency and other digital innovations is: Are there clear and tangible benefits that outweigh any costs and risks?"[2] The minds of central bankers are opening up to the possibilities and inevitabilities.

The white papers of various central banks acknowledge the complexity of such a design, and the various features to include, knowing that more features also create greater complexity and more potential points of vulnerability. The key features that are deemed necessary include low latency, defined as the round-trip time to pay for goods or services and the time to have the payment verified, high throughput to handle the expected volume should the digital currency be widely adopted, and sufficient flexibility to meet needs not yet imagined.

The technological requirements are significant. A processor of CBDC transactions may be a centralized or distributed trusted network that would have to process tens of thousands of transactions per second at peak times, with minimal latency and with the potential for growth the market demands. Such performance is far in excess of existing systems employed by commercial banks to clear interbank transactions, and likely beyond the existing capacity of even a redesigned bitcoin network.

A United States Digital Coin

In the United States, the Federal Reserve Board of Boston and the Massachusetts Institute of Technology (MIT) collaborated to define CBDC expectations and potential design criteria. Called *Project Hamilton*, their benchmark for an optimal system must have sufficient capacity to process transactions within five seconds 99% of the time. This includes transaction validation, execution, and confirmation. Such expectations are consistent with existing credit and debit card payment processing. For the United States, the team identified a minimum throughput of 100,000 transactions per second, based on current credit card and interbank transactions systems and expected future transaction volumes under widespread adoption of a CBDC. As a reference, bitcoin is designed to support three to seven transactions per second, processed in blocks that are immortalized only once every ten minutes.

Such a system must also be resilient, as measured by the need to ensure reliability should multiple data centers fail simultaneously. The desirability of a greater number of distributed nodes must also balance an overriding

---

[2] https://www.cnbc.com/2021/09/22/the-fed-is-evaluating-whether-to-launch-a-digital-currency-and-in-what-form-powell-says.html, accessed April 26, 2022.

need to ensure privacy and protection of personal data. A greater number of processing nodes creates more points of potential vulnerability. The network must build into its design sufficient robustness and the ability to adapt to future needs or unintended complications.

Finally, the design of a CBDC must determine in advance whether the system will be self-contained, will issue the CBDC to intermediaries such as banks, which then manages their interfaces with customers, or a hybrid model combining both elements. Meanwhile, as with existing digital currencies, users would maintain a wallet that can navigate the public keys within a blockchain and the private keys that ensure transaction protection at the individual level. Project Hamilton by the Boston Federal Reserve and MIT had to make some assumptions about the degree to which private user data is protected compared to the advantages of greater centralization. Finally, the system must be flexible enough to support updating and resilient to unforeseen network or equipment failures.

Despite their collection of challenging requirements, the Project Hamilton group believed that all needs can be successfully addressed through a variety of approaches.

First, they propose decoupling the two processes of transaction validation and assurance of fund availability. They recommended a processing unit that stores fund availability data that is separate from the unit that verifies transactions. In doing so, a firewall can be established that protects accounts, held in an Unspent Funds Hash Set (UHS), and also would permit subsequent improvements in each of these units without adversely compromising the other.

The second key assumption is to ensure the transaction unit is sufficiently robust to prevent double-spending and is sufficiently amenable to future optimization and failure prevention. The researchers used bitcoin as a model for transactions, but with a method that allows for funds validation without immediate probing of the UHS. The researchers label this feature *transaction-local validation*.

The third concept is to ensure the system can use the UHS to support high performance and geographically duplicated fault tolerance in a system that allows simultaneous reading and writing of transactions at its maximum design workload (Fig. 23.1).

Bitcoin is not well-suited as such a Stablecoin for a number of reasons. First, the network handles fewer than 140,000,000 transactions per year. The digital coin Amazon is contemplating exceeds that transaction volume every couple of minutes, while the Visa network exceeds annual bitcoin transactions on an average day. Both provide latency, in terms of the completion

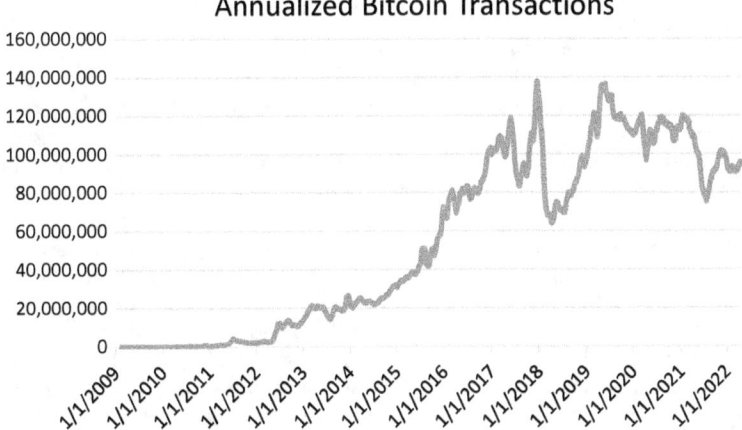

Fig. 23.1 Annual bitcoin transactions

of a recorded transaction in seconds or less, while a bitcoin transaction may take upwards of half an hour to be confirmed. Bitcoin's value also fluctuates, sometimes relatively quickly, so the value of the transaction can change before the transaction is complete.

Such issues do not arise for a CBDC. The Federal Reserve/MIT team instead determined that their architecture could support 1.7 million transactions per second with less than one second latency 99% of the time and 0.5 second latency 50% of the time. The researchers were confident that it is possible to build such a system that meets the needs of issuers, users, and the transactions processors, and is resilient to threats from malicious actors. They conclude that such a deployment is technically possible, but further design work must await a clearer articulation of the public policy goals a central bank determines must be met. They also propose alternative architectures that can meet their articulated goals, but their analysis depends on a current set of premises that may evolve with more discussion of desired public policy.

The U.S. Executive Branch Makes Strong Statement on Cryptocurrency

On March 9, 2022, the Executive Branch of the Federal Government of the United States ordered a study of how digital currencies can both benefit and increase financial market risk. President Biden also signaled a willingness to create a Central Bank Digital Currency (CBDC). With the signing of an executive order, Biden mobilized federal regulators to assess the risks of a cryptocurrency market that now approaches almost $2 trillion. These include risks to consumers, investors, and the overall economy.

> Cryptocurrencies have experienced dramatic growth in the United States in just a few years. Large investments in marketing have led about 16% of American adults to have traded or invested in cryptocurrencies. National leaders are acknowledging that the industry has moved far quicker than has its potential regulators. Biden stated, "We must take strong steps to reduce the risks that digital assets could pose to consumers, investors, and business protections." The White House noted that federal agencies must monitor cryptocurrencies' impact on financial stability, national security, and climate change.
>
> Treasury Secretary Janet Yellen added that greater regulatory measures will allow the industry to innovate more responsibly, while the nation also has the tools to combat illicit activity denominated in cryptocurrencies. This is a welcome addition to the federal government's regulatory authority.
>
> While it may be counterintuitive to see the price of bitcoin rally by 9% on the news, the dropping of this federal regulatory shoe reduces uncertainty with regard cryptocurrencies, and hence reduces at least one component of risk. With the reduction of risk, the value of bitcoin is enhanced.

Between such statements, white paper on CBDCs, and the direction set by the Administration, the world's largest economy will likely see an acceleration of the pace toward a government-sponsored Stablecoin and the banking reform necessary to accommodate it. Since many aspects of the coin have already been formulated in theory and simulation, the President's recent executive order may break the regulatory logjam. This effort follows parallel and more advanced measures in China and elsewhere.

President Biden notes the compelling interest of sovereign nations to expand an affordable financial innovations that can reduce the cost of transactions and cross-border transfers safely and affordably. Still, risks to consumers and investors must be addressed. These consumer risks include identity theft, theft of assets, and the security of financial data in an industry that has to now defied cohesive regulation. Billions of dollars have been lost in the absence of appropriate protections. These losses measured per crypto transaction processed are much larger than that of traditional financial institutions.

The president also identified the need for oversight to reduce the use of cryptocurrencies such as bitcoin to harbor and hide illicit activities. Federal authorities recognize that such expanded oversight also has a global dimension. The United States is prepared to offer global leadership to help coordinate international capital flows.

Such executive branch leadership is laudable. As the White House notes, the promotion of safe and affordable financial services, as envisioned by Satoshi Nakamoto, will allow greater and safer financial innovation that has the potential to increase the efficiency of our daily transactions. At the same time, we must protect obvious vulnerabilities for our privacy, national security, climate change, and financial resiliency. This leadership shall, in the long run, enhance the success of cryptocurrency innovation, despite the reluctance of a decidedly libertarian cryptoculture to encourage or foster regulation.

Beyond the obvious value of financial oversight to protect consumers and unsophisticated investors, the president's backing of the creation of a CBDC, first voiced by former Federal Reserve Chairman Alan Greenspan decades ago, is certainly a significant advance. The president called for coordination of various agencies within 180 days to analyze the ramifications of economic growth from the creation of a CBDC. It also calls for study of how a public coin would interact with or affect private digital coins and potentially displace other payment systems and currencies.

Meanwhile, the U.S. harbors concerns over a CBDC's implications on national security, financial crime, human rights, and the ability of the United States to project economic sanctions on nations when necessary. The United States cannot do this unilaterally. Coordination with its trading partners is necessary, and Biden promised to coordinate with the G7 nations and their finance ministers as the U.S. moves toward sponsoring a national digital coin.

This move by the chief executive of the world's largest economy, and with a timeline to match the rhetoric, may well be the step necessary to legitimize digital currencies as a safe store of value, and bring us a step forward to the realization of Satoshi's dream, except, of course, the involvement of government in the process.

24

The Disruption of the Fractional Banking System

Central banks act as the bank for commercial banks. In other words, a central bank considers the safety and soundness of our commercial banks and the soundness of the monetary system as its primary goals. Increased deployment of digital currencies by central banks must take into consideration the needs of and responses from their member banks. In addition, these member banks must be sufficiently responsive to the rapidly evolving needs of the public and their central bank and have the capacity to collaborate to meet mutual needs. This must be done within an economy which supports thousands of banks in the United States, and multiple banks in other countries, each which differs in their organization, information technology sophistication, and centrality of fintech within their strategic plans.

Satoshi harbored little trust in such a network of member banks under the auspices of a central bank. Satoshi noted that bitcoin as a substitute for money may be appealing precisely because it would make central bank monetary manipulation obsolete. Satoshi observed, "Indeed, there is nobody to act as central bank or federal reserve to adjust the money supply as the population of users grows. That would have required a trusted party to determine the value, because I don't know a way for software to know the real-world value of things."[1]

---

[1] http://p2pfoundation.ning.com/forum/topics/bitcoin-open-source?commentId=2003008%3AComment%3A9562, accessed April 19, 2022.

However, responsible central banks in developed countries have been amazingly disciplined at controlling the money supply to preserve its real-world value. It is helpful to describe how central banks and their commercial bank customers function within the fractional banking system so we may understand and appreciate the various challenges in the introduction and regulation of Stablecoins.

The fractional reserve banking system uses monetary policies of a central bank to control the size of the money supply. Central banks do this by influencing the ability of commercial banks to create money. To understand this, note that the size of the money supply, using the M1 measure, is primarily the sum of cash in circulation and demand deposits held in checking accounts at commercial banks. The term *demand deposit* refers to a deposit that can readily act as cash by issuing checks against it or in making electronic payments from it. Since checks and electronic payments from a checking account function as cash, they both behave as cash and represent a measure of the ability to transact for goods and services.

In fact, because of our confidence in the safety of the banking system, most of our purchases are made from balances held in our checking accounts, even those purchases on credit cards that defer their withdrawal from our checking accounts until when we pay the balances. Indeed, the vast majority of our transactions are made with checks, or their equivalent, rather than cash. Central banks allow us to maintain confidence in this system of monetary transactions. They do so by regulating the money creation process.

The Money Creation Process

When a bank receives a deposit, it uses that deposit to in turn issue a loan. The difference in interest earned on a loan and paid to depositors is called the *spread* and represents the largest share of banking revenue. This revenue is offset by administrative and employee costs, infrastructure costs, taxes, and shareholder's equity.

To see how a bank can create money, consider a simple example of one bank allowed to operate exclusively, and with a requirement that it holds a certain ratio of each new deposit in the form of cash reserves, with the remainder lendable by the bank. This ratio of mandated cash reserves is called the *reserve ratio* and is set by the central bank overseeing the commercial bank. Typically, this reserve ratio is set to around 10%, which means that for every hundred dollars of deposits, the bank must retain at least ten dollars in cash, and can then lend out the remaining ninety dollars.

24 The Disruption of the Fractional Banking System

Here's how a bank manages to create money. Especially in this example where we assumed an exclusive bank, but also for the banking industry as a whole, any loan made by the bank will be in the form of a deposit to the borrower's checking account. Presumably the borrower intends to make a purchase, which results in a check written against that checking account, and hence creates a simultaneous deposit of that check to the bank account of the individual with whom the borrower transacts. In other words, each new loan results in a new deposit somewhere in the banking system.

Using the example of a $100 initial deposit, a 10% reserve ratio requires $10 must be held in cash reserves. The $100 initial deposit eventually ends up as a $10 cash asset for the bank, and a $90 loan asset. However, since this loan results in a $90 deposit somewhere in the banking system, total deposits have risen from the original $100 to $190, without any additional cash injected into the system.

This second $90 deposit then requires another $9 in cash reserves and allows the bank to extend another $81 loan, which again results in a new deposit somewhere in the banking system and raises the total value of deposits to $190 + $81, or $271, again with no additional injection of cash. This process continues likewise as shown in Fig. 24.1.

You now see what is called the *deposit expansion multiplier* at work. Let us use the symbol rr to represent the reserve ratio. Then the change in required reserves ΔR is equal to the change in deposits ΔD times the reserve ratio rr.

The Bank's T-Account			
Assets		Liabilities	
Cash	Loans	Deposits	
$100	$900	$1000	Original Deposit Held in Cash and Loans
$90	$810	$900	Loan Results in New Deposit
$81	$729	$810	Loan Results in New Deposit
$72.90	$656.10	$729	Loan Results in New Deposit
*	*	*	
*	*	*	
$1000	$9000	$10,000	

Fig. 24.1 The Bank's T-Account

Total demand deposits then rises according to the formula:

$$\Delta D = \left(\frac{1}{rr}\right)\Delta R.$$

Since the reserve ratio rr is less than one, deposits rise by an amount greater than the cash available for reserves. The ratio 1/rr defines the deposit expansion multiplier. In the case of a required reserve ratio of 10%, such a deposit expansion multiplier is 10. In other words, an initial cash deposit results in total deposits, including checks deposited from new loans, of ten times the initial cash deposit. Once the banking system has fully lent the amount limited by the reserve ratio, banks find on their balance sheet cash of $100 and loans of $900 for an initial $100 cash injection.

The deposit expansion multiplier then acts as a leverage ratio of sorts. A $100 cash deposit results in the ability of the banking system to create up to $900 in new loans. Banks pay interest on $1000 of deposits ultimately, but earn interest on $900 of loans that arise from that initial $100 cash injection. In addition, banks earn a nominal return on the $100 held in mandatory cash reserves, at the central bank's discount rate. Naturally, the bank would prefer a higher deposit expansion multiplier that would arise with a lower reserve ratio. For instance, with a reserve ratio of 5%, the deposit expansion multiplier would rise to 20, which would allow banks to extend $1900 of loans from an initial $100 cash deposit and would earn interest on the full $1900 while it pays a much lower rate of interest on $2000 of deposits. Banks can more highly lever their loans for a given new cash deposit with a lower reserve ratio, and hence, earn greater profits.

Bank Liquidity

However, it is also prudent for a bank to maintain sufficient cash reserves. If a 5% cash reserve ratio was insufficient to cover expected withdrawals that may be in the form of cash, the bank would become illiquid, with insufficient liquid cash reserves to cover their needs.

Concern about maintaining sufficient cash is not typically a problem for a bank. It knows that on a given day it is likely to receive about as much cash to deposit as will be demanded by its customers in cash. Cash reserves only act as a buffer in case these two forces of cash deposits versus cash withdrawals become imbalanced. Such could occur, for instance, if there were a run on the bank following rumors of bank insolvency or illiquidity.

Indeed, a bank would prefer to not keep even 5% or 10% of their total deposits in the form of cash in their vault. For your local bank, which might have total deposits of $100 million, required cash reserves if held in their vault would exceed $10 million, and would be a profitable bounty for modern day Willie Suttons. Banks instead hold the vast bulk of their cash reserves centrally, with the regional branch of their central bank, and maintain just enough cash at each branch to cover day-to-day differences in the amount of cash coming into versus the amount of cash leaving the bank on a daily basis. This difference is typically well less than 1% of total deposits, especially with the advent of federally mandated deposit insurance that guarantees customers' bank deposits will remain safe even if a bank becomes insolvent. The local branch does benefit, though, by having its district Central Bank safekeep its cash, and earns a moderate return on their deposits in turn.

The other advantages with holding cash reserves with the central bank is that, from the central bank's perspective, they can easily monitor member banks' cash reserves, and, from the member bank's perspective, they can earn interest on any excess reserves, over and above the mandated reserves, at the rate of interest the central bank sets.

Central Bank Manipulation of the Money Supply

Central banks have a need to fine-tune the total money supply. Too great a money supply chasing the same amount of goods and services would result in spending that exceeds that capacity of an economy to produce, which results in inflation. On the other hand, to change the reserve ratio to fine-tune the money supply is impracticable, especially since it may force banks to call in loans to bolster cash reserves. Instead, a central bank steers the money supply in a more nuanced way.

Ideally, a bank would like to use their leverage power to the fullest extent, which would result in the mandated minimum cash reserves, held primarily with their central bank. But, if a customer unexpectedly switches a large account to another bank, simply by writing a check in the amount of their total deposits, the central bank, as part of the check-clearing function they offer their member banks, makes the adjustment by moving the transferred sum from cash reserves of the bank experiencing the withdrawal and into the reserves of the bank receiving the deposit. This leaves one bank short of cash reserves, even if another bank now holds excess reserves. In fact, this can occur even without moving accounts from one bank to another. Simply writing a check from one bank, and depositing it at another has the same effect. One bank's cash reserves on the central bank's ledger goes down and another bank's reserves rise.

Knowing that a bank must pay a penalty of sorts if it is found cash-poor in reserves, in the form of borrowing costs from the central bank or from other cash-rich banks, and may suffer greater scrutiny and perhaps regulatory action from the central bank for repeat offenders of the cash reserve policy, banks choose to hold some excess cash reserves over and above what is required. This reduces the ability of the bank to fully lever its cash into loans and margin interest, but it also reduces the need for banks to borrow from other banks or the central bank to prop up reserves.

Steering the level of these cash reserves is the primary tool the central bank can employ to limit or enhance bank leverage. If the central bank decides that the money supply is too low, it can encourage banks to more fully leverage by inducing banks to keep a lower amount of excess reserves. In doing so, banks can make more loans and earn more profits, but bank profitability is of only secondary concern for the central bank.

If the central bank lowers the rate of interest it offers on reserves, or the rate of interest it requires should a bank need to borrow short term from the central bank to cover insufficient reserves, the central bank is in essence encouraging its member banks to hold a lower amount of excess reserves and instead issue more loans. The central bank can then steer the effective leverage ratio of its member banks, and hence the total size of the money supply, by adjusting its key interest rate it offers member banks.

The central bank can influence the effective leverage ratio of its banks in an even more subtle way. Let's say a central bank wants to encourage its member banks to lever up more and extend more credit which, in effect, increases the money supply. A central bank can supplement member banks' excess reserves by purchasing from banks, or from banks' customers, some sort of valuable security they may hold, usually in the form of risk-free government bonds. In doing so, bank excess reserves rise by the purchase price, and banks find they have too much cash earning very little deposited in their Central Bank account.[2] In turn, banks can attempt to issue more loans by an amount equal to the purchase price of the security times the deposit expansion multiplier.

In fact, central banks do these subtle adjustments on a regular basis through what is called *open market operations*. On a day-to-day basis, a central bank will monitor excess reserves and adjust their securities purchasing and selling policy to meet their money supply goals. If they wish to contract

---

[2] During the depths of the Great Recession, the European Bank actually paid a negative interest rate on commercial bank excess reserves. In essence, banks were penalized for holding reserves rather than lend them out.

this money supply, they merely need to sell some bonds to member banks or their customers, which reduces excess reserves by the amount of the sale and contracts the money supply by an amount equal to the product of the securities sale and the deposit expansion multiplier. In effect, the commercial banking system is an accomplice in a central bank's monetary policy.

Economic Fine-Tuning

If a central bank almost never changes the reserve ratio, and perhaps changes up to quarterly the interest rate it offers for excess reserves or demands for insufficient reserves, it accomplishes frequent fine-tuning of the money supply through such open market operations. Note that its interest rate policy is not setting economy-wide interest rates, although its policies on cash reserves will have some influence on the supply of potentially loanable funds and hence other interest rates in the economy.

This collaborative dance between a central bank and its member banks has been perfected over the centuries some nations have maintained such a fractional reserve system, and just over a century of experience in the United States with its Federal Reserve. While some may differ in their opinion of the desirability of an agency of a national government to so influence the money supply and hence our ability to transact, bitcoin founder Satoshi included, economists generally agree that the system functions well in maintaining confidence in the monetary system and in stabilizing the value of our currency and inflation.

Central banks have been equally effective in maintaining monetary policies that have promoted full employment by ensuring households have available to them sufficient cash or borrowing potential at acceptable interest rates to fuel their spending needs. They have also ensured sufficient member bank liquidity and solvency through their lending and oversight capabilities. While it is certainly true that central banks have at times done too little and too late, especially in the wake of major economic displacements, economies overall have been well served by their central banks, and in their ability to moderate inflation by increasing interest rates and deleveraging member banks when spending is outpacing the ability of an economy to produce and supply goods and services. If anything, central banks over the past few decades have shown too much restraint rather than too much monetary expansion.

Central banks know and can control its member banks. For this reason, much of the discussion among central banks regarding digital Stablecoins have occurred under the premise that Stablecoins ought to be administered as part of the existing banking system. This could mean setting up private Stablecoin providers as virtual banks, with the ability to take deposits and issue loans, but under the same premises and regulatory requirements as brick-and-mortar banks. Or, it could mean that a Stablecoin is sponsored by a central bank, through a Central Bank Digital Currency (CBDC), administered in conjunction with its member banks.

From the perspective of most central banks, the simpler route would be the latter, a system of digital Stablecoins that substitute for cash just as would a check, but administered through the existing mechanisms central banks and commercial banks know and understand. The regulatory regime and principles are already in place and are well-understood, and this system has worked reasonably well for generations. On the other hand, to extend participation to some member banks may be difficult.

Dangers to Banks Too-Small-To-Be-Protected

Certainly, some member banks are sufficiently sophisticated to already offer a number of *fintech* products and avenues for banking, but other banks, especially smaller banks with deposits less than $10 billion, would likely find such a new strategic fintech thrust difficult and, for some, almost impossible to accommodate. To force its member banks to accommodate processing of a CBDC in conjunction with their existing checking accounts may force industry consolidation that would be troubling for central banks already concerned that the acceleration of the trend toward consolidation may reduce industry competitiveness and hence be costly to consumers. Such would concentrate profits and power among the same banks too-big-to-fail that so troubled Satoshi.

On the other hand, expanding the banking industry significantly by admitting a plethora of new virtual banks into the mix, with their preexisting advantage in spawning new DeFi products, potentially places traditional banks at a disadvantage that would likely be fatal for many smaller banks.

But, to do neither is perhaps even more problematic. Despite the firmly held belief among cypherpunks that bypassing traditional institutions is desirable, should privately-issued Stablecoins and DeFi lending from their reserves occur, the single most effective tool for effective macroeconomic policy is removed from national coordination. This tool of monetary control was essential in the excoriation of hyperinflation from many economies during the Great Stagflation of 1979–1981 and will be an important tool to prevent a prolonged period of inflation in post-COVID-19 economies.

This incredibly important policy debate is occurring within central banks and among legislators worldwide. However, on the political front where the issue will ultimately be decided, our legislators are mulling over two perspectives. Successful oversight is incredibly complex and requires a deep understanding necessary in the inner workings not only of central banks and the entire banking industry, but also in the nature of cryptocurrencies, which is a fascinating but perhaps even more complex subject matter in its own right. The other perspective is a laissez-faire approach touted by the cryptocurrency industry and especially bitcoin advocates and *Crypto Bros*.

Digital currencies are the wave of the future and, from the industry's perspective, shall *evolutionize* rather than revolutionize our economy. From that perspective, if we do not embrace the cryptocurrency industry, including all its aspirations, we are Luddites whose fear of change shall doom our economy to irrelevance. That perspective is one that can garner more populist support than the former approach that would incorporate CBDCs into our current banking framework.

One can imagine the political rhetoric that shall ensue if only that debate were held within the confines of Congressional hearings. It is far more likely, though, that once K-Street lobbyists get into the act in an even more engaged way than they already have, the debate shall pit economic progress against stale existing institutions. It is hard to defend big banks, which likely have the most to gain by the Stablecoin policies central bankers may prefer to adopt, especially following the excesses of too-big-to-fail policies following the beginning of the Great Recession, and central banks' role in it. We need only recall that the Genesis Block for bitcoin contained little but a headline ridiculing Britain's central bank for coming to the aid of its banking industry at the onset of the Great Recession.

25

Shock and Awe and a Call for Regulatory Action

Recall Federal Reserve Chairman Alan Greenspan's words in 1996:

> We could envisage proposals in the near future for issuers of electronic payment obligations, such as stored-value cards or 'digital cash,' to set up specialized issuing corporations with strong balance sheets and public credit ratings.[1]

Satoshi remained skeptical, though, and retorted "Banks must be trusted to hold our money and transfer it electronically, but they lend it out in waves of credit bubbles with barely a fraction in reserve. We have to trust them with our privacy, trust them not to let identity thieves drain our accounts. Their massive overhead costs make micropayments impossible."[2] Satoshi felt that the very underpinnings of the fractional banking system makes the economy susceptible to central bank corruption. Satoshi harbored no confidence in regulators. While regulation is the antithesis of what bitcoin's creator had envisioned, it is regulation that will allow Satoshi's dream to come true. If the masses lose confidence in any currency, they will flee to currencies that are perceived to be safer.

Many of the frauds in cryptocurrencies arise from what would be securities regulation violations, at least in the world in which entities like the Securities and Exchange Commission can exercise oversight.

---

[1] https://www.federalreserve.gov/boarddocs/speeches/1996/19960919.htm, retrieved February 27, 2022.
[2] http://p2pfoundation.ning.com/forum/topics/bitcoin-open-source, accessed April 19, 2022.

Ripple Labs has made the largest splash across the most dimensions in the crypto world, and perhaps the greatest challenge to regulators, with its release of the XRP coin. They had developed their coin using the usual cadre of software developers and computer scientists. But they also commissioned lawyers and lobbyists to ensure they could sway the SEC, other regulators, and Congress itself to support their coin and industry. In doing so they were accused of selling to investors cryptocurrency in excess of a billion dollars without appropriate SEC approval. This would act as a watershed case in the determination of the bounds of regulatory oversight.

A Regulatory Fight on All Fronts

Ripple Labs had followed the K-Street playbook. They hired two lobbying firms and retained former aides to President Trump and Presidential Candidate Hillary Clinton to assist in a strategy to curry the favor of the public and regulators. Ripple also hired a former chairperson of the SEC from the Obama Administration to defend itself from SEC charges.

The approach by Ripple Labs and others with regard to regulation of cryptocurrencies is based partly on the merits of new coins, but also depends on favorable public opinion to influence Congressional action. The industry is taking its case to the people through such actions as major ad buys during the Superbowl by three different cryptocurrency exchanges, and by purchase of the rights to name a National Basketball Association arena. If regulators cannot move quickly enough or in a direction satisfactory for members of the cryptocurrency industry, lobbyists, and lawyers can grease the skids.

The crypto industry expands most successfully when it can do so rapidly, for two reasons. First, the concepts of cryptocurrency are complicated, and successful regulation requires a deep understanding of arcane computer science, energy economics, and monetary theory. By moving quickly, understanding and observation is replaced by trust in advocates and obfuscation. Second, time is money. A major mining operation can lose millions of dollars in profit for each day of delay in coming online, and a cryptocurrency that fails to quickly captivate the attention in an industry that hears proposals for new coins almost daily loses the buzz it spends so much money cultivating.

Worse, if the unrelenting pressure to permit cryptocurrencies is delayed at all, the industry runs the risk of regulators calling a time out and imposing a moratorium to afford time to consider complicated factors. Time really is money in the rapidly moving crypto industry. Given the global nature of the industry delays in the United States means that currencies can take root elsewhere and remain outside of oversight reach of U.S. regulators. But unnecessary delays may also mean losing access to the lucrative U.S. investment community. Like other companies, the money to be made is in the Initial Public Offering valued at billions of dollars for a new entity, rather than the slog in maintaining that currency over time.

The corporate cryptocurrency community is sophisticated indeed. Their network quietly does work behind the scenes to influence those in positions of authority. They have assembled a "Digital Chamber of Commerce" to project an aura of respectability and have appointed former regulators and legislators from the Commodity Futures Trading Commission and Congress to act as the face of the Chamber.

The Digital Chamber and trade groups such as the Blockchain Association of cryptocurrency developers and exchanges have anted up millions to lobby on behalf of and represent the industry, with their efforts accelerating dramatically over the past year. Exchanges and proposed coins line up in advance famous actors and former legislators for their advertising campaigns and boards of directors. In the case of Ripple and the lawsuit brought against them by the SEC, these efforts sometimes employ the strategy of asking for permission and asking for forgiveness in equal measure.

The industry is reeling from accusations of creating conflicts of interest, from hiring a senior leader of the SEC within a day of their announcement of a lawsuit, to hiring a former leader of the Office of the Comptroller of the Currency, which oversees and regulates banks, just before a new digital bank is chartered. The industry is clearly attempting to coopt regulators through lucrative lobbying or employment contracts.[3]

There are revolving door rules that prevent former regulators and legislators from retiring to instantly begin lobbying former colleagues. However, these rules can be circumvented by purchasing retired regulators as generals and have them guide staff as foot soldiers for the actual lobbying efforts until revolving door rules time out. This industry is capable of offering salaries these individuals cannot afford to refuse.

The efforts are two-pronged, to prevent heavy handed regulation on coins themselves, and protect from regulation the exchanges that peddle them. If their efforts do nothing but obfuscate and delay, their investments buy time to ensure they first win in the court of public opinion by enticing as many

---

[3] https://www.wsj.com/articles/cryptocurrency-giant-binance-hires-former-top-bank-regulator-11618912800#:~:text=BlockFi%2C%20a%20cryptocurrency%20startup%2C%20said,Redfearn%2C%20as%20a%20vice%20president, accessed March 25, 2022.

Americans as they can to vest into the cryptocurrency world through the usual promises of great profits that come to pioneers who have the courage to jump in first. It is far easier to open Pandora's Box than close it afterward.

Regulatory Agency Interventions

Fortunately, the highest placed regulators, U.S. Treasury Secretary and former Federal Reserve Board chairperson Janet Yellen, and current Federal Reserve board chair Jerome Powell have a good grasp of the industry and a strong sense of some of the dangers for which they need to protect the public in their roles as regulators in chief. Both Yellen and Powell are worried about the extreme volatility of some of these products, and the inability of perhaps naive investors to properly assess the risk such volatility creates.

Even an anti-money-laundering rule proposal by the Treasury Department to require the revelation of the participants in transactions over $3,000 met with consternation from the industry, followed by unrelenting pressure to abandon this and similar initiatives. Meanwhile, any such rule proposals must go through the process of Notice of Proposed Rulemaking, at which time regulators are deluged with comments that arise from highly organized campaigns designed to delay and desist in regulation.

XRP and a New Exchange Sends Ripples Through the Banking Industry

The Ripple controversy was over whether the exchange's cryptocurrency, XRP, was a security or, instead a commodity or currency. The Ripple exchange is one of the earliest U.S. real-time settlement exchanges. Formed in 2012, it was conceived by Jed McCaleb, with developers Arthur Britto and David Schwartz. McCaleb approached Ryan Fugger, who had already developed a mechanism called OpenCoin in the mid-2000s, and was amenable to the creation of an entity called Ripple, and its associated digital currency XRP.

While banks found XRP too risky as a financial instrument, some institutions did see value in the ability of Ripple to provide a transaction communications network as an alternative to the *Society for Worldwide Interbank Financial Telecommunications* (SWIFT) network that banks use not to move funds between banks but rather to communicate in preparation and documentation of these large movements. Ripple's shared ledger and blockchain techniques offered a reasonable substitute for SWIFT, but its developers also realized that this funds transaction system could also be augmented with bank-like functions, including offering interest on funds much as banks will lend and borrow from each other at an *interbank overnight funds rate*.

The definition of a digital coin's function matters because currencies and commodities do not fall under SEC purview. The Commodity Futures Trading Commission in the late 1990s, under the influence of then influential Congressional leader Phil Gramm, decided to keep commodities and currencies, and their associated derivatives, lightly regulated, under the theory that these are instruments and assets employed by sophisticated investors and speculators who are capable of estimating and managing their risk. Often though, those enticed into crypto investing are not the sophisticated traders of commodities and foreign exchange that Gramm felt could protect themselves. While industry strategy advocates for categorization of their activities in the way most likely to avoid regulation, the SEC argued that XRP is equivalent to a potentially speculative security such as a stock, which should require full public disclosures that describe the risk of any such security offering. The SEC argues their position based on the "Howey Test", which arose from a Supreme Court ruling in The Securities and Exchange Commission v. W. J. Howey Co. in 1946. This ruling defined an investment contract, and determines SEC jurisdiction if a contract exists that (1) is an investment of money for (2) a common enterprise with (3) the expectation of profits to be (4) derived by the efforts of others. Since cryptocurrencies are typically marketed to those who are not miners themselves, it is argued that purchases of crypto is an investment that satisfies Howey and hence should fall under SEC purview.

On the other hand, the industry argues that to regulate in the absence of well-defined cryptocurrency rulemaking and policies amounts to ad hoc regulation that can do harm to the path of development of the industry. The strategy of shock and awe the crypto industry has adopted makes thoughtful policy development challenging.

To legislate and regulate successfully, agencies need to be as well organized, strategic, and coordinated as those they must oversee. Yet, various agencies and legislative committees are separately pursuing their own agendas, while the industry comes with one. In this case, the industry actually supported a House bill that called for a working group to examine potential interests and approaches. In doing so, they obtained representation on that working group. The industry is well-resourced and has an effective playbook. Those concerned about consumer protection or environmental degradation from Proof of Work mining are far less organized.

Ultimately, though, while the industry is entirely organized and united, and agencies well understand the dilemma before them, legislators in Congress are divided, with some expressing grave concerns for the protection of investors and consumers, and the other camp of the belief that the cryptocurrency industry represents an opportunity for the U.S. to be the undisputed creator of a friendly environment for digital innovation and transactions efficiency.

There is a need for a coherent and consistent regulatory environment for the blockchain, digital coins, and exchanges if blockchain and DeFi innovations are to realize their potential without imposing harm upon investors and those who will come to rely on these innovations. The challenge is to promulgate regulations that can work in this country and not simply export their regulatory responsibilities abroad.

China has its own objectives with regard to a national digital currency and has demonstrated that it prefers both mining and private sector digital currencies to go elsewhere. In the absence of International Monetary Fund leadership in this issue, the United States and the European Union are the two entities that can offer the most leadership and benefit most from collaboration. The reality is that major nations are anticipating regulation of a security that can easily be transacted over the Internet from anywhere and across borders and political jurisdictions. In such an environment, regulation is like squeezing on a balloon. Contraction somewhere results in expansion somewhere else, unless a concerted approach on behalf of regulators globally, and the public they represent, is essential.

Inevitably, regulation in the U.S. and abroad must acknowledge two aspects for which the industry would prefer minimized. The success of DeFi based on Stablecoins depends on the maintenance of sufficient reserves and insurance designed to prevent runs on reserves.

Such assurances do not only require a prudent level of reserves to maintain the value of currencies, but must also ensure the creation of mechanisms for risk management that crucially depend on accurate risk assessments and audits. Financial regulation depends critically on documentation, but the design of DeFi to manage risk and transactions typically obscures the ownership of accounts. This artifact of cryptocurrencies may then require sophisticated forensic auditing, perhaps employing artificial intelligence, to track the flows of income and wealth and attach them to their owners.

The challenges to regulators are profound and nations can ill-afford significant delays nor ineffective regulation. This balancing act will be difficult to navigate, but failure or delay is not an option. Digital currencies have proven to move ahead in the absence of regulation.

26

Bitcoin's Global Reach

Not only have individuals gravitated to cryptocurrency as if it is some magical elixir, but nations have considered it too. Some have even envisioned a decentralized system of exchange and banking, along the lines of Satoshi's vision: "Bitcoin would be convenient for people who don't have a credit card or don't want to use the cards they have."[1]

Most all nations issue their own fiat currency. At one time backed by gold, the movement by U.S. President Nixon to move the U.S. dollar off the gold standard marked the beginning of movement off the international Bretton Woods Accord, and the end of currency as a security backed by a valuable and tangible asset. Such *fiat* currencies, named from the Latin and meaning "let it be done," maintain their value by governmental decree. For instance, the declaration on the U.S. dollar states that it is backed by the full faith and credit of the United States Government.

While the value of early currencies was guaranteed by banks, and hence we use the term bank note, today the value of a fiat currency is assured by our confidence in government regulation and oversight that restricts the supply of such a currency to ensure its value. Hence, fiat money does not have an intrinsic value derived from something else of known value, but is instead valued based on its utility to act as a medium of exchange in transactions, and trust in our monetary authority.

---

[1] https://bitcointalk.org/index.php?topic=671.msg13844#msg13844, accessed April 19, 2022.

In other words, fiat currencies have value as a matter of faith and trust. Such government-issued tender has been used for more than a millennium in China, but only became the norm in the U.S. once it abandoned its agreement with other nations to maintain fixed exchange rates between the participants of the Bretton Woods conference immediately following World War II. But, once the U.S. abandoned the Gold Standard in 1971, other nations followed suit.

The Nature of Monetary Value

The nature of a fiat currency then requires its value to be determined by monetary supply and demand, not by the underlying value of some commodity. It must also be declared a form of legal tender. Before bitcoin, a governmental body made this declaration. In the digital coin world, a cryptocurrency is backed solely by the faith of its participants that a digital currency shall retain and hopefully enhance its value. The currency is thus valueless except that we are willing to accept it as a medium of exchange. By recognizing a mutually accepted medium of exchange, value is created. This value arises because more transactions are possible and are more efficient, if we all agree on a common medium of exchange.

As an example, if I have a spare personal computer which I would like to trade for a spare high-end Graphics Processing Unit, I would have to discover someone who has the spare GPU and is in search of a PC. This double coincidence of wants may be difficult to discover, and hence a mutually advantageous trade may be prevented by the costs associated with finding a suitable trading partner.

On the other hand, there may be many people who are willing to purchase my PC with a currency, and others who would accept my currency for their GPU. A successful and accepted currency saves effort and promotes more mutually advantageous trade by solving the double coincidence of wants. Because of that advantage, we give fiat currency its value, even if it has no intrinsic value.

> **An Early Form of Global Fiat Currency**
>
> Such double coincidence of wants is magnified with the development of trade over distances, especially international trade. In the Dawn of Exploration, should one who lords over an empire wish to trade with another empire, each must assemble a group of tradable goods that are equal in perceived value to those with whom we wish to trade. It is inefficient to travel great distances

to trade under the hope that we have assembled and brought with us the appropriate bundle of goods our trading partner might desire. If travel is over long distances and time, the costs of mistakes and mismatches are amplified.

If we find a mutually respected and trusted middleman who can guarantee some sort of bill of exchange, and if all parties are confident such a market maker will be willing to convert exchange insurance policies into the money or commodity they desire, both sides will then be able to trade for such bills of exchange. The market maker could be a bank, insurance company, or government. Such exchange insurance was the root of the Medici family of bankers in the Tuscan region of Italy who facilitated regional trade but also financed such trade, through Venice to the world. This is then a confidence game that depends crucially on trust in the issuing and insuring institution, and allowed explorers such as Marco Polo to establish much longer trade routes that would have been far too cumbersome without some medium of exchange. As Marco Polo noted in his *The Travels of Marco Polo*:

> All these pieces of paper are issued with as much solemnity and authority as if they were of pure gold or silver... and indeed everybody takes them readily, for wheresoever a person may go throughout the Great Kaan's dominions he shall find these pieces of paper current, and shall be able to transact all sales and purchases of goods by means of them just as well as if they were coins of pure gold.[2]

Clearly, a fiat currency, or such bills of exchange promises an insuring institution might provide, is a clear and perhaps even a competitive advantage. However, its premise is that the medium of exchange will maintain its value because of our confidence in the utility it provides us to promote exchange, but also in our confidence that the supply remains restricted. For instance, the Weimar Republic was required to make colossal reparation payments following the Great War. They paid for reparation and for an armament buildup in anticipation of a Second World War by simply printing extra Deutsche Marks. Without a commensurate increase in demand for the currency, the excess supply diluted the value of the currency. Other opportunistic nations have attempted this errant economic theory and have invariably found themselves slipping into hyperinflation.

As the value of the currency declines, traders demand more of the currency for a given exchange. In other words, the price of the good in effect rises. A feedback loop can then set in which causes transactors to flee from the inflated currency, which depresses demand and value even further, and hence requires a greater number of units of the currency to be demanded for a given

---

[2] Marco Polo (1818). *The Travels of Marco Polo, a Venetian, in the Thirteenth Century: Being a Description, by that Early Traveller, of Remarkable Places and Things, in the Eastern Parts of the World.* pp. 353–55. Retrieved February 12, 2022.

trade. In effect, inflation accelerates first because of a misguided attempt to print more currency to cover fiscal spending, and then from a collapse of confidence in the hyperinflated currency.

Sound Monetary Policy

The common element of such hyperinflation is the diversion of the currency to serve some sort of fiscal purpose. The tempting and dangerous allure of printing extra money to cover extra government spending, instead of increasing the level of taxation to cover fiscal spending, results in a flight from the currency to other stores of value. Often that alternative currency is the U.S. dollar, which has on many occasions become the de facto shadow currency for black markets that grow rapidly, despite rules that may attempt to prevent such a substitution.

Some nations recognize their inability to properly support and manage their currency, and simply adopt the U.S. dollar as the prevailing currency to piggyback on the diligence of the U.S. Federal Reserve in limiting inflation. Puerto Rico, El Salvador, Ecuador, Panama, Somalia, Turks and Caicos Islands, Zimbabwe, Guam, U.S. Virgin Islands, Timor-Leste, Palau, Marshall Islands, the British Virgin Islands, American Samoa, Federated States of Micronesia, Bonaire, Northern Mariana Islands, and the Caribbean Netherlands all accept the U.S. dollar as legal tender.[3]

In doing so, they can rely on the efforts of the U.S. Federal Reserve to maintain for them the value of their legal tender. Many of these nations have territorial relations with the United States, so such a sharing of legal tender should come as no surprise. Other nations depend so heavily on U.S. tourism that acceptance of the U.S. currency is a path of least resistance. Still others, though, adopt the U.S. dollar as a way to ensure their own prudent monetary policy by piggybacking on the Federal Reserve.

El Salvador diverged notoriously from their time-trusted policy. In 2001, the nation adopted the U.S. dollar to provide for monetary stability in a nation for which their monetary authority had lost the confidence of its public. The inflation rate that had perennially been in double digits for a generation declined to normal levels almost immediately. Indeed, the nation demonstrated a better inflation experience than did any of its Central and South American peers. In turn, El Salvador had to sacrifice that important tool of monetary control, but the anti-inflation dividends were worthwhile.

---

[3] https://www.investopedia.com/articles/forex/040915/countries-use-us-dollar.asp, retrieved March 7, 2022.

El Salvador Goes Bitcoin

Then, in September of, 2021, the President of El Salvador pledged his nation would become the first to adopt a cryptocurrency as legal tender. By adopting bitcoin, the nation was pegging its finances on a currency developed as a libertarian and anarchistic alternative to currencies sponsored by government institutions. El Salvador's experience is an institutionalization of an anti-institutional concept. It also allowed El Salvador some hope of moving away from the U.S. dollar, a currency turned convenient in Central America, but at a time in which U.S. immigration policies were deeply resented.

One of the articulated reasons to do so was to create an ability for its citizens to transact without a bank account. However, bitcoin was not a good choice. It takes upwards of half an hour for a transaction to be fully completed. And the currency fluctuates in value, sometimes significantly seemingly overnight. Despite its status as a legal tender, many merchants did not want to accept it. Reduced confidence in El Salvador's government induced the interest rate on government bonds to skyrocket compared to the U.S. Treasury benchmark.

Nonetheless, El Salvador authorities claimed that the use of bitcoin would foster participation of underbanked poor people and would facilitate the transfer of income from relatives employed in the U.S. to their El Salvadorian families. To seed the acceptance of bitcoin, the government even provided each family with a fraction of a bitcoin. The reality is that a good majority of those most poverty-stricken do not have access to the Internet to access their newfound coin. Still more coin is lost when people with little reason to use a computer or smartphone in the first place forget their wallet passwords or private key, which leaves the currency inaccessible. Satoshi deemed such losses of bitcoin an increase in wealth for everyone else since this deflation increases the spending power of remaining bitcoin holders.

A Crypto Cult of Personality in El Salvador

El Salvadorian President Nayib Bukele opted for this bitcoin experience because he considered himself technologically proficient, as many millennials are, and rejoiced as an honorary *Crypto Bro*. He believed that a step into Decentralized Finance would fling the 70% of his citizens without bank accounts into the crypto currency century. His citizens first heard of the plan when he announced it at a bitcoin conference in Miami, Florida, and he proudly participated in a social media site with fellow bitcoin evangelists a few days later as his congress approved the plan.

His plan was seeded with $150 million of bitcoin purchases, which resulted in $30 worth of bitcoin distributed to citizens willing to create a wallet and

> download their funds. Most citizens, the majority of whom do not have access to the Internet, reported that they would not participate, and businesses balked at the requirement that they accept bitcoin for payment, Few businesses had any sort of facility to transact, nor the ability to wait upwards of half an hour to determine whether the transfer was authenticated. Meanwhile, every bitcoin transaction must pay a small fee, so multiple spending of each $30 will end up generating transactions costs that fuel the bitcoin network but does nothing to feed El Salvador's hungry. To be fair, these fees are balanced off against the significant wire fees levied when relatives send money back home from abroad.
>
> Since the El Salvador experiment began, the International Monetary Fund (IMF) recommended they discontinue it. Instead Bukele doubled down by proposing a $1 billion Volcano Bond issuance, half of the proceeds to be spent on additional bitcoin accumulations, and the other half to build a Bitcoin City that would tap geothermal energy to run turbines and generate electricity for bitcoin mining. Meanwhile, economists and El Salvador businesses alike have panned the experiment.[4]

A number of nations are likely looking to the El Salvador experiment for signs of success, but there has been only one new taker since. In late April of, 2022, the Central African Republic became the second nation to adopt bitcoin as legal tender. Were a nation to experiment with alternative mediums of exchange, it should use one for which the blockchain is memorialized many times per minute rather than a handful of times per hour. Access would need to be simple, and, in the case of a digital currency, the Internet must be equally accessible. Finally, as we saw, some sort of a Stablecoin would be better for transactors, even if it would frustrate speculators.

El Salvador's experience aside, to attempt any serious solutions to the various challenges of bitcoin will require a global effort. This is an industry that permits nodes to exist anywhere they can discover copious power and an Internet connection. When China banned bitcoin, shipping containers of mining machines filled ships that migrated to the United States, Canada, Kazakhstan, and elsewhere almost overnight. When the City of Plattsburgh petitioned its power regulator to permit charging one of the world's largest mining farms a sufficient rate to cover the extra electricity it had to purchase, CoinMint's mining operation simply expanded less than a hundred miles

---

[4] https://www.bloomberg.com/news/articles/2022-03-22/crypto-world-awaits-el-salvador-s-bite-size-volcano-bitcoin-bond#:~:text=The%20government%20has%20an%20%24800,it%20a%20yield%20of%2019.5%25, retrieved March 25, 2022.

away over a weekend. They made sure their next installation was in a warehouse that could house dozens of shipping containers loaded chock-full with upwards of 100,000 miners and hence enable them to quickly relocate in the future at a moment's notice should a better deal arise. Crypto knows no borders and is a footloose industry.

The Need for Global Coordination

There are various tools that could be employed to slow down the bitcoin mining arms race and reduce electricity consumption, but they would necessarily require global adoption to be effective. These include a very hefty surtax on mining machines, given the short length of time necessary to amortize their costs. Other public policies include a fixed surcharge on electricity in the order of ten or twenty cents per kilowatt-hour applied only to such high-density users as bitcoin mining. Or, to half electricity usage, a 50% tax on mined coins could be levied.

These very severe applications of public policy are much larger than almost any imaginable product but tobacco perhaps and would require the application of these surtaxes globally, including in nations that believe they have significant excess coal to fuel the industry. Even with such Draconian measures, mining may only be halved. But, should miners merely migrate to a place like Kazakhstan when it believed it has sufficient coal-fired energy capacity, greenhouse gas emissions could actually become significantly worse. We know that such emissions know no national boundary, and hence, remain a problem for us all.

The industry can also easily go underground. Already many very small-scale hobby miners employ Antminer S9 machines, one or two at a time, to warm basements or garages, or any other area that can well-suffer the noise they create. I know of people who had access to free power at their place of employment who surreptitiously mined crypto from their offices at the expense of their employer. Renegades exist everywhere, and the profit motive, as we have seen, is a powerful motivator, especially if they subscribe to the general principles of libertarianism in which Satoshi believed. Such mining would remain anonymous and below the radar screen of possible regulators.

For these various reasons, and just like other activities for which society may not approve, there will always be bitcoin so long as there remains strong demand for those speculators, money launderers, and transactors evading detection who can tolerate the half hour latency in transaction approvals. To those who want to hide the identity behind their transactions, there will always be strong demand. And to those speculators who profit by gambling on volatility with other gamblers of their ilk, bitcoin will remain an attractive instrument. As the vast majority of more centrally controlled Proof of Stake coins become mainstream instruments for our transactions, and increasingly under regulation and oversight, bitcoin may well remain a refuge for scoundrels. Rogue operators and nations will likely always stand by to serve rogue users of a digital currency that began with so much promise and idealism, but was coopted by the very corporatization that Satoshi abhorred.

While it also has served as a way to move money easily across political and geographical boundaries, those who enjoy this feature are not the unbanked Satoshi imagined, but those more likely to launder money, avoid regulatory detection, or, when nations impose penalties such as occurred following Russia's invasion of Ukraine, bypass carefully crafted economic sanctions. These are large sums of a scale Satoshi could not have imagined and has put the price and volatility of bitcoin well beyond the great unbanked. Meanwhile, an entire secondary industry of large and profitable corporations has emerged to cater to this industry. In fact, the profits of these secondary sectors of exchanges and miner manufacturers continue to dwarf even the incredibly profitable mining farms.

27

Conclusion

So much is now known about bitcoin. So many have marveled and many more have profited from Satoshi's clever and altruistic concept. Few could have imagined the extent of the phenomenon. This book has described the varied aspects of the innovative new coin that few imagined at first. In retrospect, though, the phenomena, theory, and empirical analyses this book presents could possibly have been anticipated at the time of bitcoin's inception, if only one could imagine its spectacular price growth.

The challenge is in the protocol's richness and the coin's mysticism. When Satoshi developed the coin, perhaps only the collaborator Hal Finney also understood its technical promise. The economics of the coin even today is as baffling to computer scientists as the technical aspects of the coin have eluded economists. Bitcoin's richness and complexity, and its ability to defy redesign is both its marvel and curse. Like a science fiction creation of a genius scientist gone bad, the bitcoin footprint is sure to survive.

Bitcoin is the product of a genius who no doubt did not understand the full implications of its production on our environment and of its profits bestowed upon a subsequent generation of bitcoin evangelists. Satoshi's suspicion of existing institutions was not at all unusual among introverted but creative individuals born in the wake of Watergate, and who suffered the displacements from the follies of financial institutions too-big-to-fail. The ensuing Great Recession ensured Satoshi's generation would unlikely achieve the comfort of baby boomers before them.

Satoshi disappeared as quickly as bitcoin was sprung on the world, and far too early to ever see where this innovation would take us. It is possible that Satoshi still exists, with a bitcoin wealth that makes its creator one of the wealthiest people in the world, something Satoshi likely could not have imagined. If so, and given the hype and cultish desperation of those seeking to profit immensely from Satoshi's creation, I'd be surprised if this computer science genius will ever appear publicly.

We must all now reflect on how the planet and the currency can coexist. The world knows that large institutions develop a life of their own that is difficult to dismantle, at least until some other concept comes along that makes monolithic financial institutions obsolete. Such institutions create a culture that is amplified by marketers and protected by those well-served by the profits they create. They profit on fees, however small, for every transaction we make. Satoshi's goal to decentralize money is a great snippet of an idea, at least on the surface and in theory. But, now, barely a dozen years later, the coin has become so massive that it has taken a life of its own and has bred a new set of institutions rivalling the size of those Satoshi hoped to replace. We are at a crossroads as we try to socialize such a clever computer science concept so we can mitigate its consequences as we celebrate its innovation.

I began this book in marvel of Satoshi. But this should also be a cautionary tale. Our society is quick to profit from clever creations, but sometimes slow to see their consequences. Bitcoin's creator should not be held accountable for unintended consequences. Society must be capable of understanding the potentials and the dangers of innovations and proceed accordingly. Unfortunately, this is a cautionary tale of social innovation that is so complicated that few initially understood its utility and implications. My book had the hopeful mission to help educate my fellow citizens, our regulators, and the specialists in our various fields who toil and study often in isolation rather than in a cross-disciplinary manner.

Satoshi can't be blamed in any way for our failure to understand the implications of the coin on speculators, innovators, profiteers, malefactors, or our environment. It is our regulators who must protect us from ourselves and, at times, our creations. But, once an idea becomes an institution in itself, such regulation becomes much more difficult as positions become entrenched, and as the public is swayed by the influence of the profits our innovations foment, and often fails to account for all its costs.

Many *Crypto Bros* who have abandoned the ideals of Satoshi and the cypherpunks are able to profit immensely from bitcoin mining. I expect they understand at an intuitive level the implications of *The Bitcoin Dilemma*. They scour the planet for cheap electricity because they know they derive their profits not by inventing a better mousetrap but by diverting for themselves the cheapest power sources. But, to now, the economics have not been fully described to the extent we can see through claims that more efficient mining machines will reverse bitcoin's trend toward ever increasing energy demands.

Indeed, I have demonstrated that ever increasing innovation may even result in energy demand that accelerates even quicker than the increase in the bitcoin price. Meanwhile, not only do higher energy costs bankroll the profits of bitcoin miners, but they also pay an inefficiency premium on top of that. Obsolete fossil-fueled power plants must remain or return online to meet the energy demand of miners, at the expense of greenhouse gas emissions and higher yet electricity costs.

Our ability to treat the unintended consequences of the innovative bitcoin is confounded by all the wealth it diverted. Our only response, on behalf of our environment, is to hope the coin's popularity does not continue to accelerate and our regulators can rise to the task of truly ground-breaking oversight and remedy. Satoshi's innovation has heralded new tools for transaction efficiency, but our adoption of new coins cannot come at the expense of our few policy tools to tailor the economy toward high growth and employment and low inflation.

The challenges for society and regulators alike are substantial, and the complicated computer science concepts and economics certainly need to be absorbed and understood. I recognize the challenges, especially when an institution develops a mind and culture of its own, and when the wealth it creates also fosters an immense institutional momentum. However, we have no collective choice but to overcome these challenges. Bitcoin is not going away, and certainly digital currencies are here to stay. It is up to us to rise to the regulatory occasion.

The nature of bitcoin transactions is a world apart from what Satoshi enjoyed or expected. A recent snapshot showed that the top 1,000 bitcoin addresses represent 34.49% of all bitcoin value. This may well represent less than 1,000 individuals as many individuals use multiple public addresses, especially those with a desire to conceal identities. With a market capitalization that approached a trillion dollars, this represents an average public address value of one billion dollars for each of these individuals. Bitcoin has become the refuge of Bitcoin Billionaires and oligarchs who can hide their money nowhere else.

Satoshi's dream has been realized in some ways, and an abject failure in others. The incredibly low-transaction fee borne by users is well lower than bank wire fees, credit card merchant fees, and other similar costs. However, the entire economic system pays a much higher price. The bitcoin network

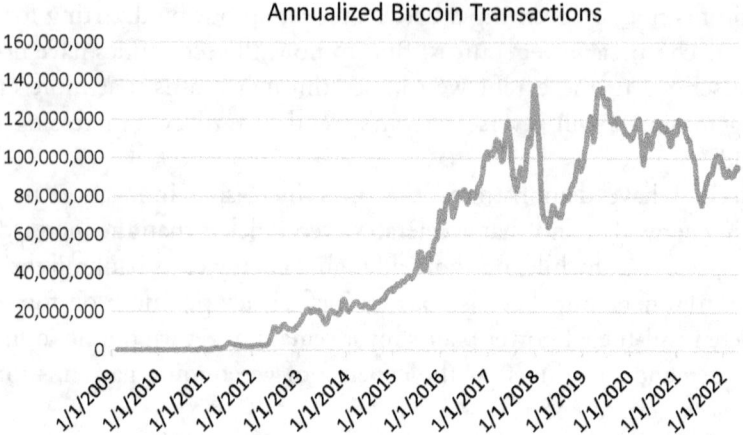

Fig. 27.1 Annual bitcoin transaction activity

processes about 250,000 transactions per day, at an average rate of three to seven transactions per second. But, the subsidies ratepayers make to the industrial electricity rate bitcoin miners negotiate, the diversion of costly fossil-fueled electricity to accommodate this greater demand, the environmental costs of fossil-fueled power generation, and the dilution of the value of the currency for holders of bitcoin as mining adds to the supply each day, all sum to a daily cost estimate of $127 million to support bitcoin mining. On a per transaction basis, these hidden costs sum to more than $500 per transaction (Fig. 27.1).

Yet, transactors themselves only see an average transaction fee of 0.0033%. While these fees seem modest, and in line with traditional debit card or bank transfer fees, but without the consumer protections other means provide to keep transactions safe, the economic system pays a much higher price.

Satoshi would be discouraged by the reality that those who transact in bitcoin are not the vast unbanked or those who wish to exercise their libertarian rights to consume goods or services that they conclude hurt no others. Instead, as the data show, most transactors are very wealthy and exchange far more in a single average transaction than the entire worth of the bitcoin network when Satoshi was active. Rather than a tool for the libertarian proletariat, bitcoin has instead become a vehicle for large speculators and investment banks, international money launderers, *Crypto Bros*, and perhaps oligarchs who wish to bypass the SWIFT system for communicating large international transactions. Meanwhile, the savings in bitcoin transactions costs are captured by the transactions costs paid to large exchanges that

Satoshi hoped to replace, and by us all for bitcoin's incredible electricity footprint.

To be fair, while the Cypherpunk ideal has been coopted by the very institutions and powerful they wished to undermine, crypto users will always find ways to transact. Bitcoin has been coopted to enable the agenda of the *Crypto Bros*, but Satoshi cannot be held responsible for it. Now, we must manage bitcoin to allow it, or more likely, the alternative Proof of Stake digital currencies it spawned, to live up to the ideal to which Satoshi subscribed.

Epilogue

Bitcoin is unrivalled in its height of market capitalization and depth of volatility, as measured by its finances, marketing efforts, and political divisiveness. The few months since the completion of this book have witnessed events that other securities may not experience over a lifetime.

The cryptocurrency has gone from a valuation approaching $70,000 to less than a third of that value in barely six months. Fortunes made have been lost many times over. Those who borrowed money to buy in at a price of $40,000 or $50,000 first earned 50% and, if they heeded the HODL mantra, have since been wiped out and may even owe twice as much as they borrowed. Anybody who bought in when the price was less than $20,000 may be okay, depending on what happens next, but that buy-in would have to have been some time during the Trump administration, and over a year before Matt Damon chided us that Fortune Favors the Brave. Everyone who responded to Damon's challenge may well have lost much or all of their investment, especially if they used borrowed money that is so facilitated by DeFi.

Some exchanges themselves who invented these new products have locked the accounts of their clients for fear of illiquidity and insolvency, and laid off almost a fifth of their workers, in the case of the huge Coinbase exchange, while some coins disappeared entirely, such as the disappearance of the stablecoin Terra.

Diehards believe crypto markets may bounce back, albeit with a new set of speculators. Time will tell if they are right.

Meanwhile, bitcoin mining continues. While *The Bitcoin Dilemma* determines that the level of electricity consumption in mining is determined primarily by the bitcoin price and the price of electricity, that result is a long run phenomenon. In the short run, how should a miner respond to the dramatic plunge in price?

Miners wear two hats. They are driven by the Gospel of Profits, and hence they will mine if they think their coins will be of greater value someday than the cost of electricity today. They are also often *Crypto Bros* who have great confidence in bitcoin and believe value for their coin will return. Finally, so long as they have sufficient cash flow to cover their electric bills and their miner financing payments or rental costs, they wish to mine knowing that, if they don't, those coins that will in their mind be again valuable someday will instead be mined by others. They see mining as a race to catch as catch can, and they are often willing to mine as speculators rather than investors.

Some have been able to secure inexpensive power, and have state-of-the-art machines. These miners can profitably produce at current low prices. Likely they would prefer to mine and hold rather than sell at current prices, so sufficient cash reserves to pay their electricity bills are crucial. However, given the deep pocket corporatization of the sector, it should come as no surprise that mining has not curtailed despite the bitcoin price carnage.

At the same time, the bitcoin mining industry has upped the lobbying ante. New York State has followed the lead of Plattsburgh and imposed a moratorium on mining powered by fossil fuel sources. Governor Kathy Hochul has yet to sign the two year moratorium. The industry has spent millions in lobbying, campaign donations, and advertising on behalf of New York State candidates with pro-crypto platforms. The public debate is fast and furious, but the public and politicians still fail to discern between the potential value of cryptocurrencies and the resource wastefulness of but one coin, bitcoin, that still dominates the vast majority of Proof-of-Work mining.

Meanwhile, ether, the major competing coin with qualities in every dimension of utility that dominate bitcoin, completed its transition to Proof-of-Stake, perhaps with even greater fervor given the loss of reward to its Proof-of-Work miners.

While the financial carnage for unsophisticated investors and some miners may be painful, the much greater scrutiny facing bitcoin may offer an avenue for more of the public to become better informed, even if it requires viewing a bit of a train wreck occuring in slow motion in front of our very eyes. Legislators are also taking notice now too. The Securities and Exchange Commission is still eyeing industry regulation because, unlike commodities such as wheat, oil, or pork bellies, the level of marketing to the general public remains feverish. The SEC's four part Howey test may help determine if a financial instrument is a security or a commodity. While the test implies that a crypto investment is a security as defined by Howey, some members of the U.S. Senate appear to be willing to wade into precedent and legislate otherwise. This so-called "Howey Test," is based on the 1946 Supreme Court case *SEC v. W.J.Howey Co.*, and determines that a financial instrument is a security if it requires an investment in money, represents a common enterprise, has the expectation of profit, and the value is derived from the efforts of others.

The decentralized nature of crypto often defies easy categorization. However, it is clear that crypto is a huge investment category. Given the incredible degree by which participants are currently trying to protect the value of bitcoin, it is becoming increasingly clear that the industry is a common enterprise in which profits are fueled by the efforts of others, especially if these "others" are often those who own the exchanges, act as custodians for customers' online wallets, and have developed algorithms for DeFi that sometimes require them to prop up the value of bitcoin.

This debate over the nature of bitcoin may nonetheless continue, even if the industry prefers to be overseen by entities such as the Commodity Futures Trading Commision. The Commission's deregulation was part of the Commodity Futures Modernization Act of 2000, fostered by the belief of Phil Gramm, the once-Congressional chair who oversaw the CFTC, that the exchange of commodities are primarily between experienced and sophisticated traders who understand the risk and need little protection from themselves. The huge losses by unsophisticated and perhaps deceived investors ought to be a cautionary tale.

These debates, on mining, and on regulation, will likely wind through state legislatures and Congress for years to come. While most informed observers can perhaps agree with the altruistic motives of Satoshi and the Cypherpunks, the subsequent divides created by those who will profit and the rest who will pay for the crypto movement are just as divisive among legislators. The debate will likely span years, which are eternities for a digital currency that has been traded for barely a decade. It may be, though, that *Crypto Bros* will suffer no problematic delays. Little regulations exist, and many opportunities abound to mine, create new Initial Coin Offerings, pump-and-dump, and market to the masses in the regulatory void that currently exists, and shall likely enjoy the regulatory vacuum for some time to come.

Appendix

Code Changes in the City of Plattsburgh in Response to Cryptocurrency Mining

J.
Moratorium on commercial cryptocurrency mining operations.
[Added 3–15-2018 by L.L. No. 3–2018].
(1)
Enactment and title. The Common Council of the City of Plattsburgh does hereby ordain and enact the City of Plattsburgh moratorium on commercial cryptocurrency mining operations in the City of Plattsburgh. This subsection shall impose a moratorium on applications or proceedings, or the issuance of approvals or permits, for commercial cryptocurrency mining operations in the City of Plattsburgh.
(2)
Authorization, purpose, and definitions.
(a)
Authorization.
[1]
Pursuant to the authority and provisions of §10 of the Municipal Home Rule Law of the State of New York and the statutory powers vested in the Common Council of the City of Plattsburgh to regulate and control land use and to protect the health, safety, and welfare of its residents, the Common Council of the City of Plattsburgh hereby declares an 18-month moratorium on all

applications, or proceedings for applications, for the issuance of approvals or permits for the commercial cryptocurrency mining operations in the City of Plattsburgh.

[2]

This moratorium will allow time for the Zoning Code and Municipal Lighting Department regulations to be amended to regulate this potential use.

(B)

Purpose.

[1]

It is the purpose of this subsection to allow the City of Plattsburgh the opportunity to consider zoning and land use laws and Municipal Lighting Department regulations before commercial cryptocurrency mining operations results in irreversible change to the character and direction of the City.

[2]

Further, it is the purpose of this subsection to allow the City of Plattsburgh time to address, through planning and legislation, the promotion of the protection, order, conduct, safety, health, and well-being of the residents of the City which are presented as heightened risks associated with commercial cryptocurrency mining operations.

[3]

It is the purpose of this subsection to facilitate the adoption of land use and zoning and/or Municipal Lighting Department regulations to protect and enhance the City's natural, historic, cultural, and electrical resources.

(c)

Definitions. As used in this section, the following terms shall have the meanings indicated:

Commercial Cryptocurrency mining

The commercial process by which cryptocurrency transactions are verified and added to the public ledger, known as the "block chain," and also the means through which new units of cryptocurrencies are released, through the use of server farms employing data processing equipment. For purposes of this definition, any equipment which requires a high-density load service, or any server farm will presumably be a commercial cryptocurrency mining operation.

Cryptocurrency
A digital currency in which encryption techniques are used to regulate the generation of units of currency and verify the transfer of funds, operating independently of a central bank.

High-Density Load Service
The provision of electrical service where the requested load density, in the portion of the premises containing the load consuming equipment, exceeds 250 kWh/ft2/year.

Server Farm
Three or more interconnected computers housed together in a single facility whose primary function is to perform cryptocurrency mining or associated data processing.

(3)
Scope of controls. During the effective period of this subsection:

(a)
The Code Enforcement Officer, Building Inspector, Planning Board, or Zoning Board of Appeals shall not accept an application for a commercial cryptocurrency mining operation.

(b)
The Code Enforcement Officer, Building Inspector, Planning Board, or Zoning Board of Appeals shall not grant any permit for a commercial cryptocurrency mining operation.

(4)
No consideration of new applications. No applications for commercial cryptocurrency mining operations or for approvals for a site plan, special use permit, building permit, or any other permit shall be approved by any board, officer, employee, or agent of the City of Plattsburgh while the moratorium imposed by this subsection is in effect. Nothing in this subsection shall be construed such as to result in any default approval for any application heard or considered during the moratorium imposed by this subsection. This moratorium shall apply to all such applications, whether pending or received prior to the effective date of this law.

(5)
Term. The moratorium imposed by this subsection shall be in effect for a period of 18 months from the effective date of this subsection. It may be terminated earlier if the Common Council determines by resolution that the purpose of the local law has been fulfilled. During the period of the moratorium, the Common Council shall endeavor to amend the local Zoning Code

and/or Municipal Lighting Department regulations to address and regulate commercial cryptocurrency mining operations.

(6)

Location. The moratorium imposed by this subsection shall apply to the territorial limits of the City of Plattsburgh.

(7)

Penalties. Any firm, person, corporation, or other entity that shall establish, place, construct, erect, or in any way site or locate a commercial cryptocurrency mining operation described in this subsection in the City of Plattsburgh in violation of the provisions of this subsection shall be subject to, in addition to any penalties prescribed by state or local law, a civil penalty of not more than $1,000 for each day or part thereof during which such violation continues. If necessary to remove any construction or property that may have taken place in violation of this subsection, then the cost of such removal, including reasonable attorneys' fees incurred by the City, shall constitute a lien and charge against any real property owned or leased by the violator located within the City and shall be collected in the same manner and at the same time as other City charges. The civil penalties provided for by this subsection shall be recoverable in an action instituted in the name of the City in any court of competent jurisdiction.

(8)

Validity. The invalidity of any provision of this subsection shall not affect the validity of any other provision of this subsection that can be given effect without such invalid provision.

cryptocurrency mining operations.

[Added 10-25-2018 by L.L. No. 6–2018].

(1)

Definitions.

Commercial cryptocurrency mining

The commercial process by which cryptocurrency transactions are verified and added to the public ledger, known as the blockchain, and also the means through which new units of cryptocurrencies are released, through the use of server farms employing data processing equipment. For purposes of this section, any equipment which requires a high-density load service, or any server farm, will constitute a commercial cryptocurrency mining operation.

Cryptocurrency

A digital currency in which encryption techniques are used to regulate the generation of units of currency and verify the transfer of funds, operating independently of a central bank.

High-Density Load Service
The provision of electrical service where the requested load density has, for any monthly billing period, either an average power demand in excess of 300 kilowatts, or an average power density in excess of 250 kilowatt hours per year per square foot, equivalent to 35.064 square feet per kilowatt, at 100% load factor. "Square footage" is defined as leased or owned boundaries of floor space devoted to the operating data processing equipment, and excludes space for offices, storage, shipping and receiving, or any other space that is not electronic processing.

Server Farm
Three or more interconnected computers housed together in a single facility whose primary function is to perform cryptocurrency mining or associated data processing.

(2)
Fire safety.

(a)
Fire suppression. An active clean agent fire protection system must be provided and maintained in good working order within any structure which contains a commercial cryptocurrency mining operation. High-sensitivity smoke detectors shall be installed and operational in order to activate this clean agent fire suppression system.

(b)
There shall be an emergency electricity termination switch installed outside of any containment structure which contains a commercial cryptocurrency mining operation.

(c)
Containment space. The equipment used in any commercial cryptocurrency mining operation shall be housed in an individually metered, electrically grounded, and metal-encased structure with a fire rating designed to resist an internal electrical fire for at least 30 min. The containment space shall contain baffles that will automatically close in the event of fire independent of a possible electric system failure.

(d)
All building requirements required by this section, including, but not limited to, heat transfer apparatuses, fire detection/suppression systems, or containment structures shall be designed by a New York State licensed engineer and in accordance with all applicable codes and standards.

(3)
Heat.

(a)

The ambient temperature inside of a containment space which houses a commercial cryptocurrency mining operation shall not exceed 120° F. at any time. No person shall be permitted to regularly inspect and work within the containment area which houses a commercial cryptocurrency mining operation if the ambient temperature within the containment area exceeds 90° F.

(b)

Any commercial cryptocurrency mining operation shall ensure that no more than 20% of the heat dissipated by the mining activity shall be released directly to the outside when the average daily temperature is less than 40° F.

(4)

Nuisance abatement.

(a)

No commercial cryptocurrency mining operation may cause adverse or detrimental effects to adjoining lessees, owners, or residents that diminish the quality of life or increase the costs of serving their business or maintaining their homes.

(b)

No commercial cryptocurrency mining operation shall produce a noise level exceeding 90 dB from a distance of 25 feet from the exterior of the containment structure.

(5)

Special use permit. A special use permit, pursuant to this chapter of the City Code, is required for any new commercial cryptocurrency mining operation, and any expansion of any pre-existing commercial cryptocurrency mining operation, in order to ensure conformance with this section.

(6)

Effective date; applicability.

(a)

This subsection shall take effect immediately upon filing in the office of the New York State Secretary of State.

(b)

This subsection shall apply to all building permit or zoning applications pending at the time it becomes effective, unless the reviewing Council or Board shall determine that its application would be impracticable or unjust in the particular circumstances.

Glossary

51% Attack an effort to artificially manipulate a blockchain of transactions by commandeering a majority of the nodes that authenticate a block through polling.

Account an identifier in a cryptocurrency wallet that attaches a public key observed within transactions in blocks on a blockchain to its owner through a private key known only by the owner and its custodial wallet.

Adam Back a British computer scientist who has been an influential colleague since the early days of bitcoin.

Address a locator, often a unique 64-digit hexadecimal, or 256-bit number that uniquely associates a transaction with the owner it represents. This address is typically the public face of the account owner, but does not identify the owner unless also accompanied by a private key.

Algorithm a set of commands in a computer science script that performs some function based on a series of calculations. For instance, a hash algorithm may return a unique number for a given set up inputs, often in the form of transactions between addresses.

Algorithmic Stablecoin an algorithm designed to ensure that the value of a Stablecoin remains relatively constant by automatically purchasing the coin when its price falls, and selling the coin when its price rises.

Algo-Trading (Algorithmic Trading) an algorithm that automatically places buy and sell orders for securities or currencies based on various rules baked into the algorithm. Such algo-trading can take advantage of trends far more rapidly than can human traders.

Trustless a trading and blockchain encoding regime that does not rely on a centralized entity to ensure accurate verification of a series of transactions.

Anarcho-capitalism a philosophy advanced by the economist Murray Rothbard which espouses the advantages of a decentralized capitalist system that can substitute for and hence thwart the influence of established institutions. Bitcoin evangelists have adopted this philosophy as the underlying motivation for a flourishing cryptocurrency industry.

Arbitrage a process of buying an asset in one market and selling in another to take advantage of slight price differences across markets or forums. Such arbitrage results in profits with low risk and also equalizes prices across markets.

Antminer S9 the first very broadly marketed and sold bitcoin mining machine that ushered in the corporate era of bitcoin mining following its availability in 2017.

ASIC an acronym for an Application Specific Integrated Circuit, which is a device that incorporates specialized circuitry to perform a primary function extremely efficiently. ASIC technologies have vastly increased the speed of processing of cryptocurrency encoding, but, due to *The Bitcoin Dilemma*, has not translated these efficiencies into reduced energy consumption across their networks.

Asset-Backed Tokens a digital claim that establishes title and ownership on a physical asset. For instance, a Stablecoin cryptocurrency allows the transfer of such titles to a coin backed by a convertible currency such as the U.S. dollar.

Astroturfing a deceptive attempt to flip public debate by conducting marketing campaigns that undermine or misrepresent legitimate public concerns. For instance, Greenwashing is an astroturfing technique to make those who contribute to the burning of fossil fuels and their generation of greenhouse gasses appear to actually contribute to the improvement of the environment.

Audit a methodical examination of a process to ensure that it obeys the underlying principles of the process. For instance, a forensic audit tracks transactions between accounts to better understand the purpose of the transactions, while a code audit in an inspection of programming code to ensure it acts as intended and without any unintended consequences.

Authentication a method that confirms the validity and authority of an entity to perform a function such as a transaction in a blockchain, the right to access a program or device, or an assurance that other rights assigned to an entity are not illegally granted to another entity without permission.

Bandwidth the capacity or rate of transmission of data across a network, typically measures in data bits per second, or megabits per second (Mbps). Greater bandwidth allows for more and more frequent transactions.

Banking Secrecy Act (BSA) an act promulgated in the United States in 1970 to combat the movement of cash from illegal activities into legal activities in an effort to conceal the illegal activity. The BSA requires the owners of transactions of certain types or size to be revealed.

Bitcoin ATM (BTM) an automated teller machine (ATM or cashpoint) that allows the user to buy and sell bitcoin.

Bitcoin the first broadly popularized and employed cryptocurrency, proposed, and developed by Satoshi in 2009. It is a Proof of Work digital currency that enjoys the largest market share, by market capitalization, of all cryptocurrencies.

Bitcoin Dilemma a counterintuitive result that demonstrates the amount of electricity consumed in Proof of Work mining increases with value of the cryptocurrency but does not decrease as new and more efficient mining machines are made available. The dilemma arises because of the way the difficulty target in Proof of Work mining adjusts as processing capacity improves.

Bitcoin Dominance (BTCD) the observation of the share of cryptocurrency values, as measured by its share market capitalization, is dominated by the bitcoin cryptocurrency.

Bitcoin Pizza a reference to two pizzas purchased for 10,000 bitcoin by Laszlo Hanyecz. This transaction, valued at approximately $420 million today, constituted the first commercial transaction of bitcoin.

Bitcointalk a popular online forum for discussion of blockchain technology, bitcoin, and cryptocurrencies in general.

Bitmain a manufacturer of bitcoin mining equipment using ASIC technologies. Bitmain also owned a bitcoin mining pool and, before divestment, a number of bitcoin mines in China.

Block Reward the amount of a cryptocurrency given to the first miner or pool of miners that successfully solve a puzzle designed to permanently encode a block in a blockchain in a way that defies subsequent tampering.

Block Size the amount of data that can be contained in a single block in a blockchain. For bitcoin, the block size is 1 megabyte, while Ethereum 1.0 can encode 8 megabyte.

Block Time the duration spanned by a given block in a chain. For bitcoin, one block is produced approximately every ten minutes, while the Ethereum 1.0 protocol encodes a block every twelve seconds.

Blockchain a sequence of blocks, or collection of data, usually in the form of transactions between addresses, that are linked serially over time to ensure one block cannot be modified without destroying the integrity of the chain. This technique maintains the integrity of transactions in a cryptocurrency over time.

Bubble a runup of asset prices in which the value of the asset exceeds its rational or intrinsic value.

Central Bank an agency charged by a national government to oversee the commercial banking industry and other financial institutions, and the responsibility to conduct monetary policy to manage inflation and unemployment. In the United States, the central bank is named the Federal Reserve.

Central Bank Digital Currency (CBDC) a digital currency issued by a central bank to act as a legal tender alongside a conventional paper currency. The offering of such a digital currency requires governmental authorization.

Central Processing Unit (CPU) an integrated circuit that performs much of the calculations and processes enabled by firmware and software programs contained in an operating system.

Cloud Mining the mining of cryptocurrency through access to miners located elsewhere and accessed through the cloud, often based on a daily rental rate for the processing power.

Cold Storage a method to store the ownership of cryptocurrencies that is not directly linked to the Internet and hence is difficult to hack or steal. These offline wallet addresses could be stored on a USB drive, on paper, or on an offline computer.

Cold Wallet a wallet which can be accessed only offline and with access to a securely held private key.

Collateralization the use of a valuable asset to offer backstop security for a loan of an alternate asset such as cash or cryptocurrency.

Collateralized Stablecoin a Stablecoin that maintains a fixed or stable value because it is predominantly or entirely backed by collateral held in a reserve account.

Confirmation the series of blocks and length of time necessary for verification of a transaction. For instance, a transaction in bitcoin is collected over a ten-minute interval and then protected and verified over another interval of approximately ten minutes before the transfer of funds can be consummated in credits and debits to individual accounts.

CPU Miner a personal computer that is employed to perform the operations necessary to add a block to a blockchain in a cryptocurrency. In their infancy, many coins can be mined with CPUs before processor competition requires more specialized mining hardware such as GPUs or ASICs.

Craig Wright a noted Australian computer scientist who was prominent in the early development of bitcoin, and who is sometimes proposed as the person behind Satoshi, the mysterious and possible pseudonym for the inventor of bitcoin.

Credit Rating a score granted by one of three agencies in the United States, or agencies in other countries, that measure the creditworthiness of an individual or entity based on their past credit history.

Crypto Debit Card a debit card that allows the cardholder to pay for transactions using cryptocurrencies held in their digital wallets.

Cryptoasset a digital asset that uses cryptographic processes and algorithms to protect the cryptocurrency blockchain.

Cryptocultist an individual who adopts the political philosophy based on libertarian values and the decentralization of financial processes that bypass governmental or large private institutions. In addition, the cryptocultist is willing to depart from the original values espoused by Satoshi in their interest in profit. They often represent their pursuit of profit in heroic terms based on the spirit of, or their preferred interpretation of Satoshi.

Cryptocurrency a digital medium of exchange for which transactions are maintained by a blockchain protected using cryptographic techniques.

Cryptographic Hash Function a program or algorithm that converts a block containing a series of transactions to a (typically) 256-bit long number in a manner that links the block to the one before and after it as a way to prevent any subsequent modification.

Cryptomillionaire an individual who accumulates the equivalent of at least a million dollars in cryptocurrency, usually through mining or cryptocurrency speculation.

Currency a medium of exchange to facilitate transactions and commerce.

Custodian an individual or agency responsible for the safekeeping and recordkeeping associated with an asset, including a digital asset protected using cryptographic techniques.

Day Trading a type of speculative trading during the hours an exchange is open that is based on the discovery of profits arising from arbitrage opportunities. The term "day" referred initially to the hours of operation of early computerized stock exchanges, with positions closed at before the exchange closes so the trader is not subjected to overnight changes in security value. With 24-h exchanges, the term now applies to a trader who tends to not hold positions at times when market activity is not monitored.

Decentralized Currency a digital currency that can be traded between peers, in a peer-to-peer network, that bypasses traditional financial institutions. In doing so, a network of decentralized nodes is able to authenticate and memorialize transactions included in a blockchain without intervention by a supervising third party.

Deep Web a loose network of websites and users that are hidden from unauthorized users and traditional search engines.

DeFi a movement that subscribes to the goal of decentralized financial transactions without the need for intervention or oversight by third parties or traditional financial institutions.

Delegated Proof of Stake (dPOS) an alternative version of the Proof of Stake model of blockchain authentication and verification that delegates verification duties to a subset of participants that are authorized to reach a consensus on authentication proposals.

Denial-of-Service (DoS) Attack a technique used to neutralize or make inaccessible a web site or function by overburdening the site with random access requests to prevent legitimate users from accessing the service.

Derivative any financial security that derives its value not based on its own intrinsic value but is instead derived based on the value of another asset or security.

Digital Currency a currency for which ownership is recorded and verified using digital means, usually over the Internet. The digital currency may or may not represent title to assets with intrinsic value.

Distributed Consensus a polling requirement that the majority or all members of a decentralized network can agree to the accuracy of a proposed candidate for authentication of a block in a blockchain.

Distributed Denial of Service (DDoS) Attack a denial of service attack in which the attack comes from a number of sources either directed or under the control of an attacking agent, often through the distribution of malware planted on unsuspecting computers.

Distributed Ledger a series of blocks in a chain that are authenticated by many nodes that are operated in a manner to prevent collusion and block corruption. The network needs not be decentralized. Distribution of a ledger makes its corruption more difficult because multiple records of blocks are recorded at numerous site.

Dorian Satoshi an Asian-American physicist some have proposed to be the true identity of Satoshi. Satoshi declared in a correspondence that s/he is not Dorian Satoshi.

Double Spend Attack a technique to corrupt a block or blocks in a chain so that the attacker can again spend a digital asset that has already been transferred to another account holder. Such double spending then can act as a theft of the cryptocurrency.

Encryption a method that converts a string of letters and numbers into another string so that the original string can be recovered only by an authorized user who has access to a code or decoding process.

Escrow a third-party custodial account that is held in trust and not released until authorized by a buyer and seller upon full completion of the terms of a transfer.

Field Programmable Gate Array (PPGA) an integrated circuit that can be modified through software or firmware to optimally perform a specific function. This technique allows a processing unit to direct more resources to certain functions as needed, rather than in fixed proportions hard-wired into a central processing unit (CPU).

Fork a departure from a predefined path in the progression of a blockchain or algorithm. Upon the fork, the new version of the blockchain or algorithm may evolve alongside the original version, with popularity dictating over time which fork is considered to best improve the process of interest. For some cryptocurrencies, such as bitcoin, a proposed fork must be approved by consensus of the nodes in the network, while in other cryptocurrency protocols, such as Ethereum, a fork may be authorized by a governing entity.

Fractional Stablecoin a digital currency for which its value is maintained by a reserve asset, such as the U.S. dollar, such that the total value of the reserve asset is less than the total value of the Stablecoin. The reserve asset may be used to trade algorithmically for the Stablecoin so that the value of the Stablecoin remains roughly constant relative to the backing asset.

Genesis Block the first recorded block in a chain. The Genesis block differs from other blocks in that it cannot contain a code that represents the value of the block that preceded it. The Genesis Block is often referred to as block 0 since it differs in syntax from the blocks the follow it.

Gold-Backed Cryptocurrency a Stablecoin that is a token that represents the value of an underlying physical quantity of gold.

Hacking a method designed to either monitor or take control of another central processor or network by an unauthorized use, usually for illicit purposes.

Hal Finney an early collaborator in the development of bitcoin and the inventor of a predecessor to bitcoin.

Hardware Wallet a digital cryptocurrency wallet that is typically removed from the network and acts as a dependable backup source for the wallet.

Hash an algorithm that takes a large or complex set of alphanumeric inputs and converts them to much more compact output such that a small change in the input results in a significant change in the output.

Hexadecimal a mathematical base represented by the numbers 0 to 9 and letters A to F. These sixteen possible values can represent 2^4 values equivalent to four binary numbers. Hence, a 256-bit long binary string can be represented by a 32-character-long hexadecimal string.

Hot Wallet a digital wallet that contains cryptocurrencies but is linked to the Internet and hence is vulnerable to potential manipulation or theft by hackers.

Inflation a rise in prices of a bundle of goods and services that acts as a measure for the depreciation in purchasing power of a currency.

Internet of Things (IoT) a widely accepted communications protocol that allows a wide variety of devices connected to a network to report and exchange data and information and permit or control access and the operation of other devices on the network that follow the same protocols.

Keylogger a malicious application that is surreptitiously planted onto the hard drive or within the firmware of a computer processor so that the attacker can observe and record keystrokes that may represent logon credentials or operations. Such an application can be delivered through email or shared resources to potentially allow a malicious attacker to gain control of the computer and either divert resources or demand a ransom for the release of the victim's computer.

Leverage the use of borrowed assets to permit the borrower to purchase more of another asset than their initial investment could afford. By earning more on the use of the borrowed asset than the interest obliged to pay for use of the asset, a borrower can earn a greater profit than otherwise possible had they been limited to their original investment. Leverage allows the user to magnify both their profits and potential losses due to movement in the speculative asset purchased.

Leveraged Tokens a token for which its value is derived by both a purchased and a borrowed security. Because of the built-in leverage, changes in the purchased fractional asset are magnified, both in gains and losses.

Malware small and difficult to detect software that can be injected onto a computer or other device that affords the malicious attacker access to the device or network.

Margin Call a notice and potential sale of assets used as collateral for a loan when the asset value falls below the amount borrowed.

Margin Trading a method to increase leverage and hence the return on an asset, net of interest paid, by borrowing to purchase more of an asset than the trader could otherwise purchase based on their own investment.

Market Capitalization (MCAP) the total value of a traded asset based on current market valuation. For instance, the value of all outstanding bitcoin at the market price has topped one trillion dollars U.S. at times.

Megahashes Per Second (MH/s) the number of hashes, in millions, that a processor can successfully calculate in one second. Common central processing units (CPUs) of 2009 vintage could perform a hash function called SHA-256, used to encode bitcoin, in excess of one megahash per second. A state-of-the-art ASIC can perform the same hash function at a rate greater than 100 million MH/s.

Mining the process of calculating, authenticating, and verifying additional blocks in a blockchain. Each block contains a set of new transactions to be validated, and nonces that represent the previous and the current block. In the case of Proof of Work, the miner following this process is awarded a specified reward or share thereof.

Mining as a Service (MaaS) the provision of mining capacity for rent over the Cloud for users who wish to mine but do not have the requisite hardware or access to a sufficiently profitable electricity rate.

Mining Contract a contract that secures the right to mine using equipment accessed over the Cloud, for a predetermined rental rate and duration.

Mining Difficulty a factor that algorithmically adjusts the difficulty of successfully calculating and authenticating a block in a blockchain so that blocks are mined at approximately a specified block duration.

Mining Farm a collection of mining machines collocated to take advantage of their combined collection of resources, network, and preferable electricity rates.

Mining Pool a coalition of miners that agree to collectively sum their processing power and share in any reward that results should an individual member of the pool successfully authenticate and calculate a block, subject to verification of the broader network.

Mining Reward a specified and potentially algorithmically adjustable reward to a miner or its pool upon successful authentication and calculation of a validated block in a blockchain.

Mining Rig a mining machine that is used for cryptocurrency mining, often as part of a mining farm or pool.

Mobile Wallet a wallet that contains a private key and holds the amount of a digital currency owned on a mobile device that can be accessed by the owner.

Moore's Law a prediction made by Gordon Moore in 1965 that computing power will double approximately every eighteen months. Moore's Law allows processor capabilities to rise and costs to fall over time. In the case of bitcoin, it results in collective network processing power that has increased by more than a factor of one trillion since 2009.

Network a collection of clients or nodes that are connected, usually through their unique Internet Protocol (IP) addresses, to collectively perform a function. In the case of bitcoin, the network represents collective processing power equivalent to approximately ten million Antminer S9 ASIC processors.

Nick Szabo the developer of Bit Gold and an early bitcoin advocate and collaborator. He also proposed the use of smart contracts that permit additional functionality for more sophisticated cryptocurrency protocols such as Ethereum 1.0 and 2.0.

Non-Fungible Token (NFT) the digital representation, or token, that represents title to a digital asset, real property, or digital intellectual capital that cannot be taken by others without permission.

Office of the Comptroller of the Currency (OCC) an office of the Federal Government of the United States that reports to the U.S. Treasury and oversees national banks, some state banks, federal savings associations, and foreign banks operating in the United States.

Open Source a software or hardware protocol that allows for free and open development and sharing of the protocol as a way to further development and benefit the broader community of participants and users.

Paper Wallet a physically printed copy of a private key, typically in the form of a hexadecimal 64-digit code or a phrase that represents the code, that affords the holder access to the contents of a digital cryptocurrency wallet.

Peer-to-Peer (P2P) the ability of individuals or their nodes to share information directly between them in a decentralized way that is not subject to monitoring. This allows parties of a distributed network to share files, tasks, and rewards in the case of Proof of Work mining.

Peer-to-Peer (P2P) Lending a method that allows participating peers to lend and borrow among themselves over a network without the need of or oversight of a middleman or authority. Such loans are typically collateralized through tokens of ownership to valuable assets.

Peg a benchmarked rate of exchange between two assets that can be maintained through algorithmic or manual intervention.

Pegged Currency an asset, such as a Stablecoin, for which its relative value is maintained through some sort of manual or algorithmic process, usually in reference to an underlying physical currency.

Phishing a technique in which a malicious hacker wins access to documents or computers by misrepresenting themselves as a legitimate entity that may do business with the victim. Such phishing could result in the revelation of critical information from the victim that may allow the hacker subsequent access to valuable documents, bank accounts, passwords, or other valuable assets or information.

Private Blockchain a form of a blockchain that is owned and employed on a proprietary basis by a single entity such as a corporation over its network.

Private Key a secret string that is necessary, in combination with a public key, to decode and hence complete access to a transaction that is protected through a public/private key combination. This asymmetric-key encryption process, in which part of the key can be viewed and referred to publicly, but cannot be completely decoded without the additional private key allows for transactions to be made within a blockchain without revelation of the originator and receiver of the transaction.

Proof of Authority (PoA) a blockchain consensus methodology that is more efficient than Proof of Work because it verifies authenticity through a streamlined process that can be administered only by a party or parties authorized to perform blockchain encryption functions.

Proof of Donation a blockchain authentication method that employs donations as an element of blockchain transfers and encryption.

Proof of Stake (PoS) a method to authenticate and encode a blockchain by consensus agreement of a group that pledges, or stakes, something of considerable value to essentially insure the validity of the blockchain authentication.

Proof of Validation (PoV) a type of Proof of Stake blockchain authentication method that ensures blockchain authentication is performed only through nodes that are validated based on some Proof of Stake.

Proof of Work (PoW) a blockchain authentication method that requires miners to solve a complex and time and energy consuming mechanism as its stake in ensuring the validity of the consensus blockchain authentication for the addition of a new block to the blockchain.

Protocol a collection of rules that specify how individual nodes and a network shall interact to collect, authenticate, and validate additions of a block to a blockchain, usually based on a consensus of nodes on a network.

Public Address an observable string, often 64 characters long in hexadecimal format, or 256 bits, that specifies a unique account which belongs to and can be accessed by an individual or entity who also has access to the private key associated with the public address.

Public Blockchain a blockchain that can be observed by the public, but which may or may not reveal the identity of transactors without an additional private kay.

Public Key an observable string, often 64 characters long in hexadecimal format, or 256 bits, that is necessary, in combination with a private key, to denote and hence complete access to a transaction that is protected through a public/private key combination. This asymmetric-key encryption process, in which part of the key can be viewed and referred to publicly, but cannot be completely decoded without both the public and private key allows for transactions to be made within a blockchain without revelation of the originator and receiver of the transaction.

Pump-and-Dump a method to drive the price of a security up by creating news stories designed to generate interest in the security, followed by a sale of the security before the news is discovered false or misleading.

Ransomware a malicious code or application placed on a victim's computer or network that allows a hacker to steal network contents or encrypt the victim's network, to be held for ransom of a specified amount and address, usually in bitcoin. If the ransom is paid, the hacker grants to the victim a code that will unlock or repair their network.

Regulated a sector or function that is overseen and controlled by another entity and set of rules, usually in the overall public interest.

Regulatory Compliance adherence to a set of rules and oversight to ensure that practices followed advance a (usually) legislated public interest.

Renewable Energy energy that is derived from a resource that, if used within certain constraints, can be provided indefinitely on a sustainable basis. Examples include solar, wind, and tidal power, although these three resources depend on the energy from the sun, which mortals can assume are almost infinitely lived. While nuclear fission and fusion can be produced in abundant amounts, the fissionable or fusionable material is exhaustible, but not easily so given the rate of human consumption. Hydrogen as a fuel source is not renewable, especially since there are few natural sources of hydrogen and hence abundant electricity must be employed to generate hydrogen.

Return on Investment (ROI) the flow of rewards, after variable costs, that can be devoted to pay over time for an initial and usually significant investment in the expansion of productive capacity.

Rug-Pull a crypto scam in which publicity is generated to hype a new coin, followed by absconding of the coin funds raised, which results in a valueless asset and defrauded investors.

Satoshi (SATS) a division of one bitcoin into a smaller unit representing a value of 0.00000001 BTC.

Satoshi the person or people attributed to the creation of bitcoin and responsible for mining the single largest batch of bitcoin owned by any one entity. There are a variety of theories about the true identity of Satoshi.

Scaling Problem a design constraint that limits the rate and quantity of transactions a specified blockchain can authenticate, encode, and verify in a given period of time.

Scaling Solution a modification of a blockchain protocol that improves throughput and expansion. For instance, Ethereum 2.0 extends the functionality of the Ethereum 1.0 protocol.

Securities and Exchange Commission (SEC) an agency of the federal government of the United States that has the regulatory duty to enforce securities and exchange laws. The agency is also responsible for proposing and promulgating securities rules, regulating associated sectors and publicly traded corporations, and other activities that could negatively affect the securities industry.

SHA-256 a sophisticated cryptographic function that generates a 256-bit code as an output for any text included in its input. It has the quality of outputting a dramatically different signature code for even a minute change in its input. This hash function is used in bitcoin Proof of work (PoW) as well as some other blockchain encoding protocols.

Shilling an attempt to use media as a repository for garnering interest in a new cryptocurrency or other asset or security. Often, social media is exploited as the object of false or misleading statements intended to move the value of a cryptocurrency.

Silk Road a broad and extensive hidden black market that allowed the transaction of illegal goods and services. It resided on the dark web, and was discontinued by the FBI in 2013 as a culmination of a series of seizures of illegally obtained bitcoin.

Soft Fork a blockchain protocol modification which, if accepted, will generally require miners to update their software to continue to mine along the new fork.

Spyware a form of malware that allows the perpetrator the ability to view records or observe keystrokes on a victim's computer or device.

Store of Value a quality of a valuable asset that allows its value to be maintained over time rather than be depreciated. Store of value is an important quality for a cryptocurrency hoping to gain wide acceptance.

Supercomputer a general-purpose computer that can attain a very high level of processing speed, typically measured in double precision floating point operations per second (FLOPS). The world's top supercomputers are approaching a speed of 1 exaflop, or 10^{18} FLOPS. A gaming PC with specialized GPU is able to attain approximately 6 teraflops, or 6×10^{12} FLOPS. A PC of 2009 vintage and a good graphics processor could process 2,526,800,000,000 FLOPS, or 2.5268×10^{12} FLOPS. Comparisons based on FLOPS is somewhat misleading because different types of processors are optimized for different types of calculations.

Supply Chain Attack a method adopted by malicious attackers to garner information of value from those who supply major corporations or government entities. In doing so, the hacker may obtain back door access to an organization's network.

Terahashes Per Second (TH/s) equal to one trillion (10^{12}) hashes per second, a useful unit of processing power for machines that process the hash algorithm. For instance, the ubiquitous Antminer S9 machine processes at approximately 13.5 TH/s.

Decentralized Autonomous Organization (The DAO) an early example of a decentralized network of nodes established by developers in 2016.

Decentralized Currency a blockchain currency that employs a decentralized network of nodes to verify, codify, and authenticate additional to a blockchain by consensus agreement of the entire network.

Digital Dollar a potential future digital currency sponsored by the U.S. Federal Reserve and tied to the U.S. dollar. Other national digital currencies are referred to as a Central Bank Digital Currency (CBDC).

Token a unit of account that represents a digital title to a unit of real or virtual value. Digital currencies are, in essence, tokens, as are Non-Fungible Tokens (NFT).

Token Economy the combination of goods and services that can be transacted in a decentralized peer-to-peer network through blockchains that can operate independently and without participation of third parties or intermediaries.

Tokenomics the social science study of token economies and the various protocols that define the supply and transactions of cryptocurrencies.

Trojan a form of malware that may enter a computer system hidden within a piece of otherwise legitimate software.

Tumbling a method of laundering of bitcoin or other cryptocurrency balances by combining parts of such balances in transactions containing other legitimate transactions as an attempt to launder cryptocurrency obtained through illicit transactions.

Two-Factor Authentication (2FA) a technique that requires two or more methods to ensure a claim of authenticity to access a network, device, or computer.

United States House Committee on Financial Services a committee of the United States House of Representatives (Congress) that oversees all financial aspects of the U.S. economy and its institutions.

Venture Capital a pool of private equity funds designed to seed and develop firms in their nascent stages under the expectation that the investment will allow the firm to grow to one of significant value and hence return high returns to the early venture capital investors.

Volatility a statistical measure of the spread in the distribution of returns, measured primarily by return variance, defined as the sum of squared deviations of returns relative to their mean return.

Wash Sale the sale of a cryptocurrency at a loss to claim a tax benefit that may offset another sale for a profit, and thereby potentially eliminate the capital gains tax owed. The wash sale investor can repurchase the digital currency they held to permit them to continue holding the cryptocurrency while they harvest the capital loss to offset a capital gain.

Web 3.0 a term that defines the next generation of services and commerce available over the internet that rely heavily on decentralized transactions and digital currencies.

Web3 Foundation an entity that formed to encourage new applications and technologies that will constitute the next generation of the Internet based on decentralized web software protocols.

When Lambo a phrase referring to when cryptocurrency holders will become rich enough to afford the purchase of a Lamborghini.

References

Ahonen, Elias, Matthew J. Rippon, and Howard Kesselman (2016). Encyclopedia of Physical bitcoins and Crypto-Currencies, April 15. ISBN 978-0-9950-8990-7.

Alsabah, Humoud, and Agostino Capponi (2020). Pitfalls of bitcoin's Proof-of-Work: R&D Arms Race and Mining Centralization (February 4, 2020). Available at SSRN: https://ssrn.com/abstract=3273982 or https://doi.org/10.2139/ssrn.3273982.

Antonopoulos, Andreas M. (April 2014). Mastering Bitcoin: Unlocking Digital Crypto-Currencies. O'Reilly Media. ISBN 978-1-4493-7404-4.

Ashlee Vance (2013). "2014 Outlook: Bitcoin Mining Chips, a High-Tech Arms Race." Businessweek, November 14. https://www.bloomberg.com/news/articles/2013-11-14/2014-outlook-bitcoin-mining-chips-a-high-tech-arms-race. Rretrieved March 3, 2022.

Back, Adam (1997). "HashCash." http://www.hashcash.org/papers/announce.txt. Rretrieved March 3, 2022.

Badea, L., and M. C. Mungiu-Pupăzan (2021). "The Economic and Environmental Impact of Bitcoin," in IEEE Access, vol. 9, pp. 48091–48104, https://doi.org/10.1109/ACCESS.2021.3068636.

Bambrough, Billy (2021). "Coinbase CEO Hits Back at Dogecoin Creator After Attack On 'Cult-Like' Bitcoin and Crypto Price Culture." https://www.forbes.com/sites/billybambrough/2021/07/16/bitcoin-has-made-so-many-wealthy-coinbase-ceo-hits-back-at-dogecoin-creator-after-attack-on-cult-like-crypto-price-culture/?sh=782cb9d16363. Rretrieved February 28, 2022.

Bamji, Zubin (2021). "We Can End Routine Gas Flaring by 2030. Here's How." Sustainable Energy For All, March 1. https://blogs.worldbank.org/energy/we-can-end-routine-gas-flaring-2030-heres-how, accessed March 18, 2022.

Barski, Conrad, and Chris Wilmer (2015). Bitcoin for the Befuddled. No Starch Press. ISBN 978-1-59327-573-0.

Baur, Dirk G., and Josua Oll (2019). "The (Un-)Sustainability of Bitcoin Investments (April 4, 2019)." Available at SSRN: https://ssrn.com/abstract=3365820 or https://doi.org/10.2139/ssrn.3365820.

Beikverdi, A., and J. Song. (2015). Trend of Centralization in Bitcoin's Distributed Network. 2015 IEEE/ACIS 16th International Conference on Software Engineering, Artificial Intelligence, Networking and Parallel/Distributed Computing (SNPD), June pp. 1–6. https://doi.org/10.1109/SNPD.2015.7176229. ISBN 978-1-4799-8676-7. S2CID 15516195.

Benetton, Matteo, Matteo Benetton, Giovanni Compiani, and Adair Morse (2021). "When Cryptomining Comes to Town: High Electricity-Use Spillovers to the Local Economy (May 14, 2021)." Available at SSRN: https://ssrn.com/abstract=3779720 or https://doi.org/10.2139/ssrn.3779720.

Benner, Katie (2022). "Justice Dept. Seizes $3.6 Billion in Bitcoin and Arrests Married Couple." *New York Times*, February 8, 2022, https://www.nytimes.com/2022/02/08/us/politics/ilya-lichtenstein-heather-morgan-bitcoin-laundering.html. Rretrieved February 28, 2022.

Biden, Joe (2022). "Executive Order on Ensuring Responsible Development of Digital Assets." https://www.whitehouse.gov/briefing-room/presidential-actions/2022/03/09/executive-order-on-ensuring-responsible-development-of-digital-assets/, accessed March 15, 2022.

Bitir-Istrate, Ioan, Cristian Gheorghiu, and Miruna Gheorghiu (2021). "The Transition Towards an Environmental Sustainability for Cryptocurrency Mining." E3S Web of Conferences, 292, 03004, https://doi.org/10.1051/e3sconf/202129403004.

Böhme, Rainer, Nicolas Christin, Benjamin Edelman, and Tyler Moore (2015). Bitcoin: Economics, Technology, and Governance. *Journal of Economic Perspectives* 29 (2): 213–238. https://doi.org/10.1257/jep.29.2.213

Bondarev, Mikhail (2020). "Energy Consumption of Bitcoin Mining." *International Journal of Energy Economics and Policy*. https://doi.org/10.32479/ijeep.9276

Boot, Patrick J., and Marysia Laskowski (2020). "The First Cryptocurrency Bank." The National Law Review. https://www.natlawreview.com/print/article/first-cryptocurrency-bank. Rretrieved March 7, 2022.

Bradstock, Felicity (2022). "The Geopolitical Impact of Cryptocurrency." Oilprice, February 12. https://oilprice.com/Geopolitics/International/The-Geopolitical-Impact-Of-Cryptocurrency.html. Rretrieved February 28, 2022.

Brito, Jerry, and Andrea Castillo (2013). "Bitcoin: A Primer for Policymakers" (PDF). Mercatus Center. George Mason University. https://www.mercatus.org/publications/technology-and-innovation/bitcoin-primer-policymakers. Rretrieved March 3, 2022.

Caughill, Patrick (2017). "Nobel Prize-Winning Economist Says Bitcoin "Ought to Be Outlawed." https://futurism.com/nobel-prize-winning-economist-says-bitcoin-ought-outlawed, November 30, 2017. Rretrieved February 28, 2022.

Chaum, D. L. (1979). Computer Systems Established, Maintained and Trusted by Mutually Suspicious Groups. Electronics Research Laboratory, University of California.

Cocco, L., R. Tonelli, and M. Marchesi. (2019). "An Agent Based Model to Analyze the Bitcoin Mining Activity and a Comparison with the Gold Mining Industry." *Future Internet* 11: 8. https://doi.org/10.3390/fi11010008.

Cocco, Luisanna, and Michele Marchesi (2016). "Modeling and Simulation of the Economics of Mining in the Bitcoin Market." Plos One. https://doi.org/10.1371/journal.pone.0164603.

Corbet, Shaen, Brian Lucey, Andrew Urquhart, and Larisa Yarovaya (2019). "Cryptocurrencies as a Financial Asset: A Systematic Analysis." *International Review of Financial Analysis* 62: 182–199, ISSN 1057-5219. https://doi.org/10.1016/j.irfa.2018.09.003.

Cornish, Chloe (2018). "Bitcoin Slips Again on Reports of US DoJ Investigation." *Financial Times*, May 24. https://www.ft.com/content/5d8f06f2-5f3a-11e8-9334-2218e7146b04. Rretrieved March 3, 2022

Crypto Climate Alliance (2021). "Guidance for Accounting and Reporting Electricity Use and Carbon Emissions From Cryptocurrency," December 15. https://cryptoclimate.org/wp-content/uploads/2021/12/RMI-CIP-CCA-Guidance-Documentation-Dec15.pdf. Rretrieved February 28, 2022.

de Vries, Alex, (2020). "Bitcoin's Energy Consumption Is Underestimated: A Market Dynamics Approach." *Energy Research & Social Science* 70: 101721, ISSN 2214-6296. https://doi.org/10.1016/j.erss.2020.101721, https://www.sciencedirect.com/science/article/pii/S2214629620302966, accessed February 28, 2022

Dean, James (2018). "Bitcoin Investigation to Focus on British Traders, US Officials Examine Manipulation of Cryptocurrency Prices." *The Times*, May 25. https://www.thetimes.co.uk/article/bitcoin-investigation-to-focus-on-british-traders-c58brwn60. Rretrieved March 3, 2022

Dittmar, Lars, and Aaron Praktiknjo (2019). "Could Bitcoin Emissions Push Global Warming Above 2°C?" *Nature Climate Change* 9 (9): 656–657. Bibcode:2019NatCC...9..656D. https://doi.org/10.1038/s41558-019-0534-5. S2CID 202859187.

DuPont, Q. (2017). The Politics of Bitcoin: Software as Right-Wing Extremism, by David Golumbia. *Journal of Cultural Economy* 10 (5): 474–476.

Dwork, Cynthia, and Moni Naor (1993). "Pricing via Processing, Or, Combatting Junk Mail, Advances in Cryptology." *CRYPTO'92: Lecture Notes in Computer Science No. 740*. Springer: 139–147. https://doi.org/10.1007/3-540-48071-4_10. https://doi.org/10.1080/17530350.2017.1322997.

Engle, Brad (2021). "The Cult of Crypto." GHP Investment Advisors, September 30. https://ghpia.com/the-cult-of-crypto/. Rretrieved February 28, 2022.

European Central Bank (October 2012). Virtual Currency Schemes (PDF). Frankfurt am Main: European Central Bank. ISBN 978-92-899-0862-7. https://www.ecb.europa.eu/pub/pdf/other/virtualcurrencyschemes201210en.pdf. Rretrieved March 3, 2022.

Federal Reserve Bank of Boston and Massachusetts Institute of Technology Digital Currency Initiative (2022). "Project Hamilton." https://www.bostonfed.org/publications/one-time-pubs/project-hamilton-phase-1-executive-summary.aspx, accessed March 15, 2022

Foley, Sean, R. Jonathan, and Talis J. Putnin (2019). "Sex, Drugs, and Bitcoin: How Much Illegal Activity is Financed Through Cryptocurrencies?" *The Review of Financial Studies* 32 (5) (May): 1798–1853. https://doi.org/10.1093/rfs/hhz015.

Foteinis, Spyros (2018). "Bitcoin's Alarming Carbon Footprint." *Nature* 554 (7691): 169. Bibcode:2018Natur.554..169F. doi:https://doi.org/10.1038/d41586-018-01625-x.

Freudenburg, W.R. (2006). Environmental Degradation, Disproportionality, and the Double Diversion: Reaching Out, Reaching Ahead, and Reaching Beyond. Rural Sociology, 71: 3-32.

Fung, Brian (2018). "State Regulators Unveil Nationwide Crackdown on Suspicious Cryptocurrency Investment Schemes." *The Washington Post*, May 21. https://www.washingtonpost.com/news/the-switch/wp/2018/05/21/state-regulators-unveil-nationwide-crackdown-on-suspicious-cryptocurrency-investment-schemes/. Rretrieved March 2, 2022.

Gandal, Neil; J.T. Hamrick, Tyler Moore, and Tali Oberman (May 2018). "Price Manipulation in the Bitcoin Ecosystem." *Journal of Monetary Economics* 95: 86–96.

Garcia, D., C.J. Tessone, P. Mavrodiev, and N. Perony (2014). "The Digital Traces of Bubbles: Feedback Cycles Between Socio-Economic Signals in the Bitcoin Economy. https://doi.org/10.1098/rsif.2014.0623.

Gervais, Arthur, Ghassan O. Karame, Vedran Capkun, and Srdjan Capkun (2013). "Is Bitcoin a Decentralized Currency?" InfoQ. InfoQ & IEEE Computer Society. https://eprint.iacr.org/2013/829.pdf. Rretrieved March 2, 2022.

Gervais, Arthur, Ghassan O. Karame, Damian Gruber, and Srdjan Capkun (2014). "On the Privacy Provisions of Bloom Filters in Lightweight Bitcoin Clients" (PDF https://eprint.iacr.org/2014/763.pdf. Rretrieved March 2, 2022.

Gkillas, K, and P. Katsiampa (2018). "An Application of Extreme Value Theory to Cryptocurrencies." *Economic Letters* 164: 109–111.

Golumbia, David (2015). Lovink, Geert (ed.). Bitcoin as Politics: Distributed Right-Wing Extremism. Institute of Network Cultures, Amsterdam. pp. 117–131. ISBN 978-90-822345-5-8. SSRN 2589890.

Gonzales-Barahona, Jesus M. (2021). "Factors Determining Maximum Energy Consumption of Bitcoin Miners." https://arxiv.org/abs/2107.10634#:~:text=Results%3A%20We%20show%20a%20basic,energy%20price%2C%20and%20amortization%20cost. Rretrieved February 28, 2022.

Goodkind, Andrew L., Benjamin A. Jones, and Robert P. Berrens (2020). "Cryptodamages: Monetary Value Estimates of the Air Pollution and Human Health Impacts of Cryptocurrency Mining." *Energy Research and Social Science* 59: 3–8.

Greenberg, P., and D. Bugden (2019). "Energy Consumption Boomtowns in the United States: Community Responses to a Cryptocurrency Boom." *Energy*

Research & Social Science 50: 162–167. https://doi.org/10.1016/j.erss.2018.12.005

Greenspan, Alan (1996). "Regulation of Electronic Payment Systems." U.S. Treasury Conference on Electronic Money & Banking: The Role of Government, Washington DC, September 19, 1996.

Griffin, John M., Amin Shams (2018). "Is Bitcoin Really Un-Tethered?" Social Science Research Network, June 13. SSRN 3195066

Handagama, Sandali (2022). "Crypto Advocates Push Back on Sweden's Call for EU Mining Ban." Coindesk, February 9, 2022, https://www.coindesk.com/policy/2022/02/09/crypto-advocates-push-back-on-swedens-call-for-eu-mining-ban. Rretrieved February 28, 2022.

Hayek, Friedrich von (October 1976). Denationalisation of Money: The Argument Refined. 2 Lord North Street, Westminster, London SWIP 3LB: The institute of economic affairs. ISBN 978-0-255-36239-9. https://mises.org/library/denationalisation-money-argument-refined. Rretrieved March 3, 2022

Horowitz, Julia (2022). "How Cryptocurrencies Could Trigger a Financial Crisis." CNN Business, February 18, 2022, https://www.cnn.com/2022/02/18/investing/premarket-stocks-trading/index.html. Rretrieved February 28, 2022

Houy, Nicolas (2019). "Rational Mining Limits Bitcoin Emissions." *Nature Climate Change* 9 (9): 655. Bibcode:2019NatCC...9..655H. doi:https://doi.org/10.1038/s41558-019-0533-6.

Huang, Jon, Claire O'Neill, and Hiroko Tabuchi (2021). "Bitcoin Uses More Electricity Than Many Countries. How Is That Possible?" *The New York Times*, September 3. ISSN 0362-4331. Retrieved 16 January 2022.

Puiu, Tibi (2021). "Nobel Prize-Winning Economist Calls Bitcoin a 'Cult.'" ZME Science, May 23, 2021. https://www.zmescience.com/science/news-science/nobel-prize-winning-economist-calls-bitcoin-a-cult/. Rretrieved February 28, 2022.

Isaac, Mike, and Kellen Browing (2022). "Crypto Enthusiasts Meet Their Match: Angry Gamers." *New York Times*, January 19. https://www.nytimes.com/2022/01/15/technology/cryptocurrency-nft-gamers.html. Rretrieved February 28, 2022.

Jackson, Rueben (2021). "The Crypto Climate Accord Walks a Fine Line Between Self-Interest and the Greater Good." Bitcoin.com, July 27. https://news.bitcoin.com/crypto-climate-accord-walks-fine-line-between-self-interest-and-greater-good/. Rretrieved March 1, 2022.

Jakobsson, Markus, and Ari Juels (1999). "Proofs of Work and Bread Pudding Protocols." Secure Information Networks: Communications and Multimedia Security. Kluwer Academic Publishers: 258–272. https://doi.org/10.1007/978-0-387-35568-9_18

Kahn, M.A., and K. Salah (2018). "IoT Security: Review, Blockchain Solutions, and Open Challenges." *Future Generat. Comput. Cyst* 82: 395–411,

Kaushik Basu (2014). "Ponzis: The Science and Mystique of a Class of Financial Frauds" (PDF), July. World Bank Group. https://openknowledge.worldbank.org/handle/10986/19358. Rretrieved March 3, 2022.

Kay, Grace (2021). "The Many Alleged Identities of Bitcoin's Mysterious Creator, Satoshi Nakamoto." Business Insider, November 28. https://www.businessinsider.com/bitcoin-history-cryptocurrency-satoshi-nakamoto-2017-12. Rretrieved March 3, 2022.

Kharif, Olga (2019). "Bakkt Plans First Regulated Options Contracts on Bitcoin Futures." bloomberg.com., October 24. https://www.bloomberg.com/news/articles/2019-10-24/bakkt-plans-first-regulated-options-contracts-on-bitcoin-futures. Rretrieved March 2, 2022

Köhler, Susanne, and Pizzol, Massimo (2019). "Life Cycle Assessment of Bitcoin Mining." *Environmental Science & Technology* 53 (23): 13598–13606, November 20. Bibcode:2019EnST...5313598K. https://doi.org/10.1021/acs.est.9b05687. PMID 31746188.

Korhonen, Outi, and Juho Rantala (2021). "Blockchain Governance Challenges: Beyond Libertarianism." Symposium on the Global Governance Implications of Blockchain, Cambridge University Press Online. https://doi.org/10.1017/aju.2021.65, https://www.cambridge.org/core/journals/american-journal-of-international-law/article/blockchain-governance-challenges-beyond-libertarianism/D34C6761D744E44FA04C3E64B4DEFE51, accessed February 28, 2022.

Krause, Max J. and Thabet Tolaymat (2018). "Quantification of Energy and Carbon Costs for Mining Cryptocurrencies." *Nature Sustainability* 1 (11): 711–718. https://doi.org/10.1038/s41893-018-0152-7. S2CID 169170289.

Kurmanaev, Anatoly (2021). Bitcoin Preaches Financial Liberty. A Strongman Is Testing That Promise." NYT. Archived from the original on 7 October 2021. Retrieved 8 October 2021.

Leising, Matthew; Mira Rojanasakul, Demetrios Pogkas, Brandon Kochkodin (2018). "Crypto Coin Tether Defies Logic on Kraken's Market, Raising Red Flags." Bloomberg, June 29.

Li, Jingming, Nianping Li, Jinqing Peng, Haijiao Cui, and Zhibin Wu (2019), Energy Consumption of Cryptocurrency Mining: A Study of Electricity Consumption in Mining Cryptocurrencies." *Energy* 168: 160–168.

Locke, Taylor (2022). "Bitcoin's 'Judas': The Co-founder of a Rival Cryptocurrency is Pushing for a Green Revolution in Mining. It's Not Going Well." Fortune, April 2, 2022, https://fortune.com/2022/04/02/bitcoin-mining-green-campaign-chris-larsen/?queryly=related_article, accessed April 7, 2022.

Lopez, Oscar; Livni, Ephrat (7 September 2021). "In Global First, El Salvador Adopts Bitcoin as Currency." *The New York Times*. Archived from the original on 28 December 2021. Retrieved 30 September 2021.

Martin, Brett A.S., Chrysochou, Polymeros, Strong, Carolyn, Wang, Di, and Jun Yao (2022). "Dark Personalities and Bitcoin®: The Influence of the Dark Tetrad on Cryptocurrency Attitude and Buying Intention." *Personality and Individual Differences*, 188, 2022.

Martin, Katie and Billy Nauman (2021). "Bitcoin's Growing Energy Problem: It's a Dirty Currency." The Big Read, May 20, 2021, https://www.ft.com/content/1aecb2db-8f61-427c-a413-3b929291c8ac, accessed March 17, 2022.

Masanet, E., Shehabi, A., Lei, N., Vranken, Harald, Koomey, Jonathan, and Jens Malmodin (2019). "Implausible projections overestimate near-term Bitcoin CO2 emissions." *Nature Climate Change* 9: 653–654. https://doi.org/10.1038/s41558-019-0535-4

Massias, H, X.S. Avila, X.S, and J.-J. Quisquater (1999). "Design of a Secure Timestamping Service with Minimal Trust Requirements." 20th Symposium on Information Theory in the Benelux, May.

Matonis, Jon (2012). "Bitcoin Prevents Monetary Tyranny", *Forbes*, October 4. http://www.forbes.com/sites/jonmatonis/2012/10/04/bitcoin-prevents-monetary-tyranny/. Rretrieved February 28, 2022

Matthew, Graham Wilson and Aaron Yelowitz (2014). "Characteristics of Bitcoin Users: An Analysis of Google Search Data." Social Science Research Network, November.

McIntosh, Rachel (2019). "Six Months After Bitwise: Wash Trading Lives on In Crypto." https://www.financemagnates.com/cryptocurrency/news/things-are-better-but-wash-trading-persists-in-crypto-heres-why/. Rretrieved February 28, 2022.

Milman, Oliver (2022). "Bitcoin Miners Revived a Dying Coal Plant—Then CO2 Emissions Soared." *The Guardian*, February 18. https://www.theguardian.com/technology/2022/feb/18/bitcoin-miners-revive-fossil-fuel-plant-co2-emissions-soared. Rretrieved February 28, 2022.

Mir, Usama (2020). "Bitcoin and its Energy Usage: Existing Approaches, Important Opinions, Current Trends, and Future Challenges." *KSII Transactions on Internet and Information Systems* 14 (8), August.

Monroe, Rachel (2022). "Why Texas's Power Grid Still Hasn't Been Fixed." *The New Yorker*, February 9. https://www.newyorker.com/news/letter-from-the-southwest/why-texasss-power-grid-still-hasnt-been-fixed. Rretrieved February 28, 2022.

Mora, C., Rollins, R.L., Taladay, K. (2018). "Bitcoin Emissions Alone Could Push Global Warming Above 2°C. *Nature Clim Change* 8: 931–933 https://doi.org/10.1038/s41558-018-0321-8

Möser, M., Böhme, R., and D. Breuker (2013). "An Inquiry into Money Laundering Tools in the Bitcoin Ecosystem." *2013 APWG eCrime Researchers Summit*: 1–14. https://doi.org/10.1109/eCRS.2013.6805780.

Moss, Sebastian (2021). "Texas Could Add 5,000MW of Cryptocurrency Mining Data Centers by 2023, Even as ERCOT Warns of Grid Vulnerability." Data Center Dynamics, November 22.

Nadarajah, S., and J. Chu (2017). "On the Inefficiency of Bitcoin." *Economic Letters* 150: 6–9.

Nakamoto, Satoshi (2008). "Bitcoin: A Peer-to-Peer Electronic Cash System" (PDF). bitcoin.org., October 31. https://bitcoin.org/en/bitcoin-paper. Rretrieved March 2, 2022.

Namcios (2022). "Illinois, Georgia Want to Give Tax Cuts for Bitcoin Miners." Bitcoin Magazine, February 18. https://bitcoinmagazine.com/business/illinois-georgia-want-to-give-tax-cuts-for-bitcoin-miners. Rretrieved February 28, 2022.

Náñez Alonso, Sergio L., Javier Jorge-Vázquez, Miguel Á. Echarte Fernández, and Ricardo F. Reier Forradellas. (2021) "Cryptocurrency Mining from an Economic and Environmental Perspective. Analysis of the Most and Least Sustainable Countries." *Energies* 14 (14): 4254. https://doi.org/10.3390/en14144254.

Newbery, Emma. (2021) "U.S. Is Now the Biggest Bitcoin Miner in the World. Should We Be Happy?" The Ascent, October 17. https://www.fool.com/the-ascent/cryptocurrency/articles/us-is-now-the-biggest-bitcoin-miner-in-the-world-should-we-be-happy/. Rretrieved February 28, 2022.

O'Dwyer, Karl J. and David Malone (2014). "Bitcoin Mining and its Energy Footprint." ISSC 2014/CIICT 2014, Limerick, June 26–27.

Odell, Matt (2015). "A Solution To Bitcoin's Governance Problem." TechCrunch, September 21. https://techcrunch.com/2015/09/21/a-solution-to-bitcoins-governance-problem/. Rretrieved March 2, 2022.

Okorie, David I. (2020). "A Network Analysis of Electricity Demand and the Cryptocurrency Markets." *International Journal of Finance and Economics* 26 (2): 3093–3108.

Orcutt, Mike (2015). "Leaderless Bitcoin Struggles to Make Its Most Crucial Decision." MIT Technology Review, May 19. https://www.technologyreview.com/2015/05/19/168128/leaderless-bitcoin-struggles-to-make-its-most-crucial-decision/. Rretrieved March 3, 2022.

Osipovich, Alexander (22 September 2019). "NYSE Owner Launches Long-Awaited Bitcoin Futures." *The Wall Street Journal*. https://www.wsj.com/articles/nyse-owner-to-launch-long-awaited-bitcoin-futures-11569153649. Rretrieved March 3, 2022.

Pagliery, Jose (2014). Bitcoin: And the Future of Money. Triumph Books. ISBN 9781629370361.

Pan, David (2022). "Nvidia's Crypto Revenue Drops as Ethereum Heads to Proof of Stake." The Star, February 26. https://www.thestar.com.my/tech/tech-news/2022/02/26/nvidias-crypto-revenue-drops-as-ethereum-heads-to-proof-of-stake. Rretrieved March 3, 2022.

Petrik, Louis (2021). "Why Most Cryptocurrency Communities Feel Like Cults to Me." Illumination, April 27. https://medium.com/illumination/why-most-cryptocurrency-communities-feel-like-cults-to-me-9027b8f97585. Rretrieved February 28, 2022.

Popper, Nathaniel (2015). "Digital Gold: Bitcoin and the Inside Story of the Misfits and Millionaires Trying to Reinvent Money." Harper, New York.

Popper, Nathaniel (13 June 2018). "Bitcoin's Price Was Artificially Inflated Last Year, Researchers Say." *The New York Times*. https://www.nytimes.com/2018/06/13/technology/bitcoin-price-manipulation.html. Rretrieved March 3, 2022.

Posner, Eric (2013). "Fool's Gold: Bitcoin Is a Ponzi Scheme—The Internet's Favorite Currency Will Collapse." Slate, April 11. https://slate.com/news-and-politics/2013/04/bitcoin-is-a-ponzi-scheme-the-internet-currency-will-collapse.html. Rretrieved March 3, 2022.

Quiroz-Gutierrez, Marco (2022). "Crypto is Fully Banned in China and 8 Other Countries." Fortune, January 4. https://fortune.com/2022/01/04/crypto-banned-china-other-countries. Rretrieved February 28, 2022.

Rainer Böhme; Nicolas Christin; Benjamin Edelman; Tyler Moore (2015). "Bitcoin: Economics, Technology, and Governance." *Journal of Economic Perspectives* 29 (2): 213–238. https://doi.org/10.1257/jep.29.2.213.

Read, Colin, "Environmental Challenges and Financial Market Opportunities (2015)." Handbook of Environmental and Sustainable Finance, Elsevier/Academic Press.

Read, Colin (2022). "The Inevitability of Escalating Energy Usage for Popular Cryptocurrencies, and Other Dimensions of Cryptocurrency Risk." submitted to the International Journal Risk and Contingency Management.

Richter, Felix (2021). "Crypto Ransom Payments Skyrocketed in 2020." https://www.statista.com/chart/25245/total-value-of-cryptocurrency-received-by-known-ransomware-addresses/. Rretrieved February 28, 2022.

Roberts, Jeff John (2022). "Ukraine, Bitcoin, and the 'World's First Crypto War'." Decrypt, February 26. https://decrypt.co/93898/ukraine-bitcoin-war. Rretrieved February 28, 2022.

Robinson, Matt, and Tom Schoenberg (2018). "U.S. Launches Criminal Probe into Bitcoin Price Manipulation." Bloomberg. Archived from the original on 24 May 2018. Retrieved 24 May 2018.

Scheltz, Marco (2021). "Blockchain Energy Consumption: Debunking the Misperceptions of Bitcoin's and Blockchain's Climate Impact." https://medium.com/@datadrivenlab/blockchain-energy-consumption-debunking-the-misperceptions-of-bitcoins-and-blockchain-s-climate-61ac57bc0709

Schinckus, Christophe, Canh Phuc Nguyen, and Felicia Chong Hui Ling (2019). "Crypto-Currencies Trading and Energy Consumption." *International Journal of Energy Economics and Policy* 10 (3): 355–364.

Sedlmeir, Johannes, Buhl, Hans Ulrich, Fridgen, Gilbert, and Robert Keller (2020). "The Energy Consumption of Blockchain Technology: Beyond Myth." *Bus. Inf. Syst. Eng* 62 (6): 599–609.

Sharma, Ruchira (2021). "'Crypto Ruined My Life': The Mental Health Crisis Hitting Bitcoin Investors." Vice.com, February 16. https://www.vice.com/en/article/akvn8z/crypto-bad-for-mental-health. Rretrieved February 28, 2022.

Sherman, Alan; Farid Javani, and Enis Golaszewski (25 March 2019). "On the Origins and Variations of Blockchain Technologies." *IEEE Security and Policy* 17 (1): 72–77. arXiv:1810.06130. doi:https://doi.org/10.1109/MSEC.2019.2893730. S2CID 53114747.

Sigalos, MacKenzie (2022). "The 'Bitcoin Family' Emigrates to Portugal for its 0% Tax on Cryptocurrencies." https://www.msn.com/en-us/money/markets/the-bitcoin-family-immigrates-to-portugal-for-its-0-25-tax-on-cryptocurrencies/ar-AATwOtb. Rretrieved February 28, 2022

Simonite, Tom (2013). "Bitcoin Millionaires Become Investing Angels." Computing News. MIT Technology Review, June 12. https://www.technologyreview.com/2013/06/12/15919/bitcoin-millionaires-become-investing-angels/. Rretrieved March 3, 2022.

Simonite, Tom (2013). "Mapping the Bitcoin Economy Could Reveal Users' Identities." MIT Technology Review, September 5. https://www.technologyreview.com/2013/09/05/176558/mapping-the-bitcoin-economy-could-reveal-users-identities. Rretrieved March 3, 2022.

Simonite, Tom (2017). "The Man Who Really Built Bitcoin." MIT Technology Review. https://www.technologyreview.com/2014/08/15/12784/the-man-who-really-built-bitcoin/. Rretrieved March 2, 2022.

Sparkes, Matthew (9 June 2014). "The Coming Digital Anarchy." *The Daily Telegraph*. London. Archived from the original on 23 January 2015. https://www.telegraph.co.uk/technology/news/10881213/The-coming-digital-anarchy.html. Rretrieved March 2, 2022.

Spross, Jeff (2017). "Is Bitcoin Worth the Energy?" *The Week*, December, 2017. https://theweek.com/articles/742253/bitcoin-worth-energy. Rretrieved February 28, 2022.

Stoll, Christian, and Lena Klaaßen, and Ulrich Gallersdörfer (2019). "The Carbon Footprint of Bitcoin." *Joule* 3 (7): 1647–1661. doi:https://doi.org/10.1016/j.joule.2019.05.012.

Tabuchi, Hiroko (2022). "China Banished Cryptocurrencies: Now, 'Mining' is Even Dirtier." *New York Times*, February 25. https://www.nytimes.com/2022/02/25/climate/bitcoin-china-energy-pollution.html. Rretrieved February 28, 2022.

Tasca, Paolo (2015). Digital Currencies: Principles, Trends, Opportunities, and Risks, Social Science Research Network, September 7. SSRN 2657598.

Tiffany, Kaitlyn (2022). "The Crypto Backlash Is Booming." *The Atlantic*, February 4. https://www.theatlantic.com/technology/archive/2022/02/crypto-nft-web3-internet-future/621479/. Rretrieved February 28, 2022.

Truby, Jon (2018). "Decarbonizing Bitcoin: Law and Policy Choices for Reducing the Energy Consumption of Blockchain Technologies and Digital Currencies." *Energy Research and Social Science* 44: 399–410.

Tschorsch, Florian, and Björn Scheuermann (2016). "Bitcoin and Beyond: A Technical Survey on Decentralized Digital Currencies." *IEEE Communications Surveys & Tutorials* 18 (3): 2084–2123. https://doi.org/10.1109/comst.2016.2535718. S2CID 5115101.

Van Hijfte, Stijn (2020). Blockchain Platforms: A Look at the Underbelly of Distributed Platforms. Morgan & Claypool Publishers. ISBN 9781681738925.

Velde, François (December 2013). "Bitcoin: A Primer" (PDF). Chicago Fed Letter. Federal Reserve Bank of Chicago. https://www.chicagofed.org/-/media/publications/chicago-fed-letter/2013/cfldecember2013-317-pdf.pdf. Rretrieved March 3, 2022.

Venkataramakrishnan, Siddharth, and Robin Wigglesworth (2021). "Inside the Cult of Crypto." *Financial Times*, September 10. https://www.ft.com/content/9e787670-6aa7-4479-934f-f4a9fedf4829. Rretrieved February 28, 2022.

Vigna, Paul, and Michael J. Casey (January 2015). The Age of Cryptocurrency: How Bitcoin and Digital Money Are Challenging the Global Economic Order (1 ed.). New York: St. Martin's Press. ISBN 978-1-250-06563-6.

Walton, Robert (2022). "Bitcoin Mining as a Grid Resource? 'It's Complicated'." Utility Dive, February 17. https://www.utilitydive.com/news/bitcoin-mining-as-a-grid-resource-its-complicated/617896/. Rretrieved February 28, 2022.

Werbach, Kevin (2022). "Testimony to Senate Committee on Agriculture, Nutrition, and Forestry—Examining Digital Assets: Risks, Regulation, and Innovation." February 9. https://www.agriculture.senate.gov/hearings/examining-digital-assets-risks-regulation-and-innovation, accessed February 28, 2022.

Wile, Rob (2014). "St. Louis Fed Economist: Bitcoin Could Be A Good Threat To Central Banks." businessinsider.com. Business Insider, April 6. https://www.businessinsider.com/interview-with-david-andolfatto-2014-4. Rretrieved March 3, 2022.

Williams, Mark T. (2014). "Virtual Currencies—Bitcoin Risk" (PDF), October 21. World Bank Conference Washington DC. Boston University. https://www.bu.edu/questrom/files/2014/10/Wlliams-World-Bank-10-21-2014.pdf. Rretrieved March 3, 2022.

Index

A

Adleman, Leonard 14
Advanced Micro Devices (AMD) 47, 138, 141, 142, 144
algorithm 29, 30, 32, 33, 43, 45, 46, 48, 50, 52, 59, 60, 64, 70, 73, 74, 78, 79, 85, 96, 131, 179, 192, 197, 232, 297, 300, 302, 308
AlphaBay 116
Amazon 187, 236, 250
Amazon Web Services 250
American Express 27
American Samoa 276
Antminer vi, 51, 57, 74, 76, 78, 81, 83, 91, 97, 107–109, 139, 179, 214, 215, 217, 234, 279, 298, 304, 308
Application Specific Integrated Circuit (ASIC) vi, 50, 51, 69, 70, 73–76, 97, 107, 127, 130, 138–141, 143, 217, 298, 299, 303, 304
ARPANet 6
Asimov, Isaac 6

authentication 23–25, 52, 54, 57, 58, 61, 67, 96, 119, 133, 145, 158, 199, 201, 221, 232, 301, 304–306

B

Back, Adam 10, 17, 201, 297
Bank for International Settlements 250
Bankman-Fried, Sam 165
Bank of Canada 183
Bank of England 19, 183
Bardeen, John 72
Barker, Greg 165
Bellcore Labs 23
Benetton 87, 124, 215, 227, 234, 237
Big Brother 5, 8, 45
Bitcoin Dilemma xii, xiii, xv, 18, 35, 36, 53, 78, 83, 85–88, 92, 93, 95–98, 112, 124, 133, 134, 137, 138, 140, 144, 170, 172, 178, 202, 213, 217, 219, 220, 225–227, 237, 282, 298, 299

Bitcoin Gold 63, 169
Bitcoin.org 15
Bitcoin SV 63
Bitcointalk 299
Bitfinex 114, 184, 185
Bitmain vi, 51, 70, 73–75, 141, 220, 299
BitTorrent 21
Bitwise Asset Management 200
blockchain vi, xiv, 15, 22–25, 27, 29, 34, 36, 45, 46, 53, 58, 69, 80, 83, 95, 115, 117, 123, 126, 130, 131, 133, 134, 144, 145, 156, 157, 161, 168, 179–182, 187–189, 191, 201, 220, 222, 223, 238, 252, 270, 272, 278, 297–308
Blockchain Association 269
BlockFi 192–196
Bloomberg TV 200
Blum, Manuel 14
Bonaire 276
Brattain, Walter 72
Brienza, Ryan 235
British Virgin Islands 276
Britto, Arthur 270
bubble 50, 129, 166, 170, 178
Bukele, Nayib 277, 278
Buterin, Vitalik 143, 145, 176

C

Canaan Creative 73–76, 220
Canada vi, 50, 113, 132, 183, 223, 249, 278
Carney, Mark 182
Central Bank 249, 250, 253, 261, 262, 264, 299, 308
Central Bank Digital Currencies (CBDC) 249–253, 255, 264, 299, 308
Central Bank of Nigeria 250
Central Bank of the Bahamas 250

Central Processor Unit (CPU) 15, 19, 46–48, 50, 53, 73, 74, 138, 140, 142, 160, 299, 300, 302
Chaum, David 9, 10, 23
China 50, 66, 75, 129–134, 136, 178, 183, 188, 228, 249, 250, 254, 272, 274, 278, 299
climate change 237
Clinton County vii
Clinton, Hillary 268
coal 75, 87, 98, 99, 126, 132, 133, 161, 216, 217, 226, 233, 234, 236, 240, 241, 279
Codd, Edgar F. 14
Commodity Futures Modernization Act 289
Commodity Futures Trading Commission (CFTC) 177, 178, 186, 269, 271
Compound Finance (COMP) 176, 177, 189
Congressional hearing 265
COVID-19 72, 265
Cramer, Jim 50
credit card 10, 56, 167, 193, 227, 251, 258, 273, 283
Cryptocultist 300
Cryptoslate.com 144

D

database 14, 22, 115
debit card 227, 229, 250, 251, 284, 300
Decentralized Exchange (DEX) 190
Decentralized Finance (DeFi) 53, 125, 134, 145, 167, 176, 187, 189–197, 199, 264, 272, 277, 301
De Forest, Lee 70
demand deposit 258, 260
deposit expansion multiplier 259, 260, 262, 263

destabilization 131
Diem 184
Difficulty Factor 79
Diffie, Whitfield 14
Digiconomist 217
Digital Chamber of Commerce 269
Dogecoin 144, 165, 170, 176, 177
Dwork, Cynthia 57

E

Eastern Caribbean Central Bank 250
eBay 116
Ecuador 276
Edison, Thomas Alva 109
Einstein, Albert 13, 14, 17, 18
e-krona 250
El Salvador 130, 276–278
eNaira 250
energy 14, 90–92, 216–218, 220, 225, 229, 306
ETH 58, 192
ether 25, 52, 57, 59, 63, 65, 139–145, 167, 175–178, 182, 183, 189, 190, 218
Ethereum 25, 52, 53, 57, 58, 63, 119, 141, 143–145, 158, 167, 176, 177, 180, 182, 187–192, 196, 197, 199, 218, 238, 250, 299, 302, 304, 307
Ethereum Classic 63
European Union 133, 249, 250, 272
Excel 22

F

Facebook 25–27, 34, 178, 190, 236
Federal Reserve 9, 183, 184, 195, 249–252, 255, 263, 267, 270, 276, 299, 308
Federal Reserve Board 251, 270
feedback loop 275
Field Programmable Gate Array (FPGA) 48–50, 302

51% attack 63, 64, 131
Finney, Hal 8, 9, 11, 16, 43–45, 49, 53, 175, 213, 281, 302
Fleming, John Ambrose 70
Floating Point Operation 179
Foley, Sean 115–117, 169, 238
fork 23, 45, 63, 142, 144, 145, 231, 302, 307
fossil fuel xvi, 98, 125, 126, 217, 220, 222, 223, 226, 228, 233, 236, 239–241, 284, 298
Friedman, Milton 20, 157, 160
Fugger, Ryan 270

G

Game Stop 163
Gekko, Gordon 20, 160, 161
Gemini 34
Genesis Block 19, 25, 30–33, 115, 265, 302
Ghash.io 66
Gnutella 21
Goodkind, Andrew 124, 224, 227, 237
Google 6, 25–27
Gospel of Profit 156, 159, 161, 241
Gospel of Satoshi 156, 161
Gramm, Phil 271
Graphics Processor Unit (GPU) 48, 49, 138–145, 274, 308
Great Recession 32, 129, 184, 193, 249, 262, 265, 281
Greenspan, Alan 9, 50, 250, 255, 267
Griffin, John 185
Guam 276

H

Haber, Stuart 23
Hamilton Project 252
Hamming, Richard 14
hard fork 23

hash 10, 17, 23, 29, 30, 32–34, 43, 46, 47, 50, 59, 64, 70, 74–76, 80, 88, 96, 132, 179, 217, 297, 303, 307, 308
hashrate 82
Hellman, Martin 15
Hochul, Kathy 288
Hong Kong 132, 184
Hougen, Matt 200
Howey 289
Hughes, Eric 7

I

integrated circuit vi, 51, 72, 74, 179, 299, 302
Intel xv, 9, 47, 72, 74–76, 81, 97, 220
Intel 8080 74
Internet xii, xiv, 6, 9, 21, 26, 55, 60, 62, 67, 82, 99, 114, 116, 117, 135, 178, 188, 272, 277, 278, 300, 301, 303, 304, 309
Internet Protocol 116, 304
intrinsic value 11, 166, 273, 274, 299, 301
I, Robot 180
Irrational Exuberance 50

J

Jakobsson, Markus 10, 56
Journal of Cryptology 23
Juels, Ari 10, 56

K

Kaseya 118
Kazaa 21
Klondike Gold Rush 73, 75
Kraken Bank 185, 186, 193
Kranton, Rachel 151
Krause, Max 238
K-Street 111, 265, 268

L

Lamborghini 164, 309
Larsen, Chris 240
Li, Jingming 208
Litecoin 143
London vii, 31, 132

M

MakerDAO 189
Manhattan Project 70, 71
Marco Polo 275
Marshall Islands 276
Massie, Suzanne 56
Mastercard 27, 125, 250
Matthews 116
McCaleb, Jed 270
McLuhan, Marshall 19
Medici 275
Meta 26, 190
Micronesia 276
miner vi, xv, 17, 31, 33, 35, 45–47, 50, 53, 56, 57, 59, 64, 69, 74–76, 78–85, 87–90, 93, 95–97, 99, 107, 131, 137, 139–141, 144, 214–216, 219, 220, 222, 224, 227, 231, 232, 235, 239, 280, 299, 304
mining farm 79, 81, 82, 108, 110, 123, 126, 215, 217, 221, 226, 235, 236, 240, 292, 294, 304
M.I.T. 64, 251, 252
Moore, Gordon xv, 9, 304
MySpace 25

N

Nakamoto, Hatoshi/Satoshi v, vi, xi–xvi, 8–13, 15–19, 23–25, 29–35, 43–49, 52, 53, 55–57, 59, 63, 64, 67, 69, 77, 78, 80, 83, 95, 96, 113, 121, 129, 131, 135, 138, 144, 156, 157, 159–161, 163, 167, 175, 177,

179–182, 186, 187, 193, 194, 197, 200, 213, 219, 223, 227, 228, 231, 232, 240, 241, 249, 254, 255, 257, 263, 264, 267, 273, 277, 279–285, 298, 300, 302, 307
Naor, Moni 57
Napster 10, 21
National Institute of Standards and Technology (NIST) 30
National Security Agency (NSA) 8, 10, 30
Neumann, John von 71
Niagara Power Authority 108
Nobel Prize 14
nonce 32, 33, 43, 46, 47, 59, 64, 96
Non-Fungible Token (NFT) 65, 145, 171, 180, 181, 188, 304, 308
Northern Mariana Islands 276
Novogratz, Mike 165, 190
nuclear 70, 71, 220, 223, 225, 232, 233, 306
Nvidia 138, 141, 142

O

Occupational Safety and Health 111
Office of the Comptroller of the Currency (OCC) 195, 196, 269, 304
Ohl, Russell 72
open market operations 262, 263

P

Palau 276
Palmer, Jackson 165, 176, 177
Panama 276
PancakeSwap 195
peak power plant 87, 98, 226
Peer-to-Peer 11, 15, 21, 305
pegged 182, 183

Plattsburgh vi, vii, 107–113, 122, 234, 235, 278, 291–294
Powell, Jerome 183, 185, 186, 250, 270
Pretty Good Privacy 9
PrimeXBT 201
Private Key 58, 305
Proof of Activity 58
Proof of Authority 58, 305
Proof of Capacity 58
Proof of Elapsed Time 58
Proof of Identity 58
Proof of Stake 23, 24, 53, 57, 58, 119, 139, 143–145, 158, 170, 180, 182, 199, 201, 217, 221, 231, 232, 236, 238, 240, 280, 285, 301, 305, 306
Proof of Work xiii, 10, 16, 23, 24, 29, 56–58, 64, 78, 83, 85, 119, 124, 130–133, 137–139, 143–145, 159, 170, 177, 180, 188, 199, 201, 202, 213, 218, 221, 236–238, 240, 271, 298, 299, 304–306
protocol xii, xiv, 11, 12, 21, 32, 33, 45, 52, 53, 55, 57, 58, 63, 67, 80, 83, 119, 141, 143–145, 158, 177, 180, 187, 188, 190, 196, 197, 199, 201, 218, 220, 223, 231, 232, 240, 250, 281, 299, 303, 305, 307
Public Key 306
Public Ledger 34
Public Service Commission 224, 234, 235
Puerto Rico 276
Pump-and-Dump 306

R

ransomware 118, 202
Read, Colin 111
Reagan, Ronald 56
Reddit 6, 170

Research and Development (R&D) 75, 141
reserve ratio 258–261, 263
reserves 61, 183–185, 194, 258–264, 272
Richter, Felix 118
Rider A 111, 124, 234, 235
Riksbank of Sweden 250
Ripple Labs 161, 240, 268–270
Rivest, Ron 14
Roaring Twenties 171
Robin Hood 163
Rug-Pull 307

safe harbor 201
Sand Dollar 250
Scaramucci, Anthony 200
Schwartz, David 270
Securities and Exchange Commission (SEC) 171, 177, 178, 182, 196, 267–269, 271, 307
SEC v. W.J.Howey Co. 289
Sedlmeir, Johannes 39
SHA-256 29, 30, 32, 33, 46, 48, 50, 59, 60, 64, 70, 73, 74, 82, 96, 179, 220, 303, 307
Shamir, Adi 14
Shams, Amin 185
Shockley, William 72
Silk Road 114, 116, 117, 307
Skybridge Capital 200
Slomp, Cornelius Jan 114, 117
S9 vi, 51, 57, 74, 76, 78, 81, 83, 88, 91, 97, 107–109, 139, 179, 214–217, 234, 235, 279, 298, 304, 308
solar 87, 220, 221, 223, 225, 233, 234, 236, 306
Somalia 276

speculation xv, 15, 45, 118, 157, 158, 163–166, 169–173, 182, 195, 199, 201, 202, 300
Stablecoin 65, 131, 132, 166, 167, 182–186, 189, 195, 231, 249, 250, 254, 264, 278, 297, 298, 300, 302, 305
store of value 135, 156, 167, 255
Stornetta, Scott 23
Structure, Conduct, Performance (SCP) 82, 85, 90
SushiSwap 195
Sutton, Willie 60
Sydney 132
Szabo, Nick 10, 16, 304

Tender 132
Terra 287
Tesla, Nikola 109, 182
Tether 184–186
The Good Wife 50
The Onion Router (TOR) 21, 30, 116
Thomas, Stefan 16, 109
TikTok 25
Timor-Leste 276
token 175–177, 180, 181, 185, 189, 302–304, 308
transaction-local validation 252
transistor 51, 72–74
Treasury 65, 254, 270, 277, 304
TrueUSD 184
Trump, Donald 65, 268
tumbling 114, 116, 117
Turing, Alan 14, 71
Turks and Caicos Islands 276
Twitter 26

Uniswap 190

United States (US) 15, 17, 21, 30, 35, 50, 61, 65, 80, 113, 114, 118, 124–127, 130, 132–136, 181–186, 189, 194–196, 215, 216, 220, 224, 225, 227–229, 231, 249, 251, 253–255, 257, 263, 268–274, 276–278, 298–300, 302–304, 307, 308
Unspent Funds Hash Set 252
U.S. Virgin Islands 276

V

Vancouver 50, 132
Van Gogh 13
Visa 27, 125, 132, 157, 187, 229, 250
volatility 131, 156, 168–170, 183–185, 189, 202, 270, 280

W

wallet 34, 45, 52, 60, 188, 192, 195, 252, 277, 297, 300, 302–305
Wall Street 20, 52, 110, 127, 129, 160, 161, 193
Warren, Elizabeth 50, 196
wash sale 114, 116, 117, 309

Web 1.0 25
Web 2.0 25
Web3 25–27, 135, 190, 309
Wei Dai 17
Weinberg, Jack 5
wind 87, 220, 221, 223, 225, 226, 233, 236, 306
Wright, Craig Steven 16, 123, 166, 300

X

XRP 268, 270, 271

Y

Yao, Andrew 14
Yellen, Janet 254, 270
YouTube 25

Z

Zencash 115, 178
Zhang, Nangeng 73
Zimbabwe 276
Zimmerman, Phillip R. 9, 44
Zuckerberg, Mark 26

GPSR Compliance

The European Union's (EU) General Product Safety Regulation (GPSR) is a set of rules that requires consumer products to be safe and our obligations to ensure this.

If you have any concerns about our products, you can contact us on

ProductSafety@springernature.com

In case Publisher is established outside the EU, the EU authorized representative is:

Springer Nature Customer Service Center GmbH
Europaplatz 3
69115 Heidelberg, Germany

www.ingramcontent.com/pod-product-compliance
Lightning Source LLC
LaVergne TN
LVHW020136080526
838202LV00048B/3953